THE OXFORD SHAKESPEARE

General Editor · Stanley Wells

The Oxford Shakespeare offers new and authoritative editions of Shakespeare's plays in which the early printings have been scrupulously re-examined and interpreted. An introductory essay provides all relevant background information together with an appraisal of critical views and of the play's effects in performance. The detailed commentaries pay particular attention to language and staging. Reprints of sources, music for songs, genealogical tables, maps, etc. are included where necessary; many of the volumes are illustrated, and all contain an index.

STEPHEN ORGEL is the Jackson Eli Reynolds Professor of Humanities at Stanford University.

THE OXFORD SHAKESPEARE

Currently available in paperback

The rest of the plays are forthcoming

OXFORD WORLD'S CLASSICS

WILLIAM SHAKESPEARE

The Winter's Tale

Edited by
STEPHEN ORGEL

OXFORD
UNIVERSITY PRESS

OXFORD

UNIVERSITY PRESS

Great Clarendon Street, Oxford OX2 6DP

Oxford University Press is a department of the University of Oxford.
It furthers the University's objective of excellence in research, scholarship,
and education by publishing worldwide in

Oxford New York

Athens Auckland Bangkok Bogotá Buenos Aires Calcutta
Cape Town Chennai Dar es Salaam Delhi Florence Hong Kong Istanbul
Karachi Kuala Lumpur Madrid Melbourne Mexico City Mumbai
Nairobi Paris São Paulo Shanghai Singapore Taipei Tokyo Toronto Warsaw

with associated companies in Berlin Ibadan

Oxford is a registered trade mark of Oxford University Press
in the UK and in certain other countries

Published in the United States
by Oxford University Press Inc., New York

British Library Cataloguing in Publication Data

Data available

Library of Congress Cataloging in Publication Data

Shakespeare, William, 1564–1616.
The winter's tale / edited by Stephen Orgel.
p. cm—(Oxford world's classics)
Includes index.
1. Orgel, Stephen. II. Title. III. Series:
PR2839.A2074 1996 822.3'3—dc20 95–52554

ISBN 978-0-19-953591-0

4

Printed in Great Britain by
Clays Ltd, St Ives plc

PREFACE

FOR references, elucidations and citations I am indebted to Leonard Barkan, John Bender, Caroline Bicks, A. R. Braunmuller, Christopher Highley, Lindsay Kaplan, Randall S. Nakayama, Paul Seaver, Willard Spiegelman, John Stokes and Marion Trousdale. Patrick Stewart gave me a fascinating afternoon discussing his experience performing Leontes, and I have learned much from Dr Robert Brofman's professional insight into Leontes' pychopathology. On the relation of textual to theatrical matters, I am grateful for the suggestions of Alan Dessen and Adrian Kiernander. For the solution to the problem of 'o'er-dyed blacks' in 1.2.130–1, I have Dr Edward Maeder and Karen Finch, OBE, to thank. John Manning called my attention to the King of Bohemia's *impresa* in Typotius. On pastoral matters I have benefited from the expertise of Paul Alpers. Philip Brett and Anthony Newcomb have been my guides through Renaissance music history and practice. Jonathan Crewe and David Riggs at different stages gave the introduction acute and sympathetic readings, and helped to bring it to its final shape. Christine Buckley has been a superlative copy-editor. Finally, the general editor has once again been exemplary, and most of his suggestions have been silently adopted.

STEPHEN ORGEL

CONTENTS

LIST OF ILLUSTRATIONS

INTRODUCTION

IN 1672 Dryden, looking back at the drama of the last age, singled out *The Winter's Tale*, along with *Measure for Measure* and *Love's Labour's Lost*, for particular criticism. These plays 'were either grounded on impossibilities, or at least, so meanly written, that the Comedy neither caus'd your mirth, nor the serious part your concernment'.[1] Tastes in comedy change, and there is no disputing them; but the impossibilities of *The Winter's Tale* are undeniable, and the degree of seriousness the play lays claim to is certainly at least arguable: Dryden could have cited the title itself—a winter's tale is proverbially a fable, a fairy tale—in defence of his assertion. The play has had many subsequent admirers, but Dryden's criticism has also been echoed in every era: Charlotte Lennox, in 1753, found the play ridiculous, and the statue 'a mean and absurd contrivance'; Hartley Coleridge, in 1851, declared 'the queen's reanimation beyond all dramatic credibility'; D. G. James, in 1937, called 'Paulina's deception of Leontes and imprisonment of Hermione . . . preposterous'; and Terry Eagleton, in 1986, declared the play's resolution to 'rest not only upon a reactionary mystification of Nature but on a logical mistake'.[2]

The play had, however, been popular in its own time, and not only at the Globe, where Simon Forman saw it in the spring of 1611.[3] Seven performances at court are recorded before 1640; it was played before the King in 1611, when it was new, and two years later it was one of fourteen dramas selected to entertain King James's daughter Elizabeth and her fiancé the Elector Palatine during the two months of celebrations preceding their marriage. In 1633 it was still being performed at court by the King's Men, 'and likt'.[4]

---

[1] From *A Defence of the Epilogue, Or, An Essay on the Dramatique Poetry of the Last Age*, quoted in *Shakespeare: The Critical Heritage*, ed. Brian Vickers (London, 1974), i. 145.

[2] The Lennox and Coleridge remarks are reprinted in the *Variorum*, pp. 352–4, 357; for the James, see *Scepticism and Poetry* (London, 1937), pp. 232–3; for Eagleton, see *William Shakespeare* (Oxford, 1986), p. 93.

[3] For Forman's account of the play, see Appendix A.

[4] Sir Henry Herbert's Office Book, p. 236; quoted in C. M. Ingleby *et al.*, *The Shakspere Allusion Book*, 2nd edn. (Oxford, 1932), p. 321. For a list of early performances, see below, pp. 62 ff.

Dryden's opinion, however, was not eccentric. After the clos-
ing of the theatres the play disappeared from the stage for a
century, and Pope was of the opinion that no more than 'some
characters, single scenes, or perhaps a few particular passages'
were Shakespeare's.[1] It was successfully revived in the 1740s
and 1750s, but during the eighteenth century achieved its
greatest popularity in Garrick's truncated version, *Florizel and
Perdita*, produced in 1756. Its reintroduction in a substantially
complete form was the work of John Philip Kemble in 1811;
thereafter it was regularly produced, often spectacularly and with
major performers. Dryden's complaints that the play was illogical
and neither funny enough nor serious enough still occasionally
reappeared in reviews and in the critical literature, but they
seemed finally to be answerable, if not answered, when Dowden,
in 1877, declared that *The Winter's Tale*, along with *Pericles,
Cymbeline*, and *The Tempest*, was neither comedy nor tragedy, but
romance, a category in which it remains firmly entrenched
today.

Genres

Dowden's generic ploy undoubtedly enabled criticism to see the
interrelations of these four plays more clearly, and probably
served to disarm the most obvious rationalistic objections to their
action. The creation and refinement of artistic categories has
been one of the primary functions of criticism from Aristotle to
Northrop Frye, and Dowden's claims for his new Shakespearian
genre in fact did little more than systematize an observation
already made by Coleridge in his *Notes on 'The Tempest'*, in
which the play is referred to as a romance. In a sense, the new
category summed up the nineteenth century's view of the late
Shakespeare. Dowden's claims for the genre itself are, moreover,
exceedingly modest—romance is defined simply as that which is
'romantic':

There is a romantic element about these plays. In all there is the same
romantic incident of lost children recovered by those to whom they are
dear—the daughters of Pericles and Leontes, the sons of Cymbeline and

---

[1] Preface to Shakespeare, 1725, in D. Nichol Smith, *Eighteenth-Century Essays
on Shakespeare* (Glasgow, 1903), p. 60; Pope is similarly dubious about *Love's
Labour's Lost* and *Titus Andronicus*.

Alonso. In all there is a beautiful romantic background of sea or mountain. The dramas have a grave beauty, a sweet serenity, which seem to render the name 'comedies' inappropriate; we may smile tenderly, but we never laugh loudly, as we read them. Let us, then name this group consisting of four plays, Romances.[1]

The new genre, however, has proved as obfuscatory as it has been enlightening; various attempts to move beyond the circularity of the definition, refine its terms, establish the genre within a tradition, have revealed a good deal about the history of romance, but perhaps nothing so much as its ultimate inadequacy as a critical category for Shakespearian drama.[2] *The Winter's Tale* and *The Tempest* were comedies to the editors of the First Folio of 1623, when the plays first appeared in print; *Cymbeline*—despite its miraculous restorations and happy ending—was a tragedy. (*Pericles* does not appear in the First Folio at all.) These are the genres whose implications we must understand if we are to see *The Winter's Tale* as Shakespeare's audiences and first readers saw it. The crucial point here is that notions of genre have changed radically since the Renaissance. Genres for us are exclusive and definitive, whereas for the Renaissance they tended to be inclusive and relational. J. C. Scaliger's immense *Poetics*, first published in 1561, is a model for the age's attitudes towards literary categorization: it is essentially a filing system, and works are characteristically filed under a number of headings. Many plays (the *Oresteia*, for example) are declared to be both comic and tragic. In the same way, *Troilus and Cressida* is declared in the preface to the 1609 quarto 'as witty as the best comedy in Terence or Plautus', while the Folio editors included it in the section of tragedies. These claims do not contradict each other. Sidney's *Defence of Poesie* is often cited decrying the mingling of 'kings and clowns' in the 'mongrel tragicomedy' of his time; the objection, however, is not to the mixture of genres, but to the failure to observe decorum. He has already justified mixed forms by observing that 'if severed they be good, the conjunction cannot be hurtful': there is a comedy of wonder and delight fully appropriate to the decorum of

[1] *Shakespeare* (New York, 1877), pp. 55–6.
[2] See, e.g., Carol Gesner, *Shakespeare and the Greek Romance* (Lexington, Kentucky, 1970); Stanley Wells, 'Shakespeare and Romance', in J. R. Brown and Bernard Harris, eds., *Later Shakespeare* (1967), pp. 49–70.

tragedy.[1] This is not to say that *The Winter's Tale*, which certainly mingles kings and clowns indecorously, would have been to Sidney's taste; but that does not distinguish it from any of the modern English plays Sidney considers—all are declared to be 'defectious in the circumstances'. But of course, Sidney died in 1586; a few seasons of Shakespeare might have moved him to revise his opinions.

Mixed genres disturb us; and since the early nineteenth century we have found ways of explaining away the comic scenes in Shakespearian tragedy, as De Quincey rescued *Macbeth* by arguing that the comedy of the drunken porter does not vitiate but rather increases the tragic momentum.[2] No doubt it does, though it is not clear that critics of Shakespeare's age would have viewed the scene in the same way: there is a large body of Renaissance critical theory that argues precisely for the necessity of comic scenes in tragedy in order to mitigate the form's overwhelming effects. Thus in Italy, tragedies were regularly performed with comic or satiric interludes between the acts, and in the Elizabethan theatre, tragedies invariably concluded with jigs.[3] When modern critics discuss the tragic impact of plays like *King Lear* and *Hamlet* on Shakespeare's audience, they invariably forget about the jigs. The mixture of genres was an essential element of the theatrical experience for Shakespeare's audience, and by the time *The Winter's Tale* was written tragicomedy had been established through an extensive critical debate as a dramatic genre of unquestionable seriousness. Thus on the frontispiece to the 1616 folio of Ben Jonson's *Works* (figure 1), the genres are anatomized: Comedy and Tragedy, on either side of the triumphal arch that surrounds the book's title and author, are surmounted by Pastoral, anatomized into its two forms, the

---

[1] The Sidney passage is in *Miscellaneous Prose*, ed. K. Duncan-Jones and Jan van Dorsten (Oxford, 1973), p. 114. For a fuller discussion, see my 'Shakespeare and the Kinds of Drama', *Critical Inquiry*, 6 (1979), 107–23.

[2] 'The Knocking at the Gate in *Macbeth*', first published in the *London Magazine*, October 1823.

[3] This has recently been called into question, but the evidence for it is quite solid. Thomas Platter, a visiting Swiss traveller, describes seeing the jig at the end of *Julius Caesar* at the Globe in 1599, and says it is customary; the Middlesex Justices in October 1612 ordered the suppression of jigs at the end of plays 'on the ground that the lewd jigs, songs, and dances so used at the Fortune led to . . . breaches of the peace' (Chambers, *Elizabethan Stage*, i. 304); and William Prynne, in 1633, says that 'now always they put at the end of every tragedy . . . a comedy or jig' (*Histriomastix*, p. 484).

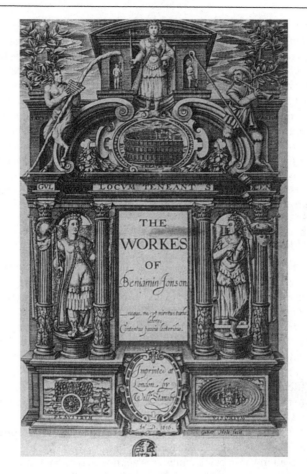

1. Ben Jonson, *Works* (1616), frontispiece: Tragedy and Comedy on either side, bucolic and satiric Pastoral above, Tragicomedy at the top.

bucolic and satiric; above these stand the two presiding deities of theatre, the rational Apollo and the ecstatic Dionysus, and between them at the top of the arch is the crowned figure of Tragicomedy, the epitome of drama.

What this means is not that we can now comfortably declare the play a tragicomedy, rather than a romance, but that we can see how fluid the concept of genre was for Shakespeare's age. To abandon the category of romance is at once to reveal that such plays as *Much Ado About Nothing, Measure for Measure, Othello*, even *The Comedy of Errors*, have at least as much to tell us about *The Winter's Tale*, even generically, as *Pericles, Cymbeline* and *The Tempest* have. It is also to abandon the fiction of Shakespeare at the age of forty-six declining into a serene old age, and producing a drama of wisdom, reconciliation and harmony. *The Winter's Tale*, like *The Tempest*, returns to issues that had concerned Shakespeare throughout his career, and its harmonies and reconciliations are as deeply embedded in the ideals, conflicts and anxieties of Jacobean culture and the historical moment as those of *The Tempest* are.

Obscurity and Elucidation

The play's problems for a modern audience are not, of course, merely generic. They are in every sense dramatic, the more so if one is aware of Shakespeare's earlier treatments of similar issues. Why does he set up the powerful tragic momentum of the opening three acts, only to disarm it with fantasy and magic? Why is Mamillius not restored, along with Hermione and Perdita; and moreover, why is the death of Mamillius—Leontes' only son and the heir to the throne—so much less of an issue dramatically than the death of his wife and the loss of his daughter? Perhaps most puzzling of all, why does Shakespeare preserve Leontes and ultimately exonerate him—why is he not treated in the fashion of all those other foolish, headstrong, misguided, tyrannical Shakespearian kings, who go to their deaths even in those cases where it is acknowledged that they are more sinned against than sinning? In fact, if we read *The Winter's Tale* in the context of Shakespeare's earlier dramas of royalty, we will be struck by how little distinction is normally accorded to the office of king, how close the dread sovereign is to the foolish, fond old man. There are in *Hamlet* no claims about the particular sanctity of kingship, nor is the murder of an anointed king represented as more heinous than the murder of anybody else. *Macbeth* does make such claims about the murder of Duncan, but not about the killing of Macbeth, who is no less a duly anointed king; and more significantly, the play has no

investment in making the king a good king—in educating
Duncan in the proper management of his thanes and his realm,
in rehabilitating Macbeth through penance, prayer, and the
advice of a good woman, in ensuring that Malcolm will not
repeat Duncan's mistakes by taking as his right-hand man a
dubiously ethical soldier like Macduff. Why, then, the intense
focus on the preservation and rehabilitation of Leontes? Why not
let him atone by dying, and resolve the tragic issues through the
accession of a new and innocent generation, on the models
provided by the endings of *2 Henry IV*, *Macbeth* and *King Lear*?
Shakespeare's source, indeed, gave him a strikingly dramatic
model: at the conclusion of Greene's *Pandosto*, the repentant king
falls in love with his still unidentified daughter; and when he
learns who she is, kills himself, to be succeeded on the throne by
his unsullied daughter and son-in-law. This is an ending that
would be perfectly consistent with the tragedy of royalty as
Shakespeare practised it, and both the preservation of Leontes
and the mode by which it is effected are unique in his drama.

The play is problematic, too, in a more specific and local sense.
It is syntactically and lexically often baffling, though this is an
aspect of the text that has been generally ignored by editors and
critics since about the middle of the last century. But if we
consider the editorial debates over such passages as Polixenes'
explanation of his need to return home (1.2.12–15), Hermione's
protestations at her trial (3.2.45–50 and 103–4), most of all,
Leontes' jealous ravings (1.2.136–44, and elsewhere), it is clear
that even where a consensus has been reached, it is based on no
real linguistic evidence. Here are two examples.

Hermione, in the course of her objections to her treatment,
says to Leontes,

> I appeal
> To your own conscience, sir, before Polixenes
> Came to your court how I was in your grace,
> How merited to be so; since he came,
> With what encounter so uncurrent I
> Have strained t'appear thus . . .
>
> (3.2.44–9)

For the past hundred years or so, the last two lines have been
taken to mean 'with what behaviour so unacceptable I have

transgressed that I should appear thus (i.e. on trial)'. This interpretation represents the consensus of three mid-Victorian editors, Halliwell, Staunton and White, and it has become, for us, simply the meaning of the passage. But to gloss the passage in this way is, at the very least, to conceal more than a century of debate and bafflement. The lines were, in fact, considered incomprehensible by most eighteenth-century editors including Johnson, who wrote of them, 'These lines I do not understand; with the licence of all editors, what I cannot understand I suppose unintelligible, and therefore propose that they may be altered . . .' Johnson's testimony in this matter is especially apropos, given his characteristic genius for finding a plain prose sense in the most elaborately conceited Shakespearian verse. In default of an interpretation, he produced a felicitous, if unconvincingly rationalized, emendation: 'With what encounter so uncurrent *have I | Been stained* to appear thus?' Even this, though it certainly makes a kind of sense, depends on its emendation to render the crucially ambiguous words *encounter* and *uncurrent* comprehensible. A detailed consideration of the history of similar attempts at elucidation would show no more than the relevant *OED* entries, for *encounter, uncurrent,* and *strain*: that the modern interpretation represents an essentially arbitrary selection of meanings from among a list of diverse and often contradictory possibilities, and does not so much resolve the linguistic problem as enable us to ignore it. The confident tone of the gloss conveying this interpretation will give no hint of two centuries of uncertainty, debate and disagreement.

A number of Hermione's speeches are similarly ambiguous, but they nevertheless constitute relatively simple cases; though particular expressions are obscure, Hermione's general drift is clear enough for us to see what we have to get her words to mean. Leontes' invective in Act I gives us no such confidence. Here is the famous crux as it appears in the First Folio:

> Can thy Dam, may't be
> Affection? thy Intention stabs the Center.
> Thou do'st make possible things not so held,
> Communicat'st with Dreames (how can this be?)
> With what's vnreall: thou coactiue art,
> And fellow'st nothing. Then 'tis very credent,
> Thou may'st co-ioyne with something, and thou do'st,

8

(And that beyond Commission) and I find it . . .

$$(1.2.136-43)$$

Find *what*? From Rowe onward, the passage has defied any consensus. Indeed, it is one of the rare places where Rowe, normally the most tolerant of editors, felt moved to radical revision:

> Can thy Dam? may't be—
> Imagination! thou dost stab to th' Center.

This can hardly be called emendation. And though no subsequent editor was persuaded, most editions since Rowe's time have adopted his equally radical repointing, whereby 'may't be—' stands alone, and 'Affection', no longer a predicate nominative in the simple question 'may it be affection?', is now the vocative subject of a new sentence, 'Affection, thy intention stabs the centre!'[1]

I have not proposed a new reading or declared the matter solved (though I cannot help remarking that I find some of the problems greatly simplified if we reject the ubiquitous and quite unnecessary repunctuation). What interests me is how little attention the editorial tradition has paid to the fact of a drama that speaks in this way—few commentators get beyond Pafford's observation that 'the speech is meant to be incoherent': Leontes is crazy, and his language is an index to his character. The problem with this is not merely that it commits the play to the imitative fallacy, but that this sort of linguistic opacity is not at all limited to Leontes. Hermione, Camillo, Antigonus and Polixenes all exhibit it on occasion as well. It is a feature of the play, and one to which I have tried to be true in the commentary.[2]

---

[1] The essential lexical work on the passage is that of Hallett Smith, 'Leontes' *Affectio*', *ShQ* 14 (1963), 163–6, which, however, depends on the eighteenth-century revision of the text. Charles Frey has an incisive discussion of the issues raised by the speech in *Shakespeare's Vast Romance* (New York, 1980), esp. p. 77; other provocative readings are in J. V. Cunningham, *Woe or Wonder* (Denver, 1960), pp. 110–12, Carol Thomas Neely, '*The Winter's Tale*: The Triumph of Speech', *SEL* 15 (1975), 324–7, and Jonathan Smith, 'The Language of Leontes', *ShQ* 19 (1968), 317–18. For a sensible counter-argument, that the speech makes better sense if 'affection' is not the technical philosophical term but the normal vernacular word for love, passion, or lust, see Maurice Hunt, 'Leontes' "Affection" and Renaissance "Intention" ', *University of Mississippi Studies in English*, 4 (1983), 49–55.

[2] For important and interestingly divergent discussions of the relationship between language and speaker in the late plays see James Sutherland, 'The Language of the Last Plays', in John Garrett, ed., *More Talking of Shakespeare*

What is concealed in the process of editorial interpretation (Johnson's methods constitute a striking exception) is the effort of will, or even wilfulness, involved in selecting from among the ambiguities of an open and fluid text a single, paraphrasable sense. Elucidation assumes that behind the obscurity and confusion of the text is a clear and precise meaning, and that the obscurity, moreover, is not part of the meaning. And since the editorial process is committed to elucidation, it is largely helpless before a text that is genuinely obscure. But what does it mean that a play speaks incomprehensibly? What are the implications for drama of a text that works in this way?—as *The Winter's Tale* undeniably does, if we think of it as a transaction between actors and audiences rather than between editors and readers; for even if we were persuaded that we had successfully elucidated all the play's obscurities, no actor can speak meaning, rather than words, and no audience, least of all Shakespeare's in 1611, comes supplied with the necessary glosses. Of course, we assume that we are, by elucidating, recovering meaning, not imposing it; but is this assumption really defensible? How do we know that the obscurity of the text was not in fact precisely what it expressed to the Renaissance audience? In this respect, the claims of Spenser for the 'dark conceit' of *The Faerie Queene*, of Chapman and Jonson for the virtues of the mysterious in poetry, may be more relevant to Shakespeare than our construction of literary history commonly assumes. A plain prose paraphrase may not, after all, be the bottom line in unlocking the mysteries of an occluded text.

We need to remember that the Renaissance tolerated, and indeed courted, a much higher degree of ambiguity and opacity than we do; we tend to forget that the age often found in incomprehensibility a positive virtue. The discontinuity between image and text in Renaissance iconographic structures has in recent years become a commonplace; symbolic imagery was *not* a universal language—on the contrary, it was radically indeterminate, and always depended on explanation to establish its meaning. When the explanation was not provided—as was often the case—the spectators remained unenlightened. But this was not a problem: 'no doubt', as Ben Jonson put it, 'their grounded

(London, 1959), pp. 144–58, and Anne Barton, 'Leontes and the Spider', in her *Essays, Mainly Shakespearean* (Cambridge, 1994), pp. 161–81.

judgements did gaze, said it was fine, and were satisfied'.[1] This particular observation described the response of uneducated spectators, but even writing for an intellectual élite, Jonson strove for what he called 'more removed mysteries',[2] and his printed texts included explanatory commentaries designed, as he put it, finally, months or years after the event, 'to make the spectators understanders'.[3] The satisfaction in such cases derived precisely from the presence of the mystery, which assured the audience at abstruse spectacles, whether groundlings or scholars, that they participated in a world of higher meaning. We are familiar with such strategies in court masques, but they are also not alien to popular drama. *Pericles*, which Jonson attacked for pandering to popular taste, includes a procession of knights bearing symbolic shields and mottoes which require elucidation to be understood, but which are not elucidated.

All editors subscribe, however uncomfortably, to some version of Burckhardt's Renaissance, an integrated culture that still spoke a universal language. For theatre historians, this view of the period was, or at least should have been, seriously compromised when Aby Warburg analysed two of the learned spectators' accounts of the famous Medici *intermezzi* of 1589, probably the best documented of the great Renaissance festivals, and observed that the meaning of the performance, and indeed the very identity of the symbolic figures, was opaque to even the most erudite members of the audience.[4] Since Warburg's essay was published in 1895, it is time Renaissance studies began to take it into account: it bears on our general sense of the nature of Renaissance public discourse as a whole. The spectator of *The Winter's Tale* in 1611, we implicitly assume, would have understood it all. What we are recovering, we tell ourselves, is only what every Renaissance audience already knew. I want to argue on the contrary that Shakespeare's audience was more like the

---

[1] *Part of the Kings entertainment, in passing to his Coronation*, in C. H. Herford, P. and E. Simpson, eds., *Ben Jonson*, vol. vii (1941), p. 91, ll. 266–7.

[2] *Hymenaei*, lines 16–17.

[3] *Love's Triumph Through Callipolis*, line 1.

[4] Aby Warburg, 'I Costumi Teatrali per gli Intermezzi del 1589', *Atti dell'Accademia del Reale Istituto Musicale di Firenze: Commemorazione della Riforma Melodrammatica* (Florence, 1895), pp. 125–6. For a recent study with a similar point, see A. R. Braunmuller, ' "To the Globe I rowed": John Holles Sees *A Game At Chess*', *ELR* 20 (1990), pp. 340–56.

audience constructed by Warburg than like the audience constructed by Burckhardt; that what Polixenes' 'sneaping winds' speech (1.2.12 ff.), or Hermione's courtroom questions (3.2.44–9, 104–6), or Leontes' jealous ravings conveyed to the Renaissance audience was pretty much what they convey to us: intensity, vagueness and obscurity. It is clear that the King of Bohemia is insisting he must go home, that the Queen is complaining about her treatment, that Leontes is wildly jealous; if anything is clear about their reasoning it is that it is utterly unclear, despite the attempts of almost three centuries of commentary to clarify it. How we interpret this obscurity—as a function of character, or of the Sicilian court, of the language of kings, of the complexities of public discourse, of the nature of stage plays themselves in the Renaissance—is the real textual question, and it remains an open one. The Shakespearian text, characteristically, gives us no guidance on the matter. We do it wrong when we deny that it is problematic and has always been so, and reduce it to our own brand of common sense.[1]

Mysteries of State

However historically conditioned we may find them, Shakespeare's plays are certainly not, in any simple or direct sense, mirrors of his world, and to undertake to find particular historical figures brought to life in them, as criticism has from time to time been fond of doing, is certainly naïve. But the central political phenomenon of the age, James I, was rapidly redefining the nature of the monarchy in England, and Shakespearian drama cannot have been insensitive to the new attitudes, especially since Shakespeare's company was under the direct patronage of the King. For the first time in two centuries the Divine Right of Kings became a serious political philosophy, and the mystical side of kingship, so ironically treated in Shakespeare's histories of the 1590s, and so infrequently invoked by Elizabeth, was now essential to the crown—King James even reintroduced the practice of touching to cure the King's Evil. 'The mystery of state' was

[1] A. R. Braunmuller isolates the primary problem with analyses of speech in the play when he observes that 'most discussion of fact, fancy and style has centered on the characters' ignorance or certitude, rather than the audience's': 'Narrative Speech and the Hinge of *The Winter's Tale*' (forthcoming).

a continual refrain in all James's utterances, 'the mystery of the king's power', the 'secretest drifts' of policy.[1] James represented the royal mind as programmatically occluded, a politic obscurantism that may certainly be reflected in the linguistic obscurity of Leontes' (or Macbeth's, or Cymbeline's) court: this is the Jacobean language of authority. In the new King's realm, the issue of elucidation became critical, and not merely in the literary sense. In 1607, for example, John Cowell, Regius Professor of Civil Law and Vice-Chancellor of the University of Cambridge, published his compendious *Interpreter: or book containing the signification of Words: Wherein is set forth the true meaning of all . . . such words and terms as are mentioned in the law writers or statutes . . . requiring any Exposition.* The book's fate testifies precisely to the dangers of elucidation: it was suppressed by royal proclamation because of its absolutist interpretation of such terms as 'prerogative' and 'subsidy'[2]—an interpretation that King James certainly did not find unsympathetic, but that was, precisely for that reason, better left a mystery.

James was as withdrawn and uncharismatic as Elizabeth had been outgoing; he resisted, as a matter of principle, any questioning of the royal judgement, and was especially concerned with maintaining and strengthening the royal prerogatives. The sonnet prefixed to *Basilicon Doron* sums up the royal position succinctly:

> God gives not kings the style of gods in vain,
> For on his throne his sceptre do they sway . . .

The same point in virtually the same language was repeated to Parliament in 1610, during the debates over the Great Contract, which would have provided the King with a permanent annual revenue, thereby making the Crown largely independent of Parliament's advice and control: 'Kings are justly called gods, for that they exercise a manner or resemblance of divine power upon earth', and James went on to insist that Parliament not presume to call the royal prerogative in question.[3] Nor should the

---

[1] The phrases are from a speech to the Star Chamber in 1616 and from the *Basilicon Doron*; cited in Jonathan Goldberg's essential study of the interrelationships between the King and the arts, *James I and the Politics of Literature* (Baltimore, 1983), p. 56.

[2] See the note on the entry for STC 5900, and the article on Cowell in the *DNB*.

[3] McIlwain, p. 307.

Commons presume to advise him 'how to govern, for that was his craft, and to meddle with that would be to lessen him'.[1] John Chamberlain observed that this 'bred generally much discomfort to see our monarchical power and royal prerogative strained so high and made so transcendent every way'.[2] Leontes' insistence, in 2.3, that he is not accountable to his advisers, and his lords' and Paulina's equally tenacious questions and protestations, are informed by a debate that persisted throughout James's reign. It is to the point that Leontes is, in the dramatic contest, ultimately the loser. Parliament similarly declined to ratify the Great Contract. William R. Morse, considering the political implications of the play, shrewdly observes that 'whatever the commitment of the court faction around James I to the ideology of absolutism, whatever their estimate of the hegemony of their position in 1610, the evidence of the drama suggests that the emergent [anti-absolutist] ideology is already passing into a kind of cultural dominance, consigning the absolutist culture of the court to a residual status thirty years before political events confirm the shift'.[3]

Lord Thomas Howard in 1611 analysed for Sir John Harington the difference in style between the new King and his predecessor: 'Your Queen did talk of her subjects' love and good affections, and in good truth she aimed well; our King talketh of his subjects' fear and subjection, and herein I think he doth well too, as long as it holdeth good.'[4] The cautionary conclusion is an index to an *arrière pensée* that was increasingly apparent throughout the realm. In 1606, only three years after the King's accession, Harington himself summed up what had passed from the royal style, a masterful, irresistible, machiavellian sense of theatre: 'We all did love her, for she said she loved us.'[5]

No less than Howard and Harington, Shakespeare in the first decade of the new reign rethinks the nature of kingship through

---

[1] The paraphrase is D. H. Willson's, *King James VI and I* (Oxford, 1967), p. 246.

[2] Letter to Ralph Winwood, 24 May 1610; *Letters*, i. 301. For a summary of the historical situation, on which this paragraph is based, see Willson, *King James VI and I*, pp. 243–70.

[3] 'Metacriticism and Materiality: The Case of Shakespeare's *The Winter's Tale*', *ELH* 58 (1991), pp. 283–304; the passage cited is on pp. 288–9.

[4] *Nugae Antiquae*, ed. Henry Harington and Thomas Park (London, 1804), i. 395; the passage, with an enlightening discussion, is cited in Jonathan Goldberg, *James I and the Politics of Literature*, pp. 28 ff.

[5] *Nugae Antiquae*, p. 360.

Macbeth, King Lear, Cymbeline, The Winter's Tale, and finally *Henry VIII* (a play significantly titled, for its first audiences, *All is True*), both in terms of how much beyond the merely political is invested in the office, and of what sorts of sanctions there might be to contain a king who abuses his prerogatives—the sanctions only now, for Shakespeare, begin to include divine ones. Indeed, to Sir Henry Wotton in 1614, the first performance of *All is True* was 'sufficient in truth within a while to make greatness very familiar, if not ridiculous'.[1] Shakespeare and the King's Men were, for this spectator, approaching too close to the monarchy, unveiling too much of the mysteries of state. What, then, would King James have thought of *The Winter's Tale*, a play about a monarch whose dogged adherence to James's deepest convictions about the independence, indeed the sanctity, of the royal judgement brings him to the edge of tragedy? It could not have offended him; he paid his players to perform it repeatedly at court for his entertainment. Perhaps he allowed the title to guide his response, and considered it no more than a tragicomic fable. But perhaps too he saw in it a confirmation of an equally basic tenet of his political philosophy, most forcefully argued in *The True Law of Free Monarchies*: that however bad a king may be, he is still the king.

It also cannot be irrelevant to *The Winter's Tale* that there was a royal family at the centre of English society for the first time since the death of Henry VIII.[2] James I's drama was of necessity a family drama, since his virtue as a successor to Elizabeth lay not only in his legitimate claim and his Protestantism, but even more in the fact that he came furnished with three heirs. The negotiations for the marriages of the elder two, Prince Henry and Princess Elizabeth, were actively pursued throughout the decade. The fact that Elizabeth eventually married the future King of Bohemia is certainly mere coincidence as far as the play is concerned, since Prince Frederick had no hereditary connection with the Bohemian throne and was not offered it until 1619, but

---

[1] Quoted in Chambers, *Elizabethan Stage*, ii. 419.

[2] Jonathan Goldberg analyses the political implications of James as *paterfamilias* in 'Fatherly Authority: The Politics of Stuart Family Images', in *Rewriting the Renaissance*, ed. Margaret W. Ferguson *et al.* (Chicago, 1986), 3–32. David Bergeron's *Shakespeare's Romances and the Royal Family* (Lawrence, Kansas, 1985) discusses the Jacobean royal family in relation to Jacobean literature and to Shakespearian drama in particular.

the subject of royal marriages was an especially timely one when the play was first performed, and by 1613 the possibility of Frederick's being offered the Bohemian crown had at least been rumoured.[1] A more sombre coincidence was the swift and mysterious death of Prince Henry in November 1612, probably of typhoid fever. By the time the King's Men revived *The Winter's Tale* at court in late 1612 or 1613 to entertain the royal fiancés, the play would have had an eerie topicality.

The King's relation to his heir was part of a complex family drama. James and Prince Henry were in fact by 1611 political opponents, James a programmatic pacifist eager for accommodations with the Catholic powers on the continent, Henry a militant Protestant, eager to lead an army of liberation through Germany and the Low Countries. By the age of fourteen, the Prince's military ambitions were being noted with enthusiasm throughout the country, and by the time he was formally declared Prince of Wales in 1610, his popular following made him a serious rival to the King in matters of public and foreign policy. The exchange at the opening of *The Winter's Tale* about the extravagant popular expectations invested in Leontes' young son Mamillius, with its implied lack of enthusiasm for Leontes, is a reflection of the Jacobean situation:

ARCHIDAMUS ... You have an unspeakable comfort of your young prince Mamillius. It is a gentleman of the greatest promise that ever came into my note.

CAMILLO I very well agree with you in the hopes of him. It is a gallant child, one that, indeed, physics the subject, makes old hearts fresh. They that went on crutches ere he was born desire yet their life to see him a man. (1.1.32–8)

—and, tacitly, to see him succeed his father.

---

[1] The Spanish ambassador reported in 1613 that King James had said 'he doubted not but that his son-in-law should have the title of a King within a few years'. The ambassador enquired privately what this meant, and was told that it was 'in respect of the Crown of Bohemia' (which was elective, not hereditary). The French, he was told, secretly supported the plan. The ambassador considered it 'a thing almost impossible'. (Carola Oman, *Elizabeth of Bohemia* (London, rev. edn., 1964), p. 88, citing SP 81.12.323.) Since in 1613 this was news to the Spanish ambassador, who had excellent informants, it could not have surfaced by 1611, but it must have had some currency among at least some members of the audience, and certainly among the royal party, around the time of the wedding.

Leontes' Jealousy

Though the play declares itself an old tale, it implicitly asserts—
like so much of the literature of any traditionally oriented
society—the truth of its fables, and it is very much true to the
assumptions of its culture. Its realities are not the facts of history
but the terrifying truths of the inner life—the destructiveness of
jealousy, the creations of sexual fear, the complexities of love, the
imponderable unpredictability of family relationships and deep,
long-lasting friendships, the divided loyalties inherent in even the
most devoted service. The insistent theme is time; but a time
removed from history and located within the family, time as
defined by generations, by youth and age, by the relations
between parents and children, and by the blood-brotherhood of
male bonding starting in early childhood. If Sicily is initially
represented as a kingdom of old age, it is the potential of infancy,
the term of Hermione's pregnancy, that measures the drama that
follows, and opens the space of Leontes' jealousy:

> Nine changes of the watery star hath been
> The shepherd's note since we have left our throne
> Without a burden. Time as long again
> Would be filled up, my brother, with our thanks,
> And yet we should for perpetuity
> Go hence in debt. And therefore, like a cipher,
> Yet standing in rich place, I multiply
> With one 'we thank you' many thousands more
> That go before it.   (1.2.1–9)

Here time is first simply change, dependent on the mutable
moon. Immediately after, at line 3, it is a medium that can be
filled (with thanks), and then, just as abruptly, it is infinite, and
its capacity cannot be satisfied—despite the multiplication of
value Polixenes describes in line 6, he sees himself as perpetually
in debt to Leontes. Love, friendship, brotherhood, hospitality,
are here represented as incurring overwhelming debts; and
Polixenes' hyperbole is like Othello's, or Romeo's, or Orsino's,
view of their love, without the counterweight provided by the
deflating rhetoric of Desdemona and Juliet or the comic tone of
Twelfth Night. Kingship and friendship are hospitality, but also
competition, and always falling short. The best friend is also
the rival who always makes you feel insecure. The ultimate

competitor is that other twin, whose face is 'a copy out of mine' (121), 'as like as eggs' (129), your son, the heir to your throne. And your wife, though she acts in your interests, even on your instructions, may in fact, with the identical words and manner, betray you.

Such a view of friendship, hospitality and family ties is clearly more ominous than comfortable, and though Leontes' passion appears suddenly and utterly unexpectedly, it is nevertheless in its way inevitable, the mirror image of Polixenes' unstable hyperbole. The 'notoriously unmotivated jealousy of Leontes', in S. L. Bethell's phrase,[1] has been a major stumbling block for the play, the first of its many improbabilities. Coleridge, however, undertook to vindicate Shakespeare's psychological acuity here, through an invidious comparison with *Othello*:

> The idea of this delightful drama is a genuine jealousy of disposition, and it should be immediately followed by the perusal of *Othello*, which is the direct contrast of it in every particular. For jealousy is a vice of the mind, a culpable tendency of the temper, having certain well known and well defined effects and concomitants, all of which are visible in Leontes, and, I boldly say, not one of which marks its presence in *Othello*.[2]

Coleridge then proceeds to cite a number of characteristics that are in fact shared by both figures:

> first, an excitability by the most inadequate causes, and an eagerness to snatch at proofs; secondly, a grossness of conception, and a disposition to degrade the object of the passion by sensual fancies and images; thirdly, a sense of shame of his own feelings exhibited in a solitary moodiness of humour, and yet from the violence of the passion forced to utter itself, and therefore catching occasions to ease the mind by ambiguities, equivoques, by talking to those who cannot, and who are known not to be able to, understand what is said to them,—in short, by soliloquy in the form of dialogue, and hence a confused, broken, and fragmentary manner; fourthly, a dread of vulgar ridicule, as distinct from a high sense of honour, or a mistaken sense of duty; and lastly, and immediately consequent on this, a spirit of selfish vindictiveness.

These obviously describe Othello as well as Leontes.

And yet there is, of course, a radical difference between the two plays that has nothing to do with character. What Coleridge's

---

[1] *The Winter's Tale: A Study* (1947), p. 48.
[2] *Lectures on Shakespeare*, 1818, cited in the *Variorum*, p. 366.

account omits is simply the plot: Othello inhabits a dramatic world of deliberate, malicious misrepresentation, of the fabrication of evidence and misinformation, whereas the self-generating nature of Leontes' passion is clear throughout. It is often argued that Othello is culpably gullible, his sense of self so fragile that his love would have ended tragically even without Iago; but credible as we may find this, it is an argument that writes the hero into another play—Iago is an essential part of *Othello*. In this respect, Leontes' jealousy, violent and unsubstantiated, is in fact realistic, far more true to human experience than Othello's super-rationalized passion, which has a villain for its agent. Emilia, at a critical moment in *Othello*, punctures the play's claim that jealousy is caused by the plotting of villains and the stealing of handkerchiefs:

> DESDEMONA
> Alas the day, I never gave him cause.
> EMILIA
> But jealous souls will not be answered so.
> They are not ever jealous for the cause,
> But jealous for they're jealous. It is a monster
> Begot upon itself, born on itself.
>
> (3.4.155–9)

It is in Emilia's interests to produce this observation, since she herself is part of the villainy—she committed the crucial theft and is protecting her guilty husband; nevertheless, her wisdom is self-evidently true, and has the force of a commonplace. The lack of any external motivation is, in this formulation, a defining feature of the passion, and Leontes' psychology in the opening acts consequently seems, in contrast with Othello's, strikingly modern in its dramatic recognition of the compulsiveness of paranoid behaviour, and more generally, of the self-generating and autonomous nature of consciousness itself.

The evidence of Hermione's adultery, therefore, is produced from within; Leontes' reasoning is characteristically circular and his syntax utterly ambiguous:

> Too hot, too hot!
> To mingle friendship far is mingling bloods.
> I have *tremor cordis* on me; my heart dances,
> But not for joy, not joy. This entertainment

> May a free face put on, derive a liberty
> From heartiness, from bounty, fertile bosom,
> And well become the agent—'t may, I grant.
> But to be paddling palms and pinching fingers,
> As now they are, and making practised smiles
> As in a looking-glass, and then to sigh, as 'twere
> The mort o'th' deer—O, that is entertainment
> My bosom likes not, nor my brows.
>
> (1.2.107–18)

Here the evidence of innocence and guilt is identical—it is, indeed, precisely the concession of the possibility of innocence, '' t may, I grant', that produces its reversal, the conviction of culpability. Leontes' language has a tendency to produce lists, with each item generating the next, and the items often synonymous ('From heartiness, from bounty, fertile bosom'); these remain harmless until the abstract 'entertainment' and 'liberty' are particularized. The suspicious quality of 'paddling palms and pinching fingers' obviously derives solely from the way Leontes describes them, but the invocation of the 'smiles | As in a looking-glass' and the 'sigh, as 'twere | The mort o'th' deer', with their implications of solitude and separation, abandons any sense of the actual social scene taking place before us—two people talking—and makes it impossible to know from the text whether any of this is happening at all.

The question of evidence then becomes critical:

> Mamillius,
> Art thou my boy? . . .
>   —what, hast smutched thy nose?
> They say it is a copy out of mine.
>   . . . they say we are
> Almost as like as eggs—women say so,
> That will say anything. But were they false
> As o'er-dyed blacks, as wind, as waters, false
> As dice are to be wished by one that fixes
> No bourn 'twixt his and mine, yet were it true
> To say this boy were like me.
>
> (1.2.118–34)

The evidence that Mamillius is Leontes' son is physical evidence, the evidence of likeness; but even this, as Leontes presents it, turns out to be hearsay, the word of women, who 'will say anything'—testimony only impeaches evidence. The inadmissibility of the testimony is then confirmed by a series of comparisons demonstrating the untrustworthiness of women, 'as false as o'er-dyed blacks', etc., another self-generating list, which is then itself refuted by an act of mere assertion—'yet were it true | To say this boy were like me'. Truth has been made independent of evidence.

Something has already been said about the problems of the subsequent 'Affection' passage, and I have undertaken to analyse its linguistic and syntactic complexities in the commentary. I wish here to pause over the sequence of pronouns, revealingly characteristic of Leontes' syntax:

> With what's unreal thou coactive art,
> And fellow'st nothing. Then 'tis very credent
> Thou mayst co-join with something, and thou dost,
> And that beyond commission, and I find it,
> And that to the infection of my brains . . .
>
> (140–4)

The 'it' that Leontes finds refers to 'something', which refers to 'nothing', which is 'what's unreal' in line 140. In finding 'it', Leontes has, literally, found nothing.[1]

The nothing that he finds, like Cordelia's nothing, grows and multiplies:

> Is whispering nothing?
> Is leaning cheek to cheek? Is meeting noses?
> Kissing with inside lip? Stopping the career
> Of laughter with a sigh?—a note infallible
> Of breaking honesty! Horsing foot on foot?
> Skulking in corners? Wishing clocks more swift?
> Hours minutes? Noon midnight? And all eyes
> Blind with the pin and web but theirs, theirs only,
> That would unseen be wicked? Is this nothing?
> Why then the world and all that's in't is nothing,
> The covering sky is nothing, Bohemia nothing,
> My wife is nothing, nor nothing have these nothings
> If this be nothing.   (1.2.281–93)

---

[1] For a detailed analysis of this and similar grammatical strategies, see J. P. Thorne, 'The grammar of jealousy: A note on the character of Leontes', *Edinburgh Studies in English and Scots*, ed. A. J. Aitken *et al.* (1971), pp. 55–65.

But the terrifying void thus evoked is only another version of Polixenes' hyperbole of negation, the 'cipher | Yet standing in rich place' that multiplies his unremitting, endlessly insufficient gratitude. Leontes' nothing is embodied in Perdita, loss personified, but she too is like Polixenes' cipher 'standing in rich place', through whom her Bohemian stepfather, 'a most homely shepherd . . . from very nothing, and beyond the imagination of his neighbours, is grown into an unspeakable estate' (4.2.37–40). In a sense such refigurations are redemptive, restoring Leontes to sanity, persuading him that he has indeed seen nothing; but they also reveal how controlled the play's terms are by Leontes' mind.

Motivation

Psychological motivation and dramatic motivation are two different things; however fantastic the depiction of Othello's passion, it has, at least until very recently, proved far more compelling than Leontes' to audiences and readers. Editors and critics, indeed, have often undertaken to supply what Shakespeare omits, a rational basis for Leontes' delusion, arguing that Leontes may in fact have perfectly good grounds for his jealousy, that Hermione, though innocent, may have presented the appearance of impropriety.[1] Directors, following suit, sometimes give Hermione and Polixenes a suspiciously intimate pantomime to justify Leontes' outburst 'Too hot, too hot'; or alternatively, they have the couple behave as Leontes describes them, but indicate by the dreamlike quality of their acting, or of the lighting, that we are seeing them through Leontes' eyes. These, of course, are not

---

[1] Quiller-Couch and Dover Wilson, for example, assume that when Hermione speaks of 'Th'offences we have made you do', etc. (1.2.82–5), 'Leontes is intended by Shakespeare to overhear these equivocal words as he comes forward from behind' (New Shakespeare *Winter's Tale*, p. 133). Howard Felperin, in a brilliantly mischievous essay, observes that the text in fact gives us no real reason to believe in Hermione's innocence ('Tongue-Tied, Our Queen?', in his collection *The Uses of the Canon* (Oxford, 1990), 35–55). Felperin is playing devil's advocate, but Nevill Coghill quite seriously asks 'Who can fail to wonder whether the man [i.e. Polixenes] so amicably addressing this expectant mother may not be the father of her child? For what other possible reason can Shakespeare have contrived the conversation so as to make him specify nine changes of the inconstant moon? These things are not done by accident' ('Six Points of Stage-craft in *The Winter's Tale*', *Sh. Survey* 11 (1958), p. 33).

neutral assumptions, and have consequences for the play as a whole; in performance, this is, after all, the single crucial moment determining the degree of Leontes' delusion. But if Leontes' jealousy is reasonable, an honourable mistake, how are we to feel about the rest of the play, the sixteen years of loss, self-castigation and penance? Lear asserts, credibly, that he is more sinned against than sinning, Othello that he is 'an honourable murderer'; but nobody in *The Winter's Tale*, nobody except editors and critics, undertakes to exculpate Leontes.

Emilia's wisdom to the contrary notwithstanding, however, the question of motivation is in fact addressed by the play. Leontes does undertake to account for his passion, or at least to provide a psychological context for it. After his first flash of violent jealousy, he explains his distracted manner to Hermione and Polixenes in this way:

> Looking on the lines
> Of my boy's face, methoughts I did recoil
> Twenty-three years, and saw myself unbreeched,
> In my green velvet coat, my dagger muzzled
> Lest it should bite its master and so prove,
> As ornaments oft do, too dangerous.
>
> (1.2.152–7)

The return to childhood here is also a retreat from sexuality and the dangers of manhood exemplified in unmuzzled daggers. Leontes sees himself 'unbreeched', not yet in breeches: Early Modern children of both sexes were dressed in skirts until the age of seven or so; the 'breeching' of boys was the formal move out of the common gender of childhood, which was both female in appearance and controlled by women, and into the world of men.

The childhood to which Leontes imagines himself returning has been described by Polixenes as Edenic, and specifically pre-sexual:

> what we changed
> Was innocence for innocence—we knew not
> The doctrine of ill-doing, nor dreamed
> That any did. Had we pursued that life,
> . . . we should have answered heaven
> Boldly, 'not guilty', the imposition cleared
> Hereditary ours.

This is a world without vice and without temptation, in which even original sin appears to have been dealt with. There are no women in it, only the best friend, an emotional twin.

At this point Hermione enters the fantasy with a pertinent observation: 'By this we gather | You have tripped since.' Polixenes agrees; the fall from grace is a fall into sexuality:

> O my most sacred lady,
> Temptations have since then been born to's, for
> In those unfledged days was my wife a girl;
> Your precious self had not yet crossed the eyes
> Of my young playfellow.

Hermione both protests and concurs:

> Of this make no conclusion, lest you say
> Your queen and I are devils. Yet go on;
> Th'offences we have made you do we'll answer,
> If you first sinned with us, and that with us
> You did continue fault, and that you slipped not
> With any but with us.
>
> (1.2.67–85)

However good-natured their banter, Hermione's projected conclusion is the logical one: 'your queen and I are devils'. Her teasing view of marriage as a continuing state of sin with diabolical agents repeats the view of sexuality implicit in the men's fantasy.

It is impossible to say what particular word or gesture triggers Leontes' paranoid jealousy, but the translation of the inseparable friend into the dangerous rival and of the chaste wife into a whore is similarly implicit in the fantasy, its worst-case scenario, so to speak, replicating the situation Shakespeare had imagined with such detailed intensity in the Dark Lady sonnets. All this is predicated simply on the move out of childhood and into sexuality—in Polixenes' account, 'ill-doing' is a 'doctrine', an education out of innocence, and knowledge, the forbidden fruit, is explicitly carnal.[1] It is also, as Leontes later observes, fatal:

---

[1] J. I. M. Stewart, in *Character and Motive in Shakespeare* (1949), pp. 35–6, sees Leontes' behaviour as the belated guilty reaction to an adolescent love affair between Leontes and Polixenes. Half a century later, the theory seems rather quaint, and quite anachronistic: there is no evidence that suppressed guilt over adolescent homosexuality was a Renaissance problem. But it does have its value

> There may be in the cup
> A spider steeped, and one may drink, depart,
> And yet partake no venom, for his knowledge
> Is not infected; but if one present
> Th'abhorred ingredient to his eye, make known
> How he hath drunk, he cracks his gorge, his sides
> With violent hefts. I have drunk, and seen the spider.
>
> (2.1.39–45)

Leontes' assumption here, that knowledge is not a defence against poison but is itself the poison, is entirely consistent with Polixenes' account of childhood as an Edenic innocence destroyed by carnal knowledge, and is, indeed, an obvious extension of it. Similarly, Polixenes' implication that the knowledge of 'ill-doing' comes in dreams—'we knew not | The doctrine of ill-doing, nor dreamed | That any did'—is terrifyingly realized in Leontes' subsequent behaviour, conditioned by his dangerously circular conviction of the absolute identity of his wife's adultery with his own fantasy, the ambiguous assurance that 'Your actions are my dreams' (3.2.80). The two kings remain 'as twinned lambs', two versions of the same psyche.

And when Leontes retreats from the implications of this fantasy, he is retreating not only from women and sex: he is retreating from his place in one of the very few normative families in Shakespeare—families consisting of father, mother and children. Most families in Shakespeare have only one parent; the very few that include both parents generally have only one child, and when that configuration appears, it tends to be presented as Leontes' marriage is presented, as exceedingly dangerous to the child: for example, Juliet and her parents, Coriolanus and Virgilia, Cymbeline, his queen, and Innogen,[1] Macduff and Lady Macduff,[2] the Duke and Duchess of York in *Richard II* arguing about whether to denounce their child as a traitor. It is a

---

in indicating that the crucial relationship is between the two men, not between husband and wife. For relevant historicized views of homosocial relationships in the Renaissance, see Alan Bray, *Homosexuality in Renaissance England* (1982), Eve Kosofsky Sedgwick, *Between Men* (New York, 1985), Chapters 1 and 2, Bruce R. Smith, *Homosexual Desire in Shakespeare's England* (Chicago, 1991), and Jonathan Goldberg, *Sodometries* (Stanford, 1993).

[1] I use the Oxford editors' spelling of the name.

[2] Macduff later implies that there are more children ('all my pretty ones'), but dramatically we see only the single son, immediately before his murder.

configuration that, with the single exception of the Page family in *The Merry Wives of Windsor*, appears nowhere else in comedy.

Marriage is a dangerous condition in Shakespeare. We are always told that comedies end in marriages. A few of Shakespeare's do, but the much more characteristic Shakespearian conclusion comes just before the marriage, and sometimes, as in *Love's Labour's Lost* and *Twelfth Night*, with an entirely unexpected delay or postponement—and in the case of the former, with no certainty whatever that the proposed nuptials will in fact eventually take place. Plays that continue beyond the point where comedy ends, with the older generation defeated and a happy marriage successfully concluded, depict the condition as utterly disastrous: *Romeo and Juliet*, *Othello*. Most Shakespearian marriages of longer duration are equally disheartening, with shrewishness, jealousy and manipulativeness the norm in comedy, and real destructiveness in tragedy: Oberon and Titania, the Merry Wives, Capulet and Lady Capulet, Claudius and Gertrude, Macbeth and Lady Macbeth, Cymbeline and his queen, Posthumus and Innogen. The trusting, articulate, openly affectionate marriage of Brutus and Portia is all but unique in Shakespeare.[1]

The Jacobean family, like the Jacobean state, is a patriarchy, and Shakespearian drama reflects a deep cultural ambivalence about the place of women in it. Lady Macbeth, Gertrude, Goneril and Regan represent the dark side of the irresistible independence, grace and intelligence of Portia, Rosalind, Helena. The encroachment of women on masculine prerogatives was increasingly a subject of warning and exhortation, from sermons and pamphlets to royal proclamations. In 1620, according to John Chamberlain, King James commanded the Bishop of London to instruct the clergy 'to inveigh vehemently and bitterly in their sermons against the insolency of our women, and their wearing of broad-brimmed hats, pointed doublets, their hair cut short or shorn, and some of them stilettos or poniards, . . . adding withal that if pulpit admonitions will not reform them he would proceed by another course'.[2] This admonition was directed against a

---

[1] See *Julius Caesar* 2.1.233 ff. The only Shakespearian marriage that is specifically depicted as sexually happy, moreover, is the incestuous marriage of Claudius and Gertrude, a murderer and an adulteress.

[2] *Letters of John Chamberlain*, ed. Norman E. McClure (Philadelphia, 1939), ii. 286–7.

masculine fashion in women's clothing; Linda Woodbridge has anatomized the developing disapproval of this style for women, culminating in two pamphlets published in 1620, *Hic Mulier*, an attack on women in male dress, and *Haec-Vir*, a reply attacking male effeminacy, which is held to be responsible for the fashion—if men were really men, the argument goes, women would be women.[1] It is clear, however, that the new cultural phenomenon was not the style of dress but the anxiety it provoked:[2] how are women to be kept in their place?

This was obviously not a new issue in British society. John Knox's collective libel *The Monstrous Regiment of Women* appeared in 1558 warning England and Scotland of the dire consequences attendant on the fact that both countries were ruled by women. Thirty-five years later such Shakespearian queens as the Margaret of *Henry VI*, Part 3 and Tamora in *Titus Andronicus* could still serve as exemplary figures for Knox's admonition. But the polemic gains an extraordinary energy at the moment when women are, in fact, effectively excluded from the structures of authority. In all King James's insistence on his status as patriarch, the matriarch is utterly elided, incorporated or even rendered superfluous. His marriage provides the model for his monarchy: upon his accession in 1603, he declared to Parliament that 'I am the husband and the whole island is my lawful wife; I am the head, and it is my body.'[3] The imagery derives from St Paul on marriage, and the two statements are presented as synonymous. Mothers become unnecessary; he himself will be 'a loving nourish-father' who will provide his subjects with 'their own nourish-milk'.[4] James conceives himself as the head of a single-parent family.

'Your queen and I are devils': Hermione's banter participates in a basic cultural anxiety. In a sense Leontes' fears need no explanation because they are merely the cultural currency of the age, articulated continually in sermons and pamphlets, and in

---

[1] Linda Woodbridge, *Women and the English Renaissance* (Urbana, 1986), pp. 139–51.

[2] For example, Simon Shepherd cites a number of texts from the 1580s and 1590s that similarly remark, with varying degrees of interest and disapproval, the popularity of masculine female clothing. See *Amazons and Warrior Women* (Brighton, 1981), esp. Chapter 6.

[3] McIlwain, p. 272.

[4] Ibid., p. 24.

royal tirades against 'the insolency of our women'. If we ask why feminine manners and fashions should occupy the royal attention at all, it is perhaps sufficient to observe that in *The Winter's Tale* Antigonus' good-humoured inability to control his wife represents one manifest limit of Leontes' royal authority. In the drama it is a salutary limit, certainly; but even here the relation between husband and wife is ambiguous, presented comically and ironically, hardly a model marriage; and as for their sense of family life, they are as parents scarcely more humane than Leontes: Antigonus mentions their three daughters once, only to threaten to 'geld' them (2.1.147), and this remark constitutes the only indication from either of them that their family extends beyond themselves. And though Paulina's behaviour is certainly vindicated, the instrument of restoration and reconciliation, the play's ambivalence about her is clear—even her admirers impugn her shrewish tongue and her harsh manner. Is this what Rosalind and Portia become in middle age? Or is the witty, articulate heroine no longer a believable figure for the Shakespeare of 1610?[1]

Hermione's Trial

In the course of her trial for adultery and treason, Hermione confronts her husband with his fantasies:

> My life stands in the level of your dreams,
> Which I'll lay down

and Leontes replies,

> Your actions are my dreams.
> You had a bastard by Polixenes,
> And I but dreamed it.
> (3.2.79–82)

It is a characteristic moment confounding knowledge and fantasy, uncovering the threats inherent in conventionally innocent

---

[1] It is perhaps relevant that Moll Cutpurse, the witty, articulate heroine of Middleton's and Dekker's *The Roaring Girl*, produced in the same year as *The Winter's Tale*, is a transvestite. For an acute and original discussion of Paulina's subversive behaviour in relation to the changing concept of authorship in the Renaissance, see Jane Tylus, *Writing and Vulnerability in the Late Renaissance* (Stanford, 1993), pp. 165 ff.

behaviour—hospitality, sociable conversation, expressions of affection for old friends: these are rendered malevolent through the operation of dreams.[1] The 'level' in Hermione's metaphor is the target in archery, what is aimed at. 'My life stands in the level of your dreams' means 'I stand within the fatal range of your delusions', 'you take aim at me through your dreams', with the dream providing not the fairy fables and lovers' toys of an earlier Shakespeare, but the deadly reality of the marksman preparing to shoot. In this context, 'Your actions are my dreams' is no more than the literal truth, and Leontes' sarcasm, 'You had a bastard by Polixenes, | And I but dreamed it', is an accurate expression of the paranoid dubiety of the play's world.

Leontes' paranoia is, however, not merely a tragic delusion; it too has clear cultural co-ordinates. To begin with, it registers the fears of a patriarchal society about the power of women, exemplified in sexual power. But more specifically than this, the issue of bastardy was one that haunted the English monarchy for three generations; even King James lived under the shadow of his mother's reputation for profligacy, and had feared that the charge that he was illegitimate, the child not of Darnley but of Mary Stuart's secretary David Rizzio, would keep him from the English throne. The question of Perdita's legitimacy is one with complex social and legal implications.

Hermione's trial is the mirror of a critical moment in English history. The idea of a queen charged with adultery and treason on trial for her life would still have had considerable resonance in the England of 1610—so much resonance, indeed, that in Shakespeare's drama about the romance of Henry VIII and Anne Boleyn, its tragic conclusion cannot be so much as hinted at (ninety years after the events, the continuing necessity for politic silence gives a particular poignancy to the play's contemporary title *All is True*).[2] The offspring of that marriage, Elizabeth, like Perdita declared illegitimate by an act of the royal imagination,

[1] Garrett Stewart discusses dream as a metatheatrical strategy in *A Midsummer Night's Dream* and *The Winter's Tale* in 'Shakespearean Dreamplay', *ELR* 11 (1981), pp. 44–69; see also Marjorie Garber's *Dream in Shakespeare* (New Haven, 1974), esp. pp. 163–86, for an overview.

[2] Horace Walpole was the first to call attention to the similarities between Hermione's trial and that of Anne Boleyn; see *Historic Doubts on the Life and Reign of King Richard the Third . . .* (1768), ed. P. W. Hammond (Gloucester, 1987), pp. 108–9.

had the taint of her bastardy to contend with throughout her long reign. Her official iconography included continual allusions to both the Virgin Mary and the phoenix, vainly enlisting typology and symbology to assert the immaculateness of her own conception. Even from the throne, half a century later, there was no way to countermand the royal patriarch's fantasy of cuckoldry—in this context, the insane dream is not Leontes' paranoid invention, but the idea that after so many years of anonymity and exile, Perdita can be retroactively legitimized.

Elizabeth's claim to the English throne derived from her father's will, which established the line of succession.[1] Parliament had in fact granted Henry VIII the authority to legitimize bastards, so that, in the absence of a male heir, his natural son Henry Duke of Richmond could succeed him. He did not, in fact, use this authority (Richmond died shortly after the act was passed), nor did he ever legitimize either Mary Tudor, who had been bastardized by the nullification of the King's marriage to Katherine of Aragon, or Elizabeth.[2] But the fact of the king's authority over his children's bastardy is significant, and relevant.

Under English law, however, Elizabeth was in fact not illegitimate, nor would Perdita have been. Lord Chief Justice Coke explains the applicable law in this way:

We term them all by the name of bastard that be born out of lawful marriage. By the Common Law, if the husband be within the four seas, that is, within the jurisdiction of the King of England, if the wife hath issue, no proof is to be admitted to prove the child a bastard . . . unless the husband hath an apparent impossibility of procreation, as if the husband be but eight years old. . . . But if the issue be born within a month, or a day, after marriage between parties of lawful age, the child is legitimate.[3]

[1] Even this was ambiguous, since the earlier Act specifically excluding her from the succession (28 Henry VIII) had never been revoked, and was therefore also still in force.

[2] Mary had herself legitimized by an Act of Parliament on her accession (this was probably technically unnecessary, since the return to Roman Catholicism meant that Henry's marriage to her mother was once again held to be valid), but for Elizabeth the issue of her bastardy was far more complicated, and she declined to reopen it. 'Thus the question of Elizabeth's "legitimacy" was ignored and continued to trouble her for many years to come' (J. B. Black, *The Reign of Elizabeth* (Oxford, 1936), p. 15).

[3] *First Part of the Institutes of the Laws of England* (4th edn., 1639), Book 3, Sec. 399, p. 244.

That is, the child of a legally married woman is legitimate, even if the husband denies paternity, unless a manifest impossibility is involved. At her trial, an extraordinary number of charges was brought against Anne Boleyn: four lovers were indicted (of whom only one confessed, under the threat of torture), and she was accused in addition of an incestuous liaison with her brother. This proliferation testifies primarily to the inherent weakness of the legal aspects of the royal case; though since adultery against the King was taken to constitute treason, the single confession would presumably have been sufficient to send the Queen to her death. (In this context, Leontes' and Polixenes' identification of each other as brothers and twins in effect adds the charge of incest to Hermione's indictment—in *Pandosto* the Queen is accused of 'most incestuous adultery'; see Appendix B, p. 241.) But all this was in fact irrelevant to the question of whether Elizabeth was a bastard: whatever Anne Boleyn was guilty of could, under the law as elucidated by Justice Coke, have no effect on her daughter's legitimacy—in order to bastardize Elizabeth, Henry would have had to show that his marriage to Anne had been invalid, something he attempted to do but failed.[1] Elizabeth's bastardy was, like Perdita's, a pure creation of the royal will.

There is, of course, in Hermione's case no admissible testimony, because there is no agreement about what constitutes evidence. What for Leontes is empirical, 'the sensible and true avouch' of his own eyes, is to Hermione merely 'surmises, all proofs sleeping else | But what your jealousies awake' (3.2.110–11). The appeal to the oracle is in itself an acknowledgement of the radical fallibility of human justice, the impossibility of determining truth through the processes available to human reason. The play certainly assumes the oracle's infallibility, though this, for a Renaissance audience, may have constituted yet another of its improbabilities. There was, by Shakespeare's time, a considerable literature denying any divine inspiration to the ancient

---

[1] Henry, in addition to raising all the charges of multiple adultery, incest and treason, undertook to have his marriage to Anne invalidated on the grounds of his own previous liaison with her sister: to sleep with one's husband's brother, or one's wife's sister, was incestuous under canon law, and to have had carnal relations with two sisters or two brothers was held to constitute a sufficient affinity to prevent a subsequent marriage to one of them. The line of argument was valid, but it was considered politically inexpedient to pursue it.

oracles, and Leontes' rejection of Apollo's word is entirely consistent with orthodox Christian opinion.[1] More to the point,
however, is Leontes' sudden reversal of his decision, what for him
proves the truth of the oracle:

> SERVANT
> The prince, your son, with mere conceit and fear
> Of the Queen's speed, is gone. . . .
>
> > Is dead.
>
> LEONTES
> Apollo's angry, and the heavens themselves
> Do strike at my injustice.
>
> (3.2.142–5)

This constitutes a significant rearrangement of the events as
Shakespeare found them in *Pandosto*, where the King's change of
heart is a direct and immediate response to the reading of the
oracle, and the news of the boy's death comes only after
Pandosto's apology and repentance. Shakespeare erects upon the
accidents and misfortunes of Greene's plot a far more complex
moral psychology for his hero. The events as Greene presents
them have a clear logical structure; but there is no logical
connection between the death of Mamillius and Leontes' sudden
conviction of divine retribution: Leontes has, in fact, been given
a perfectly reasonable physiological explanation for Mamillius'
death; he invents and elects to believe a metaphysical one. The
process is no different from that by which he had convinced
himself of Hermione's guilt. Being released from one's delusions
and restored to one's senses has nothing to do with a return to
rationality.

Mamillius' Death

Stanley Cavell, in a superb essay considering the play in the
context of philosophical scepticism, begins by anatomizing the
problematic nature of Mamillius' death:

Shall we say that the absent boy is meant to cast the shadow of finitude
or doubt over the general air of reunion at the end of the play, to

---

[1] For example, Hobbes dismisses 'the ambiguous or senseless answers of the
priests at Delphi, Delos, Ammon, and other famous oracles' (*Leviathan*, i. 12).
Felperin develops this point in 'Tongue-Tied, Our Queen', pp. 38–41.

emblematize that no human reconciliation is uncompromised, not even one constructible by the powers of Shakespeare? Or shall we say that in acquiring a son-in-law the loss of the son is made up for? Would that be Hermione's—the son's mother's—view of the matter? Or shall we take the boy's death more simply symbolically, as standing for the inevitable loss of childhood? Then does Perdita's being found mean that there is a way in which childhood *can*, after all, be recovered? But the sixteen years that Perdita was, as it were, lost are not recovered.[1]

This is one of the very few discussions of the play to take its losses seriously. The more usual critical position is exemplified in Hazelton Spencer's rapt account of the play's conclusion: 'each theme (except the plaintive little motif of Mamillius) is restated, and all are combined, in the magnificent counterpoint of the fifth act'.[2] Spencer's account is hyperbolic but nevertheless accurate: the play certainly does not make much of the death of Mamillius. But why is the death of the treasured child, the only son, the heir to the throne, no more than a 'plaintive little motif'?

The relation between fathers and sons in the play is a complex mix of opposites, 'Now my sworn friend and then mine enemy', as Polixenes puts it (1.2.165), and Leontes seeing himself in his child's face is also seeing the childhood twin and rival. The question that Leontes' scrutiny initiates, are you really mine, is quickly answered—they are 'as like as eggs' (l. 129)—but Leontes' next question calls Mamillius' very childishness in doubt: 'Mine honest friend, | Will you take eggs for money?' (159–60)—are you an innocent, are you really the child you seem? Mamillius denies it: 'No, my lord, I'll fight.' He denies it again with Hermione and her women at the opening of Act 2, refusing to play, and to be spoken to 'as if | I were a baby still'—there is no nostalgia for childhood innocence in the depiction of this child. Nor will he be told stories; it is he who proposes the winter's tale (2.1.25 ff.), a tale of sprites and goblins beginning 'There was a man dwelt by a churchyard . . .', a tale about a man who lives with the continual evidence of death and loss about him. Mamillius' tale is the story of Leontes: the child has already been destroyed by Leontes' sin, Mamillius' innocence by Leontes' knowledge.

Cavell finely anatomizes the Oedipal implications of this scene:

---

[1] *Disowning Knowledge* (Cambridge, 1987), p. 193.
[2] *The Art and Life of William Shakespeare* (New York, 1940), p. 367.

Think of the boy whispering in his mother's ear, and think back to her having shown that her fantasy of having things told in her ear makes her feel full [1.2.90–1]. . . . Then the scene of the boy's telling a tale is explicitly one to cause jealousy (as accordingly was the earlier scene of telling between Hermione and Polixenes, which the present scene repeats, to Leontes' mind); hence the son's death reads like the satisfaction of the father's wish.[1]

If this remains too narrowly within its Freudian categories, we may observe that the rivalry between King and heir has been implied at the very outset, and was, moreover, a potent political reality in Jacobean England. At Prince Henry's death, it was widely believed, even by Queen Anne, that he had been poisoned, and the King himself was not beyond suspicion—he was in many respects the logical suspect.[2] If the story of Oedipus is somewhere behind Leontes and Mamillius, it is a version of the story in which Laius wins.

Hermione's Death

If Leontes' metaphysical understanding of Mamillius' death represents a higher truth than the physiological account the messenger gives, it is worth observing first that only Leontes views the matter in this way, and second that in his response to the terrible news, while acknowledging his culpability, he also accommodates himself to his loss very easily. Hermione's swoon is not taken seriously—'Her heart is but o'ercharged; she will recover'; Heaven is squared with an apology, and all past errors are assumed to be easily rectifiable:

> Apollo, pardon
> My great profaneness 'gainst thine oracle.
> I'll reconcile me to Polixenes,
> New woo my queen, recall the good Camillo,
> Whom I proclaim a man of truth, of mercy . . .
>   (3.2.151–5)

In a sense, Leontes' ultimate salvation lies precisely in his ability to make metaphysical leaps of faith, to move beyond the imme-diacies of facts and evidence—it is an ability that Paulina will

---

[1] *Disowning Knowledge*, p. 196.
[2] See J. W. Williamson, *The Myth of the Conqueror* (New York, 1978), 166–8.

invoke in the final scene as an essential element in the restoration of Hermione: 'It is required | You do awake your faith' (5.3.94–5). Hamlet's sudden conviction that 'There's a special providence in the fall of a sparrow' (5.2.165–6) is similarly enabling, and equally illogical. To call Leontes' accommodation to the death of his child easy is not to deny the realities of the feeling involved, but it is to see it as a psychological strategy that we may feel leaves the King, from the moral point of view, unpleasantly intact. Even in coming to his senses, Leontes' ego remains resolutely unbruised: 'I have too much believed mine own suspicion' (3.2.149)—as Cavell pertinently asks, how much would be enough?[1] The death of his son and wife, the loss of his daughter, are to be lessons for him—terrible lessons—but that is all they will be. It is Antigonus who suffers death for the abandonment of Perdita; Leontes remains at the centre of the play's moral universe. The restored Hermione accepts him back at the play's end, Perdita reappears to provide him with the heir his actions have destroyed: the preservation and continuance of the king is throughout the critical issue.

This bears, too, on our sense of Paulina's independence. Her passionate resistance to Leontes' commands produces some of the most thrilling moments in the play. But elsewhere she speaks essentially as the king's externalized conscience, at times in an almost Spenserian fashion, as if Leontes has actually succeeded in incorporating her. Announcing the death of Hermione, she expresses the moral realities that Leontes cannot acknowledge: that everything does not take place inside his head, that losses cannot be restored simply by repenting, that feelings have no effect on facts:

> O thou tyrant,
> Do not repent these things, for they are heavier
> Than all thy woes can stir; therefore betake thee
> To nothing but despair.
>
> (3.2.205–8)

But in fact, at his first gesture of repentance, she at once withdraws the charge, declares herself 'a foolish woman' (l. 225) and asks forgiveness—women, in this world, even the best and most truthful, must not go too far: the truth itself, as

---

[1] *Disowning Knowledge*, p. 196.

Shakespeare's *All is True* bore witness, can go too far. Paulina is the most powerful moral voice in the play, but her role is increasingly defined within the limits of the play's monarchical and patriarchal assumptions. The moral voice, in this context, is the one that devotes itself single-mindedly to the continual articulation of the hard facts of Leontes' life, the voice of the architect of his long catharsis.

One of those hard facts is the death of Hermione. Initially, Paulina's report is our evidence, and like Leontes, we have no reason not to believe it. The evidence, indeed, is the same as the evidence of Mamillius' death: the report of an eyewitness. But the play goes further than this. At the end of the scene, Leontes demands to see the bodies of his wife and son, and says he will have them buried in a single grave (ll. 232–4). This is important, because it was quite unnecessary for Shakespeare to include it. If he had wanted to leave some question about Hermione's death, Leontes could easily have said nothing, or could have said that he could not bear to be confronted with the evidence of his crimes. Leontes is our guarantee that the two deaths are real: if Mamillius is dead, so is Hermione; and by the same token, if Leontes is being deceived by Paulina about the reality of death, so are we being deceived by Shakespeare. What this means is not that at the play's conclusion, Hermione really is a statue come to life (we have the word of Hermione herself that this is not the case), but that Shakespearian drama does not create a consistent world. Rather it continually adjusts its reality according to the demands of its developing argument.[1]

---

[1] There are a number of places where Shakespearian drama subsequently misrepresents action we have seen taking place, as, for example, in Iachimo's and Pisanio's egregiously inaccurate accounts of their roles in the events of the play at the end of *Cymbeline*, or in the famous double time-scheme of *Othello*, which requires our belief in a whole sequence of events for which there is literally no time in the play's structure. Nor is the device unique to Shakespeare, or to the Renaissance: Hitchcock was criticized for employing it in *Stage Fright*. In a flashback at the beginning of the film, Charlotte Inwood (played by Dietrich) appears in her lover's flat wearing a bloodstained dress, which she leaves with him. But at the end the lover confesses that this version of events is false: it was he who subsequently put the blood on the dress, as a way of manufacturing evidence of Charlotte's guilt. The blood in the flashback is the same kind of misrepresentation as Hermione's death. For a fuller discussion, see my essay 'Shakespeare Imagines a Theatre', in *Shakespeare Man of the Theatre*, ed. Kenneth Muir *et al.* (Newark, Del., 1983), 34–46.

Pastoral

To anyone familiar with the tremendous variety and vitality of Renaissance pastoral (as of its Virgilian and Theocritean models), the modern division of the mode into idyllic and realistic visions, the critical dichotomy of 'soft' and 'hard', will seem absurdly reductive. Indeed, the play that established tragicomedy as a serious genre in the Renaissance was itself a pastoral, Guarini's *Il Pastor Fido* (1590, first translated into English anonymously in 1602); and for most of the dramatists of Shakespeare's age, pastoral was the mode in which tragedy and comedy became inseparable. The lives of shepherds, Renaissance pastoral assumes, exhibit within a small compass all the elements of human life—that is why it is worth attending to: not because it is an escapist fantasy about the golden age, but because of its moral and emotional capaciousness.

In *The Winter's Tale* the tragicomic aspects of the mode are epitomized at once in those two touchstones of theatrical perversity, the shipwreck on the seacoast of Bohemia and the bear that devours Antigonus. The bear, indeed, has been shown by Louise Clubb to constitute, in itself, a tragicomic topos in sixteenth-century continental drama, a generic commonplace.[1] As for the Bohemian seacoast, which Shakespeare found in *Pandosto* and retained, it is not an error, but one of the elements stamping the play as a moral fable—like the title itself, it removes the action from the world of literal geographical space as it is removed from historical time.[2] Despite the fact that Shakespeare plays are not

[1] 'The Tragicomic Bear', *Comparative Literature Studies*, 9 (1972), 17–30. Other particularly useful discussions of the bear are Dale B. J. Randall, ' "This is the Chase": or the Further Pursuit of Shakespeare's Bear', *Shakespeare Jahrbuch*, 121 (1985), pp. 89–95, which calls attention to Horace's complaint, in *Epistles* II.1.185–6, against audiences who 'call in the middle of a play for a bear or for boxers'; Dennis Biggins's ' "Exit Pursued by a Beare": A Problem in *The Winter's Tale*', *ShQ* 13 (1962), pp. 3 ff.; and Michael Bristol's 'In Search of the Bear', *ShQ* 42 (1991), pp. 145–67, which places the bear in the context of both Renaissance folklore and seasonal economics. Daryl Palmer relates the bear to Hermione's invocation of her imperial Russian father, pointing out that the Russian emperor best known to Shakespeare's age was Ivan IV ('the Terrible', d. 1584), who murdered his son and, according to Purchas, amused himself 'with letting bears loose in throngs of people': 'Jacobean Muscovites: Winter, Tyranny and Knowledge in *The Winter's Tale*', *ShQ* 46 (1995), 323–39.

[2] In *Pandosto* the kingdoms are reversed; Pandosto is King of Bohemia and Egistus King of Sicilia. But Bohemia still has a seacoast: Egistus 'provided a navy of ships and sailed into Bohemia to visit his old friend and companion' (see

notable for geographical accuracy, the setting has provoked several centuries of complaint and specious explanation. In 1619, Jonson told Drummond of Hawthornden that 'Shakespeare in a play brought in a number of men saying they had suffered shipwreck in Bohemia, where there is no sea near by some 100 miles'.[1] Hanmer resolved the problem by declaring the Folio's compositor to be at fault and changing Bohemia to Bithynia. No subsequent editor followed his lead, though both Garrick, for his version of the play, *Florizel and Perdita*, and Charles Kean for his famous production at the Princess's Theatre in 1856, set the pastoral scenes in Bithynia (see below, pp. 69–74).[2] But Furness observed that since Jonson complained about the play's geography four years before the Folio was printed, the error must have been Shakespeare's. Several critics (one as recently as 1955) have argued that since for brief periods in the thirteenth and early sixteenth centuries Bohemia was part of the Austrian empire, it therefore did have a seacoast—this is rather like arguing that since the 1536 Act of Union Wales has been on the North Sea. But most commentators have been content to explain the error away as Pafford and Schanzer do, by observing that it is simply adopted from Greene. However, if there is a problem, this merely shifts it from Shakespeare to Greene.

It is, of course, entirely possible that both writers found Bohemia a pleasantly euphonious name (by early 1610 it had the additional merit of its staunch and embattled Protestantism) and considered the facts of geography irrelevant to the fairy-tale world of the story. But the seacoast of Bohemia seems also to have had a special resonance in Jacobean England. The *Variorum* cites three instances in which references to the Bohemian coast are used to characterize a particularly foolish or ignorant speaker; S. L. Bethell argues on the basis of these that the setting was an old joke, analogous in modern times to references to the Swiss Navy or Wigan Pier, and suggests that if W. S. Gilbert 'presented us with an admiral in the Swiss navy', this would be

Appendix B, p. 235). For a speculation on the reason for the reversal, see below, pp. 45–6.

[1] *Conversations with Drummond*, in *Ben Jonson*, ed. Herford and Simpson, vol. ii, ll. 208–10.

[2] For the printed version of *Florizel and Perdita*, Garrick returned the play to Bohemia.

a good indication to a Savoy audience of 'the degree of reality to be attributed to his plot'.[1] If this is correct, the setting of the pastoral scenes would then be, like Shakespeare's title, an alienating device, and an index to both tone and genre.

In any case, the relevance of seacoasts to Bohemia in the Renaissance imagination is in fact demonstrable: Wenceslaus IV, King of Bohemia (1361–1419), took as his *impresa* a storm-tossed ship, with the motto *Tempestati Parendum* ('stormy weather must be prepared for') (see figure 2). I am not suggesting that Greene and Shakespeare were familiar with the ancient King of Bohemia's *impresa*, but rather that the ruler of this landlocked country found a ship in a storm an appropriate emblem of his condition for moral and ethical reasons, not geographical ones.

Antigonus' vision of Hermione and his encounter with the bear make it clear that pastoral is no more a golden world than the Sicilian court is. It is violent and dangerous, nature at its wildest; it exhibits, moreover, from the outset the same problems of knowledge, judgement and interpretation as the world Antigonus has left. And if faith is required for Leontes' ultimate salvation, it provides no help in Antigonus' case, merely misleading him and demonstrating his naïvety. His belief in a providential universe convinces him that since fate has brought him to Bohemia, Perdita must be Polixenes' child; and despite his earlier adamant assertion of Hermione's innocence, he interprets his vision of her 'In pure white robes, | Like very sanctity' (3.3.21–2) to imply her death, and if her death, her guilt as well. He arrives at this conviction not passionately or maliciously, but through reason and faith (under the circumstances, his return to Sicily would scarcely be auspicious). And the bear assures us that nature in this play is no kinder than civilization.

Antigonus' death is another of the play's unrestored losses. He is the faithful servant to an irrational and vindictive master. He has been criticized for obeying Leontes, but however barbarous the King's orders may be, the alternative to obeying them is to see Perdita burnt. He commits himself and the infant to the protection of Providence—naïvely, no doubt, but that is the point. Paulina essentially writes him off as soon as he leaves (see 3.2.228–9), and when, at the play's end, Camillo is offered as a

---

[1] *The Winter's Tale: A Study*, pp. 32–5.

2. *Impresa* of Wenceslaus IV, King of Bohemia, from Jacobus Typotius, *Symbola Divina & Humana Pontificum Imperatorum Regum* (Prague, 1601–3).

replacement, there is no question of her remaining true to her husband's memory: he is, in the play's terms, a total loss. But the fatal bear is also the pivot on which the play turns from tragic to comic, the index to a radical change not of subject but of tone.[1] 'Though authority be a stubborn bear,' says the Clown late in Act 4, 'yet he is oft led by the nose with gold' (4.4.795–6): by this time there are even ways of dealing with the savagery of

---

[1] Nevill Coghill calls the bear 'a dramaturgical hinge, a moment of planned structural antithesis', 'Six Points of Stage-craft in *The Winter's Tale*', *Sh. Survey*, 11 (1958), p. 35.

authority and bears. Antigonus' death, as the Clown recounts it, becomes a black comedy; the abandoned infant, as the shepherd takes it up, is assumed to be the offspring of 'some stair-work, some trunk-work, some behind-door work' (3.3.71–2)—to be, in fact, exactly what Leontes had claimed—but this is now no impediment to pity, charity, love. Bohemia, as the play develops, is hardly an ideal world, except perhaps for disguised princes and con-men looking for easy marks; but it offers a set of alternatives to the dramatic issues of Sicily, a way of rethinking and re-enacting them.

The most striking of these, in terms of dramaturgy, is the introduction of a narrator, Time personified, as Chorus to Act 4—the tale begun by Mamillius and interrupted by the drama of Leontes now becomes the play. Criticism has on the whole been unhappy with this; Hazlitt considered it (along with Antigonus on the coast of Bohemia) one of the play's 'slips or blemishes';[1] Quiller-Couch used it as a prime example of the play's 'flagrant specimens of inferior artistry',[2] and Dover Wilson rescued Shakespeare from it by declaring it the work of a collaborator.

The presentation of a narrator had been, in *Pericles*, a consciously archaizing device, reviving moral Gower to supply the authority for Shakespeare's only morality play. The expedient had been popular but artistically dubious, according to Ben Jonson, who saw the play exactly as Shakespeare intended, but in the worst way—not as a drama but as 'a mouldy tale, . . . stale | As the shrive's crust, and nasty as his fish'.[3] In *The Winter's Tale*, Time's narration expresses quite a different kind of moral authority. The speech is unnecessary for the purposes of conveying information; everything we learn from Time is repeated at once in the ensuing dialogue between Camillo and Polixenes. But the move from action to narration is another pivot, turning the drama we have experienced with such immediacy into a tale with a teller who both claims control over the apparently free play of the characters and offers a disturbingly amoral overview:

> I that please some, try all; both joy and terror
> Of good and bad, that makes and unfolds error . . .

[1] *The Characters of Shakespeare's Plays* (1817), in A. R. Waller, ed., *Collected Works* (1902), i. 324.

[2] New Shakespeare *Winter's Tale*, pp. xxv, 159.

[3] 'On *The New Inn*: Ode. To Himself', 21–3.

Through the operation of Time both good and bad experience
both joy and terror; some are pleased, all are tried; both error
and its painful revelation are Time's responsibility. *Veritas filia
temporis*, 'Truth', the aphorism says, 'is the daughter of Time';
but this has ceased to be a comforting commonplace—the only
truth revealed is, ironically, 'error'. Nor do human institutions,
such as the orderly operation of what we normally understand
as time (or, as Capell shrewdly suggested, such as the dramatic
unities)[1] constrain this figure, for

> it is in my power
> To o'erthrow law, and in one self-born hour
> To plant and o'erwhelm custom.

Like the Chorus in *Henry V* impugning the power of the stage,
reducing the theatre's representations to its physical limita-
tions, Time returns *The Winter's Tale* to its source, a narrative
which declares itself, in its subtitle, *The Triumph of Time*. The
difference, however, is that we have become Time's creatures
too.[2]

Nature and Art

Theocritus wrote his idylls from the Alexandrian court for an
audience of powerful, educated and sophisticated readers; pastoral is, in its inception, embedded in the courtly. The mode had
always been available as a way of talking about that other world
of ambition, privilege and power. For George Puttenham, in
1589, its primary character was indirection, 'under the veil of
homely persons and in rude speeches to insinuate and glance at
greater matters, and such as perchance had not been safe to have
been disclosed in any other sort'.[3] Alexander Barclay, in the first
English eclogues, published in 1515, explains that through his
shepherds he delineates 'the miseries of courtiers and courts of all
princes in general'.[4] The involvement of court with pastoral was

---

[1] Cited in the *Variorum*, p. 156.

[2] The best discussion of time in the play is Inga-Stina Ewbank's 'The Triumph
of Time in *The Winter's Tale*', *REL* 5 (1964), pp. 83–100.

[3] *The Arte of English Poesie* (1589), i. 18; the text is modernized.

[4] Beatrice White, ed., *Eclogues of Alexander Barclay* (1928), p. 1.

not, moreover, a poetic fiction in Shakespeare's England. Keeping sheep was big business, enclosures had been an increasingly serious economic and political issue for almost a century, and the impulse of pastoral poetry to represent the world of shepherds as pretty and harmless has a political dimension that is quite invisible to us. The idyllic pastoral is predicated on the satiric pastoral—Barclay's shepherds, like Spenser's in *The Shepheardes Calender*, are as likely to curse their masters as to celebrate their country pleasures. The double edge of the mode is evident in the double vision of Rosalind and Celia, fresh from court, overhearing the shepherd Silvius elegantly complaining about love, and then receiving a straightforward lesson from his colleague Corin in the hard economics of the pastoral life.[1]

The presence of aristocrats in the rustic world, therefore, is of the essence of pastoral. It is also, however, a threat to it, and is sometimes positively destructive: the effects of Florizel's and Polixenes' presence at the sheep-shearing are, in their way, entirely conventional. When, in Book VI of *The Faerie Queene*, the knight of Courtesy enters the pastoral world in pursuit of the Blatant Beast, he finds the traditional *otium* and love in the person of Pastorella, but he also abandons his knightly quest, intrudes upon and disrupts a dance of rustic deities, and drives away the Graces, the source not only of poetry but of the Courtesy he himself embodies. The classic model for the destructive intrusion of royalty into pastoral is invoked by Perdita herself: the appearance of Dis, King of the Underworld, to carry Proserpina off from the Sicilian field of Enna as she gathers the flowers Perdita catalogues.

Perdita's catalogue has a long history relating to love and death. In Theocritus, the lovesick Polyphemus offers Galatea lilies and poppies, flowers respectively of winter and summer; Adonis' bier is strewn with garlands and blossoms in Bion's elegy, and Moschus calls on roses, anemones, hyacinths, and 'flowers in sad clusters' to mourn for the dead Bion.[2] Virgil, elaborating Polyphemus' offer, has the shepherd Corydon tempt

---

[1] *As You Like It* 2.4. The pioneering discussion of the relation between pastoral and the Elizabethan wool industry is Louis Adrian Montrose's 'Eliza, Queene of the shepheardes', *ELR* 10 (1980), 153–82.

[2] Theocritus, *Idyll* 11, 56–7; Bion, *Idyll* 1, *Lament for Adonis*, 75–6; Moschus, *Idyll* 3, *Lament for Bion*, 5–7

the disdainful youth Alexis with flowers in profusion, precisely enumerated:

> for you the nymphs
> bring—look!—baskets of lilies; a fair naiad
> gathers pale wallflowers and the buds of poppies,
> and blends narcissus and the fragrant dill,
> then interweaves with cassia and sweet herbs
> soft hyacinth and yellow marigold . . .[1]

Renaissance examples abounded (see the note on 4.4.104–27), but for English poetry, Shakespeare's catalogue established the norms of the topos, both in its elaboration and detail, and in its extraordinary expressive range.

'O Proserpina, | For the flowers now that frighted thou letst fall | From Dis's wagon . . .': the ensuing list depicts the natural world as engaged in a cosmic love affair, and thereby evokes a nature that is no longer Virgilian but Ovidian. Indeed, the association of the flower catalogue with the rape of Proserpina derives from Ovid. In the *Metamorphoses*, she is gathering only 'violets or white lilies' (5.392), but in the *Fasti*, the list is extensive: her companions picked marigolds, violets, poppies, hyacinth, amaranth—thyme, rosemary, sweet clover, roses, and '*sine nomine flores*'—'nameless flowers', more flowers than can be catalogued; she herself picked crocuses and white lilies (4.435–42). Why is the rape of Proserpina being invoked in the middle of a country sheep-shearing festival? It acknowledges, to begin with, the dangerous aspects of pastoral love affairs, and thereby serves as another version of Polixenes' Edenic myth; but it also reverses it: in this case the interloper is male, the innocence destroyed female. The mythological association of flowers with rape, indeed, is already implicit in the scene in the very persona Florizel has devised for Perdita: he has costumed her as Flora, goddess of flowers (4.4.2–3, 9–10). The costume does more than reflect his name; Flora, according to Ovid, was at first the simple nymph Chloris, beloved of Zephyrus, the west wind. He pursued her, she fled, but he seized her and raped her, and then to make amends filled the earth with flowers

[1] Eclogue 2, 45–50; the translation is by the editor, and appears in *Poetry* 116 (1970), 353–5.

44

and gave her dominion over them—'*arbitrium tu, dea, floris habe*'.[1] Florizel several times denies that his intentions are anything but honourable; but in the allusive structure of the play, the rape has already been committed twice. Florizel himself, indeed, cites three additional examples as precedents for his own behaviour:

> The gods themselves,
> Humbling their deities to love, have taken
> The shapes of beasts upon them. Jupiter
> Became a bull and bellowed; the green Neptune
> A ram and bleated; and the fire-robed god,
> Golden Apollo, a poor humble swain,
> As I seem now.

> (4.4.25–31)

The scene invokes myths in which male sexuality is characteristically disguised, violent, compulsive, often bestial, but also an essential part of nature; and through it—through acts of sexual violence against women—the world is filled with flowers and poetry.[2]

The Proserpina story is also a story about time, refining and redefining both the terms of Time's chorus and the very concept of a winter's tale. It is a myth that explains the cycle of seasons: the abduction of Ceres' daughter, like the loss of innocence in Eden, is responsible for the fact that winter exists at all, that the 'perpetual spring and harvest' of Spenser's Garden of Adonis, or the eternal round of growing and reaping that Ceres promises Ferdinand and Miranda, can be no more than a poetic fiction.[3] But the cycle also includes a time of restoration and reconciliation, with the annual return of Proserpina to her home in Sicily. If Shakespeare took the Proserpina story as an underlying fable for the play, rather than as a mere local allusion, it would explain why he switched the locations he found in *Pandosto*, so that

---

[1] *Fasti*, 5.212

[2] Paul Alpers sees Florizel's pastoral guise, and more specifically his Ovidian allusions, as an antidote to the destructive hyperbole of the opening scenes, a redemptive and liberating mode of idealization: 'After the anguish of Leontes' Sicily, where fantasies of bestial sex and the wearing of horns poison the imagination . . . Florizel . . . provides an alternative to a courtly habit of hyperbolic asseveration that is implicated in the tragedy of the first three acts' (*What Is Pastoral?*, forthcoming).

[3] See *Faerie Queene* 3.6.42; *Tempest* 4.1.114–15.

Perdita's return, as 'Welcome hither, | As is the spring to th'earth' (5.1.150–1), would be to Sicily, not to Bohemia, and would thus be true to the myth.[1]

Nature, as Perdita presides over it, excludes 'the fairest flowers o'th' season . . . carnations and streaked gillyvors, | Which some call nature's bastards'; as cultivated flowers, they do not grow naturally in her garden, 'and I care not | To get slips of them' (4.4.81–5). The term 'bastard' was used for hybrids; it also meant 'counterfeit', a sense which colours the botanical usage (ironically, the child who is prejudicially called 'natural' provides the prejudicial epithet for the art that usurps nature). In her resolute resistance to bastards, Perdita doubtless shows herself to be her father's daughter, but her brief debate with Polixenes on the uses of art extends beyond the play and is informed by topoi reaching back to antiquity. Kermode in his introduction to the Arden *Tempest* gives an excellent overview of the matter, citing parallel passages from Florio's Montaigne and Puttenham's *Arte of English Poesie* expressing Perdita's and Polixenes' positions respectively, and observes that the latter commonplace can be found as far back as Democritus.[2] Polixenes' view, that the hybridizer's art is learned from nature and acts as its agent to improve it, is countered by Perdita's, that anything that interferes with nature will necessarily corrupt it. The 'bastard' flower, she implies, is thus correctly characterized, an index to our own corruption as it is the creation of our illicit pleasure. This, in fact, constitutes her ultimate moral position: her objection to the 'art' is not to its practice (she agrees that 'the art itself is nature') but to the impulse motivating it, which is to produce a more attractive flower,

> No more than, were I painted, I would wish
> This youth should say 'twere well, and only therefore
> Desire to breed by me.
>
> (4.4.101–3)

---

[1] E. A. J. Honigmann calls attention to the play's Ovidian background, and includes a similar speculation on the reversal of the locations, in 'Secondary Source of *The Winter's Tale*', *Philological Quarterly*, 34.4 (1955), pp. 27–38.

[2] *The Tempest* (1954), pp. xxxv–xxxvi; Pafford argues that the importance of the debate has been greatly overstated, but nevertheless gives extensive quotations from the sources cited by Kermode. Both discussions are indebted to Harold S. Wilson, 'Nature and Art in *The Winter's Tale*', *Shakespeare Association Bulletin*, 18 (1943), pp. 114–20. See the note on 4.4.87–103.

The ironies inhabiting this brief exchange are obvious: the invocation of the art that mimics nature, Giulio Romano's lifelike sculpture, is essential to the play's resolution, the embodiment of restoration, forgiveness, grace; and marrying 'A gentler scion to the wildest stock' (l. 93) is precisely what Florizel proposes in marrying Perdita, and what Polixenes adamantly forbids. But the ironies are, in human terms, rather less telling than criticism has found them; our opinions, even philosophical ones, are not invariably consistent—if this is a failing, it is a very ordinary one—and what we believe to be right for flowers we need not necessarily believe to be right for our children. It is the violence of Polixenes' response to his son's rustic fiancée that is surprising, not its failure to coincide with his botanical observations.

Marriage Negotiations

To the England of 1611, however, Polixenes' reaction would have appeared less surprising. Royal marriages were an essential diplomatic instrument, to which the preferences of the young people involved were scarcely relevant. The negotiations for King James's two elder children were matters of national policy and international relations, and had polarized public and court opinion for a decade. Such arrangements had nothing to do with romance; throughout the Renaissance, the *politique* marriage seemed the most likely way to resolve the European power struggles. When in *The Tempest* Prospero marries his daughter to the son of his ancient enemy he is acting fully in accordance with the political wisdom of the age. It is fortunate that Ferdinand pleases Miranda, but that is no part of the reason he was selected. His own wishes are no more consulted than Miranda's are: Prospero's magic arranges the matter, and the children do what is expected of them.

King James's pacifism led him to prefer Roman Catholic matches for his children, both as a way of insulating England from the religious hostilities that kept the continent in a continual state of war, and as a way of preventing England in the next generation from entering the conflict on either side. Though he publicly informed Prince Henry in *Basilicon Doron* that 'I would rathest have you to marry one that were fully of your own religion',[1] in practice he made it clear that to marry his children to Protestants would have been a waste of good diplomatic currency. In the year of the Prince's death, 1612, James was negotiating marriages for him with the French Princess Christine, the Spanish Infanta, and a princess of Savoy; Princess Elizabeth's marriage to the Prince of Piedmont, nephew of the King of Spain, was to have been part of the latter arrangement. All these matches were favoured by Queen Anne, who by this time had converted to Roman Catholicism; but she had no more say in the matter than her children did. Prince Henry, unlike his father, was a militant Protestant, and strongly expressed both his distaste for an ecumenical marriage and his support of the Elector Palatine's suit for his sister—the latter's virtue as a brother-in-law lay in his Protestantism, not his charm. Nevertheless, Henry was constrained to write reassuring his father of his firm conviction that it was 'for your Majesty to resolve what course is most convenient to be taken by the rules of State', merely observing that 'my part to play, which is to be in love with any of them, is not yet at hand'.[2]

Polixenes' outrage that Florizel should presume to select his own bride, and to do so secretly, must be seen in this context. Florizel's hand is in every sense a royal property, and not at his disposal. (Nor, indeed, does the play itself have much to say in favour of romance: the only reason Florizel is vindicated is that Perdita ultimately turns out to be the princess who would have been his father's choice.) Such matters are relevant not only to the rarefied world of court policy and international diplomacy, though of course the higher one was on the social scale the more relevant they became. The enormous degree of authority upper-class and wealthy parents exercised over their children's marital arrangements is difficult for us to imagine, but a contemporary example may help to provide a perspective. In 1568, a few months after their marriage, Bess of Hardwick and her fourth husband George Talbot, Earl of Shrewsbury, drew up a contract relating to their heirs. The problem this extraordinary document was designed to resolve is that in Elizabethan marriages where both sides owned property, the land settled on the wife was hers

---

[1] McIlwain, p. 35; 'rathest' = most prefer, the superlative of rather.

[2] Letter of 5 October 1612, quoted by Williamson, *The Myth of the Conqueror*, pp. 138–9.

only in her lifetime; it could not be passed on to her children by a previous marriage—Bess had eight. She was past childbearing, and she and the Earl therefore uséd their respective offspring to consolidate and strengthen their own financial arrangements. The agreement stipulated that two of Bess's children marry two of the Earl's; I summarize David Durant's extensive account:

Gilbert Talbot, the Earl's second son, then aged fourteen was to marry before Easter Bess's second daughter Mary, who was twelve. If Mary died before the marriage or 'before carnal knowledge between them', then Gilbert was to marry Bess's youngest daughter Elizabeth. If Mary was bereft of Gilbert by some disaster, then she was to marry one of the Earl's other sons. A further marriage was proposed between Bess's eldest son, then eighteen, and the Earl's youngest daughter, who was at most eight at the time. Again all mischance was covered by offering alternative brothers and sisters in descending and ascending order of ages. In the event, all the partners originally chosen lived and did as they were told.[1]

This system was obviously not felt to be unproblematic. Egeus' insistence in *A Midsummer Night's Dream* that, in accordance with 'the ancient privilege of Athens' (1.1.41), his daughter either marry a man she does not love or suffer death is depicted as obviously tyrannical, though legally valid, and is ultimately overruled, as a principle of equity, by Theseus; and George Wilkins's play *The Miseries of Enforced Marriage* (1607) is clearly not written in the service of a radical or revolutionary ideology. At the same time, legislation in the period was directed toward increasing parental control over children's marriages, not decreasing it. The Canons of 1604 raised the age of consent from twelve for girls, fourteen for boys, to twenty-one. This meant that children under the age of twenty-one could not marry without their fathers' or guardians' consent, and, perhaps more to the point, that fathers could now negotiate marriages for their children without the children's consent throughout their adolescence. (Florizel is about twenty-three[2] and thus, under English law, free to contract his own marriage, which is what makes his behaviour especially reckless.) Polixenes' (or Egeus', or Capulet's) irrationality and vindictiveness are, in this context, no more arguments against patriarchal authority than Lear's foolishness,

---

[1] David N. Durant, *Bess of Hardwick* (1977), pp. 56–7.
[2] Florizel is the same age as Mamillius, and Mamillius' age at 1.2.154–5 would be about seven; Act 4 takes place sixteen years later.

Macbeth's villainy or Richard II's malfeasance are arguments in favour of democracy: fathers are morally obligated to act in their children's best interests, but no failure to do so can vitiate their authority. A bad king, as King James insists in *The True Law of Free Monarchies*, is still the king.

But Polixenes' indignation goes beyond accusations of unprincely behaviour; it is malicious and sadistic, and the fury of his threats against Perdita and the old Shepherd recalls us to the courtly world of Leontes' rage—pastoral is, once again, no escape.

Autolycus

The largest figure in the play's pastoral landscape is neither shepherd nor courtier, but the ballad-seller, pedlar, con-man and thief Autolycus. When Simon Forman saw the play at the Globe in 1611, it was Autolycus, 'the rogue that came in all tattered like colt-pixie',[1] who left the strongest impression, even morally: the message Forman took away from the theatre was not about the dangers of unwarranted jealousy but to 'Beware of trusting feigned beggars or fawning fellows'. The name means literally 'the wolf himself', or 'the wolf by himself', 'the lone wolf'; the mythical Autolycus was Odysseus' maternal grandfather, of whom Homer says that he 'outdid all men in stealing and swearing', and credits Odysseus' wiliness to him.[2] In Ovid, Autolycus is a twin: his mother, Chione, was seen by Mercury and Apollo at the same time, and both determined to have her—once again, the love story is a rape story. Apollo waited for darkness, but Mercury with his caduceus put her to sleep in broad daylight and raped her. Apollo, more cautious and for once more deceitful, gained access to her at nightfall in the form of an old woman and seduced her; and in one pregnancy she gave birth to Autolycus, the child of Mercury, and Philammon, the child of Apollo. The twins inherited their respective fathers' talents: Autolycus, as the son of the patron of thieves and liars, became a master of cunning—Ovid says 'he could make white

---

[1] A mischievous sprite or hobgoblin, especially in the shape of a ragged colt luring men to follow it and then disappearing (*OED*). For Forman's account of the play, see Appendix A.

[2] *Odyssey* 19.294–6.

black and black white, a worthy heir of his father's art'. Philammon, as the child of the god of music, became a famous musician—the ballad-singing Autolycus is impersonating his twin.[1] The myth is relevant both to the twinship fantasy of Leontes and Polixenes and to the larger and more vexing question of the determination of paternity.

Autolycus invokes both his lupine nature and his mythical ancestry when he says, using the term for the birth of an animal, that he was 'littered under Mercury', born when the planet was in the ascendant, and he deprecatingly describes himself as, like his father, a petty thief, 'a snapper-up of unconsidered trifles' (4.3.25–6). In this he is part of another mythology, modern and culturally specific, a figure from the underworld of Elizabethan cony-catching pamphlets, which inform his language as they provide sources for his trickery. The parallel figure in Greene's *Pandosto*, Dorastus' servant Capnio, accounts only for Autolycus' practical function in Shakespeare's plot, enabling the lovers to elope successfully, but the roguery and wit derive from the rich literature of cozenage and vagabondage, several of the most influential examples of which are also by Greene.[2] Recent studies of masterless men, those dispossessed in increasingly large numbers from the land, or from their traditional places in villages or on the great estates, indicate how pervasive and visible a problem the rootless poor had become by the end of the sixteenth century. A. L. Beier, analysing the political implications of social dislocations, poverty and demographic shifts, observes that vagrancy came to be explained as a kind of witchcraft, a conspiratorial form of essential evil, to which theft and cozenage were endemic but incidental. Vagabondage was 'the classic crime of status, the social crime *par excellence*. Offenders were arrested not because of their actions, but because of their positions in society.' But Arthur Kinney, citing this observation, goes on to point out that the literary representation of roguery in the period is not at all

---

[1] The story is in *Metamorphoses* 11.303–17.

[2] Dover Wilson and Quiller-Couch called attention to Shakespeare's indebtedness to Greene's *Second Part of Cony-Catching* and *Third Part of Cony-Catching* (1592) in the trick Autolycus plays on the Clown at 4.3.49 ff., which is described in the former, and in two of Autolycus' set-pieces, the 'What a fool honesty is' speech (4.4.592 ff.) and his account of the requisite qualities for a cutpurse, 'To have an open ear . . .' (4.4.666 ff.). See the New Shakespeare *Winter's Tale*, pp. xxii, 176, 177.

imbued with the sort of fear and moral outrage this suggests. The pamphlets tend to have the tone of jest books; the criminal acts they describe are not incidental but essential, performed, like those of Autolycus, for our entertainment. 'The Tudor dispossessed . . . in a rising capitalist society were appropriated as a commodity themselves by the writers of rogue pamphlets.'[1] And by the same token the trickster and charlatan Autolycus, the essential entertainer, is the figure in this play closest to the playwright.

Mercury is not only the god of theft and lying; he is also, paradoxically, the god of eloquence and, in a mystical Egyptian incarnation, presides over the profound truths of hermetic philosophy (so called from Hermes, his name in Greek, identified with the Egyptian Thoth, god of wisdom). He is, moreover, the inventor of the lyre: Apollo is the god of music, but the enabling instrument of his art was created and given to him by Mercury. And if Autolycus' ballads are Mercurial and anti-Apollonian in their mendacity and irrationality, they nevertheless prove entirely persuasive and invariably find purchasers. Autolycus' ability to produce documentary confirmations of the most fantastic of their claims provides a wry commentary on the questions of evidence that fill the play. The ballads serve, indeed, as indices to the nature of and capacity for belief, rustic models for all those events that are said to be like incredible old tales—Antigonus' fatal encounter with the bear, Perdita's reappearance, Hermione's restoration, *The Winter's Tale* itself—but must nevertheless be believed. They are also prototypes of Paulina's equally unlikely but pre-eminently artistic charade at the play's conclusion, for which she requires that 'You do awake your faith'—requires what in any other context would be called gullibility. Autolycus is as essential a part of that conclusion as Paulina. The liar and thief holds the key to Perdita's identity and unwittingly provides Leontes and Polixenes with the crucial fact transforming the shepherdess to a princess, as it also elevates shepherd and clown to the gentry, Mercury, liar and thief, is also the Olympian mes-

---

[1] See the excellent introduction to Kinney's collection of rogue pamphlets *Rogues, Vagabonds, and Sturdy Beggars* (Amherst, Mass., 2nd edn., 1990), p. 5, which also cites the Beier quotation above. Ovidian sources for Autolycus are discussed in Jonathan Bate, *Shakespeare and Ovid* (Oxford, 1993), pp. 228–9.

senger, the bringer of good news and good fortune, the god of information.

The rogue and tale-teller moves in all the play's worlds. He has been the Prince's servant at court, but he can go unrecognized by Florizel through the simple expedient of a false beard—a quintessential actor, all his representations are taken for truth. He is, in the course of the action, whatever his costume dictates: pedlar, shepherd, gentleman. But more than this, he bridges the gap between stage and audience; he is the master of the aside, continually revealing his disguises, tricks and plots to us. Paulina keeps the secret of her redemptive witchcraft to herself, but we are placed in collusion with Autolycus. And the most subversive figure in the play is, precisely through the thoroughness of his subversion, ultimately the most socially responsible: what he ultimately subverts is not authority, but its errors and misuses. He explains his motives in determining to conceal the escape of Florizel and Perdita: 'If I thought it were a piece of honesty to acquaint the King withal, I would not do't. I hold it the more knavery to conceal it; and therein am I constant to my profession' (4.4.675–8). There is no threat in this subversion; quite the contrary. In being most a knave, he is most serviceable to the interests not only of the young couple, but of the two kings.[1]

Paulina's Gallery

The statue Paulina claims to produce at the play's conclusion is part of a large art collection, and Paulina's house includes a gallery containing 'many singularities' (5.3.10–12). Collecting was not a novelty in England in 1610. Richard Haydocke in 1598 noted 'many noblemen then furnishing their houses with the excellent monuments of sundry famous and ancient masters, both Italian and German',[2] and English collectors in the first decade of the seventeenth century began for the first time to be serious connoisseurs, dispatching experts to the continent to buy for them, and concerned with acquiring expertise of their own.

---

[1] Stephen Greenblatt's classic essay 'Invisible Bullets' uses Thomas Harman's *Caveat for Common Cursitors, Commonly Called Vagabonds* (1566) to make a similar point about the uses of roguery in the *Henry IV* plays; see *Shakespearean Negotiations* (Oxford, 1988), pp. 51–6.

[2] From the Preface to his translation of Paolo Lomazzo's *Trattato, A Tracte containinge the Artes of curious Painting, Caruinge & Buildinge* (Oxford, 1598), p. 6.

3, 4. The Earl and Countess of Arundel before their gallery. Paintings by Daniel Mytens, c.1616.

In 1609, the Earl of Exeter was advising the Earl of Shrewsbury to purchase paintings by Palma Giovane and sculpture by Giambologna,[1] suggestions both shrewd and in the best modern taste. Prince Henry became a passionate collector of paintings and bronzes,[2] and the Earl and Countess of Arundel were about to embark on the creation of the most important art collection of the age in England, rivalled only by the royal collection after Charles I came to the throne. (See figures 3 and 4.) By 1610 Inigo Jones's outstanding expertise was being employed: he had almost certainly travelled in Italy by this time,[3] and was advising first the Earl of Rutland on artistic matters, and later Prince Henry.

On the continent conspicuous collections of great art had for more than a century been an attribute of princely magnificence, and Henry VIII had to some extent undertaken to emulate his contemporaries Francis I and Charles V in this respect. But neither Elizabeth nor James had much interest in the arts as such, and neither had any interest whatever in increasing the royal collection. Prince Charles, however, inherited most of his brother's treasures, and, with the advice and encouragement of two of his father's favourites, Somerset and Buckingham, added constantly to them. By the mid-1630s the Caroline royal pictures constituted one of the greatest art collections in the world. There was more in this acquisitive passion than aesthetics and conspicuous consumption. Just as, in the sixteenth century, artists came increasingly to be considered not mere craftsmen but philosophers and sages (thus the greatest artist of the age is referred to, in the account of his funeral, as 'the divine Michelangelo'), so increasingly in the period great art was felt, in a way that was at once pragmatic and quasi-mystical, to be a manifestation of the power and authority of its possessor. Great artists became essential to the developing concept of monarchy, to realize and deploy the imagery of legitimacy and greatness.

[1] David Howarth, *Lord Arundel and his Circle* (New Haven, 1985), p. 21.

[2] For an overview of the prince's collections, see Roy Strong, *Henry Prince of Wales* (1986), pp. 184–219.

[3] The evidence for this is inferential, but fairly conclusive: he was referred to in 1605 as 'a great traveller', and was invited to accompany Arundel to Italy in 1613 'by means of his language and experience in those parts'. See John Harris, Stephen Orgel and Roy Strong, *The King's Arcadia: Inigo Jones and the Stuart Court* (1973), p. 17.

The extent to which the power of art became a practical reality in England may be gauged by a brief comparison of two large royal expenditures. In 1627, in the midst of the long and disastrous war England waged with Spain and subsequently with France, the Duke of Buckingham led an expedition to relieve a beleaguered Huguenot garrison at La Rochelle. But his troops proved insufficient, and in urgent need of reinforcements and pay for the soldiers, he appealed to the King. Charles believed wholeheartedly in the cause, but money was difficult to find; after three weeks, £14,000 and 2,000 additional troops were committed to the enterprise. These proved utterly inadequate, and Buckingham was forced to retreat ignominiously. Throughout this period, however, Charles was eagerly negotiating for the magnificent art collection of the Gonzaga Dukes of Mantua, which had recently come on the market. For this he paid, in 1627 and 1628, a total of £25,500.[1] To this monarch, a royal gallery was worth far more than a successful army.

The history of collecting provides one context within which Paulina's imaginary statue must be viewed. Another is more directly topical: in 1605 James had commissioned statues of Queen Elizabeth and Mary Queen of Scots as tomb effigies for their monuments in Westminster Abbey—James's treasonous mother was to be rehabilitated by being reburied among the kings and queens of England. Elizabeth's statue was completed in 1607, Mary's before 1612; both statues were lifelike, in the sense that they were painted, as Hermione's is said to be, and as effigies always were in the period.[2] The royal patron of the King's Men was not a connoisseur or a collector, but he nevertheless relied on the power of art to memorialize, reconcile and restore.

Shakespeare's selection of Giulio Romano as the peerless sculptor of Paulina's commission has occasioned much commentary, which is briefly reviewed in the note to 5.2.95. Giulio, though famous as a painter and architect, is not known to have made statues. The ultimate authority for his excellence as a sculptor, however, is an impeccable one: Vasari quotes Giulio's epitaph,

[1] See Oliver Millar, *The Queen's Pictures* (New York, 1977), pp. 40–2.

[2] Glynne Wickham calls attention to the relevance of the effigies in the course of an unconvincing argument for the play as part of the investiture ceremonies for Henry as Prince of Wales; see 'Romance and Emblem: A Study in the Dramatic Structure of *The Winter's Tale*', in David Galloway, ed., *The Elizabethan Theatre III* (1973), pp. 94–5.

in which he is praised specifically for his skill at making lifelike sculpture. Therefore whether Giulio in fact was or was not a sculptor (and the epitaph is difficult to argue away), the problem as far as Shakespeare is concerned is surely solved: Giulio *was* known in the Renaissance as a sculptor. But it is also worth remarking on the fact that in a period when connoisseurship was rapidly developing and actively pursued, Shakespeare, or whoever was advising him, should have gone not to a gallery or to the art market to find his paragon (say Michelangelo, Cellini, or Giambologna), but to the text that constitutes the beginning of art history.[1]

The Statue in the Chapel

Giulio Romano's statue is, in the most literal sense, the evidence of things not seen, said to have been sculpted by an artist whose statues, if he did in fact make any, Shakespeare could have known only by reading or hearsay, a work created out of pure inference from a narrative. The play's conclusion depends in other ways as well on the evidence of things not seen: the fact that the meeting of the two kings and the recognition of Perdita are only reported in 5.2, not dramatized, has been considered a fatal dramatic flaw, an index to Shakespeare's failing powers. For Quiller-Couch, it was another of the play's 'flagrant specimens of inferior artistry', 'a hopelessly scamped and huddled-away situation'.[2] Cavell, however, sees the scene's narratives as not only functional but essential in relation to the questions of knowledge the play is concerned with, pointing out that 'an answer to the question "How do you know?" is provided by specifying how you can tell'.[3] The function of language is to tell, and narration is a crucial form of knowledge in the play. Nevertheless, the

[1] The larger significance of Vasari to the notions of art and nature in the play is discussed by Leo Salingar, 'Shakespeare and the Italian Concept of Art', in his collection *Dramatic Form in Shakespeare and the Jacobeans* (Cambridge, 1986). Ben Jonson in *Timber* cites Giulio among 'six [in fact seven] famous painters in Italy: who were excellent, and emulous of the Ancients': Raphael, Michelangelo, Titian, Correggio, Sebastiano del Piombo, Giulio Romano and Andrea del Sarto; he gives as his source Antonio Possevino's *Bibliotheca Selecta* (Rome, 1593). See C. H. Herford, P. and E. Simpson, *Ben Jonson*, viii. 612, and ix. 260. Giulio and four of the others are also named in *Underwoods* 76.

[2] New Shakespeare *Winter's Tale*, p. xxv.

[3] *Disowning Knowledge*, p. 201.

difference between knowing because you have seen (e.g. 'How she holds up the neb, the bill to him', 1.2.181) and knowing because you have been told (e.g. 'I say she's dead—I'll swear't', 3.2.201) obviously has nothing to do with empiricism; both these statements are, in context, true, but any reasonable inference that may be drawn from either is ultimately false. In fact, one of the most striking aspects of the intellectual life of the play is its insistent separation of interpretation and belief from knowledge; and it makes no difference whether the knowledge is constituted by what we observe or what we are told.

The dangers of knowledge, the spider in the cup, remain, at the play's end, potent. Even the destructive carnal knowledge of Polixenes' childhood fantasy is part of the reconciliation scene, as Leontes declares his attraction to Perdita (5.1.222–3), and must be recalled to propriety by Paulina. The incestuous passion of father for daughter had provided the tragic denouement of *Pandosto*, and even in *The Winter's Tale*, radically as Shakespeare has diminished the episode, the daughter is as much a threat to her mother as Mamillius had been to his father. But the passion is also essential to Shakespeare's comic denouement. Paulina chides Leontes:

> Your eye hath too much youth in't. Not a month
> Fore your queen died, she was more worth such gazes
> Than what you look on now.
>
> (5.1.224–6)

It is precisely Leontes' incestuous feeling for Perdita that Paulina redirects toward Hermione. The invidious comparison is, of course, merely vindictive unless Hermione is alive, but if Leontes is being recalled to reality here, it is a reality that has been systematically concealed, for sixteen years and half the play, from both him and us.

Early in the play Leontes accuses Paulina of being 'A mankind [i.e. mannish] witch' (2.3.67), at once masculine and the essence of feminine evil. The charge of witchcraft is evoked both by her sharp tongue and her denial of her place within the patriarchy, her refusal to be silenced by her husband and her defiance of the King himself. It implies in a larger sense that women constitute a subversive group, a threat to the social and political order— Leontes in the same place calls Paulina 'a most intelligencing

bawd', both a spy and a whore or a whoremonger. The charge
follows logically from the King's conviction that women 'will say
anything', that they are characteristically false, 'as o'er-dyed
blacks, as wind, as waters', etc. (1.2.130–1). Leontes returns to
the charge of witchcraft in the final scene, but now it is
redemptive. He apostrophizes the statue:

> O royal piece!
> There's magic in thy majesty, which has
> My evils conjured to remembrance . . .
> (5.3.38–40)

The work of art, the visible embodiment of the lost queen,
supersedes Paulina's sixteen years of recounting as the medium
of remembrance. Memory, the imitation of life, has become
magic. Paulina, pursuing her charade to make the statue move,
denies that she is 'assisted | By wicked powers' (90–1), but the
King, by fiat, permits her to practise witchcraft legally: 'If this be
magic, let it be an art | Lawful as eating' (110–11).

The recalling of the charge of witchcraft only to disarm it, the
invocation of the virtuous magic verging on the miraculous, is
obviously related to a complex of claims to transcendence in the
play. Paulina's demand that 'You do awake your faith' has
generally been taken as an acknowledgement that, for all its
classical details, the play is in essential ways Christian. Indeed,
there are allusions to original sin, grace, the burning of heretics,
Whitsun pastorals, Judas Iscariot,[1] Leontes is said to have 'per-
formed | A saint-like sorrow' (5.1.1–2); and Bethell concludes
that the play follows 'the Christian scheme of redemption'.[2] There
is certainly something in this; and the very fact that Paulina
claims to have kept the statue not in her gallery but in a chapel
makes the religious association explicit. It is also difficult to
believe that the emphasis in the play's resolution on the evidence
of things not seen, the primacy of the spirit over the letter,

---

[1] See 1.2.73–4, 79; 2.3.114; 4.4.134; 1.2.414.

[2] *The Winter's Tale: A Study*, pp. 38, 76. Along with this go some much more
dubious claims—that Leontes' and Hermione's near-tragedy is 'based on the
sanctions of true love in Christian marriage', and that Shakespeare is an advocate
'of the pleasantly human love-story with wedding bells as its happy ending' (p.
117). The pleasantly human love stories of Proteus and Sylvia, Hero and Claudio,
Helena and Bertram, to say nothing of Romeo and Juliet and Desdemona and
Othello, are presumably not included in this advocacy, but in any case, the
question is what happens after marriage.

salvation through faith—on the tenets, in short, of Pauline Christianity—does not account for Paulina's name. There are, in addition, the wary disclaimers of any 'superstitious', i.e. Roman Catholic, overtones: Perdita, kneeling before the image, denies that ''tis superstition' (5.3.43), just as Antigonus had allowed himself 'for this once, yea superstitiously' to believe in the miraculous vision of Hermione (3.3.39).

Nevertheless, no one, Protestant or Catholic, in the England of 1610 would have endorsed the notion that true Christianity is legalized magic—this is the stuff of Protestant satires on Popery, and the very suggestion in any other context would certainly have resulted in an indictment for blasphemy. To see magic merely as an allegory of religion, and thereby simply to transfer our attention from witchcraft to theology, is to miss the sense of why magic must be legitimized, why it remains an element in the play at all. Hermione, after all, is not a statue; unlike Paulina, she makes no pretence to the miraculous, asserting merely

> that I,
> Knowing by Paulina that the oracle
> Gave hope thou wast in being, have preserved
> Myself to see the issue.
>
> (5.3.125–8)

Why then the claim of occult powers in restoring her?

To begin with, magic is related to the sexual jealousy of the first half of the play. The action of Paulina's that elicits the initial charge of witchcraft is her attempt to make Leontes acknowledge the child he believes to be the issue of his wife's adultery: witchcraft and bawdry are aspects of each other. Thus Brabanzio assumes that Othello has bewitched Desdemona, and subsequently Iago revises the charge to make Desdemona the witch;[1] this is offered as a logical explanation for the behaviour of a woman who ignores the patriarchal imperatives. *A Midsummer Night's Dream* goes further, making magic an indispensable element in all society's erotic arrangements, whether in getting them wrong or setting them right. The notion of magic as an erotic control mechanism is overtly expressed in *The Tempest*, in which Prospero's art is employed to produce the most literally far-fetched of suitors for Miranda, but also to prevent any sexual

---

[1] See 1.1.173–5, 1.3.60–106 and 3.3.214–15.

relationship between them until his plans are realized and their marriage is properly solemnized.

It is surely not irrelevant that King James took an intense interest in witchcraft; his treatise on *Daemonologie*, and his attitude generally, represent a significant regression from the prevailing late Elizabethan attitudes, which were highly sceptical of the whole subject. At the same time, though the practice of magic was illegal, prosecutions diminished significantly after about 1585, and very few cases are recorded in the early seventeenth century. Martin Ingram concludes that 'in late Elizabethan and early Stuart times witchcraft and magical practices were not of major concern either to the ecclesiastical authorities or to the majority of the people'.[1] But as prosecutions diminished, stage magic and diabolism flourished: in addition to *Macbeth*, *Pericles*, *The Tempest* and Jonson's *Masque of Queens*, Jacobean England saw Middleton's *The Witch*, Dekker, Ford and Rowley's *Witch of Edmonton*, the anonymous *Merry Devil of Edmonton*, Jonson's *Devil is an Ass* and *Mercury Vindicated from the Alchemists at Court*, as well as updated versions of the perennial favourite *Doctor Faustus*—and of course the debunking play *The Alchemist*. The conjuror's art is the art of theatre.

The interrelationships of art, magic, religion and theatre form a topos for aesthetic experience in the age. 'Picture', Ben Jonson wrote in his commonplace book, 'is the invention of Heaven: the most ancient, and most akin to Nature'; the work of art 'doth so enter and penetrate the inmost affection (being done by an excellent artificer) as sometimes it o'ercomes the power of speech and oratory.'[2] Hence the effect of Paulina's statue on Leontes: 'I like your silence; it the more shows off | Your wonder' (5.3.21–2). The same evocation of wonder is the end of theatre throughout Renaissance treatises on the art: Francesco Robortello's influential commentary on Aristotle's *Poetics* (1548) observes that spectacle is the essence of drama, since it is the necessary expression of the text, and goes on to locate the effect of drama in its power to evoke wonder through its depiction of

---

[1] *Church Courts, Sex and Marriage in England, 1570–1640* (Cambridge, 1987), p. 97.

[2] *Timber: or Discoveries*, in C. H. Herford, P. and E. Simpson, eds., *Ben Jonson*, vol. viii (Oxford, 1947), lines 1523, 1526.

the marvellous.[1] And Sebastiano Serlio, instructing the Renaissance in the design of stage sets and machinery, asserts that 'among all the things that may be made by men's hands, thereby to yield admiration, pleasure to sight, and to content the fantasies of men', theatrical artifice is pre-eminent.[2] This is how drama, for the Renaissance theorist, brought about the therapeutic catharsis that Aristotle described—not through the power of poetic language or heroic action but through the marvels of representation and spectacle.

Art, magic and theatre come together for Shakespeare most explicitly in the figure of Prospero, and Paulina's revelation of the statue is a miniature version of the masque Prospero presents as he brings his plans to a successful conclusion. Prospero's art is quintessentially theatrical: he has at his command a troupe of actors, the spirits of nature led by Ariel, and all the resources of the Jacobean stage—thunder and lightning machinery, flying devices, disappearing banquets, even a closet of costumes, the 'glistering apparel' that so fatally distracts Stefano and Trinculo from their conspiracy. Paulina requires much less in the way of apparatus, only a discovery curtain and a Hermione capable of standing absolutely motionless for eighty lines; but her demand for a suspension of disbelief, her invocation of wonder, and most of all, her claims for the therapeutic quality of her performance sound much more like Renaissance apologias for theatre than like any Renaissance version of religious experience.

The Statue in the Theatre

For audiences and critics since the early nineteenth century, the statue scene has been of the essence, epitomizing the divided life of the play, an utterly implausible device that is nevertheless overwhelmingly moving. Simon Forman, however, in his account of the performance he saw of *The Winter's Tale* at the Globe in 1611, makes no mention of Hermione's statue coming to life. This, as our only contemporary report, has been proposed as

---

[1] *In Librum Aristotelis de arte poetica explicationes* (1548), p. 57. For a discussion of such claims in relation to Jacobean theatre, see my essay 'The Poetics of Spectacle', *New Literary History*, 2 (1971), pp. 367–89.

[2] The passage is quoted from the first English translation, *The First Book of Architecture* (1611), fol. 24 (N1ʳ).

evidence that the statue scene is a revision, and that in its initial form, the play followed its source in leaving the queen dead; but Forman is too unreliable a witness to support such an inference: his accounts of both *Macbeth* and *Cymbeline* also vary significantly from the texts.[1] The most we can conclude from Forman's evidence is that what at least one Jacobean spectator took home from *The Winter's Tale* for contemplation and moral enlightenment did not include the miracle of the living statue. But however eccentric a witness Forman may be, he is not at all eccentric in one respect: although *The Shakspere Allusion Book* records twenty allusions to the play in the seventeenth century (about on a par with *Lear* and *Henry V*; almost double the number for *As You Like It*), not one of these refers to the statue or the resurrection of Hermione. Outside the text of the play, no reference whatever to the statue scene survives from the seventeenth century.

From the time the play reappeared on eighteenth-century stages, however, the statue scene increasingly became its emotional centre. It was so popular, indeed, that it was often played by itself, as a prelude or coda to another drama. In the nineteenth century, it became a miniature sentimental warhorse, guaranteed to put any audience, even the most provincial, in a receptive mood or send them home with tears in their eyes. An 1891 playbill preserved in Goodspeed's Opera House in East Haddam, Connecticut, is characteristic: it promises an overture, a burlesque called *A Musical Surprise*, 'the popular two-act farce entitled *A Box of Monkeys*', and—not as the evening's conclusion, but as a curtain-raiser to the two comedies—the statue scene from *The Winter's Tale*. Guarini's conviction that tragicomedy was the essence of theatre remained as valid for the age of Ibsen and Pinero as it had been for that of Shakespeare and Jonson.

But despite the seemingly obvious theatrical power of the resurrection of Hermione, when *The Winter's Tale* returned to the stage in the mid eighteenth century, its producers invariably

---

[1] As does his account of *Richard II*; but the performance he saw was clearly not of Shakespeare's play. Forman's notes were made in a journal of 'common policy', moral notes for guidance in his everyday affairs; they record what he found ethically useful in the play—the truth eventually comes to light; don't trust charming mountebanks.

located the dramatic life of the play in its pastoral scenes.[1] It was revived for the first time since the 1630s in 1741, initially at Goodman's Fields and then at Covent Garden; it was not a success, and the subsequent interpolation of a ballet of shepherds and shepherdesses did not rescue it—though the fact that shepherds and shepherdesses seemed the solution is certainly to the point. A decade later the play succeeded on the stage in two competing versions which all but reduced it to its pastoral elements. Macnamara Morgan's *The Sheep-Shearing, or Florizel and Perdita* opened at Covent Garden in 1754 to an enthusiastic reception; and from 1756 ran against Garrick's *Florizel and Perdita, a Dramatic Pastoral* in Drury Lane. Morgan's play omits the statue scene entirely. It is concerned with the romance of the two young people in apparent defiance of class boundaries; Leontes and Hermione do not appear at all, and the problems of the socially unequal marriage are resolved by the revelations of Antigonus, who is not dead but has remained in Bohemia disguised as Perdita's shepherd father—the bear has gone the way of the statue. Garrick, however, returned the action's denouement to the statue scene, and despite the fact that Hermione appears nowhere else in the play, Mrs Pritchard's queen was considered one of her finest roles. The scene itself, however, was not universally admired as a way of concluding the action. Dennis Bartholomeusz quotes a review in the *London Chronicle* which complains of the improbabilities of the conception:

Her having lived sequestered for many years might be allowed, if she did not stand for a statue at last. This circumstance is certainly childish, as is likewise the pretended revival of her by music. Had Hermione been discovered to us in a rational manner, the close would have been pathetic, whereas at present, notwithstanding many strokes of fine writing, reason operates too strongly against the incident . . . (p. 32)

Audiences till the end of the century were in fact able to choose the ending they preferred; Morgan's and Garrick's versions continued to be the alternative forms in which *The Winter's Tale* appeared on the London stage until John Philip Kemble in 1802 restored, if not the original text, at least Leontes' passion and

---

[1] See the excellent, detailed stage history by Dennis Bartholomeusz, *The Winter's Tale in performance in England and America*, 1611–1976 (Cambridge, 1982), the primary source for the following account.

Hermione's trial to the play—Kemble finally based his production on the Folio text only after 1811.

For a full account of *The Winter's Tale*'s stage history, the reader may be referred to Bartholomeusz's excellent account. I shall focus here on a group of representations of the final scene as a touchstone to changing theatrical attitudes toward the play. Rowe's Shakespeare in 1709, the first with illustrations, chose

5. Nicholas Rowe, *The Works of Mr. William Shakespear*, 1709. Frontispiece to *The Winter's Tale*.

6. Mrs Pritchard as Hermione in Garrick's *Florizel and Perdita*, engraving after a lost painting by R. E. Pine, *c*.1760.

7. Elizabeth Farren as Hermione, *c*.1780. Engraving after Johann Zoffany.

the statue scene for the play's frontispiece (figure 5). The realization cannot be derived from stage practice, since the play had not been performed since at least 1642, but the artist's imagination gives the moment of Hermione's revival a dramatic authority that it was not to have again in the theatre for almost a century. The costumes are a curious mixture of Roman for the men and largely contemporary for the women (Polixenes, just behind Leontes, however, is in a variety of exotic dress, presumably intended as Bohemian), but what is most striking about the scene is the absolute dominance of Hermione, her sceptre raised in a gesture of command. We will look in vain among the women for one who does not express surprise; there is no Paulina here acting as stage manager.

Fifty years later, Mrs Pritchard's equally commanding Hermione (figure 6) wears classical drapery that suggests a shroud, but she also wears a large pendent cross—since the first three acts of the play are omitted from Garrick's version, and Hermione's reference to the oracle in the last scene is cut, nothing in the text contradicted this assertion of her Christian faith. A generation after, Elizabeth Farren's Hermione, also in Garrick's version (figure 7), is notably more stylish, and a good deal younger. In place of the Christian symbolism, the iconography returns the play to the classical world: the pedestal on which she leans shows putti performing two scenes from Euripides' *Alcestis*, Herakles leading the queen back from the dead, and the reuniting of Alcestis and Admetus. In contrast, Elizabeth Hartley, in 1780 in Drury Lane (figure 8), is strictly contemporary, wearing an elaborate coiffure and an informal evening gown (court dress at this period would have called for a hoopskirt), and is posed in a neoclassical niche that suggests Marie Antoinette rather than Alcestis.

John Philip Kemble's *Winter's Tale*, first produced in 1802, though a revised and by no means complete version of the Folio text, did nevertheless restore the drama of the first three acts to the play. It also had the benefit of Mrs Siddons as Hermione (figure 9). This became one of her most famous roles, which she continued to play until her retirement. Hazlitt, reviewing the production in its first season, praised her 'monumental dignity and noble passion', and doubted that he would ever see the role done so well again (a number of critics of her later performances found her too monumental, austere and inhuman). The print

8. Mrs Hartley as Hermione, *c.*1780, from *The Westminster Magazine.*

conveys her monumentality, in an unadorned dress, leaning on a draped column, the whole image projecting an elegant and melancholy simplicity, stylistically perfectly in tune with both ancient Greece and Regency taste.

Figure 10 shows Macready's statue scene in 1837; the Hermione is Helen Faucit. The décor exhibits the same stylistic anachronisms as Rowe's frontispiece had done more than a century earlier, and indeed, as the play does itself: the statue is classical, but Leontes' palace is Gothic, and the niche in which

9. Mrs Siddons as Hermione, Drury Lane, 1802. Engraving by J. Alais after a painting by Adam Buck.

Hermione stands is decorated in the best contemporary fashion, with festoons and putti. The men's costumes are medieval, the women's Victorian. Most significant of all, Paulina is at last in evidence, controlling the scene, and the centre of attention is not the impassive queen, but Leontes' expression of surprise and joy.

Charles Kean in 1856 presented a spectacular and thoroughly archaeologized version of the play, a problematic venture,

10. Macready's statue scene, Covent Garden, 1837.

11. Original design for Kean's statue scene by I. Dayes, 1856. From the *Illustrated London News*.

considering Shakespeare's casualness about time. Leontes' Sicily was firmly, if arbitrarily, placed in the fourth century BC, and all anachronisms were excised: there were therefore no references to Whitsun pastorals, saint-like sorrows, the emperor of Russia, Giulio Romano. Sir George Scharf, the eminent archaeologist and draughtsman (subsequently the first director of the National Portrait Gallery), was engaged to provide authentic costumes and properties; these were derived from the palpable evidence of vase paintings and ancient artefacts: Shakespeare's fairy tale became a re-creation of the ancient world, historically rationalized. To deal with the fact that Bohemia did not exist in the fourth century, Hanmer's emendation of the country's name to Bithynia was adopted (Garrick had similarly set *Florizel and Perdita* in Bithynia for the stage production, though in the printed version he returned the play to Shakespeare's Bohemia). Figure 11 shows the artist's design for the statue scene, archaeologically authentic in everything except perhaps the lighting. Hermione, played by Ellen Tree (Mrs Kean), stands in a columned shrine, a slim figure classically draped; Leontes, Perdita, Polixenes and Paulina are in deep shadow, surrounded by a multitude of witnesses.

According to Ellen Terry, however, who made her debut playing Mamillius in this production at the age of nine (figure 12), Kean's archaeology was defeated by his Hermione's modesty and sense of herself. Bartholomeusz quotes from Terry's reminiscences:

> No matter what character Mrs Kean was assuming, she always used to wear her hair drawn flat over her forehead and twisted tight round her ears in a kind of circular sweep . . . And then the amount of petticoats she wore. Even as Hermione she was always bunched out by layer upon layer of petticoats in defiance of the fact that classical parts should not be dressed in superfluity of raiment. (pp. 86–7)

Indeed, Terry observes that though the costumes were purely and even pedantically classical, the 'actors and actresses seemed unable to keep their own period and their own individuality out of the clothes directly they got them on their backs. In some cases the original design was quite swamped' (p. 86). Figure 13 is a photograph of Mrs Kean as Hermione: for all her drapery, she is immediately identifiable as a Victorian matron, much more insistently of her period than the equally individualized and unidealized Hermione of Mrs Pritchard in figure 9; and it must

12. Ellen Terry as Mamillius and Charles Kean as Leontes, Princess's Theatre, 1856.

be admitted that, to modern eyes, it is difficult to accommodate this unglamorous, definitively middle-aged figure to the romance of reconciliations and restored losses at the play's conclusion. But this in a sense is our problem: the image is true to the play in a way that few interpreters, theatrical or critical, have been willing to be. Mrs Kean's Hermione takes seriously the losses and the passage of time—as, in fact, Kean's text did not: Leontes' observation that 'Hermione was not so much wrinkled, nothing

13. Mrs Kean (Ellen Tree) as Hermione, 1856.

14. Ellen Terry as Hermione, His Majesty's Theatre, 1906.

73

15. Mary Anderson as Hermione, Lyceum, 1887.

| So agèd as this seems' (5.3.28–9) was cut, as it regularly was from eighteenth- and nineteenth-century performing texts, until Beerbohm Tree in 1906—with Ellen Terry as the most agelessly beautiful of Hermiones—restored it (figure 14).

The denial of the realities of time in the play reached a logical apogee when Mary Anderson, in 1887, for the first time played both Hermione and Perdita (figures 15 and 16) to Forbes-Robertson's Leontes. Costumes were by Alma-Tadema, and the production strove above all to be pre-eminently tasteful. To this end the text was heavily cut; references to sexuality, and to the

16. Mary Anderson as Perdita, Lyceum, 1887.

darker passions generally, including Leontes' soliloquies on his jealousy, were omitted, as were most references to Hermione's pregnancy and Paulina's recriminations after Mamillius' and Hermione's death. The performing time consequently was little over two hours, and the success of the production was immense and unqualified: it lasted 164 nights, and was the longest-running production of *The Winter's Tale* in England or America in the nineteenth century,[1] exceeded in this century only by Peter

---

[1] Bartholomeusz, pp. 116–17.

Brook's production at the Phoenix Theatre in 1951, with Gielgud as Leontes, Diana Wynyard as Hermione, and Flora Robson as Paulina.

The doubling of Hermione and Perdita is more a *tour de force* for the actress than a viable option for the play, but its theatrical value—and it is difficult to see it as anything but a sentimental-izing device—has been felt by many actresses and directors since 1887. In Mary Anderson's case, it necessitated depriving Perdita of her lines in the last scene, and the *Times*'s reviewer found the device distracting and ineffective: 'The beauty of the scene . . . is seriously impaired by the presence among the company of the strange, veiled, speechless figure, who keeps her back to the audience and is addressed as Perdita.'[1] To restore the mother meant silencing the daughter. When Judi Dench doubled Her-mione and Perdita at Stratford in 1969, Trevor Nunn devised an ingenious way of allowing Hermione to perform a quick change into Perdita, thus enabling the daughter to retain her lines, but few viewers found the device persuasive—to Bartholomeusz, 'the trick seemed obvious and technically distracting' (p. 122). And yet the idea of doubling the roles remains attractive, if only as an antidote to the hardest truths of the play. It renders nugatory, for example, Leontes' moment of lust for the unrecognized Perdita (and consequently, this was one of the few bits of sexual innuendo that Mary Anderson's production felt safe in retain-ing): if Leontes is merely affirming his unaltered love for his wife, the dangers of incest and the tension between the generations need not be considered, and in the passage of sixteen years, nothing at all has been lost.

In 1912, Granville Barker returned the full text of the play to the stage in a genuinely innovative production. Eschewing any pretence to the historical, it was set on a thrust stage with sets by Norman Wilkinson recalling both post-impressionist paintings and Léon Bakst's sets for Diaghilev's ballet; the costumes by Albert Rothenstein were based on Giulio Romano—anachronism was returned to the heart of the play. Even for unsympathetic critics the production came as a revelation—in the sourest of the reviews, Rebecca West insisted on 'the quite unmistakable dull-ness of the first half', but conceded that 'Mr Barker's setting of

---

[1] Quoted by Bartholomeusz, p. 122.

the play helps one to forget it'.[1] Henry Ainley's Leontes was praised for its 'passion and obstinacy and spasmodic fierceness, the weak man's counterfeit of strength',[2] and Lillah McCarthy's Hermione, for those who admired it, was 'delightfully unstagy', a triumph of tact and restraint.[3] One critic who did not admire it was again Rebecca West:

Miss McCarthy enjoys the undoubted advantages of beauty and health, which gave her a kind of exciting vitality that makes her animation delightful. But in all reflective and dignified parts she becomes nerveless and stolid, mooing her more sonorous lines and acting a little more smugly. When Hermione is unveiled she looks not so much like a statue as like the Marble Arch. Like it she lacks poise and significance. And like it she is out of place, as we remember with regret in thinking of her successes in comedy.[4]

Whatever the merits of its individual performances, Granville Barker's conception of the play was rightly seen as revolutionary, reopening the text to the full range of interpretive possibility.

What the Statue Does Not Say

The catharsis engineered by Paulina depends, of course, on sixteen years of suffering and penance on Leontes' part. Nothing is said of what Hermione has undergone during the sixteen years; and indeed, the play's stagecraft renders the question irrelevant: she has been dead. Her classic prototype, Alcestis, is similarly silent about her experience, as is the restored Hero of *Much Ado About Nothing*: this is the mark of the good woman, and as we have seen, the parallel with Alcestis was noted as early as the eighteenth century.[5] Our only contemporary observer, Simon Forman in 1611, did not even consider Hermione's resurrection worth mentioning—not only does he not report the statue coming to life, but even her reappearance as part of the final reconciliation goes unremarked. For modern audiences, the reunion of husband and wife is the essential element in the

---

[1] Review in the *Daily Herald*, 23 September 1912.

[2] Review in the *Referee*, quoted in Bartholomeusz, p. 151.

[3] See the comments cited in Bartholomeusz, p. 155.

[4] *Daily Herald*, 23 September 1912.

[5] W. W. Lloyd did a detailed comparison of the plays in 1856 (cited in the *Variorum*, p. 357); for a more recent discussion see Martin Mueller, 'Hermione's Wrinkles, or Ovid Transformed', *Comparative Drama*, 5 (1971), 226–39.

denouement, but this may well be an anachronistic reaction: Leontes' courtiers continually urge him to remarry, and Paulina prevents him from doing so precisely because Hermione could have been produced at any time, the royal family reconstituted, new heirs born.[1] The oracle would not thereby have been fulfilled, but clearly no one at court except Paulina believes that it needs to be. For Shakespeare's age, the restoration of Perdita is the crucial element; even Hermione says she has preserved herself to see Perdita, not Leontes.

Perdita's disappearance for sixteen years is, moreover, in its cultural context, not quite the sort of tragic loss it appears to us. The children of aristocratic families were often sent away to be raised, and both Prince Henry and Princess Elizabeth were taken from their mother in infancy and brought up by surrogate parents.[2] (Mamillius and Florizel are being raised at home, but the tensions and dangers are obvious—they are, indeed, in a sense the subject of the play.) Queen Anne certainly saw somewhat more of her children over the years than Hermione sees of Perdita, but the idea of the royal family as a unit, with the children an essential part of it, is not a Renaissance one. In the

---

[1] Janet Adelman, as part of a passionate and ingenious attempt to discover an independent space for women in the final moments of the play, argues that while it is true that the containment of women's power is a primary and ultimate concern, nevertheless 'The Winter's Tale restores the mother to life and makes the father's generativity and authority contingent on her return.' She then proposes a contrast with Pericles: 'If Pericles could allow the mother back only by ruthlessly excising her sexual body, The Winter's Tale insists on the recovery—within patriarchal limits—of that body'. But The Winter's Tale is no less ruthless: Hermione is restored only when she is past childbearing—a fact which surely affects any claims about 'the father's generativity'. Generative sexuality is as dangerous at the end of the play as it had been at the beginning. I imagine, therefore, that we would also disagree here about the extent of patriarchal limits. See Suffocating Mothers (1992), pp. 220–36; the passage quoted is on p. 236. Valerie Traub seems to me to come much closer to the force of the concluding scene: 'Rather than a victory for the wronged heroine, the final scene works as wish-fulfillment for Leontes, who not only regains his virtuous wife and loses his burden of guilt, but also reassumes his kingly command of all social relations' (Desire and Anxiety (1992), p. 45).

[2] Prince Henry was sent to the household of the Earl of Mar at the age of a few weeks, Princess Elizabeth to Alexander, Lord Livingstone (later Earl of Linlithgow), at three months. Neither rejoined their parents until the move to England, when Henry was nine and Elizabeth seven, after which both children continued to live in separate households. For an incisive discussion of the practice of giving away children in the period, see Patricia Fumerton, Cultural Aesthetics (Chicago, 1991), Chapter 2.

culture at large, husbands and wives often lived apart for long periods, as Shakespeare and his wife did for over twenty years. We have assumed that this implies an unhappy marriage; but the practice was not unusual, and indeed was the norm in aristocratic alliances where more than one household was maintained. The tragic loss that Perdita represents is not the loss of her company, or of the opportunity to watch her grow, or of the role we believe her parents should have had in the formation of her character, but the loss of an heir, as the oracle says: 'the King shall live without an heir if that which is lost be not found'. That is what is found, the essential thing. The fact that so many audiences and critics since the eighteenth century have seen this ending as profoundly satisfactory says much for the tenacity of patriarchal assumptions as the subtext to aesthetic judgements. Once the crucial loss is restored, everything returns to its proper place; even Paulina acknowledges her proper status to be that of the obedient wife—to somebody, to anybody, to whomever the king chooses. What is restored, finally, in this quintessentially Jacobean drama, is royal authority.

The Date, Early Performances, and the Text

Simon Forman recorded in his journal that he had seen *The Winter's Tale* at the Globe on 15 May 1611.[1] This is the only external evidence for the date of the play. There seems in addition to be a reference to Jonson's masque *Oberon*, which includes a dance of satyrs, in the Servant's introduction of the 'saltiers' in 4.4.332, 'One three of them, by their own report, sir, hath danced before the King'. *Oberon* was performed at court on New Year's Day, 1611.[2] If the Servant's line is in fact an allusion, it would mean that the composition of the play was still in progress in early January.

But, as Stanley Wells points out, both the passage and the dance may be an interpolation after the play was complete:

---

[1] Bodleian MS Ashmole 208, fols. 201ᵛ–202ʳ; see below, Appendix A. Forman also gives accounts of *Cymbeline*, *Macbeth*, and a non-Shakespearian *Richard II*, all of which he saw at the Globe in 1611. The relevant passages are reprinted in Chambers's *Shakespeare*, ii. 337–41.

[2] Chambers also proposed that the bear alludes to the bears that draw Oberon's chariot, but later decided that Shakespeare was more likely indebted to the bear in *Mucedorus*; see *William Shakespeare*, i. 489.

The passage introducing this dance could be omitted without disturbing any of the dialogue; no one comments upon the dance afterwards; moreover, the Clown's comment that 'My father and the gentleman are in sad talk' [4.4.308] would be naturally followed, after the exit of Autolycus and his clients, by Polixenes' 'O, father, you'll know more of that hereafter' [4.4.338], which indicates that they have been carrying on a conversation which we have not heard. Polixenes' comment is not nearly so natural after the satyr dance, since it suggests that he had been talking to the Old Shepherd rather than attending to the dance he had himself insisted on witnessing. There is no reason to doubt Shakespeare's authorship of the passage introducing the dance, but it could be a late addition. (*Textual Companion*, p. 601).

Earlier versions of this argument are energetically rejected by Pafford (p. xxii), but his reasons are less than cogent.

In any case, there is no reason to doubt that the play was new to the stage in the season when Forman saw it in 1611. It was performed at court on 5 November in the same year, probably in the Banqueting House,[1] and again sometime between December and February 1612–13 as one of the fourteen plays presented by the King's Men during the festivities preceding the wedding of King James's daughter Elizabeth to Prince Frederick the Elector Palatine. Court performances thereafter are recorded on 7 April 1618, possibly sometime in 1619,[2] on 18 January 1624 before the Duchess of Richmond while the King was absent, and finally for the Caroline court on 16 January 1634. There is no record of a subsequent performance before the mid eighteenth century.

The play was first printed in the Folio of 1623; it was the last of the comedies, as *The Tempest* was the first. The only entry for it in the Stationers' Register is that of 8 November 1623, where it is listed among the sixteen plays included in the Folio that have not previously been entered. From the fact that the play has a

[1] In October, 1611, James Maxwell was paid 'for making ready... the Banqueting House there [at Whitehall] three several tymes for playes' (Audit Office, Declared Accounts, Bundle 389, Roll 49, fol. 10b, in the PRO). Since the King's Men were paid for performing *The Tempest*, *The Winter's Tale* and one other play at court in late October and early November, the conclusion is reasonable (though not inescapable) that these were the plays for which Maxwell was preparing the Banqueting House during October. The fact that the Banqueting House was selected, rather than the court theatre the Cockpit-in-Court, implies nothing about how the play was regarded; the Banqueting House was being used as a performing space for entertainments of all kinds, including bear-baiting, at this period. See the introduction to my Oxford *Tempest*, p. 3.
[2] Chambers, ii. 346.

special set of signatures and that the play preceding it, *Twelfth Night*, ends on a recto and *The Winter's Tale* begins on the next recto (leaving the only blank verso in the section of comedies other than the final verso of *The Winter's Tale* itself), it has been deduced that the copy for the play arrived late at the printer's, after the setting of the section of histories was already in progress.[1] If this is the case, the fact that the play was placed last has as little significance as the fact that *The Tempest* was placed first.[2]

Despite the complexity of the language, it is a clear text, relatively free of printer's errors.[3] A number of idiosyncrasies indicate that the copy was prepared for the press by the scribe Ralph Crane, who was employed from time to time by the King's Men, and is generally agreed to have been responsible for preparing the Folio texts of *The Tempest*, *The Two Gentlemen of Verona*, *The Merry Wives of Windsor* and *Measure for Measure* in addition to *The Winter's Tale*. From the fact that Sir Henry Herbert licensed a new copy of the play for performance on 19 August 1623 because 'the allowed book was missing',[4] Greg concluded, reasonably, that since the 'allowed book' would have been the prompt copy, Crane was working from Shakespeare's foul papers; his argument has been elaborated by T. H. Howard-Hill, who concludes that 'Crane made two transcripts from foul papers, one to replace the prompt-book which was missing before a new prompt-book was relicensed . . . , and the other as copy for the Folio'. He continues, however, with an important and salutary caveat regarding the assumptions that can be derived from the knowledge that Crane was working from Shakespeare's autograph:

By the time Crane had copied his source twice (or, indeed, only once) many of the obscurities of his copy had been smoothed out. The texts of

---

[1] Charlton Hinman concludes that copy for *The Winter's Tale* was not available to the printer before December 1622, and that Crane's transcript was prepared after those of the other four comedies; see *The Printing and Proof-Reading of the First Folio of Shakespeare* (Oxford, 1963), ii. 521.

[2] See the introduction to my Oxford *Tempest*, pp. 58–9.

[3] Detailed discussion of the typography and orthography is in Pafford, '*The Winter's Tale*: Typographical Peculiarities in the Folio Text', *Notes & Queries*, 206 (May, 1961), 172–8; information on the division of labour among the compositors is tabulated in Charlton Hinman, *Printing and Proof-Reading of the First Folio of Shakespeare* (Oxford, 1963), ii. 496–503.

[4] E. K. Chambers, *William Shakespeare* (Oxford, 1930), i. 488.

all five comedies have been described by modern editors as 'good', an opinion justified by the small number of errors which have been detected in them. Crane, however, was not prone to write rubbish; the kind of nonsense set up by a baffled compositor in the first quarto of *Lear* is never found in his transcripts, and even when he may be suspected of error, the reading of his transcript is at the least plausible. If his sophistication of his texts had been less, more could be discovered of the nature of his copy. The 'goodness' of [the five texts prepared by Crane] means little more than that the printer's copy was free from obvious error. The general level of Crane's accuracy was high, but he was not reluctant to interfere with his text, consciously or unconsciously, when its meaning was obscure to him. Certainly, there is more of his orthography in these texts than the author's. These considerations should encourage editors to regard the 'correctness' of the texts printed from Crane transcripts with renewed scepticism.'[1]

Two of Crane's hallmarks clearly visible in *The Winter's Tale* are the thorough division of the play into acts and scenes and the tendency (not invariably followed in this case) to mass entrances at the beginning of a scene, in accord with classical, continental and, perhaps most relevant, Jonsonian precedent, rather than indicating them at the appropriate points in the action—such scribal practices produced an elegant reading text, but the undifferentiated entries would also have rendered it useless for purposes of performance. It is possible, however, that the massed entries have been too easily dismissed. Pafford identified eight scenes in which the initial entrances require adjustment because some characters are not in fact on stage at the outset. But Alan Dessen, in a thoughtful and painstaking essay, makes a case for the dramatic cogency of at least some of the massed entries, 'the potential theatrical effect of figures who are onstage but silent', and argues that we need to consider them on a case by case basis, especially since Crane's practice in *The Winter's Tale* is inconsistent.[2]

Some unusual features of the play's language may also be ascribed to Crane; these include idiosyncratic spellings, the use

---

[1] *Ralph Crane and Some Shakespeare First Folio Comedies* (Charlottesville, 1972), pp. 132–3. See also Howard-Hill's article 'Knight, Crane and the copy for the Folio *Winter's Tale*', *Notes & Queries*, 211 (April, 1966), 139–40.

[2] In 2.1, for example, Dessen writes, 'consider the theatrical effect if a silent Leontes (with or without attendant lords) is a silent observer of his queen and son for some thirty lines. Such a stage image would echo his observation of Hermione and Polixenes in 1.2' ('Massed Entries and Theatrical Options in *The Winter's Tale*', *Shakespeare Studies*, forthcoming).

of apostrophes to indicate words which are conceived to be missing (e.g. 'Who taught' this?', 2.1.11; ''Beseech you all', 2.1.112)—both of which largely disappear in modernized editions—and the relatively dense punctuation with a liberal use of brackets and hyphens. But the complexity and obscurity of the verse can only be authorial.

EDITORIAL PROCEDURES

I HAVE followed the procedures set up by the General Editor, described in detail in *Henry V*, edited by Gary Taylor (Oxford, 1982), pp. 75 ff. Modernization has followed the principles established in Stanley Wells's 'Modernizing Shakespeare's Spelling', in Wells and Taylor, *Modernizing Shakespeare's Spelling, with Three Studies in the Text of 'Henry V'* (Oxford, 1979). In the collations, insignificant variations in speech headings (e.g. Sheephearde, Florizell) have not been recorded, and obvious misprints (e.g. 'presenrly' for 'presently', 2.2.46) have been silently corrected. Punctuation is collated only where a significant syntactical question is involved. Since all asides and speech directions (e.g. *to Camillo*) are editorial, only those that are original to this edition have been collated. Both the Folio's apostrophes to signal the presumed omission of a word (see above) and the division into acts and scenes are assumed to be scribal, and have not been collated. Changes to stage directions are noted in the collations, but where the specified action is clearly implied by the dialogue, the change is neither bracketed in the text nor attributed to a particular editor. Disputable alterations are printed within broken brackets (⌐¬) .

Quotations and references to other Shakespeare plays are from the Complete Oxford Shakespeare, Compact Edition (Oxford, 1988).

Abbreviations and References

The following abbreviations are used in the introduction, explanatory notes and collations. The place of publication is London unless otherwise specified.

EDITIONS OF SHAKESPEARE

F, F1	The First Folio, 1623
F2	The Second Folio, 1632
F3	The Third Folio, 1663
F4	The Fourth Folio, 1685

Alexander	Peter Alexander, *Works*, The Tudor Shakespeare (1951)
Bevington	David Bevington, *Works*, third edition (Glenview, 1980)
Cambridge	W. G. Clark and W. A. Wright, *Works*, The Cambridge Shakespeare, 9 vols. (Cambridge, 1863–6)
Capell	Edward Capell, *Comedies, Histories, and Tragedies*, 10 vols. (1767–8)
Collier	John Payne Collier, *Works*, 8 vols. (1842–4)
Dyce	Alexander Dyce, *Works*, 6 vols. (1857)
Halliwell	J. O. Halliwell[-Phillipps], *Works*, 16 vols. (1853–65)
Hanmer	Thomas Hanmer, *Works*, 6 vols. (Oxford, 1743–4)
Hudson	H. N. Hudson, *Works*, 11 vols. (Boston, 1851–6)
Johnson	Samuel Johnson, *Plays*, 8 vols. (1765)
Keightley	Thomas Keightley, *Plays*, 6 vols. (1864)
Kermode	Frank Kermode, *The Winter's Tale*, The Signet Shakespeare (New York, 1963)
Malone	Edmond Malone, *Plays and Poems*, 10 vols. (1790)
Maxwell	Baldwin Maxwell, *The Winter's Tale*, The Pelican Shakespeare (New York, 1956)
Oxford	Stanley Wells and Gary Taylor, eds., *Complete Works*, The Oxford Shakespeare (Oxford, 1986)
Pafford	J. H. P. Pafford, *The Winter's Tale*, The Arden Shakespeare (1963)
Pope	Alexander Pope, *Works*, 6 vols. (1723–5)
Quiller-Couch	John Dover Wilson and Arthur Quiller-Couch, *The Winter's Tale*, The New Shakespeare (Cambridge, 1931)
Rann	Joseph Rann, *Dramatic Works*, 6 vols. (Oxford, 1786–94)
Riverside	G. B. Evans (textual editor), *The Riverside Shakespeare* (Boston, 1974)
Rowe	Nicholas Rowe, *Works*, 6 vols. (1709)
Rowe 1714	Nicholas Rowe, *Works*, 8 vols. (1714)
Schanzer	Ernest Schanzer, *The Winter's Tale*, The New Penguin Shakespeare (Harmondsworth, 1969)
Sisson	C. J. Sisson, *Complete Works* (1954)
Staunton	Howard Staunton, *Plays*, 3 vols. (1858–60)
Steevens	Samuel Johnson and George Steevens, *Plays*, 10 vols. (1773)

Theobald	Lewis Theobald, *Works*, 7 vols. (1733)
Variorum	Horace Howard Furness, *The Winter's Tale*, A New Variorum Edition (Philadelphia, 1898)
Warburton	William Warburton, *Works*, 8 vols. (1747)
White	R. G. White, *Comedies, Hostories, Tragedies, and Poems* (Boston, 1859)
Wilson	John Dover Wilson and Arthur Quiller-Couch, *The Winter's Tale*, The New Shakespeare (Cambridge, 1931)

OTHER WORKS

Abbott	E. A. Abbott, *A Shakespearian Grammar*, third revised edition (1870). References are to paragraph numbers.
Bethell	S. L. Bethell, *The Winter's Tale: A Study* (1947)
Bullough	Geoffrey Bullough, *Narrative and Dramatic Sources of Shakespeare*, volume 8 (1975)
Cavell	Stanley Cavell, *Disowning Knowledge in Six Plays of Shakespeare* (Cambridge, Mass., 1987)
Cercignani	Fausto Cercignani, *Shakespeare's Works and Elizabethan Pronunciation* (Oxford, 1981)
Chamberlain, *Letters*	Norman E. McClure, ed., *Letters of John Chamberlain*, 2 vols. (Philadelphia, 1939)
Chambers	E. K. Chambers, *The Elizabethan Stage*, 4 vols. (Oxford, 1923)
Chambers, *William Shakespeare*	E. K. Chambers, *William Shakespeare*, 2 vols. (Oxford, 1930)
Coleridge	S. T. Coleridge, *Notes and Lectures* (London, 1849)
Dent	R. W. Dent, *Shakespeare's Proverbial Language: An Index* (Berkeley and Los Angeles, 1981)
DNB	*The Dictionary of National Biography*, Compact Edition (Oxford, 1975)
Douce	Francis Douce, *Illustrations of Shakespeare*, 2 vols. (1807)
ELH	*ELH (Journal of English Literary History)*
ELR	*English Literary Renaissance*
Florio	John Florio, *Queen Anna's New World of Words* (1611)
Greg	W. W. Greg, *The Shakespeare First Folio* (Oxford, 1955)
Grigson	Geoffrey Grigson, *The Englishman's Flora* (1955)

Howard-Hill	T. H. Howard-Hill, *Ralph Crane and Some Shakespeare First Folio Comedies* (Charlottesville, 1972)
Kökeritz	Helge Kökeritz, *Shakespeare's Pronunciation* (New Haven, 1953)
McIlwain	C. H. McIlwain, ed., *The Political Works of James I* (Cambridge, Mass., 1918)
MLR	*Modern Language Review*
Noble	Richmond Noble, *Shakespeare's Biblical Knowledge and Use of the Book of Common Prayer* (1935)
OED	*The Oxford English Dictionary*, second edition (Oxford, 1989)
Onions	C. T. Onions, *A Shakespeare Glossary*, second edition (1919), reprinted with addenda (Oxford, 1958)
Partridge	Eric Partridge, *Shakespeare's Bawdy* (1948)
PMLA	*PMLA (Publications of the Modern Language Association of America)*
REL	*Review of English Literature*
RES	*Review of English Studies*
Schmidt	Alexander Schmidt, *A Shakespeare Lexicon*, fourth edition (revised by G. Sarrazin), 2 vols. (Berlin and Leipzig, 1923)
SEL	*Studies in English Literature*
ShQ	*Shakespeare Quarterly*
Sh. Survey	*Shakespeare Survey*
Sisson, *New Readings*	C. J. Sisson, *New Readings in Shakespeare*, 2 vols. (Cambridge, 1956)
STC	A. W. Pollard *et al.*, eds., *A Short-Title Catalogue of Books Printed in England, Scotland, & Ireland* 1475–1640, second edition (1986)
Textual Companion	Stanley Wells and Gary Taylor, *William Shakespeare: A Textual Companion* (Oxford, 1987)
Tilley	M. P. Tilley, *A Dictionary of the Proverbs in England in the Sixteenth and Seventeenth Centuries* (Ann Arbor, 1950)
Walker	W. S. Walker, *Critical Examination of the Text of Shakespeare* (1859)
Whalley	P. Whalley, *An Enquiry into the Learning of Shakespeare* (1748)

The Winter's Tale

THE PERSONS OF THE PLAY

LEONTES, King of Sicilia

MAMILLIUS, young prince of Sicilia

CAMILLO
ANTIGONUS
CLEOMENES   } four lords of Sicilia
DION

A MARINER

A JAILER

HERMIONE, Queen to Leontes

PERDITA, daughter to Leontes and Hermione

PAULINA, wife to Antigonus

EMILIA, a lady attending on Hermione

POLIXENES, King of Bohemia

FLORIZEL, prince of Bohemia

OLD SHEPHERD, reputed father of Perdita

CLOWN, his son

AUTOLYCUS, a rogue

ARCHIDAMUS, a lord of Bohemia

MOPSA
DORCAS   } shepherdesses

Other Lords, Ladies, Gentlemen, and Servants

Shepherds and Shepherdesses

TIME as Chorus

THE PERSONS OF THE PLAY] F (The Names of the Actors) *at end of play*   A MARINER] *not in* F   A JAILER] *not in* F   MOPSA] *not in* F   DORCAS] *not in* F   Other . . . Gentlemen] Other Lords, and Gentlemen F   TIME as Chorus] *not in* F

The Winter's Tale

1.1 *Enter Camillo and Archidamus*

ARCHIDAMUS If you shall chance, Camillo, to visit Bohemia on the like occasion whereon my services are now
on foot, you shall see, as I have said, great difference
betwixt our Bohemia and your Sicilia.

CAMILLO I think this coming summer the King of Sicilia   5
means to pay Bohemia the visitation which he justly
owes him.

ARCHIDAMUS Wherein our entertainment shall shame us;
we will be justified in our loves. For indeed—

CAMILLO Beseech you—   10

ARCHIDAMUS Verily I speak it in the freedom of my knowledge. We cannot with such magnificence—in so rare—
I know not what to say. We will give you sleepy drinks,
that your senses, unintelligent of our insufficience, may,
though they cannot praise us, as little accuse us.   15

CAMILLO You pay a great deal too dear for what's given
freely.

ARCHIDAMUS Believe me, I speak as my understanding
instructs me, and as mine honesty puts it to utterance.

CAMILLO Sicilia cannot show himself over-kind to Bohe-   20
mia. They were trained together in their childhoods,

1.1.8 us;] F (~:); ~, THEOBALD

1.1.6 **Bohemia** the King of Bohemia

8–9 **Wherein . . . loves** i.e. our hospitality
will be inadequate, but the love that
prompts it will vindicate us. F separates
the clauses with a colon. Theobald, followed by many editors, replaced the
colon with a comma, so that the lines
read 'Wherein our entertainment shall
shame us, we will be justified in our
loves.' This gives an undeniably easier
sense, but Archidamus' next speech,

emphasizing the absolute insufficiency of
Bohemian entertainment, suggests that
F's syntax is correct.

11–12 **in . . . knowledge** as my knowledge permits me to do

13 **sleepy** sleep-inducing (*OED* 3)

14 **that** so that
unintelligent unaware

20–1 **Sicilia . . . Bohemia** the King of Sicilia . . . the King of Bohemia

21 **trained** educated

and there rooted betwixt them then such an affection
which cannot choose but branch now. Since their more
mature dignities and royal necessities made separation
of their society, their encounters, though not personal,   25
hath been royally attorneyed with interchange of gifts,
letters, loving embassies, that they have seemed to be
together, though absent, shook hands as over a vast,
and embraced as it were from the ends of opposed
winds. The heavens continue their loves.   30

ARCHIDAMUS I think there is not in the world either malice
or matter to alter it. You have an unspeakable comfort
of your young prince Mamillius. It is a gentleman of the
greatest promise that ever came into my note.

CAMILLO I very well agree with you in the hopes of him.   35
It is a gallant child, one that, indeed, physics the subject,
makes old hearts fresh. They that went on crutches ere
he was born desire yet their life to see him a man.

ARCHIDAMUS Would they else be content to die?

CAMILLO Yes, if there were no other excuse why they   40
should desire to live.

ARCHIDAMUS If the King had no son, they would desire to
live on crutches till he had one.   *Exeunt*

1.2   *Enter Leontes, Hermione, Mamillius, Polixenes,*
⌈*Camillo*⌉

POLIXENES
Nine changes of the watery star hath been
The shepherd's note since we have left our throne
Without a burden. Time as long again

26 hath] F1; have F2

22–3 **rooted ... branch** 'trained', with
its relevance to espaliered trees or trel-
lised vines, may have suggested the
horticultural metaphor; but the plant
that roots is their affection for each
other, not the two stocks.
23 **branch** mature, flourish
25 **encounters** literally, meetings face to
face
personal in person
26 **hath** emended by F2 to 'have', but the
usage is not uncommon: compare
'Hath all his ventures failed?' (*Merchant*

3.2.265). See Abbott 338 (Third person
plural in -th).
26 **attorneyed** represented by deputies
28 **vast** immense distance
29–30 **from ... winds** i.e. from diametric-
ally opposite points of the compass, where
the winds are imagined to originate
30 **continue** subjunctive ('may the heavens ...')
36 **physics the subject** is a tonic for the
people
1.2.0.2 *Camillo* It is not clear when he
re-enters after the first scene. Ringler

Would be filled up, my brother, with our thanks,
And yet we should for perpetuity   5
Go hence in debt. And therefore, like a cipher,
Yet standing in rich place, I multiply
With one 'we thank you' many thousands more
That go before it.
LEONTES   Stay your thanks awhile,
And pay them when you part.
POLIXENES   Sir, that's tomorrow.   10
I am questioned by my fears of what may chance
Or breed upon our absence, that may blow
No sneaping winds at home, to make us say,
'This is put forth too truly.' Besides, I have stayed
To tire your royalty.
LEONTES   We are tougher, brother,   15
Than you can put us to't.

('The Number of Actors in Shakespeare's Early Plays', in *The Seventeenth-
century Stage*, ed. G. E. Bentley (1968),
p. 114) claims that 'it is clear that he
does not re-enter until Leontes exclaims
"What, Camillo there?"' (l. 207), but
from the subsequent conversation it is
evident that Camillo has witnessed at
least some part of the preceding action.
Theobald, followed by almost all editors,
adds 'and attendants'. Whether this is
correct or not would depend on whether
the scene is played as a formal court
scene or a more intimate domestic one.
Since there is no function for or reference to attendants anywhere in the
scene, I have followed F.

1 **changes ... star** changes of the moon
('watery' because of its association with
the tides), hence months

2 **note** observation

3–6 **Time ... debt** 'Even if I spent another
nine months thanking you, I would still
depart your perpetual debtor.'

6–9 **like ... it** 'I am like a zero, which
itself is nothing, but by its placement
(after a number) multiplies the thousands of thanks that precede it'; the
metaphor plays on the proverbial 'He
is a cipher among numbers' (Dent
C391).

11 **I ... of** my anxiety demands of me

12–14 **that ... truly** 'so that no destructive events may arise at home to per-

suade me that my fears were only too
well founded'. Some editors (e.g. Furness, Schanzer) take 'that' to imply a
wish rather than a contingency, and
gloss 'O that no biting winds', etc. The
passage has suffered much elucidation.
It is clear that Polixenes is saying he
must go home, but his reasons are elliptical and obscure, and his metaphor
changes in mid-sentence. The kingdom
is conceived as a garden; with the gardener absent, the plants have no protection against the 'sneaping winds',
whatever these may be. Attempts to
make 'This is put forth too truly' part of
the same metaphor have resulted in out-
right revision or paraphrases that wander very far from the text. Thus, Hanmer
saw 'put forth' as implying the unseaso-
nal appearance of buds, and therefore
read 'early' for 'truly'—some editors
have adopted this, but it makes the relevance of the metaphor even more obscure; and Quiller-Couch and Dover
Wilson, who thought Hanmer's emendation was 'probably right', saw the
sneaping winds as Polixenes' response to
the conspiracy or faction he fears is
breeding at home, and which, were he
on the spot, could be nipped in the bud.

13 **sneaping** biting, killing with cold

15 **royalty** majesty (*OED* 1b)

15–16 **We ... to't** i.e. I am equal to any
such test. To put (a person) to it = to force
one to do one's utmost (*OED*, put, 28c, b).

95

POLIXENES   No longer stay.

LEONTES

One sev'night longer.

POLIXENES   Very sooth, tomorrow.

LEONTES

We'll part the time between's then; and in that
I'll no gainsaying.

POLIXENES   Press me not, beseech you, so.
There is no tongue that moves, none, none i'th' world,   20
So soon as yours could win me. So it should now,
Were there necessity in your request, although
'Twere needful I denied it. My affairs
Do even drag me homeward, which to hinder
Were, in your love, a whip to me; my stay,   25
To you a charge and trouble. To save both,
Farewell, our brother.

LEONTES   Tongue-tied, our queen? Speak you.

HERMIONE

I had thought, sir, to have held my peace until
You had drawn oaths from him not to stay. You, sir,
Charge him too coldly. Tell him you are sure   30
All in Bohemia's well; this satisfaction
The bygone day proclaimed—say this to him,
He's beat from his best ward.

LEONTES   Well said, Hermione.

HERMIONE

To tell he longs to see his son were strong;
But let him say so then, and let him go;   35
But let him swear so and he shall not stay—
We'll thwack him hence with distaffs.
(*To Polixenes*) Yet of your royal presence I'll adventure
The borrow of a week. When at Bohemia
You take my lord, I'll give him my commission   40

---

19 **I'll . . . gainsaying** 'I won't take no for
    an answer'
21 **could** that could
24–5 **which . . . me** 'to prevent me from
    going, though you did it out of love,
    would be to torture me'
27 **Tongue-tied** 'To be tongue-tied' is
    cited as proverbial by Tilley (T416), but
    considered dubious by Dent.

31–2 **this . . . proclaimed** we were as-
    sured of this yesterday
32 **say** i.e. if you say
33 **ward** defence (in fencing)
34 **tell** say
   strong i.e. a powerful argument
36 **But** only
38 **adventure** venture

To let him there a month behind the gest
Prefixed for's parting—yet, good deed, Leontes,
I love thee not a jar o'th' clock behind
What lady she her lord. You'll stay?

POLIXENES   No, madam.

HERMIONE

Nay, but you will?

POLIXENES   I may not, verily.

HERMIONE   Verily?   45
You put me off with limber vows; but I,
Though you would seek t'unsphere the stars with oaths,
Should yet say, 'Sir, no going.' Verily,
You shall not go—a lady's 'verily' 's
As potent as a lord's. Will you go yet?   50
Force me to keep you as a prisoner,
Not like a guest; so you shall pay your fees
When you depart, and save your thanks. How say you?
My prisoner or my guest? By your dread 'verily',
One of them you shall be.

POLIXENES   Your guest, then, madam.   55
To be your prisoner should import offending,
Which is for me less easy to commit
Than you to punish.

HERMIONE   Not your jailer, then,
But your kind hostess. Come, I'll question you
Of my lord's tricks and yours when you were boys.   60

1.2.49 'verily' 's] F (Verely'is)

41 **let him there** either leave him there,
or allow him to stay (and thus repay
with interest the week borrowed in
l. 39)

   behind As is usual in the Renaissance,
the future is not ahead but behind us,
i.e. still to come: compare l. 62, and 'at
my back I always hear | Time's wingèd
chariot hurrying near' (Marvell, *To his
Coy Mistress*, 21–2).

   gest any of the stages of a royal progress; hence, the predetermined date of
the visit (not, as the *OED* says, the time
allotted for the royal stay)

42 **good deed** indeed

43 **jar** tick (*OED sb.*[1] I.2)

44 **What lady she** whatever lady (Abbott
255); Onions explains 'lady she' as

'titled lady', but it is more likely simply
a pronominal doubling for emphasis, as
in 'The skipping king he ambled up and
down', *1 Henry IV* 3.2.60.

46 **limber** flaccid, flabby

52–3 **pay . . . depart** Upon their release,
prisoners were liable for the payment of
fees to the jailer and to various clerks of
the court. Under the Penitentiary Act of
1779, the local government became responsible for the fees, but only in new
prisons built as a result of the Act and
administered under it; prisoners in old-
style jails continued to be liable, and the
practice did not finally disappear until
the mid 19th century.

56 **should . . . offending** would imply that
I had committed an offence

97

You were pretty lordings then?

POLIXENES   We were, fair Queen,
Two lads that thought there was no more behind
But such a day tomorrow as today,
And to be boy eternal.

HERMIONE   Was not my lord
The verier wag o'th' two?   65

POLIXENES
We were as twinned lambs that did frisk i'th' sun,
And bleat the one at th'other; what we changed
Was innocence for innocence—we knew not
The doctrine of ill-doing, nor dreamed
That any did. Had we pursued that life,   70
And our weak spirits ne'er been higher reared
With stronger blood, we should have answered heaven
Boldly, 'not guilty', the imposition cleared
Hereditary ours.

HERMIONE   By this we gather
You have tripped since.

POLIXENES   O my most sacred lady,   75
Temptations have since then been born to's, for
In those unfledged days was my wife a girl;
Your precious self had then not crossed the eyes
Of my young playfellow.

HERMIONE   Grace to boot!

---

62 **behind** to come: see l. 41
65 **wag** 'a mischievous boy (often as a
    mother's term of endearment)' (*OED*)
67 **changed** exchanged
68–9 **we . . . ill-doing** we had not been
    taught to sin
71–2 **our . . . blood** 'had the weakness of
    our animal spirits not been fortified by
    the passionate blood of maturity' (Ker-
    mode)
73–4 **the . . . ours** Either 'the hereditary
    imposition having been cleared', or 'if
    the hereditary imposition had been
    cleared'. The 'hereditary imposition' is
    that of original sin, the charge of which
    we are guilty by heredity; commenta-
    tors are evenly divided over whether
    Polixenes is making himself and Leontes
    guilty of no sin except that, or saying
    that had they remained as they were

they would have been free of that sin
as well. Lines 68–9, implying that 'ill-
doing' is something we learn, not something that comes naturally to us, would
seem to support the latter interpretation.
The problem, however, is more doctrinal
than syntactical: the ambiguity is solid-
ly grounded in the nominative absolute
of the text, and the question is how far
one wants to allow Polixenes' Edenic
fantasy to extend.

77 **unfledged** immature, inexperienced
79 **Grace to boot** Usually explained as an
    exclamation like 'Heaven help us!', on
    the model of 'St George to boot' (*Richard
    III* 5.6.31; 5.3.301 in the traditional
    numbering), but it could also mean
    '(you pay me) compliments in addition'.
    To boot = into the bargain (*OED*, boot,
    sb.[1] I.1).

Of this make no conclusion, lest you say   80
Your queen and I are devils. Yet go on;
Th'offences we have made you do we'll answer,
If you first sinned with us, and that with us
You did continue fault, and that you slipped not
With any but with us.
LEONTES   Is he won yet?   85
HERMIONE
He'll stay, my lord.
LEONTES   At my request he would not.
Hermione, my dearest, thou never spok'st
To better purpose.
HERMIONE   Never?
LEONTES   Never but once.
HERMIONE
What, have I twice said well? When was't before?
I prithee tell me; cram's with praise, and make's   90
As fat as tame things—one good deed dying tongueless
Slaughters a thousand waiting upon that.
Our praises are our wages. You may ride's
With one soft kiss a thousand furlongs ere
With spur we heat an acre. But to th' goal—   95
My last good deed was to entreat his stay.
What was my first? It has an elder sister,
Or I mistake you—O, would her name were Grace!
But once before I spoke to th' purpose? When?
Nay, let me have't—I long.
LEONTES   Why, that was when   100

---

80 **Of . . . conclusion** don't follow out
that argument
83–4 **that . . . that** if . . . if
91 **tame things** overfed domestic animals
91–2 **one . . . that** failure to praise one good
deed destroys a thousand contingent others
94 **furlongs** A furlong is an eighth of a
mile; literally 'furrow-length', it originally was the length of the ploughed
furrow in a standard field, but was used
also to translate the Latin and Greek
stadium/stadion, both as the unit of
linear measurement and as the running-
track (so called because that at Olympia
was a *stadion* in length), hence the specific association of furlongs with racing.

95 **heat** 'to run swiftly over, as in a race'
(*OED* B.I.1c, the only citation for this
sense), normally used only as a noun,
e.g. 'dead-heat'
acre furlong; 'a definite measure of
land, originally as much as a yoke of
oxen could plough in a day . . . normally . . . understood to consist of 32
furrows of the plough, a furlong in
length' (*OED*)
98 **Grace** The applicable meanings range
from seemliness and courtesy to the
theological virtue that would counteract
the implications of sinfulness and devilry
in Hermione's banter about marriage at
ll. 81–6.

Three crabbèd months had soured themselves to death
Ere I could make thee open thy white hand
And clap thyself my love; then didst thou utter
'I am yours for ever.'

HERMIONE   'Tis grace indeed.
Why, lo you now, I have spoke to th' purpose twice.   105
The one for ever earned a royal husband,
Th'other, for some while a friend.

    ⌈ *She gives her hand to Polixenes* ⌉

LEONTES (*aside*)   Too hot, too hot!
To mingle friendship far is mingling bloods.
I have *tremor cordis* on me; my heart dances,
But not for joy, not joy. This entertainment   110
May a free face put on, derive a liberty
From heartiness, from bounty, fertile bosom,
And well become the agent—'t may, I grant.
But to be paddling palms and pinching fingers,

103 And] F2; A F1

101 **crabbèd** perverse, contradictory (from the gait of the crab), and, from the notoriously sour fruit the crab (= crab-apple), sour-tempered (hence 'had soured themselves to death')

103 **clap** 'to strike (hands) reciprocally in token of a bargain' (*OED sb.²* III.7); compare 'and so clap hands and a bargain', *Henry V* 5.2.130–1. 'To enter with alacrity and briskness upon anything' (*OED* IV.15b) also seems relevant: 'Shall we clap into't [a song] roundly?' (*As You Like It* 5.3.10).

108 **mingling bloods** Scholastic philosophy, descending from Aristotle, held that the basic component of semen was blood, and therefore that sexual intercourse was a mingling of bloods (see *De Generatione Animalium* i. 18–19, and Aquinas, *Summa Theologia* IIIa (Supp.), 54.1 ad 4).

109 **tremor cordis** A condition ascribed by Galen to overheated blood, for which bloodletting was the prescribed treatment. But sixteenth- and seventeenth-century medical practice rejected this diagnosis, and considered *tremor cordis* not a disease but a common symptom, an involuntary palpitation of the heart as an indication of an indeterminate disorder with an almost infinite range.

Christopher Wirtzung's *General Practise of Physicke* (London, 1617) lists as possible causes 'abundant moisture . . . in the closet of the heart . . ., pain of the stomach, . . . offense of the heart, of the liver, the lights, . . . wind, ill damps, corrupted blood, . . . great heat, sudden and great cold, great emptiness, great sorrow, fright, great fear, and other motions of the mind' (p. 263).

109–10 **my . . . joy** 'To have one's heart dance (or leap) for joy' was proverbial (Dent H331.1).

110–11 **entertainment . . . on** (*a*) this behaviour may look innocent (perhaps, but not necessarily, dishonestly); (*b*) an innocent nature may behave this way. Leontes considers the possibility that Hermione's actions may in fact be blameless, but the syntax of his sentence is utterly ambiguous: either 'entertainment' or 'face' may be the subject, and the former construction would imply culpability much more clearly than the latter.

112 **heartiness** cordiality
fertile bosom naturally generous affection

113 **well . . . agent** be praiseworthy behaviour in the doer

114 **paddling palms** paddle = 'to finger idly, playfully or fondly' (*OED* 2b). Iago

As now they are, and making practised smiles   115
As in a looking-glass, and then to sigh, as 'twere
The mort o'th' deer—O, that is entertainment
My bosom likes not, nor my brows. Mamillius,
Art thou my boy?
MAMILLIUS   Ay, my good lord.
LEONTES   I'fecks!
Why, that's my bawcock—what, hast smutched thy
    nose?   120
They say it is a copy out of mine. Come, captain,
We must be neat—not neat, but cleanly, captain.
And yet the steer, the heifer and the calf
Are all called neat.—Still virginalling
Upon his palm?—How now, you wanton calf,   125
Art thou my calf?
MAMILLIUS   Yes, if you will, my lord.
LEONTES

Thou want'st a rough pash, and the shoots that I have
To be full like me; yet they say we are
Almost as like as eggs—women say so,
That will say anything. But were they false   130
As o'er-dyed blacks, as wind, as waters, false

similarly ascribes Desdemona's and
Cassio's manual activity to lust:

  IAGO . . . Didst thou not see her paddle
  with the palm of his hand? . . .
  RODERIGO Yes, that I did, but that was
  but courtesy.
  IAGO Lechery, by this hand . . .
              (*Othello* 2.1.253–6)

116–17 **as . . . deer** as the deer sighs at its
death. ('To blow a mort' is to sound the
hunting horn when the deer has been
killed, and Leontes' image is usually
incorrectly explained as analogizing the
sighs to the sound of the horn, rather
than to what it denotes.)
118 **brows** alluding to the horns that were
said to grow on the cuckold's forehead
119 **I'fecks** A mild oath, a distortion of 'in
faith'.
120 **bawcock** fine fellow (from *beau coq*), a
colloquial endearment
122 **not neat** Leontes remembers that the
word also means horned cattle.
124 **virginalling** fingering, as if playing

the virginals
125 **wanton** playful, frolicsome; often
used of children, though the most common sense in the period was 'lascivious',
which is obviously relevant to what is
on Leontes' mind. 'As wanton as a calf'
was proverbial (Dent W38.1).
127 **pash** head (a colloquial or dialect word
for which this is *OED*'s earliest citation)
shoots i.e. the mature bull's horns
129 **Almost . . . eggs** The similarity of
eggs was proverbial; see Dent E66.
130–1 **false . . . blacks** This is generally
taken to mean unreliable as black cloth
made weak by over-dyeing: black dye
contained vitriol, which is caustic and if
used too liberally or too often tended to
rot the fabric. But in its historical context, the falseness is more basic: since
the 15th century, protectionist legislation on behalf of the dyers' guilds required that all wool cloth be first dyed
red or blue. Other colours were achieved
by overdyeing (e.g. with yellow over
blue to produce green); all black wool

As dice are to be wished by one that fixes
No bourn 'twixt his and mine, yet were it true
To say this boy were like me. Come, sir page,
Look on me with your welkin eye. Sweet villain,   135
Most dear'st, my collop—can thy dam, may't be
Affection!—thy intention stabs the centre.
Thou dost make possible things not so held,
Communicat'st with dreams—how can this be?
With what's unreal thou coactive art,   140

140 unreal thou] RANN; vnreall: thou F1; unreal, thou F3, F4, ROWE

was overdyed, blue over red, red over
blue, or black over either of these, and
therefore 'false' by definition. Over-
dyeing in black was also frequently done
to hide mistakes or accidents in dyeing.
131 **wind . . . waters** Both proverbially
false; see Dent W412, W86.1.

133 **bourn** bounds
135 **welkin eye** Johnson, followed by
nearly all editors, thought the reference
was to the eye's colour, blue as the sky.
OED, citing only this passage, more cau-
tiously explains the term as 'a heavenly
or blue eye', but cites no other instance
of 'welkin' as a colour word. Heavenly
(or bright, shining, radiant) eye seems a
preferable gloss. Shakespeare does not
use the word adjectivally elsewhere.
136 **collop** a bit of meat, hence a piece of
Leontes' flesh; 'used of offspring' (*OED*
3b). Tilley records as a proverb 'It is a
dear collop that is taken out of the flesh'
(C517).
136–7 **can . . . centre** This, and the line of
argument that proceeds from it, constitute a crucial, and crucially ambiguous, index to Leontes' psychology, and
have prompted much inconclusive discussion. 'Affection' in the context means
passion or lust (*OED* 3), though Capell,
followed most notably by Kermode,
made the passion Leontes' jealousy. This
would require, at the very least, radical
repunctuation: the affection syntactically clearly belongs to 'thy dam'. But
the referent of 'thy intention' is unclear,
and upon this depends the meaning of
the remainder of the speech. If 'thy'
refers to 'affection' personified, then
Leontes is saying that the purposes of
Hermione's lust cut to his heart (or to
the centre of the universe; if 'thy' in-

dicates an address to himself, he is
saying that his meaning has got to the
heart—of the matter, as well as his own.
Whether it is then Hermione's passion
that 'dost make possible things not so
held, | Communicat'st with dreams', or
Leontes' recognition of its significance, is
indeterminable; but this is surely to
the point: in talking about Hermione,
Leontes is also talking about himself.
137 **intention** The relevant senses are
'meaning, significance, import' (*OED* 3)
and 'purpose' (*OED* 4). Pafford and Maxwell, presumably on the basis of *OED* 8,
'intensification', take the word to mean
'intensity', but it is the direction, not the
force, of the passion that is in question.
138–9 **Thou . . . dreams** (*a*) Lust facili-
tates what had been thought impossible,
realizes fantasies and desires (or perhaps,
does the impossible in dreams); (*b*) I can
now believe things I had thought impossible, I am in touch with the world of
fantasies and desires. For the claim of
communication with dreams, compare
3.2.79–80: 'My life stands in the level of
your dreams'; 'Your actions are my
dreams.'
140 **With . . . art** Most editors since F3
have emended the punctuation of F1's
'With what's unreal: thou coactive
art', either by reducing the colon to a
comma, or (without exception from the
time of Rann, 1787) by removing the
punctuation entirely. If F1's colon has
its modern significance, 'what's unreal'
is in apposition with 'dreams', and these
are what 'thou communicat'st with';
and in that case the rest of the sentence
means 'you are compulsive and consort
with nothing'. This is certainly a
possible reading, no more confusing
than the rest of the passage. The prob-

And fellow'st nothing. Then 'tis very credent
Thou mayst co-join with something, and thou dost,
And that beyond commission, and I find it,
And that to the infection of my brains
And hard'ning of my brows.

POLIXENES   What means Sicilia?   145

HERMIONE
He something seems unsettled.

POLIXENES   How, my lord?

LEONTES
What cheer? How is't with you, best brother?

HERMIONE   You look
As if you held a brow of much distraction.
Are you moved, my lord?

LEONTES   No, in good earnest.
How sometimes nature will betray its folly,   150
Its tenderness, and make itself a pastime
To harder bosoms! Looking on the lines
Of my boy's face, methoughts I did recoil
Twenty-three years, and saw myself unbreeched,

---

147 What ... brother?] F; *continuing Polixenes' speech* HANMER   147–8 You ... distraction] *as* THEOBALD; *one line in* F

lems with it are that 'and fellow'st nothing' seems to paraphrase 'with what's
unreal thou coactive art', and that *coactive* apparently means for Shakespeare
not compulsory or acting under compul-
sion, its usual meaning in the period,
but 'acting in concert', which makes
better sense with 'and fellow'st nothing'.
Compare *Troilus* 5.2.120, 'But if I tell
how these two did co-act'.

141–3 **fellow'st ... it** For a discussion of
the syntax, see the Introduction, p. 9.

141 **credent** credible

143 **beyond commission** exceeding your
warrant, i.e. unlawfully

145 **What means Sicilia?** 'Why do you
appear so distracted?'; not an indication
that Polixenes has overheard Leontes'
baffling monologue.

146 **something** somewhat

147 **What ... brother?** Hanmer, followed most notably in this century by
Pafford and Bevington, gave this to
Polixenes on the grounds of dramatic
consistency. Pafford argues in addition

that 'the phrase "how is't with you?"
almost always carries the sense of "are
you feeling well?"', and is therefore
inappropriate as a query to Polixenes.
Most editors have felt, however, that this
is neatening the play too much: Leontes
has not been conspicuous for consistency up to this point, and in any case,
'how is't with you' here is no more
precise in meaning than 'What cheer?',
with which it is parallel.

150 **nature** Here, natural affection, the
feeling between parent and child.

151–2 **make ... bosoms** provide amuse-
ment for those who are more hard-
hearted

153 **methoughts** A common variant of
'methought', probably formed (incorrectly) by analogy with 'methinks'; *OED* records no example earlier than Shakespeare.
recoil 'to go back in memory' (*OED* 3c),
a rare usage, and the only Shakespearian
example of the word in this sense

154 **Twenty-three years** i.e. back to Mamillius' age. Most commentators estimate this at seven, which would make

In my green velvet coat, my dagger muzzled   155
Lest it should bite its master and so prove,
As ornaments oft do, too dangerous.
How like, methought, I then was to this kernel,
This squash, this gentleman. Mine honest friend,
Will you take eggs for money?

MAMILLIUS   No, my lord, I'll fight.   160

LEONTES
You will? Why, happy man be's dole! My brother,
Are you so fond of your young prince as we
Do seem to be of ours?

POLIXENES   If at home, sir,
He's all my exercise, my mirth, my matter;
Now my sworn friend and then mine enemy;   165
My parasite, my soldier, statesman, all.
He makes a July's day short as December,
And with his varying childness cures in me
Thoughts that would thick my blood.

LEONTES   So stands this squire
Officed with me. We two will walk, my lord,   170

157 do] ROWE; do's F

Leontes thirty, though Pafford argues for
ten, citing the fact that Pandosto, who is
'about fifty' when Fawnia is sixteen,
would be thirty-three or thirty-four at
this point. But boys started wearing
breeches well before the age of ten,
and often before seven: 'After the boy
was from five to seven years old, he was
"breeched", skirts being discarded, an
important family occasion' (C. W. and
P. Cunnington, *Handbook of English Costume in the 17th Century*, 3rd edn.
(1972), p. 196).

154 **unbreeched** not yet in man's breeches

155 **muzzled** Probably tipped, as fencing
foils are. Pafford suggests that the dagger may have been locked into its sheath
so that it was merely ornamental, but
adds that there is no evidence of such a
practice.

159 **squash** an unripe pea-pod (*OED sb.*[1]
1). Malvolio describes Cesario/Viola as
'Not yet old enough for a man, nor
young enough for a boy; as a squash is
before 'tis a peascod' (1.5.151-2).

160 **Will ... money?** 'To take eggs

for money', i.e. to be fobbed off
with something of little value, to be
imposed upon, was proverbial (Dent
E90).

161 **happy ... dole** Proverbial (Dent
M158), meaning 'may your lot be that
of a happy man'.

164 **He's ... exercise** 'I spend all my time
with him'; exercise = 'habitual occupation or employment' (*OED* 2)

166 **parasite** toady, flatterer

168 **childness** 'childish humour' (*OED*:
the only citation before 1856)

169 **Thoughts ... blood** Not simply
melancholic thoughts (though melancholy came to be associated with 'too
heavy and viscid a blood'—see *OED* 1,
quot. 1722), but those of 'direst
cruelty', as Lady Macbeth calls on the
'spirits | That tend on mortal thoughts'
to 'Make thick my blood' (*Macbeth*
1.5.39-42).

169-70 **So ... me** This young man plays
the same role with me. 'Squire' is medieval chivalric language, literally, a
young man of good birth attending on a
knight.

And leave you to your graver steps. Hermione,
How thou lov'st us show in our brother's welcome;
Let what is dear in Sicily be cheap—
Next to thyself and my young rover, he's
Apparent to my heart.
HERMIONE   If you would seek us,   175
We are yours i'th' garden—shall's attend you there?
LEONTES
To your own bents dispose you; you'll be found
Be you beneath the sky. (*Aside*) I am angling now,
Though you perceive me not how I give line.
Go to, go to!   180
How she holds up the neb, the bill to him!
And arms her with the boldness of a wife
To her allowing husband.

                         Exeunt Polixenes and Hermione
                         Gone already!
Inch-thick, knee-deep, o'er head and ears a forked one!
(*To Mamillius*) Go play, boy, play—thy mother plays,
        and I   185
Play too, but so disgraced a part, whose issue
Will hiss me to my grave; contempt and clamour
Will be my knell. Go play, boy, play. There have been,
Or I am much deceived, cuckolds ere now,
And many a man there is, even at this present,   190

---

183 *Exeunt . . . Hermione*] ROWE (*subs.*) (*after* 'wife', *l.* 182); *not in* F

171 **graver** more dignified
175 **Apparent** heir apparent, as in 'apparent to the crown', *Richard Duke of York* (i.e. *3 Henry VI*) 2.2.64
176 **shall's** See Abbott 215 (us for we in 'shall's').
179 **give line** play you along (continuing the fishing metaphor); i.e. give you the rope to hang yourselves. 'To give someone line' was proverbial: Dent L304.1.
181 **neb** Originally a bird's beak, and hence the mouth; but *OED* gives no instance of the usage before this one, and the appositive that immediately follows, 'the bill', may imply that the metaphor needed to be explained. Robert Armin, in *The Two Maids of More-clack* (1609), uses 'neb' as a

synonym for 'buss', i.e. 'kiss' (cited under neb *v.*, a).
184 **o'er . . . forked one** The proverb is 'over head and ears in love' (Dent H268): Leontes begins by talking about Hermione, but the 'head and ears' inevitably bring to mind the cuckold's horns, and he concludes with himself, the 'forked one'.
186 **so disgraced a part** that of the acquiescent cuckold
186–7 **whose . . . me** whose conclusion will cause me to be hissed. Quiller-Couch and Dover Wilson, followed by Kermode, gloss 'issue' as the actor's exit. This produces a more consistent theatrical metaphor, but there is no evidence that the word was ever used in this sense.

Now, while I speak this, holds his wife by th'arm,
That little thinks she has been sluiced in's absence,
And his pond fished by his next neighbour, by
Sir Smile, his neighbour—nay, there's comfort in't
Whiles other men have gates, and those gates opened,   195
As mine, against their will. Should all despair
That have revolted wives, the tenth of mankind
Would hang themselves. Physic for't there's none;
It is a bawdy planet, that will strike
Where 'tis predominant; and 'tis powerful, think it,   200
From east, west, north and south; be it concluded,
No barricado for a belly. Know't;
It will let in and out the enemy
With bag and baggage—many thousand on's
Have the disease and feel't not. (*To Mamillius*) How
        now, boy?   205

MAMILLIUS

I am like you, they say.

LEONTES   Why, that's some comfort.

What, Camillo there?

CAMILLO   Ay, my good lord.

LEONTES

Go play, Mamillius; thou'rt an honest man.

                                        Exit Mamillius

206 you, they] F2; you F1   208.1 *Exit Mamillius*] ROWE; *not in* F

192 **sluiced** flushed out, swilled (with seminal fluid), a sense antedating the examples in *OED* 4 by more than a century.
194–6 **there's . . . will** The comfort is proverbial: 'to have company in misery' (Dent C571).
195 **gates** as in sluice gates
197 **revolted** faithless
199–200 **It . . . predominant** the planet (Venus) that controls lechery will wreak destruction whenever it is in the ascendant. Planet-struck = 'stricken by the supposed malign influence of an adverse planet' (*OED*).
200 **think it** believe it
202 **No barricado** 'there is' understood. The first barricades so designated were casks (Fr. *barriques*) filled with earth or stone, and erected in the streets of Paris on the *journée des barricades* in 1588, when Henri III was driven from the city by adherents of the Duc de Guise. The word first appears in English in the 1590s, in the Spanish form used by Shakespeare.
204 **bag and baggage** slang for the scrotum and its contents
on's of us (Abbott 182)
206 **I . . . say** F2's emendation of F1's 'I am like you say', accepted by all editors. Collier's alternative suggestion, 'I am like you, you say', has been considered (e.g. by Pafford and Schanzer) a more likely reading bibliographically, which is doubtless true, but the degree of likelihood is not, even for these editors, great enough to be decisive. Mamillius is picking up Leontes' 'they say we are | Almost as like as eggs' (128–9).

Camillo, this great sir will yet stay longer.

CAMILLO

You had much ado to make his anchor hold;   210
When you cast out, it still came home.

LEONTES   Didst note it?

CAMILLO

He would not stay at your petitions, made
His business more material.

LEONTES   Didst perceive it?
(*Aside*) They're here with me already, whisp'ring,
        rounding,
'Sicilia is a . . .'—so forth; 'tis far gone   215
When I shall gust it last.—How came't, Camillo,
That he did stay?

CAMILLO   At the good Queen's entreaty.

LEONTES

At the Queen's be't; 'good' should be pertinent,
But so it is, it is not. Was this taken
By any understanding pate but thine?   220
For thy conceit is soaking, will draw in
More than the common blocks. Not noted, is't,
But of the finer natures? By some severals
Of headpiece extraordinary? Lower messes
Perchance are to this business purblind? Say.   225

CAMILLO

Business, my lord? I think most understand
Bohemia stays here longer.

LEONTES   Ha?

CAMILLO   Stays here longer.

---

211 **still . . . home** always came back

213 **material** important (*OED*)

214 **They're . . . already** people already
understand my situation
rounding talking secretly (*OED*, round,
*v.*²). The word is cognate with rune,
mystery or magic charm.

215 **so forth** and so on. Leontes avoids
saying 'cuckold'.

215–16 **'tis . . . last** it must be far gone,
since I am the last to perceive it. Proverbial wisdom: 'The cuckold is the last
that knows of it' (Dent C877).

216 **gust** literally 'taste'

219 **so it is** as matters stand
taken perceived

221 **thy . . . draw in** your understanding
will absorb

222 **common blocks** ordinary blockheads
(block = the mould for shaping hats)

223 **But . . . natures** except by more sensitive minds
severals individuals

224 **Lower messes** inferior classes. A mess
was a group, usually of four, that dined
together, and hence were on the same
social level.

225 **purblind** utterly blind

LEONTES

Ay, but why?

CAMILLO

To satisfy your highness and the entreaties
Of our most gracious mistress.

LEONTES   Satisfy?   230
Th'entreaties of your mistress? Satisfy?
Let that suffice. I have trusted thee, Camillo,
With all the nearest things to my heart, as well
My chamber-counsels, wherein, priest-like, thou
Hast cleansed my bosom; ay, from thee departed   235
Thy penitent reformed. But we have been
Deceived in thy integrity, deceived
In that which seems so.

CAMILLO   Be it forbid, my lord!

LEONTES

To bide upon't—thou art not honest; or,
If thou inclin'st that way, thou art a coward,   240
Which hoxes honesty behind, restraining
From course required; or else thou must be counted
A servant grafted in my serious trust,
And therein negligent; or else a fool,
That seest a game played home, the rich stake drawn,   245
And tak'st it all for jest.

CAMILLO   My gracious lord,
I may be negligent, foolish and fearful;
In every one of these no man is free,
But that his negligence, his folly, fear,
Among the infinite doings of the world,   250
Sometime puts forth. In your affairs, my lord,

---

251 forth. In] THEOBALD; forth in F

230–1 **Satisfy ... mistress** i.e. sexually.
  Compare *Romeo* 2.1.167–8:
  ROMEO
  O, wilt thou leave me thus unsatisfied?
  JULIET
  What satisfaction canst thou have tonight?
234 **chamber-counsels** intimate secrets
238 **seems so** i.e. seems to be integrity
239 **bide** insist (*OED* 2b)
241 **hoxes ... behind** hamstrings the
  hind legs of honesty. The metaphor al-

ludes to the practice of deliberately lam-
ing cattle by cutting the great tendon
behind the knee in the hind legs.
Quiller-Couch and Dover Wilson suggest
that the conceit 'sprang from a quibble,
or perhaps a false etymology which
identified "coward" with "cowherd".'
242 **counted** accounted
243 **grafted** deeply fixed, implanted
245 **played ... drawn** played to the end,
  the valuable prize won
251 **Sometime puts forth** appears at times

If ever I were wilful-negligent,
It was my folly; if industriously
I played the fool, it was my negligence,
Not weighing well the end; if ever fearful   255
To do a thing where I the issue doubted,
Whereof the execution did cry out
Against the non-performance, 'twas a fear
Which oft infects the wisest. These, my lord,
Are such allowed infirmities that honesty   260
Is never free of. But beseech your grace
Be plainer with me, let me know my trespass
By its own visage—if I then deny it,
'Tis none of mine.

LEONTES   Ha' you not seen, Camillo—
But that's past doubt; you have, or your eyeglass   265
Is thicker than a cuckold's horn—or heard—
For to a vision so apparent Rumour
Cannot be mute—or thought—for cogitation
Resides not in that man that does not think—
My wife is slippery? If thou wilt confess,   270
Or else be impudently negative,
To have nor eyes, nor ears, nor thought, then say
My wife's a hobby-horse, deserves a name
As rank as any flax-wench that puts to

273 hobby-horse] ROWE 1714; Holy-Horse F

253 **industriously** deliberately
255 **weighing ... end** sufficiently considering the consequences
257-8 **Whereof ... non-performance** i.e. the subsequent performance of the action revealed that not to have done it would have been wrong
260 **allowed** permissible
265 **eyeglass** Probably not 'the crystalline lens of the eye' (*OED* 1, citing only this passage)—the eye was not regarded as having a lens, though it was sometimes analogized to one—but rather, as Furness argued, the vitreous humour, so called, according to Vicary's *Anatomy* (1548), 'because he is like glass, in colour very clear' (cited in the *Variorum*).
266 **thicker** more opaque; thick = 'dull of perception' (*OED* 9). Compare Feltham's *Resolves* (1628): 'She is thick-sighted,

and cannot see them' (cited in the *OED* under 'thick-sighted').
267 **to ... apparent** as to something so plain to see
268-9 **cogitation ... think** i.e. you must have thought about it if you can think at all
270 **slippery** 'licentious, wanton, unchaste; of doubtful morality' (*OED* 5)
271-2 **be ... nor** shamelessly deny that you have
273 **hobby-horse** whore (what you ride for your pleasure): Rowe's emendation of F's *Holy-Horse* has been universally accepted. Compare *Othello* 4.1.150-3, Bianca to Cassio, on the handkerchief: 'This is some minx's token, and I must take out the work. There, give it your hobby-horse. Wheresoever you had it, I'll take out no work on't.'
274 **flax-wench** country girl

Before her troth-plight—say't, and justify't.   275

CAMILLO

I would not be a stander-by to hear
My sovereign mistress clouded so without
My present vengeance taken. 'Shrew my heart,
You never spoke what did become you less
Than this, which to reiterate were sin   280
As deep as that, though true.

LEONTES   Is whispering nothing?
Is leaning cheek to cheek? Is meeting noses?
Kissing with inside lip? Stopping the career
Of laughter with a sigh?—a note infallible
Of breaking honesty! Horsing foot on foot?   285
Skulking in corners? Wishing clocks more swift?
Hours minutes? Noon midnight? And all eyes
Blind with the pin and web but theirs, theirs only,
That would unseen be wicked? Is this nothing?
Why then the world and all that's in't is nothing,   290
The covering sky is nothing, Bohemia nothing,
My wife is nothing, nor nothing have these nothings
If this be nothing.

CAMILLO   Good my lord, be cured
Of this diseased opinion, and betimes,
For 'tis most dangerous.

LEONTES   Say it be, 'tis true.   295

CAMILLO

No, no, my lord!

LEONTES   It is—you lie, you lie!

---

274 **puts to** goes to it, 'puts out'

275 **troth-plight** betrothal (not, as Pafford believes, marriage). The point is that the betrothal was popularly, though not legally, held to confer sexual privileges— this is the issue in the charges against Claudio in *Measure for Measure*—but the flax-wench does not even wait for her engagement.

278 **present** immediate
     'Shrew beshrew, 'a plague on'

281 **As . . . true** as deep as her adultery, if she were guilty of it. Nowhere does Camillo imply any doubts about Hermione's innocence, but his hyperbole syntactically admits the possibility that

Leontes' assertion is true.

283 **career** literally, a horse's full-speed gallop (*OED* 2)

285 **honesty** chastity
     Horsing . . . foot i.e. mounted, but not on horseback

286 **Wishing . . . swift** The fantasy changes: Leontes up to this point has been imagining the lovers together, but they would wish time to move faster only if they were separated.

288 **pin and web** an eye disease combining ulceration with opacity of the cornea (*OED*, pin, *sb.*[1] 11)

292 **nothing . . . nothings** these nothings mean nothing

294 **betimes** soon

I say thou liest, Camillo, and I hate thee,
Pronounce thee a gross lout, a mindless slave,
Or else a hovering temporizer that
Canst with thine eyes at once see good and evil,   300
Inclining to them both. Were my wife's liver
Infected as her life she would not live
The running of one glass.

CAMILLO   Who does infect her?

LEONTES

Why, he that wears her like her medal, hanging
About his neck, Bohemia, who, if I   305
Had servants true about me that bare eyes
To see alike mine honour as their profits,
Their own particular thrifts, they would do that
Which should undo more doing. Ay, and thou,
His cupbearer, whom I from meaner form   310
Have benched and reared to worship, who mayst see
Plainly as heaven sees earth and earth sees heaven
How I am galled, mightst bespice a cup
To give mine enemy a lasting wink,
Which draught to me were cordial.

CAMILLO   Sir, my lord,   315
I could do this, and that with no rash potion,
But with a ling'ring dram that should not work
Maliciously, like poison; but I cannot
Believe this crack to be in my dread mistress,
So sovereignly being honourable.   320
I have loved thee—

299 **hovering temporizer** vacillating opportunist
301-2 **Were . . . life** i.e. if the organ were as infected as the behaviour that springs from it. The liver was the seat of the passions in the old physiology.
303 **running . . . glass** an hour
304 **her medal** a medal with her portrait
305 **who** Syntactically, as l. 308 makes clear, 'to whom' is required. Abbott 274 gives many analogous examples.
306 **bare** bore
308 **thrifts** gains, advantages
310 **cupbearer** The officer of the royal household in charge of serving the wine. In *Pandosto*, Franion, the Camillo char-

acter, is the King's cupbearer, not his guest's: see Appendix B, p. 237.
310 **meaner form** lower rank
311 **benched . . . worship** seated in and raised to a place of honour. A *bencher* is 'one who officially sits on a bench; a magistrate, judge, assessor, senator', etc. (*OED* 2).
314 **give . . . wink** close my enemy's eyes for good
315 **cordial** comforting, medicinal
316 **rash** quick acting
318 **Maliciously** violently (*OED* 2)
319 **crack** flaw (*OED* 8)
320 **sovereignly** surpassingly (*OED* 1)
321 **I . . . thee** This has occasioned much debate. Theobald objected that Camillo

LEONTES   Make that thy question, and go rot!
  Dost think I am so muddy, so unsettled,
  To appoint myself in this vexation? Sully
  The purity and whiteness of my sheets—
  Which to preserve is sleep, which being spotted   325
  Is goads, thorns, nettles, tails of wasps—
  Give scandal to the blood o'th' prince, my son,
  Who I do think is mine and love as mine,
  Without ripe moving to't? Would I do this?
  Could man so blench?

CAMILLO   I must believe you, sir;   330
  I do, and will fetch off Bohemia for't—
  Provided that when he's removed your highness
  Will take again your Queen as yours at first,
  Even for your son's sake, and thereby for sealing
  The injury of tongues in courts and kingdoms   335

323–4 Sully . . . sheets] *as* THEOBALD; *one line in* F

could not call his sovereign 'thee', and
gave the line to Leontes. Johnson said he
was unconvinced, but nevertheless concurred in the alteration, as did Warburton. Most subsequent editors have
agreed that the pronoun is a problem,
though since the 18th century the line
has generally not been reassigned.
Dover Wilson believed he had resolved
the difficulty with the awkward emendation 'T'have loved the—'. But Paulina
calls Leontes 'thee', and much worse, in
3.2 (see especially ll. 173 ff.): the notion
that Leontes cannot be addressed in this
way depends on anachronistic attitudes
towards kingship. James I complained
constantly that he was not treated with
enough respect, and one of the major
innovations of Charles I was the reform
and codification of court protocol. In
any case, it is surely a mistake to see the
court of legendary Sicilia as a literal
reflection of Jacobean court practice—
had James I decided to have his daughter
Elizabeth exposed in infancy, he would
not have been permitted to do so.

321 **Make . . . rot** Replying to Camillo's
doubts about the Queen's guilt: 'if you
dispute that, go to the devil!'

323 **appoint** With ironic legalistic overtones: 'ordain or nominate a person to

an office or to perform functions', 'arraign' (*OED* 12, 18).

329 **ripe . . . to't** fully matured reasons for
it

330 **so blench** go so far astray; but
'blench' has implications that contradict
Leontes' claim that he is facing an ugly
truth: the word means swerve aside,
normally to *avoid* something, shy away
from something, flinch, avert one's eyes.
Compare Hamlet on the King's reaction
to the play: 'If a but blench, | I know
my course' (2.2.599–600).

331 **fetch off** Another *double entendre*: the
expression means both kill and rescue.

334–5 **for sealing . . . tongues** in order to
silence slander. The prepositional phrase
in conjunction with 'thereby' has been
considered syntactically awkward, at
times unacceptably so. Capell found the
phrase 'one of the poet's hardinesses',
but no 18th-century commentator proposed emending it. The Cambridge editors, followed in this century notably by
Schanzer, attempted to rectify the line
by reading 'forsealing' (= shutting up
tight), a word not recorded in the *OED*.
Dover Wilson, following a suggestion of
Kellner's, emended to 'forestalling'. The
degree of awkwardness is a matter of
opinion, but it is perhaps sufficient to
point out that syntactical infelicities are

Known and allied to yours.

LEONTES   Thou dost advise me
Even so as I mine own course have set down.
I'll give no blemish to her honour, none.

CAMILLO
My lord, go then, and with a countenance as clear
As friendship wears at feasts keep with Bohemia   340
And with your Queen. I am his cupbearer;
If from me he have wholesome beverage,
Account me not your servant.

LEONTES   This is all.
Do't, and thou hast the one half of my heart;
Do't not, thou splitt'st thine own.

CAMILLO   I'll do't, my lord.   345

LEONTES
I will seem friendly, as thou hast advised me.   *Exit*

CAMILLO
O miserable lady! But for me,
What case stand I in? I must be the poisoner
Of good Polixenes, and my ground to do't
Is the obedience to a master, one   350
Who in rebellion with himself will have
All that are his so too. To do this deed,
Promotion follows—if I could find example
Of thousands that had struck anointed kings
And flourished after, I'd not do't. But since   355
Nor brass, nor stone, nor parchment bears not one,
Let villainy itself forswear't. I must
Forsake the court; to do't or no is certain

---

339 My lord] This edition; *a separate line in* F

not uncommon in *The Winter's Tale*,
particularly in the first two acts.

339 **My . . . clear** One of a number of alex-
andrines in the play. F prints 'My lord,'
as a separate line, probably because the
compositor needed to fill space on this
page.
340 **keep** stay
347 **for** as for
349 **ground to do't** basis for doing it
351 **in . . . himself** a rebel to his true nature, as Brutus describes the condition of

the conspirators 'Between the acting of
a dreadful thing | And the first motion':
'the state of man, | Like to a little
kingdom, suffers then | The nature
of an insurrection' (*Julius   Caesar*
2.1.63–9).
352 **so** i.e. rebels
  To do if I do (Abbott 357)
356 **Nor . . . parchment** Compare Sonnet
65, line 1: 'Since brass, nor stone, nor
earth, nor boundless sea'.
  bears not one records a regicide who
prospered

To me a break-neck. Happy star reign now!
Here comes Bohemia.
    Enter Polixenes
POLIXENES   This is strange—methinks   360
My favour here begins to warp. Not speak?
Good day, Camillo.
CAMILLO   Hail, most royal sir!
POLIXENES
What is the news i'th' court?
CAMILLO   None rare, my lord.
POLIXENES
The King hath on him such a countenance
As he had lost some province, and a region   365
Loved as he loves himself. Even now I met him
With customary compliment, when he,
Wafting his eyes to th' contrary and falling
A lip of much contempt, speeds from me and
So leaves me to consider what is breeding   370
That changes thus his manners.
CAMILLO   I dare not know, my lord.
POLIXENES
How, dare not? Do not? Do you know and dare not?
Be intelligent to me—'tis thereabouts;
For to yourself what you do know you must,
And cannot say you dare not. Good Camillo,   375
Your changed complexions are to me a mirror,
Which shows me mine changed too; for I must be
A party in this alteration, finding

359 **To . . . break-neck** destruction for
    me
    Happy . . . now i.e. I need good luck
    now
361 **warp** shrink, shrivel (*OED* 15b)
363 **None rare** nothing special
368 **Wafting . . . contrary** turning his
    eyes away
    falling letting droop
372–3 **How . . . thereabouts** 'What do
    you mean, dare not? Do you mean you
    do not know? Or do you mean you
    know but fear to know? Be intelligible to
    me—it must be something like that.' 'Be
    intelligent to me' means both 'let me
    understand you' and 'tell me what you

know': 'intelligent' = 'giving information, communicative' (*OED* 4). The passage is often emended, since Capell, to
'Do you know and dare not | Be intel-
ligent to me?', which gives a simpler
but weaker sense; and there is a parallel
to 'do you know and dare not' at
4.4.449.
374–5 **For . . . not** 'you cannot tell yourself you dare not know—you know
what you know'
376 **complexions** Not simply the changing
appearance of the face, but the disposition, habit of mind (*OED* 3); possibly in
the plural to refer to Leontes' behaviour
as well.

Myself thus altered with't.

CAMILLO   There is a sickness

Which puts some of us in distemper, but   380

I cannot name the disease, and it is caught

Of you, that yet are well.

POLIXENES   How caught of me?

Make me not sighted like the basilisk.

I have looked on thousands, who have sped the better

By my regard, but killed none so. Camillo,   385

As you are certainly a gentleman, thereto

Clerk-like experienced, which no less adorns

Our gentry than our parents' noble names,

In whose success we are gentle, I beseech you,

If you know aught which does behove my knowledge   390

Thereof to be informed, imprison't not

In ignorant concealment.

CAMILLO   I may not answer.

POLIXENES

A sickness caught of me, and yet I well?

I must be answered. Dost thou hear, Camillo,

I conjure thee by all the parts of man   395

Which honour does acknowledge, whereof the least

Is not this suit of mine, that thou declare

What incidency thou dost guess of harm

Is creeping toward me; how far off, how near,

Which way to be prevented, if to be;   400

If not, how best to bear it.

CAMILLO   Sir, I will tell you,

Since I am charged in honour, and by him

That I think honourable; therefore mark my counsel,

---

383 **basilisk** or cockatrice, a mythical
    serpent whose look was fatal; 'to kill
    like a basilisk' was proverbial (Dent
    B99.1).
384 **sped** prospered
385 **By** as a consequence of (Abbott 146)
386–7 **thereto ... experienced** in addi-
    tion an accomplished scholar
387 **which** a thing which (Abbott 271)
388 **gentry** with the additional sense of
    'good breeding' (*OED* 1c)
389 **In ... gentle** in succeeding whom we
    are noble

392 **ignorant concealment** concealment
    that keeps me in ignorance. Compare
    Tempest 5.1.66–8, 'their rising senses |
    Begin to chase the ignorant fumes that
    mantle | Their clearer reason.'
395 **conjure** implore, 'charge or appeal to
    solemnly' (*OED* II)
395–6 **parts . . . acknowledge** obliga-
    tions imposed by honour on man, ack-
    nowledged by honourable men
398 **incidency** incident, with a proleptic
    force; 'a thing . . . liable to befall'
    (*OED* 2)

Which must be ev'n as swiftly followed as
I mean to utter it, or both yourself and me   405
Cry lost, and so goodnight.
POLIXENES   On, good Camillo.
CAMILLO
I am appointed him to murder you.
POLIXENES
By whom, Camillo?
CAMILLO   By the King.
POLIXENES   For what?
CAMILLO
He thinks, nay with all confidence he swears,
As he had seen't, or been an instrument   410
To vice you to't, that you have touched his Queen
Forbiddenly.
POLIXENES   O then my best blood turn
To an infected jelly, and my name
Be yoked with his that did betray the best!
Turn then my freshest reputation to   415
A savour that may strike the dullest nostril
Where I arrive, and my approach be shunned,
Nay, hated too, worse than the great'st infection
That e'er was heard or read.
CAMILLO   Swear his thought over
By each particular star in heaven, and   420
By all their influences; you may as well
Forbid the sea for to obey the moon

---

406 **Cry . . . goodnight** declare lost, and
so farewell forever
407 **him** the man who is. Abbott's explanation of the pronoun as an old dative,
implying '*by* him' (Leontes), is dubious
(220).
410 **As** as if
411 **vice** force (as with the use of a vice)
(*OED* 2)
414 **his . . . best** that of Judas
415 **freshest** perfectly pure
416 **savour** smell
dullest least sensitive
419 **Swear . . . over** Either prevail over his
opinion by swearing (on the analogy,
suggested by Pafford, of 'o'ersway'), or
by swearing bring it over to your side (in
which case 'swear over' would be ana-

logous to 'win over'). There are no recorded parallels for either usage, though
Malone called attention to the similar
expression 'to swear a person down',
and Halliwell cited its appearance in
Measure 5.1.241, 'Though they would
swear down each particular saint'.
When Shakespeare uses 'overswear'
in *Twelfth Night*, it means 'outswear':
'all those sayings will I overswear'
(5.1.267).
421 **influences** in astrology, 'the supposed
flowing or streaming from the stars . . .
of an etherial fluid acting upon the character and destiny of men, and affecting
sublunary things generally' (*OED*)
422 **for to** to (Abbott 152)

As or by oath remove or counsel shake
The fabric of his folly, whose foundation
Is piled upon his faith, and will continue   425
The standing of his body.
POLIXENES   How should this grow?
CAMILLO
I know not; but I am sure 'tis safer to
Avoid what's grown than question how 'tis born.
If therefore you dare trust my honesty
That lies enclosèd in this trunk, which you   430
Shall bear along impawned, away tonight.
Your followers I will whisper to the business,
And will by twos and threes at several posterns
Clear them o'th' city. For myself, I'll put
My fortunes to your service, which are here   435
By this discovery lost. Be not uncertain,
For by the honour of my parents, I
Have uttered truth—which if you seek to prove,
I dare not stand by; nor shall you be safer
Than one condemnèd by the King's own mouth,   440
Thereon his execution sworn.
POLIXENES   I do believe thee;
I saw his heart in's face. Give me thy hand;
Be pilot to me and thy places shall
Still neighbour mine. My ships are ready, and

---

440 condemnèd] F2; condemnd F1

423 **or . . . or** either . . . or
424 **fabric** edifice (*OED* 1), structure (*OED* 3)
425 **faith** settled belief
426 **The . . . body** as long as his body survives
430 **trunk** body
431 **bear . . . impawned** take with you as a pledge
433 **several** different
  posterns side or back gates; postern = 'any door or gate distinct from the main entrance' (*OED*)
436 **this discovery** my revealing this to you
438 **prove** test
440 Since F reads 'condemnd' here, rather than 'condemned', many editors, following Capell, have rectified the metre by

ending the line with 'thereon' from l. 441. Some emendation is required, and I have chosen the smaller one made by F2. But line 441 is a long one, and either the omission of an apparently superfluous -e or the removal of a final 'thereon' to the next line would be a reasonable expedient for a compositor pressed for space.
441 **Thereon . . . sworn** and whom he thereupon swore to have executed
442 **I . . . face** 'The face is the index of the heart' was proverbial—as was 'the face is no index to the heart' (Dent F1, F1.1). Shakespeare alludes to both proverbs in the same passage in *Twelfth Night* 1.2.44–7.
443 **places** offices, honours

My people did expect my hence departure   445
Two days ago. This jealousy
Is for a precious creature. As she's rare,
Must it be great; and as his person's mighty,
Must it be violent; and as he does conceive
He is dishonoured by a man which ever   450
Professed to him, why his revenges must
In that be made more bitter. Fear o'ershades me.
Good expedition be my friend, and comfort
The gracious Queen, part of his theme, but nothing
Of his ill-ta'en suspicion. Come, Camillo,   455
I will respect thee as a father if
Thou bear'st my life off hence. Let us avoid.

CAMILLO

It is in mine authority to command
The keys of all the posterns. Please your highness
To take the urgent hour. Come sir, away.   *Exeunt*   460

2.1   *Enter Hermione, Mamillius and Ladies*

HERMIONE

Take the boy to you; he so troubles me
'Tis past enduring.

FIRST LADY   Come, my gracious lord,
Shall I be your playfellow?

MAMILLIUS   No, I'll none of you.

---

457 off hence. Let] F (off, hence: Let)
  2.1.0.1 *Enter . . . Ladies*] ROWE; *Enter Hermione, Mamillius, Ladies: Leontes, Antigonus, Lords.* F

451 **Professed** professed friendship (*OED*, profess, 3b)
453–5 **Good . . . suspicion** 'May my hasty departure assist me and bring comfort to the Queen, who is involved in his ill-conceived suspicion, but is not the object of it.' The passage has been much discussed, and more than once declared incomprehensible. The problems are how Polixenes' sudden departure, which logically would increase Leontes' suspicion, can be thought to comfort Hermione, and how Hermione can be considered 'no part' of Leontes' suspicion. The usual explanation is that Polixenes believes that Leontes is suspicious only of him and does not

conceive the Queen to be at fault, and that therefore his departure will comfort Hermione by removing the sole offending party. If this is correct, Shakespeare is asking a great deal of a very elliptical passage. Kermode ingeniously suggests that 'Perhaps "expedition" is not the subject of "comfort"—then he is merely wishing the Queen comfort in the troubles he is leaving her to, and the vagueness of the expression matches the emptiness of the wish'.

457 **off hence. Let** Many editors print 'off. Hence!—Let', a possible reading of F's punctuation; but 'bear'st my life off' seems to require some modifier.
  avoid depart

FIRST LADY

  Why, my sweet lord?

MAMILLIUS

  You'll kiss me hard, and speak to me as if   5
  I were a baby still. (*To another lady*) I love you better.

SECOND LADY

  And why so, my lord?

MAMILLIUS   Not for because

  Your brows are blacker; yet black brows, they say,
  Become some women best, so that there be not
  Too much hair there, but in a semicircle   10
  Or a half moon made with a pen.

SECOND LADY   Who taught this?

MAMILLIUS

  I learned it out of women's faces. Pray now,
  What colour are your eyebrows?

SECOND LADY   Blue, my lord.

MAMILLIUS

  Nay, that's a mock. I have seen a lady's nose
  That has been blue, but not her eyebrows.

FIRST LADY   Hark ye,   15

  The Queen, your mother, rounds apace. We shall
  Present our services to a fine new prince
  One of these days, and then you'd wanton with us
  If we would have you.

SECOND LADY   She is spread of late

  Into a goodly bulk—good time encounter her!   20

2.1.8–9 **black . . . best** The conventional Petrarchan ideal of golden-haired beauty was a frequent subject of poetic debate, generally ironic. Biron defends Rosaline's black hair against the gibes of the King, Dumaine and Longueville (*LLL* 4.3.264 ff.), and the matter is given more sinister overtones in Sonnets 130–2.

11 **Who . . . this?** Who taught you this? F here, as at a number of other places, has an apostrophe to indicate the omission of a notional word; the practice is a feature of Ralph Crane transcriptions, most pronounced in the Folio in *The Winter's Tale* and *The Tempest*. See the Introduction, p. 83.

16 **rounds** i.e. in her pregnancy; Shakespeare does not use the verb in this sense elsewhere, and this passage is the *OED*'s only citation before the 19th century.

17 **prince** a royal child of either sex; not, as the *OED* claims (6), exclusively male. Queen Elizabeth referred to herself as a prince and Bellaria is a prince throughout *Pandosto* (e.g. Appendix B, p. 242). Compare *Tempest* 1.2.174.

18 **wanton** play, without pejorative overtones, "said esp. of a child or young animal' (*OED* 1b)

20 **good . . . her** May she have a successful childbirth. Compare *All is True* (i.e. *Henry VIII*) 5.1.20–2, of Queen Anne's

HERMIONE

What wisdom stirs amongst you? Come, sir, now
I am for you again. Pray sit you by us,
And tell's a tale.

MAMILLIUS   Merry or sad shall't be?

HERMIONE

As merry as you will.

MAMILLIUS

A sad tale's best for winter; I have one   25
Of sprites and goblins.

HERMIONE   Let's have that, good sir.
Come on, sit down, come on, and do your best
To fright me with your sprites; you're powerful at it.

MAMILLIUS

There was a man—

HERMIONE   Nay, come sit down, then on.

MAMILLIUS

Dwelt by a churchyard—I will tell it softly,   30
Yon crickets shall not hear it.

HERMIONE

Come on, then, and give't me in mine ear.

Enter Leontes, Antigonus and Lords

LEONTES

Was he met there? His train? Camillo with him?

LORD

Behind the tuft of pines I met them; never
Saw I men scour so on their way. I eyed them   35
Even to their ships.

LEONTES   How blest am I
In my just censure, in my true opinion!
Alack for lesser knowledge! How accursed
In being so blest! There may be in the cup

25–6 I . . . goblins] DYCE; *one line in* F   32.1 *Enter . . . Lords*] ROWE (*subs.*)   38 knowledge!] HANMER; knowledge, F

labour: 'The fruit she goes with | I pray
for heartily, that it may find | Good
time, and live.'

25 **A . . . winter** Winter's tales were,
like old wives' tales, proverbially idle
stories to pass the time; see Dent

W513.1.
31 **Yon crickets** i.e. the chattering ladies
35 **scour** go in haste, run (*OED* 1b)
37 **censure** judgement
38 **Alack . . . knowledge!** Would that I
knew less!

A spider steeped, and one may drink, depart,   40
And yet partake no venom, for his knowledge
Is not infected; but if one present
Th'abhorred ingredient to his eye, make known
How he hath drunk, he cracks his gorge, his sides
With violent hefts. I have drunk, and seen the spider.   45
Camillo was his help in this, his pander.
There is a plot against my life, my crown;
All's true that is mistrusted—that false villain
Whom I employed was pre-employed by him;
He has discovered my design, and I   50
Remain a pinched thing, yea, a very trick
For them to play at will—how came the posterns
So easily open?
LORD   By his great authority,
Which often hath no less prevailed than so
On your command.
LEONTES   I know't too well.   55
    (*To Hermione*) Give me the boy. I am glad you did not
        nurse him.
Though he does bear some signs of me, yet you
Have too much blood in him.
HERMIONE   What is this? Sport?

40–5 **A spider ... hefts** Folk wisdom taught that spiders mixed with food or drink would render it poisonous: Tilley (S749) and Dent (S749.1) note several relevant proverbs, and Furness cites Bacon's speech prepared for the Overbury murder case, asserting that the murderers employed 'a volley of poisons; arsenic for salt, great spiders and cantharides for pig sauce or partridge sauce'. The crucial element for Leontes, however, is that the victim must know he has been poisoned in order for the venom to work. Editors since Staunton have cited as a parallel a passage from Middleton's *No Wit, No Help Like a Woman's* (*c.*1612, pub. 1657). A rich widow, believing she has learned of her fiancé's faithlessness, determines to withdraw from the marriage contract:

Have I so happily found

What many a widow has with sorrow tasted,
Even when my lip touched the contracting cup,
Even then to see the spider? (2.1.390–3).
But Middleton's point is perfectly rational: if the spider is poisonous, then *safety* lies in seeing it—one knows not to drink. In Shakespeare, however, the spider is poisonous only in conjunction with the knowledge of it, and this assumption appears to be unique— if not to Shakespeare, at least to Leontes.

44 **gorge** The term signified both the throat and the contents of the stomach.

45 **hefts** retching

48 **mistrusted** suspected

50 **discovered** revealed

51 **pinched** diminished, shrunken; tortured, afflicted (*OED*, pinch, 5–7)
    trick toy, game

52 **posterns** See note on 1.2.433.

LEONTES
Bear the boy hence; he shall not come about her.
Away with him, and let her sport herself   60
With that she's big with, for 'tis Polixenes
Has made thee swell thus.

Exit a lady with Mamillius

HERMIONE   But I'd say he had not,
And I'll be sworn you would believe my saying,
Howe'er you lean to th' nayward.

LEONTES   You, my lords,
Look on her, mark her well; be but about   65
To say she is a goodly lady, and
The justice of your hearts will thereto add
'Tis pity she's not honest. Honourable;
Praise her but for this her without-door form,
Which on my faith deserves high speech, and straight   70
The shrug, the hum or ha, these petty brands
That calumny doth use—O, I am out!
That mercy does, for calumny will sear
Virtue itself; these shrugs, these hums and has,
When you have said she's goodly, come between,   75
Ere you can say she's honest. But be't known,
From him that has most cause to grieve it should be,
She's an adultress!

HERMIONE   Should a villain say so,
The most replenished villain in the world,
He were as much more villain—you, my lord,   80

62 *Exit . . . Mamillius*] CAPELL (*subs.*); *not in* F

62 **But I'd say** I'd merely say; Hermione's
conditional implies a hypothetical situation, one that she has not yet taken
seriously.
64 **to th' nayward** towards denial (*OED*'s
only example of 'nayward')
68 **honest. Honourable** on the one hand
chaste, and on the other worthy of honour, i.e. by her birth or high place
('holding a position of honour; of distinguished rank', *OED* 2). Many editors
from Theobald on have repunctuated F's
'honest: Honorable' to combine the
concepts, reading 'honest, honourable'
or even 'honest-honourable' (Walker).
Leontes is decrying the fact that Her-

mione's honourable condition is not accompanied by an inner honesty, but it is
to the point that he separates the concepts and assumes that 'honourable' has
no moral implications.
69 **without-door** outward: Compare 'All
of her that is out of door most rich'
(*Cymbeline* 1.6.15).
72 **out** mistaken. Compare 'Like a dull
actor now | I have forgot my part, and
I am out' (*Coriolanus* 5.3.40–1).
73–4 **calumny . . . Virtue** Proverbial:
Dent E175.
75 **come between** interrupt you
79 **replenished** complete

Do but mistake.

LEONTES   You have mistook, my lady,
Polixenes for Leontes. O thou thing,
Which I'll not call a creature of thy place
Lest barbarism, making me the precedent,
Should a like language use to all degrees,   85
And mannerly distinguishment leave out
Betwixt the prince and beggar. I have said
She's an adultress, I have said with whom.
More, she's a traitor, and Camillo is
A federary with her, and one that knows   90
What she should shame to know herself
But with her most vile principal—that she's
A bed-swerver, even as bad as those
That vulgars give bold'st titles; ay, and privy
To this their late escape.

HERMIONE   No, by my life,   95
Privy to none of this—how will this grieve you
When you shall come to clearer knowledge, that
You thus have published me! Gentle my lord,
You scarce can right me throughly then to say
You did mistake.

LEONTES   No; if I mistake   100
In those foundations which I build upon,
The centre is not big enough to bear

---

83 **place** rank

85 **degrees** levels of society

90 **federary** accomplice; an otherwise unrecorded form. Shakespeare uses 'fedary'
in *Measure* and *Cymbeline*, and many
editors have assumed that 'federary' is
simply a misprint, especially since it
gives the line an extra syllable. But the
error, if there is one, is more complicated. A 'fedary', or 'feudary', from
medieval Latin *feodum*, is not an accomplice but a feudal dependant or vassal;
Shakespeare's usage, perhaps under the
influence of 'confederate', incorrectly as-
sociates it etymologically with *foedus*, a
league or confederacy—the word in
Cymbeline is spelled foedarie. But the
correct English formation from *foedus*
(gen. *foederis*) would in fact be federary,
not fedary: it looks as if Shakespeare is
correcting himself, or being corrected.

91 **shame** be ashamed

92 **But . . . principal** A baffling exception.
The sense is probably, 'even when she is
alone with Polixenes', but it is difficult to
see why this should be thought to pre-
clude Hermione's shame.
   principal the actual perpetrator of . . .
a crime (*OED* 7a); legal language

93 **bed-swerver** adultress; *OED*'s only
citation for the word. Swerver = offender
or transgressor—Florio uses the term to
translate *trasgressore*.

94 **That . . . titles** whom common people
call by the coarsest names

98 **published** publicly proclaimed, de-
nounced (*OED*, publish, 3)

99 **throughly** thoroughly
   to say by saying (Abbott 356)

102 **centre** of the universe; here, the
earth, as the centre of the Ptolemaic
system

A schoolboy's top. Away with her to prison.
He who shall speak for her is afar off guilty—
But that he speaks!

HERMIONE   There's some ill planet reigns.   105
I must be patient till the heavens look
With an aspect more favourable. Good my lords,
I am not prone to weeping, as our sex
Commonly are, the want of which vain dew
Perchance shall dry your pities; but I have   110
That honourable grief lodged here which burns
Worse than tears drown. Beseech you all, my lords,
With thoughts so qualified as your charities
Shall best instruct you measure me, and so
The King's will be performed.

LEONTES   Shall I be heard?   115
HERMIONE

Who is't that goes with me? Beseech your highness
My women may be with me, for you see
My plight requires it. (*To the ladies*) Do not weep,
     good fools,
There is no cause. When you shall know your mistress
Has deserved prison, then abound in tears   120
As I come out; this action I now go on
Is for my better grace. Adieu, my lord.

---

104 **afar off** indirectly
105 **But . . . speaks** he who merely speaks
     ill astrologically malignant
106–7 **till . . . favourable** i.e. till the pla-
     nets shed a more beneficent influence.
     Aspect = 'the relative positions of the
     heavenly bodies as they appear to an
     observer on the earth's surface at a
     given time' (*OED* II.4).
113 **qualified** tempered
114 **measure** judge (*OED* 6)
115 **Shall . . . heard?** Leontes' order to
     imprison Hermione has not been
     obeyed.
118 **fools** 'a term of endearment or pity'
     (*OED*, fool, *sb.*[1] 1c)
121 **this . . . on** Variously explained.
     Johnson took *action* in its legal sense, as
     an indictment, charge or accusation. A
     person cannot be said to 'go on' an
     indictment, but, as Pafford suggests, 'go
     on' may be elliptical for 'go to prison

on'; the interpretation is weak but
possible. Quiller-Couch and Dover
Wilson (taking a line that had been
considered and rejected by Furness) saw
the metaphor as a military one: 'she is
undertaking a campaign for her honour'. This seems to make the action too
voluntary, and has not generally been
accepted. Schanzer suggests a theatrical
metaphor, '*action* meaning the acting of
plays', hence the expression means 'the
part I now have to play'. This is attractive; there is, however, no record of 'go
on an action' being used in the sense of
'perform a play'. Kermode offers an unproblematic reading: 'I embark on this
course (to add to my honesty and
credit)'. Action, in any case, has a wide
range of meaning; and there is no reason to assume that Hermione's metaphor cannot be, like so many in the
play, a mixed one.

I never wished to see you sorry; now
I trust I shall—my women, come, you have leave.

LEONTES
Go, do our bidding; hence!   125

Exeunt Queen, guarded, and ladies

LORD
Beseech your highness call the Queen again.

ANTIGONUS
Be certain what you do, sir, lest your justice
Prove violence, in the which three great ones suffer,
Yourself, your Queen, your son.

LORD   For her, my lord,
I dare my life lay down, and will do't, sir—   130
Please you t'accept it—that the Queen is spotless
I'th' eyes of heaven, and to you—I mean
In this which you accuse her.

ANTIGONUS   If it prove
She's otherwise, I'll keep my stables where
I lodge my wife; I'll go in couples with her;   135
Than when I feel and see her no farther trust her;
For every inch of woman in the world,
Ay, every dram of woman's flesh, is false
If she be.

LEONTES   Hold your peaces.

LORD   Good my lord—

ANTIGONUS
It is for you we speak, not for ourselves.   140

125.1 *Exeunt . . . ladies*] THEOBALD (*subs.*); *not in* F

122 **grace** honour or credit, with an overtone of the religious sense. Dent records
(as a 'Christian commonplace' rather
than a proverb) 'Afflictions are sent us
by God for our good' (A53).

133 **which** of or in which (Abbott 394)
134–5 **I'll . . . wife** Obscure, and much debated. The general sense seems to be
that if Hermione is not chaste, then all
women are animals, and Antigonus will
treat his wife as he does his horses
(though if this is correct, the passage
would make better sense if the elements
were reversed: 'I'll lodge my wife where
I keep my stables'). Quiller-Couch and

Dover Wilson, following a suggestion
of Nicholson's, took this to mean specifically locking her up away from the
stallions; the interpretation is endorsed
by Pafford, but it is by no means implied.
135 **I'll . . . her** i.e. I won't let her out of
my sight; in couples = leashed together
(*OED*, couple, 1b)
136 **Than** Most editors since Pope's second
edition have thus interpreted F's 'Then';
the words were orthographically not distinguished in Shakespeare's time.
138 **dram** Literally, one-eighth of an ounce
of liquid (1.8 ml.), or one-sixteenth of an
ounce of avoirdupois weight (1.8 g.);
hence the tiniest bit.

You are abused, and by some putter-on
That will be damned for't—would I knew the villain,
I would land-damn him! Be she honour-flawed,
I have three daughters; the eldest is eleven,
The second and the third nine and some five;   145
If this prove true, they'll pay for't. By mine honour,
I'll geld 'em all—fourteen they shall not see
To bring false generations. They are co-heirs,
And I had rather glib myself than they
Should not produce fair issue.

LEONTES   Cease, no more!   150
You smell this business with a sense as cold
As is a dead man's nose; but I do see't and feel't,
As you feel doing thus ⌈*striking his own breast*⌉, and
   see withal
The instruments that feel.

ANTIGONUS   If it be so,
We need no grave to bury honesty;   155
There's not a grain of it the face to sweeten
Of the whole dungy earth.

LEONTES   What! Lack I credit?

LORD

I had rather you did lack than I, my lord,
Upon this ground; and more it would content me

---

153 *striking . . . breast*] This edition; *laying hold of his arm* HANMER; *striking him* RANN

141 **putter-on** instigator, plotter (*OED*, putter, 8)
143 **land-damn** The only recorded use of this expression, which has never been satisfactorily explained. The *Variorum* claims that 'landam' is a Cotswold word meaning 'to abuse with rancour', and that 'land-damned' is a Yorkshire term for the denunciation of slanderers, but neither can be authenticated. The word sounds like contemporary slang; 'land' may be a version of the verb 'lam', to beat or thrash—the similar 'lambaste' is first recorded in 1637.
145 **some five** about five
147 **geld** spay
148 **false generations** illegitimate children (as opposed to 'fair issue', l. 150)
149 **glib** geld, perhaps in the larger sense of 'deprive myself of my posterity'

151 **smell** 'pay some slight attention to' (*OED* II.6b)
153 **As . . . thus** Leontes performs some stage business here. Editors have suggested variously that he pulls Antigonus' nose or beard, grasps his arm, strikes him, or some piece of furniture, or himself, or feels something with his hands. Schanzer observes that 'you' is most likely to be impersonal—if it referred to Antigonus, one would expect 'as you feel *my* doing thus'. Different directors will conceive the action differently; I have proposed the simplest and most powerful gesture consistent with an impersonal 'you'.
   withal besides (Abbott 196)
157 **dungy** foul, filthy (*OED* 2)
   Lack I credit? 'Am I not to be trusted?'

To have her honour true than your suspicion,   160
Be blamed for't how you might.
LEONTES   Why, what need we
Commune with you of this, but rather follow
Our forceful instigation? Our prerogative
Calls not your counsels, but our natural goodness
Imparts this; which if you or stupefied,   165
Or seeming so in skill, cannot or will not
Relish a truth like us, inform yourselves
We need no more of your advice. The matter,
The loss, the gain, the ord'ring on't
Is all properly ours.
ANTIGONUS   And I wish, my liege,   170
You had only in your silent judgement tried it,
Without more overture.
LEONTES   How could that be?
Either thou art most ignorant by age,
Or thou wert born a fool. Camillo's flight
Added to their familiarity—   175
Which was as gross as ever touched conjecture,
That lacked sight only, naught for approbation
But only seeing, all other circumstances
Made up to th' deed—doth push on this proceeding.
Yet, for a greater confirmation—   180
For in an act of this importance 'twere
Most piteous to be wild—I have dispatched in post
To sacred Delphos to Apollo's temple

---

162 **but ... follow** 'why do we not instead follow' (Abbott 385)

163 **instigation** incentive

163–5 **Our ... this** 'My royal authority
doesn't require your advice; I am,
rather, telling you this out of the goodness of my nature.' Leontes takes King
James's line in the continuing debate
over the extent of the royal prerogative,
which was increasingly at issue in this
period. See the Introduction, pp. 12 ff.

165 **which** as regards which (Abbott 249)
or stupefied whether stunned

166 **seeming ... skill** artfully pretending
to be so

167 **Relish** appreciate

172 **overture** disclosure (*OED* 2)

175 **familiarity** intimacy

176 **touched   conjecture**   was   apprehended by reasoning

177 **naught for approbation** (lacked)
nothing for proof

179 **Made up** added up

182 **wild** rash

182–3 **I ... temple** In *Pandosto*, it is the
Queen who asks that the oracle be consulted. See the Introduction, p. 31.

182 **post** haste

183 **Delphos** Delos, birthplace of Apollo
and site of one of the three major oracles
of ancient Greece; the name was commonly given as Delphos in the Renaissance, presumably by analogy with
Delphi, though the two places were not
confused. Delphos is the form found
in *Pandosto*. (See Terence Spencer,

Cleomenes and Dion, whom you know
Of stuffed sufficiency. Now from the oracle   185
They will bring all, whose spiritual counsel had
Shall stop or spur me. Have I done well?
LORD Well done, my lord.
LEONTES
Though I am satisfied and need no more
Than what I know, yet shall the oracle   190
Give rest to th' minds of others, such as he
Whose ignorant credulity will not
Come up to th' truth. So have we thought it good
From our free person she should be confined,
Lest that the treachery of the two fled hence   195
Be left her to perform. Come, follow us;
We are to speak in public, for this business
Will raise us all.
ANTIGONUS   To laughter, as I take it,
If the good truth were known.   *Exeunt*

2.2   *Enter Paulina, a Gentleman, and attendants*
PAULINA
The keeper of the prison, call to him;
Let him have knowledge who I am.   *Exit Gentleman*
                                        Good lady,
No court in Europe is too good for thee;
What dost thou then in prison?
          Enter Gentleman with the Jailer
                                        Now, good sir,
You know me, do you not?
JAILER   For a worthy lady,   5
And one who much I honour.
PAULINA   Pray you then,

2.2.0.1 *Enter . . . attendants*] HANMER (*subs.*); *Enter Paulina, a Gentleman, Gaoler, Emilia.* F
2 *Exit Gentleman*] ROWE (*after l.* 1); DYCE; *not in* F   4 *Enter . . . Jailer*] ROWE (*subs.*); *not in* F

'Shakespeare's Isle of Delphos', *MLR* 47   194 **free** easily accessible
(1952), 199–202.)   195 **treachery** The 'plot against my life,
                                                     my crown', 2.1.47.
185 **stuffed sufficiency** 'abilities more   198 **raise** rouse
    than enough' (Johnson)   2.2.2 **have knowledge** be told
186 **all** the whole truth   6 **who** For 'whom': Abbott 274.
191 **he** i.e. Antigonus

Conduct me to the Queen.

JAILER   I may not, madam;
To the contrary I have express commandment.

PAULINA
Here's ado, to lock up honesty and honour from
Th'access of gentle visitors. Is't lawful, pray you, 10
To see her women? Any of them? Emilia?

JAILER
So please you, madam,
To put apart these your attendants, I
Shall bring Emilia forth.

PAULINA   I pray now, call her.
Withdraw yourselves. *Exeunt Gentleman and attendants*

JAILER   And madam, 15
I must be present at your conference.

PAULINA
Well, be't so; prithee.   *Exit Jailer*
Here's such ado to make no stain a stain
As passes colouring.
  Enter Jailer with Emilia
      Dear gentlewoman,
How fares our gracious lady? 20

EMILIA
As well as one so great and so forlorn
May hold together. On her frights and griefs,
Which never tender lady hath borne greater,
She is, something before her time, delivered.

PAULINA
A boy?

EMILIA A daughter, and a goodly babe, 25
Lusty, and like to live. The Queen receives
Much comfort in't, says 'My poor prisoner,
I am innocent as you.'

15 *Exeunt . . . attendants*] THEOBALD (*subs.*); *not in* F 17 *Exit Jailer*] CAPELL; *not in* F 19 *Enter . . . Emilia*] F2 (*Enter Emilia*); *not in* F

9 **honesty and honour** Recalling Leontes' charge that Hermione was 'honourable' but not 'honest', 2.1.68.
10 **gentle** noble
13 **put apart** send away
16 **conference** conversation
18–19 **ado . . . colouring** i.e. the effort

taken to produce this stain exceeds that of the whole craft of dyeing, with a quibble on colour as reason or excuse (*OED* 12b), hence, the effort is also in defiance of reason
22 **On** as a result of
23 **Which** than which

PAULINA   I dare be sworn.
These dangerous, unsafe lunes i'th' King, beshrew them!
He must be told on't, and he shall; the office   30
Becomes a woman best. I'll take't upon me;
If I prove honey-mouthed, let my tongue blister,
And never to my red-looked anger be
The trumpet any more. Pray you, Emilia,
Commend my best obedience to the Queen;   35
If she dares trust me with her little babe,
I'll show't the King and undertake to be
Her advocate to th' loud'st. We do not know
How he may soften at the sight o'th' child—
The silence often of pure innocence   40
Persuades when speaking fails.
EMILIA   Most worthy madam,
Your honour and your goodness is so evident
That your free undertaking cannot miss
A thriving issue—there is no lady living
So meet for this great errand. Please your ladyship   45
To visit the next room, I'll presently
Acquaint the Queen of your most noble offer,
Who but today hammered of this design,
But durst not tempt a minister of honour
Lest she should be denied.
PAULINA   Tell her, Emilia,   50
I'll use that tongue I have; if wit flow from't
As boldness from my bosom, let't not be doubted
I shall do good.
EMILIA   Now be you blessed for it.
I'll to the Queen; please you come something nearer.

---

28 **innocent as you** The innocence of babies was proverbial (Dent B4).

29 **lunes** lunacies
30 **on't** of it
32 **blister** Lies proverbially blister the tongue (Dent R84).
33–4 **to . . . trumpet** The metaphor is of a military herald in his red uniform preceded by a trumpeter; red-looked = appearing in red.
38 **to th' loud'st** as loudly as possible

43 **free** generous
44 **thriving issue** successful outcome
45 **meet** suitable
   Please if it please
46 **presently** immediately
48 **hammered of** hammered on, i.e. repeatedly discussed (*OED*, hammer, 4a, b)
49 **tempt . . . honour** call upon an agent of high rank; tempt = try, attempt (*OED* I.1)
51 **wit** wisdom, reasoning power

JAILER

  Madam, if 't please the Queen to send the babe,   55

  I know not what I shall incur to pass it,

  Having no warrant.

PAULINA   You need not fear it, sir;

  This child was prisoner to the womb, and is

  By law and process of great nature thence

  Freed and enfranchised, not a party to   60

  The anger of the King, nor guilty of—

  If any be—the trespass of the Queen.

JAILER I do believe it.

PAULINA

  Do not you fear; upon mine honour, I

  Will stand betwixt you and danger.   *Exeunt*   65

2.3   *Enter Leontes*

LEONTES

  Nor night nor day no rest. It is but weakness

  To bear the matter thus; mere weakness, if

  The cause were not in being—part o'th' cause,

  She, th'adultress; for the harlot King

  Is quite beyond mine arm, out of the blank   5

  And level of my brain, plot-proof; but she

  I can hook to me—say that she were gone,

2.3.0.1 *Enter Leontes*] CAPELL (*subs.*); *Enter Leontes, Seruants, Paulina, Antigonus, and Lords.*
F; *Enter Leon., Ant., Lords and other Attendants* ROWE

54 **please . . . nearer** i.e. into the next
    room (see ll. 45–6)
    something somewhat

56 **to pass it** in letting it pass
2.3.0.1 F's stage direction is *Enter Leontes,
    Servants, Paulina, Antigonus, and Lords.*
    But since Paulina does not in fact enter
    until l. 26, it is clear that the opening
    direction simply indicates the personnel
    of the scene (see the Introduction,
    p. 82). Rowe, followed by many editors,
    made Leontes' first speech an extended
    aside with Antigonus and the Lords on
    stage; Capell, followed by a smaller but
    still substantial number, had Antigonus
    and the Lords enter later with Paulina,
    and saw the opening speech as a solilo-
    quy. In terms of dramatic logic the latter

seems the preferable alternative.
3 **in being** still in existence.
3–5 **part . . . arm** Leontes conceives his
    rest to be dependent on the execution of
    the adulterers, but then pulls himself up
    short, remembering that Polixenes is out
    of his reach.
4 **harlot** lewd. The word was a general
    term of opprobrium for both sexes,
    though by the early 17th century the
    noun was used primarily for women.
5–6 **blank | And level** Shooting terms,
    bull's eye and the action of aiming at it;
    compare Q2 *Hamlet* 4.1.42 (Add. Pass.
    I. 3 in the Complete Oxford text), 'As
    level as the cannon to his blank'.
7 **hook** The metaphor is of a grappling
    hook.

Given to the fire, a moiety of my rest
Might come to me again. Who's there!

Enter a Servant

SERVANT   My lord?

LEONTES How does the boy?   10

SERVANT

He took good rest tonight; 'tis hoped
His sickness is discharged.

LEONTES   To see his nobleness
Conceiving the dishonour of his mother!
He straight declined, drooped, took it deeply,
Fastened and fixed the shame on't in himself,   15
Threw off his spirit, his appetite, his sleep,
And downright languished. Leave me solely; go,
See how he fares.   *Exit Servant*
                        Fie, fie, no thought of him;
The very thought of my revenges that way
Recoil upon me—in himself too mighty,   20
And in his parties, his alliance; let him be
Until a time may serve. For present vengeance,
Take it on her—Camillo and Polixenes
Laugh at me, make their pastime at my sorrow;
They should not laugh if I could reach them, nor   25

---

9 *Enter a Servant*] This edition; *Enrer (for 'Enter')* F2 (*beside* 'My lord—'); *Enter Servant*
ROWE (*after* 'there!') 12–13 To . . . mother!] F (To . . . Mother.); To . . . Mother, F2; To
see his nobleness! | Conceiving the dishonour of his mother, ROWE 18 *Exit Servant*]
THEOBALD (*subs.*); *not in* F

8 **Given . . . fire** 'Death by fire was the
punishment for women found guilty of
high treason or of petty treason (the
latter consisted in the murder, or con-
nivance at the murder, of husband or
master). Leontes believes Hermione to be
guilty of both forms of treason (see
3.2.[13–16])' (Schanzer).
  moiety portion (originally a legal term,
lit. 'half')
9 **Who's there!** A command for attend-
ance, not a question.
12–13 **To . . . mother!** Rowe, followed by
most editors, punctuates, 'To see his
nobleness! | Conceiving the dishonour
of his mother,'. There is no textual jus-
tification for this; and since it provides
Leontes with a neater and more rational

train of thought, it is dramatically un-
desirable.
13 **Conceiving** apprehending, understanding
14 **He . . . deeply** The line has been called
metrically deficient, but compare 'Blow,
winds, and crack your cheeks! Rage,
blow' (*Lear* 3.2.1).
15 **on't** of it (Abbott 181)
17 **solely** alone
18 **no . . . him** 'Let me not think of Polixenes'; Leontes reverts to his earlier
train of thought.
19–20 **thought . . . Recoil** For the lack of
agreement between subject and verb,
see Abbott 412 (confusion of proximity).
21 **parties** allies

Shall she, within my power.
> *Enter Paulina with a baby, Antigonus, Lords and*
> *Servants*

LORD   You must not enter.

PAULINA
Nay, rather, good my lords, be second to me!
Fear you his tyrannous passion more, alas,
Than the Queen's life? A gracious, innocent soul
More free than he is jealous!

ANTIGONUS   That's enough.   30

SERVANT
Madam, he hath not slept tonight, commanded
None should come at him.

PAULINA   Not so hot, good sir;
I come to bring him sleep. 'Tis such as you
That creep like shadows by him and do sigh
At each his needless heavings, such as you   35
Nourish the cause of his awaking. I
Do come with words as medicinal, as true—
Honest as either—to purge him of that humour
That presses him from sleep.

LEONTES   What noise there, ho?

PAULINA
No noise, my lord, but needful conference   40
About some gossips for your highness.

LEONTES   How?
Away with that audacious lady! Antigonus,
I charged thee that she should not come about me;
I knew she would.

ANTIGONUS   I told her so, my lord,
On your displeasure's peril and on mine   45
She should not visit you.

---

26 *Enter . . . Servants*] SCHANZER (*subs.*); *Enter Paulina.* F   39 What] F2; Who F1

27 **be second to** assist
30 **free** guiltless (*OED* 7); also noble, honourable (*OED* 4)
35 **heavings** groans (*OED*, heave, 8)
37 **medicinal** trisyllabic, 'med'cinal'
38 **humour** mental illness, in the old physiology caused by an imbalance in the humours
39 **presses him** weighs upon him (and keeps him from sleeping). The metaphor changes its reference from medicine to judicial torture.
41 **gossips** Here used in its literal sense, godparents for the infant's baptism.

LEONTES   What, canst not rule her?
PAULINA
From all dishonesty he can; in this,
Unless he take the course that you have done—
Commit me for committing honour—trust it,
He shall not rule me.
ANTIGONUS   La you now, you hear,   50
When she will take the rein I let her run,
But she'll not stumble.
PAULINA   Good my liege, I come—
And I beseech you hear me, who professes
Myself your loyal servant, your physician,
Your most obedient counsellor; yet that dares   55
Less appear so in comforting your evils
Than such as most seem yours—I say I come
From your good Queen.
LEONTES   Good Queen!
PAULINA
Good Queen, my lord, good Queen, I say good Queen,
And would by combat make her good, so were I   60
A man the worst about you!
LEONTES   Force her hence.
PAULINA
Let him that makes but trifles of his eyes
First hand me! On mine own accord I'll off,
But first I'll do my errand. The good Queen—
For she is good—hath brought you forth a daughter;   65
Here 'tis; commends it to your blessing.
⌈*She lays down the baby*⌉

66 *She . . . baby*] ROWE (*subs.*); not in F

47 **dishonesty** dishonourable action
49 **Commit . . . honour** send me to prison
   for acting honourably—'sin' is the word
   one would expect after 'committing'.
50 **La you** 'An exclamation . . . to call attention to an emphatic statement'
   (*OED*).
51–2 **When . . . stumble** Antigonus offers
   as praise the comparison of Paulina with
   a horse, which had been rejected in
   2.1.134–5.
53, 55 **professes, dares** Often changed by
   editors from Rowe onward to 'profess'

and 'dare', but the construction is not
uncommon: 'the verb is often in the
third person, though the antecedent be
in the *second* or *first*', with the relative
pronoun being treated as a third person
subject (Abbott 247). Compare *Lear*
2.2.448, 'If it be you that stirs these
daughters' hearts'.
56 **comforting** countenancing
60 **by . . . good** prove her good through
   trial by combat
61 **worst** least manly; lowest in degree

LEONTES   Out!
  A mankind witch! Hence with her, out o'door!
  A most intelligencing bawd!
PAULINA   Not so—
  I am as ignorant in that as you
  In so entitling me, and no less honest   70
  Than you are mad; which is enough, I'll warrant,
  As this world goes, to pass for honest.
LEONTES   Traitors!
  Will you not push her out? *(To Antigonus)* Give her
    the bastard,
  Thou dotard, thou art woman-tired, unroosted
  By thy Dame Partlet here. Take up the bastard,   75
  Take't up, I say; give't to thy crone.
PAULINA   For ever
  Unvenerable be thy hands if thou
  Tak'st up the princess by that forcèd baseness
  Which he has put upon't.
LEONTES   He dreads his wife.
PAULINA
  So I would you did; then 'twere past all doubt   80
  You'd call your children yours.
LEONTES   A nest of traitors!

---

67 **mankind** 'masculine, virago-like' (*OED*
3); also 'furious, fierce, mad' (*OED*,
mankind, *a.*²). The charge of transgress-
ing gender boundaries is intimately related to that of both witchcraft and
sexual licence; compare Banquo on the
witches, 'You should be women, | And
yet your beards forbid me to interpret |
That you are so', *Macbeth* 1.3.43–5,
and Patroclus on Achilles' refusal to
fight, 'A woman impudent and mannish
grown | Is not more loathed than an
effeminate man', *Troilus* 3.3.210–11.
See the Introduction, pp. 26 ff., 58 ff.
68 **intelligencing** carrying information,
i.e. as a go-between for Polixenes and
Hermione
72 **As . . . goes** 'Thus goes the world' was
proverbial (Dent 884.1).
74 **woman-tired** henpecked (from 'tire', in
falconry 'to pull or tear with the beak',
OED II.2)

74 **unroosted** pushed from your perch
75 **Partlet** In the stories of Reynard the
fox, the name of the hen; hence 'the
proper name of any hen; . . . also applied, like "hen", to a woman' (*OED*).
Falstaff calls Mistress Quickly 'Dame
Partlet the hen', *1 Henry IV* 3.3.51.
76 **crone** Both old woman and old ewe,
two separate words apparently unre-
lated etymologically.
78–9 **forcèd . . . upon't** the name of bastard that he has forced upon it. 'Forced'
has the additional sense of wrongly im-
puted; compare 3.1.16, 'So forcing
faults upon Hermione'.
81 **You'd . . . yours** Under English law,
the children of a legally married woman
were legitimate, and therefore entitled
to inherit, even if the husband denied paternity. See the Introduction,
p. 30.

ANTIGONUS
    I am none, by this good light.
PAULINA   Nor I, nor any
    But one that's here, and that's himself; for he
    The sacred honour of himself, his Queen's,
    His hopeful son's, his babe's betrays to slander,   85
    Whose sting is sharper than the sword's; and will not—
    For as the case now stands, it is a curse
    He cannot be compelled to't—once remove
    The root of his opinion, which is rotten
    As ever oak or stone was sound.
LEONTES   A callet   90
    Of boundless tongue, who late hath beat her husband
    And now baits me! This brat is none of mine,
    It is the issue of Polixenes.
    Hence with it, and together with the dam
    Commit them to the fire.
PAULINA   It is yours;   95
    And might we lay th'old proverb to your charge,
    So like you, 'tis the worse. Behold, my lords,

85-6 **slander . . . sword's** The observation was a commonplace; Dent doubts that it was proverbial (S521.1), but compare 'Words hurt more than swords', W839.

87-8 **as . . . to't** Leontes cannot be legally compelled to 'remove | The root of his opinion', but were he not the King, under English law Hermione would have a case. To defame a woman's honour was actionable in both civil and ecclesiastical courts; when the person defamed was a commoner the act was a tort and could be redressed by a fine, but defaming an aristocrat was a more serious matter touching the public good. Under Elizabeth, to slander the Queen was treasonable. Edward Coke discusses a relevant case in his *Reports* of a woman whose fiancé refused to marry her after being told maliciously that she had had an illegitimate child. She brought a civil action against the slanderer and won, and the defendant was ordered to pay her £200. The case was appealed, on the grounds that slander was a spiritual matter and could not be

tried in the common law, but the appeal was lost. In this case it was considered sufficient to assign a monetary value to the woman's honour (the record does not show whether the fiancé found it sufficient and proceeded with the marriage); but had the plaintiff been an upper-class woman, a public recantation would have been required. (See J. H. Baker and S. F. C. Milsom, *Sources of English Legal History* (London, 1986), p. 490.) 'As the case now stands' Leontes cannot be sued for slander only because no court has jurisdiction over the King.

90 **callet** 'a lewd woman, trull, strumpet, drab' (Leontes extends the charge against Hermione to Paulina); also a scold (*OED*)

91 **beat** Pronounced 'bait', punning on 'baits' in the next line.

92 **baits** persecutes, harasses (*OED* 4)

96 **old proverb** Dent L290. Staunton cited the proverb in Overbury's character of *A Sargeant* (pub. 1614): 'The devil calls him his white son; he is so like him that he is the worst for it.'

Although the print be little, the whole matter
And copy of the father—eye, nose, lip,
The trick of 's frown, his forehead, nay, the valley,   100
The pretty dimples of his chin and cheek, his smiles,
The very mould and frame of hand, nail, finger.
And thou good goddess Nature, which hast made it
So like to him that got it, if thou hast
The ordering of the mind too, 'mongst all colours,   105
No yellow in't, lest she suspect, as he does,
Her children not her husband's.

LEONTES   A gross hag!
And losel, thou art worthy to be hanged,
That wilt not stay her tongue.

ANTIGONUS   Hang all the husbands
That cannot do that feat, you'll leave yourself   110
Hardly one subject.

LEONTES   Once more, take her hence!

PAULINA

A most unworthy and unnatural lord
Can do no more.

LEONTES   I'll ha' thee burnt!

PAULINA   I care not;
It is an heretic that makes the fire,
Not she which burns in't. I'll not call you tyrant;   115

---

98 **print** image, likeness (*OED* 2a); with 'matter' and 'copy' (ll. 98–9), alluding specifically to the printing process

100 **trick** 'a characteristic expression . . . ; a peculiar feature; a distinguishing trait' (*OED* 8b)
   valley Not recorded as a physiognomical term: furrow in the brow? cleft or depression in the chin or upper lip?

104 **got** begot

105 **colours** characters, natures; compare *Lear* 2.2.134, 'This is a fellow of the selfsame colour', where the quarto reads 'nature'.

106 **yellow** Traditionally the colour of jealousy; *OED* 2 cites Dekker and Webster's *Northward Ho!*: 'Jealous men are either knaves or coxcombs, be you neither; you wear yellow hose without cause.'

106–7 **suspect . . . husband's** Malone observed, 'In the ardour of composition Shakespeare seems to have forgotten the difference of sexes. No suspicion that the

babe in question might entertain of her future husband's fidelity could affect the legitimacy of her off-spring.' Most editors have concurred, at least to the extent of seeing a problem in the passage, which has generally been accounted for by the confusion of the moment—Pafford explains 'that it is the deliberate expression by Shakespeare of the kind of mistake which an excited woman [or man?] might make', Schanzer that 'it is one of the many comic touches in the scene by means of which Shakespeare mitigates its tragic impact'. But there is no reason to assume that Paulina does not mean exactly what she says. She argues that it would be as fantastic for Perdita to suspect the legitimacy of her children as it is for Leontes to do so.

108 **losel** scoundrel

114–15 **It . . . in't** i.e. you are the heretic, not I

But this most cruel usage of your Queen,
Not able to produce more accusation
Than your own weak-hinged fancy, something savours
Of tyranny, and will ignoble make you,
Yea, scandalous to the world.

LEONTES (*to Antigonus*)　　　　On your allegiance,　　　120
Out of the chamber with her! Were I a tyrant,
Where were her life? She durst not call me so
If she did know me one. Away with her.

PAULINA
I pray you, do not push me; I'll be gone.
Look to your babe, my lord, 'tis yours—Jove send her　125
A better guiding spirit. What needs these hands?
You that are thus so tender o'er his follies
Will never do him good, not one of you.
So, so; farewell, we are gone.　　　　　　*Exit*

LEONTES (*to Antigonus*)
Thou, traitor, hast set on thy wife to this.　　　130
My child? Away with't! Even thou, that hast
A heart so tender o'er it, take it hence
And see it instantly consumed with fire.
Even thou, and none but thou. Take it up straight.
Within this hour bring me word 'tis done,　　　135
And by good testimony, or I'll seize thy life,
With what thou else call'st thine. If thou refuse,
And wilt encounter with my wrath, say so;
The bastard-brains with these my proper hands
Shall I dash out. Go, take it to the fire,　　　140
For thou set'st on thy wife.

ANTIGONUS　　　　　　I did not, sir;
These lords, my noble fellows, if they please,
Can clear me in't.

LORDS　　　　　　We can; my royal liege,
He is not guilty of her coming hither.

LEONTES You're liars all!　　　145

---

118 **something** somewhat
120 **On . . . allegiance** To disobey after
this would be treasonable; compare
Lear banishing Kent: 'Hear me, rec-
reant; on thine allegiance, hear me!',

1.1.166.
126 **What . . . hands?** 'Keep your hands
off me.'
139 **proper** own
141 **set'st on** didst incite

LORD

Beseech your highness, give us better credit.
We have always truly served you, and beseech
So to esteem of us; and on our knees we beg,
As recompense of our dear services
Past and to come, that you do change this purpose,   150
Which being so horrible, so bloody, must
Lead on to some foul issue. We all kneel.

LEONTES

I am a feather for each wind that blows.
Shall I live on to see this bastard kneel
And call me father? Better burn it now   155
Than curse it then. But be it; let it live.
—It shall not neither. (*To Antigonus*) You, sir, come
      you hither,
You that have been so tenderly officious
With Lady Margery, your midwife there,
To save this bastard's life—for 'tis a bastard,   160
So sure as this beard's grey. What will you adventure
To save this brat's life?

ANTIGONUS   Anything, my lord,
That my ability may undergo,
And nobleness impose—at least thus much;
I'll pawn the little blood which I have left   165
To save the innocent—anything possible.

---

147 **beseech** The object 'you' is understood; the Folio text has an apostrophe
after the word to indicate an elision.
149 **dear** both loving and valuable
152 **issue** outcome
153 **I . . . blows** Leontes' sense of himself
is proverbial (Dent F162).
158 **officious** The earlier meaning, 'ready
to do kind offices, eager to please, atten-
tive', was still the primary one in
Shakespeare's time, but the modern
sense, 'unduly forward, meddlesome',
had appeared by the turn of the century
(OED 1, 3).
159 **Lady Margery** 'Margery-prater' is another name for the hen, and therefore,
contemptuously, for woman; compare
'Dame Partlet', l. 75.
midwife The term implicates Paulina in

both the birth of the child and the concealment of its true paternity. The midwife's oath, administered from about
1540 as part of the licensing process,
included a promise not to 'permit or
suffer that woman being in labour or
travail shall name any other to be the
father of her child, than only he who is
the right true father thereof' (see
Thomas R. Forbes, *The Midwife and the
Witch* (New Haven, 1966), p. 145).
161 **this beard's grey** Antigonus' beard;
Leontes is about thirty. Malone, followed
by many editors, suggested that Leontes
pulls at the beard here, though a gesture
towards it would be sufficient to make
the point.
adventure dare to undertake
165 **pawn** risk

LEONTES

It shall be possible. Swear by this sword
Thou wilt perform my bidding.

ANTIGONUS   I will, my lord.

LEONTES

Mark, and perform it, seest thou? For the fail
Of any point in't shall not only be   170
Death to thyself, but to thy lewd-tongued wife—
Whom for this time we pardon. We enjoin thee,
As thou art liegeman to us, that thou carry
This female bastard hence, and that thou bear it
To some remote and desert place quite out   175
Of our dominions, and that there thou leave it,
Without more mercy, to it own protection
And favour of the climate. As by strange fortune
It came to us, I do in justice charge thee,
On thy soul's peril and thy body's torture,   180
That thou commend it strangely to some place
Where chance may nurse or end it. Take it up.

ANTIGONUS

I swear to do this, though a present death
Had been more merciful.

⌈*He picks up the baby*⌉

                         Come on, poor babe,
Some powerful spirit instruct the kites and ravens   185
To be thy nurses. Wolves and bears, they say,
Casting their savageness aside, have done
Like offices of pity. Sir, be prosperous
In more than this deed does require; and blessing
Against this cruelty fight on thy side,   190
Poor thing, condemned to loss.   *Exit*

---

184 *He . . . baby*] This edition; *not in* F

169 **fail** This is the noun in Shakespeare's time; *OED* first records 'failure' in 1641.
177 **it** its; 'occasionally *it*, an early provincial form of the old genitive, is found for *its*, especially when a child is mentioned' (Abbott 228)
178 **strange** alien (as the child of Polixenes)
181 **commend it strangely** 'commit it . . . as a stranger' (Johnson)

182 **nurse or end** 'Mend or end' was proverbial (Dent M874); compare 'clear or end', 3.1.18.
183 **present** immediate
188–9 **prosperous . . . require** be more prosperous than this deed deserves
191 **loss** The operative senses are 'ruin' and 'estrangement' (*OED* 1, 2c); compare 3.3.50.

LEONTES   No, I'll not rear
  Another's issue.
    Enter a Servant
SERVANT   Please your highness, posts
  From those you sent to th'oracle are come
  An hour since. Cleomenes and Dion,
  Being well arrived from Delphos, are both landed,   195
  Hasting to th' court.
LORD   So please you, sir, their speed
  Hath been beyond account.
LEONTES   Twenty-three days
  They have been absent—'tis good speed, foretells
  The great Apollo suddenly will have
  The truth of this appear. Prepare you, lords;   200
  Summon a session that we may arraign
  Our most disloyal lady; for as she hath
  Been publicly accused, so shall she have
  A just and open trial. While she lives
  My heart will be a burden to me. Leave me,   205
  And think upon my bidding.   *Exeunt*

3.1   *Enter Cleomenes and Dion*
CLEOMENES
  The climate's delicate, the air most sweet,
  Fertile the isle, the temple much surpassing
  The common praise it bears.
DION   I shall report,
  For most it caught me, the celestial habits—
  Methinks I so should term them—and the reverence   5
  Of the grave wearers. O, the sacrifice,
  How ceremonious, solemn and unearthly
  It was i'th' offering!
CLEOMENES   But of all, the burst

197 account] F (accompt)

197 **beyond . . . days** 'beyond account' =
   unprecedented—the precedent here is
   Pandosto, where the trip to Delphos
   alone takes three weeks.
199 **suddenly** very quickly

201 **session** judicial investigation
3.1.1 **delicate** delightful (*OED* 1)
2 **isle** Delphos, or Delos (see 2.1.183 and
  note)
4 **habits** garments

And the ear-deaf'ning voice o'th' oracle,
Kin to Jove's thunder, so surprised my sense   10
That I was nothing.
DION   If th'event o'th' journey
Prove as successful to the Queen—O, be't so!—
As it hath been to us rare, pleasant, speedy,
The time is worth the use on't.
CLEOMENES   Great Apollo
Turn all to th' best! These proclamations   15
So forcing faults upon Hermione
I little like.
DION   The violent carriage of it
Will clear or end the business when the oracle,
Thus by Apollo's great divine sealed up,
Shall the contents discover; something rare   20
Even then will rush to knowledge. Go—fresh horses;
And gracious be the issue.   *Exeunt*

3.2   *Enter Leontes, Lords and Officers*
LEONTES
This sessions, to our great grief we pronounce,
Even pushes 'gainst our heart. The party tried,
The daughter of a king, our wife, and one
Of us too much beloved. Let us be cleared
Of being tyrannous, since we so openly   5
Proceed in justice, which shall have due course
Even to the guilt or the purgation.
Produce the prisoner.
OFFICER
It is his highness' pleasure that the Queen
Appear in person here in court.

3.2.0.1 *Enter . . . Officers*] THEOBALD (*subs.*); *Enter Leontes, Lords, Officers: Hermione (as to her Triall) Ladies: Cleomines, Dion.* F

11 **event** outcome
14 **is . . . on't** has been well spent; on't = of it (Abbott 182)
14–15 **Apollo . . . best** The proverb is 'God turn all to good' (Dent 227.1).
17 **carriage** 'execution, conduct, management' (*OED* 10)
18 **clear . . . business** settle the matter one way or another. 'Mend or end' was

proverbial (Dent M874); compare 'nurse or end', 2.3.182.
19 **great divine** head priest
20 **the . . . discover** reveal its contents
22 **issue** outcome
3.2.1 **sessions** trial
 7 **purgation** acquittal; 'the action of clearing . . . from the accusation or suspicion of crime or guilt' (*OED* 9)

Enter Hermione as to her trial, Paulina and Ladies
                              Silence!   10

LEONTES Read the indictment.

OFFICER Hermione, Queen to the worthy Leontes, King of
  Sicilia, thou art here accused and arraigned of high
  treason in committing adultery with Polixenes, King of
  Bohemia, and conspiring with Camillo to take away the   15
  life of our sovereign lord the King, thy royal husband;
  the pretence whereof being by circumstances partly laid
  open, thou, Hermione, contrary to the faith and allegiance of a true subject, didst counsel and aid them for
  their better safety to fly away by night.   20

HERMIONE

  Since what I am to say must be but that
  Which contradicts my accusation, and
  The testimony on my part no other
  But what comes from myself, it shall scarce boot me
  To say 'not guilty'; mine integrity,   25
  Being counted falsehood, shall, as I express it,
  Be so received. But thus: if powers divine
  Behold our human actions, as they do,
  I doubt not then but innocence shall make
  False accusation blush and tyranny   30
  Tremble at patience. You, my lord, best know,
  Whom least will seem to do so, my past life

---

10 *Enter . . . Ladies*] THEOBALD (*subs.*); *Enter* F2 (*after* 'Silence.'); *not in* F   Silence!] *Silence.*
(*as stage direction*) F

10 **Silence** F prints the word in italics in
the margin, treating it as a stage direction. F2 retains the stage direction, and
adds an entry for unnamed characters—
in F, the entry of Hermione and her
ladies is part of the opening stage direction. Most editors since Rowe have made
the word part of the Officer's speech,
implying some commotion caused by
Hermione's entrance. But F's reading
may be correct: E. A. J. Honigmann
cites an analogous stage direction during Queen Katherine's trial in *All is True*
(i.e. *Henry VIII*, 2.4.10.1–3), and observes that this sort of 'very special silence'
is appropriate here as well ('Re-enter the
stage direction: Shakespeare and some
contemporaries', *Sh. Survey* 29 (1976),

pp. 117–25).
17 **pretence** intention, design (*OED* 3)
21 ff. Hermione's speech is closely adapted
from *Pandosto*; see Appendix B,
pp. 245–7.
31 **patience** With an overtone of its original sense, 'suffering'.
32 **Whom** For 'who', and almost invariably, since Rowe, emended; but *Tempest*
has two comparable examples: 'You,
brother mine, . . . whom, with Sebastian
. . . would here have killed your king'
(5.1.75–8), and 'thou hast met us here,
whom three hours since | Were
wrecked upon this shore' (5.1.138–9).
These may simply be errors (and it may
be relevant that both texts derive from
Ralph Crane copies); but they may also

Hath been as continent, as chaste, as true
As I am now unhappy, which is more
Than history can pattern, though devised   35
And played to take spectators. For behold me,
A fellow of the royal bed, which owe
A moiety of the throne; a great king's daughter,
The mother to a hopeful prince, here standing
To prate and talk for life and honour fore   40
Who please to come and hear. For life, I prize it
As I weigh grief, which I would spare; for honour,
'Tis a derivative from me to mine,
And only that I stand for. I appeal
To your own conscience, sir, before Polixenes   45
Came to your court how I was in your grace,
How merited to be so; since he came,
With what encounter so uncurrent I
Have strained t'appear thus—if one jot beyond
The bound of honour, or in act or will   50
That way inclining, hardened be the hearts
Of all that hear me, and my near'st of kin
Cry 'fie' upon my grave.

be expressive: all occur at moments
of high anxiety, and seem to show
the character—or Shakespeare on the
character's behalf—changing direction
abruptly in mid-sentence. See also
4.4.356 and 420.

34 **which** i.e. my unhappiness
35 **history** narrative (of any sort, whether
   true or imagined, and including drama,
   as in l. 36)
   pattern provide precedent for (*OED* 2)
36 **take** appeal to
37 **owe** own
38 **a moiety** a part of (lit., half)
39 **hopeful prince** prince for whom there
   are great hopes
41–2 **For . . . spare** 'Life is to me now only
   grief, and as such only is considered by
   me; I would, therefore, willingly dismiss
   it' (Johnson); for = as to; weigh =
   value; spare = avoid, give up (*OED* II.
   7b).
43 **a . . . mine** my children's inheritance
   from me
44 **stand** fight (compare 'take a stand')
45 **conscience** inmost thought, inward

knowledge (*OED* 1)
48–9 **With . . . thus** Since the mid 19th
   century this has been taken to mean
   'with what behaviour so unacceptable I
   have transgressed that I should appear
   thus (on trial)'; the passage has been
   much discussed, and was considered incomprehensible by Johnson and most
   other 18th-century editors. The modern
   consensus was established by Halliwell,
   Staunton and R. G. White; it is probably
   as close as one can come to a paraphrase, but the sense thus produced is at
   best very elliptical, and will be impossible to convey in the theatre, and it
   may be that, as with a number of
   speeches of Leontes and Polixenes, its
   obscurity is an essential part of its
   meaning. Encounter = both behaviour
   and 'amatory interview' (*OED* 3, 2b);
   uncurrent = 'not commonly accepted or
   recognized' (*OED* 2); strain = 'trans-
   gress the strict requirements of (one's
   conscience)' (*OED* 11b). See the Introduction, pp. 7–8.
49 **jot** iota, the smallest letter, hence the
   least bit

LEONTES   I ne'er heard yet
That any of these bolder vices wanted
Less impudence to gainsay what they did   55
Than to perform it first.
HERMIONE   That's true enough,
Though 'tis a saying, sir, not due to me.
LEONTES
You will not own it.
HERMIONE   More than mistress of
Which comes to me in name of fault I must not
At all acknowledge. For Polixenes,   60
With whom I am accused, I do confess
I loved him, as in honour he required;
With such a kind of love as might become
A lady like me; with a love even such,
So, and no other, as yourself commanded;   65
Which not to have done I think had been in me
Both disobedience and ingratitude
To you and toward your friend, whose love had spoke
Even since it could speak, from an infant, freely,
That it was yours. Now for conspiracy,   70
I know not how it tastes, though it be dished
For me to try how. All I know of it
Is that Camillo was an honest man,
And why he left your court the gods themselves,
Wotting no more than I, are ignorant.   75
LEONTES
You knew of his departure, as you know
What you have underta'en to do in's absence.
HERMIONE   Sir,
You speak a language that I understand not.
My life stands in the level of your dreams,

54–6 **wanted ... first** 'It is apparent that
according to the proper, at least according to the present, use of words, "less"
should be *more*, or "wanted" should be
had. But Shakespeare is very uncertain
in his use of negatives. It may be necessary once to observe, that in our language, two negatives did not originally
affirm, but strengthen the negation'
(Johnson).

59 **Which ... fault** that which is now
being called a fault, i.e. her honourable
love for Polixenes
62 **required** was entitled to
71 **dished** served up
75 **Wotting** if they know
79 **in ... dreams** within range of your delusions. The level is the target in arch-
ery, what is aimed at.

Which I'll lay down.

LEONTES   Your actions are my dreams.   80
You had a bastard by Polixenes,
And I but dreamed it. As you were past all shame—
Those of your fact are so—so past all truth;
Which to deny concerns more than avails; for as
Thy brat hath been cast out, like to itself,   85
No father owning it—which is, indeed,
More criminal in thee than it—so thou
Shalt feel our justice, in whose easiest passage
Look for no less than death.

HERMIONE   Sir, spare your threats.
The bug which you would fright me with I seek.   90
To me can life be no commodity;
The crown and comfort of my life, your favour,
I do give lost, for I do feel it gone,
But know not how it went. My second joy,
And first fruits of my body, from his presence   95
I am barred like one infectious. My third comfort,
Starred most unluckily, is from my breast,
The innocent milk in it most innocent mouth,
Haled out to murder; myself on every post
Proclaimed a strumpet; with immodest hatred   100
The childbed privilege denied, which 'longs
To women of all fashion; lastly, hurried
Here, to this place, i'th' open air, before
I have got strength of limit. Now, my liege,

---

80 **Which** i.e. my life
83 **of . . . fact** guilty of your crime; 'crime' was the commonest meaning of 'fact' in the 16th and 17th centuries (see *OED* 1c).
84 **concerns . . . avails** 'is of more importance than of use to you' (Schanzer)
85–6 **like . . . it** as the outcast it is, disowned even by its father
90 **bug** 'bugbear, hobgoblin, bogey; scarecrow' (*OED* 1)
91 **commodity** advantage, profit. Compare Falstaff, 'I will turn diseases to commodity', *2 Henry IV* 1.2.249–50.
93 **give** consider
97 **Starred . . . unluckily** born under most inauspicious stars
98 **it** its (Abbott 228). See 2.3.177 and

note.
99 **on . . . post** where public notices were fixed
100 **immodest** excessive
101 **childbed privilege** of bedrest after childbirth
     'longs belongs
102 **fashion** ranks
103 **i'th' open air** Fresh air was considered dangerous to invalids. The phrase may imply that the trial scene takes place outdoors, or it may modify 'hurried', i.e. not even brought in a closed carriage.
104 **strength of limit** The modern consensus interprets this to mean 'the strength which returns to a woman in a given period after childbirth' (Pafford). *OED* 2f

Tell me what blessings I have here alive,   105
That I should fear to die! Therefore proceed.
But yet, hear this—mistake me not: no life,
I prize it not a straw, but for mine honour,
Which I would free—if I shall be condemned
Upon surmises, all proofs sleeping else   110
But what your jealousies awake, I tell you
'Tis rigour and not law. Your honours all,
I do refer me to the oracle.
Apollo be my judge.
LORD   This your request
Is altogether just; therefore bring forth,   115
And in Apollo's name, his oracle.
                  ⌈*Exeunt certain Officers*⌉

HERMIONE

The Emperor of Russia was my father.
O that he were alive, and here beholding
His daughter's trial! that he did but see
The flatness of my misery, yet with eyes   120
Of pity, not revenge!
      ⌈*Enter Officers, with Cleomenes and Dion*⌉
OFFICER

You here shall swear upon this sword of justice
That you, Cleomenes and Dion, have

116.1 *Exeunt . . . Officers*] CAPELL; *not in* F   121.1 *Enter . . . Dion*] CAPELL (*subs.*); *not in* F

cites this passage and *Measure* 3.1.216–
17, 'between which time of the contract
and limit of the solemnity', for 'limit' as
a prescribed time, but the latter example
is not relevant: 'limit' there means not
a period of time, but a *terminus ad quem*,
the date fixed for Mariana's marriage to
Angelo. Pafford cites a more persuasive
instance, *Richard III* 3.3.7, 'The limit of
your lives is out'. But this example is
much less elliptical than Hermione's,
and the expression in relation to
childbed is otherwise unparalleled. By
1664, the phrase was already being
emended; in F3, F4 and Rowe, 'limit'
became 'limbs'. Pope and Hanmer concurred, and replaced the now missing
syllable by starting the next sentence
with 'And'. Subsequent editors rejected
the emendation, but there was no agree-

ment throughout the 18th and 19th
centuries about how to interpret the
phrase—Johnson, unable to see how it
meant what it must mean, returned to
the emendation (here to 'limb') with
cautious approval, though he stopped
short of adopting it. Halliwell's simple
gloss, 'a limited degree of strength', is
attractive, though again the usage is
unparalleled. It is perhaps sufficient to
observe that this is one of many places
where the text seems to court a deliberate obscurity.

108 **not a straw** Proverbial: Dent S917.
112 **rigour . . . law** unlawful cruelty, se-
      verity without law. The normal expres-
      sion is 'the rigour of the law'.
120 **flatness** absoluteness (*OED* 5b, citing
      only this passage)

Been both at Delphos, and from thence have brought
This sealed-up oracle, by the hand delivered   125
Of great Apollo's priest, and that since then
You have not dared to break the holy seal,
Nor read the secrets in't.

CLEOMENES *and* DION   All this we swear.

LEONTES

Break up the seals and read.

OFFICER (*reads*) 'Hermione is chaste, Polixenes blameless,   130
Camillo a true subject, Leontes a jealous tyrant, his
innocent babe truly begotten, and the King shall
live without an heir if that which is lost be not
found.'

LORDS

Now blessèd be the great Apollo!

HERMIONE   Praisèd!   135

LEONTES

Hast thou read truth?

OFFICER   Ay, my lord, even so
As it is here set down.

LEONTES

There is no truth at all i'th' oracle.
The sessions shall proceed; this is mere falsehood.

        Enter a Servant

SERVANT

My lord, the King, the King!

LEONTES   What is the business?   140

SERVANT

O sir, I shall be hated to report it.
The prince, your son, with mere conceit and fear
Of the Queen's speed, is gone.

LEONTES   How? Gone?

SERVANT   Is dead.

LEONTES

Apollo's angry, and the heavens themselves

---

130 *reads*] CAPELL; *not in* F   136–7 Ay . . . down] CAPELL; *one line in* F   139.1 *Enter a Servant*] ROWE 1709; *not in* F

139 **mere** complete   'a morbid affection or seizure of the body
141 **to report** for reporting   or mind' (*OED* 11)
142 **conceit** thinking, with an overtone of   143 **speed** fortune (*OED* 3b)

Do strike at my injustice.

Hermione falls to the ground

How now there! 145

PAULINA

This news is mortal to the Queen—look down

And see what death is doing.

LEONTES   Take her hence.

Her heart is but o'ercharged; she will recover.

I have too much believed mine own suspicion.

Beseech you tenderly apply to her 150

Some remedies for life.

Exeunt Paulina and Ladies, carrying Hermione

Apollo, pardon

My great profaneness 'gainst thine oracle.

I'll reconcile me to Polixenes,

New woo my Queen, recall the good Camillo,

Whom I proclaim a man of truth, of mercy; 155

For, being transported by my jealousies

To bloody thoughts and to revenge, I chose

Camillo for the minister, to poison

My friend Polixenes; which had been done,

But that the good mind of Camillo tardied 160

My swift command, though I with death, and with

Reward, did threaten and encourage him,

Not doing it, and being done. He, most humane,

And filled with honour, to my kingly guest

Unclasped my practice, quit his fortunes here— 165

Which you knew great—and to the hazard

---

145 *Hermione . . . ground*] This edition; *Hermione faints* ROWE 1709; *not in* F   151 *Exeunt . . . Hermione*] ROWE 1709; *not in* F

148 **o'ercharged** overburdened, oppressed

161–3 **I . . . done** I threatened him with death if he failed to do it, and promised to reward him if he did it. For the construction, compare 4.4.372–3; for 'being done' see Abbott 378 (Participle without noun).

165 **Unclasped my practice** revealed my plot

166 **Which . . . hazard** F2 regularizes the short line by reading 'certain hazard'. The emendation has no authority, but it has appealed to editors with a devotion

to neatness. Pafford writes, 'without *certain* the line in F is metrically incomplete: with it the counterbalance with *incertainties* in [the next line] is typically Shakespearean'. Wells and Taylor concur that F2's reading 'mends the metre and improves the sense'. But the metre needs no mending: occasional short lines (and occasional long ones—see l. 163) are common enough in Shakespeare; and as Furness points out, in speaking, the line requires a pause after 'great'. As for the improvement of sense,

Of all incertainties himself commended,
No richer than his honour. How he glisters
Through my rust! And how his piety
Does my deeds make the blacker!
    Enter Paulina
PAULINA   Woe the while!   170
O cut my lace, lest my heart, cracking it,
Break too!
LORD   What fit is this, good lady?
PAULINA
What studied torments, tyrant, hast for me?
What wheels, racks, fires? What flaying, boiling?
In leads or oils? What old or newer torture   175
Must I receive, whose every word deserves
To taste of thy most worst? Thy tyranny,
Together working with thy jealousies—
Fancies too weak for boys, too green and idle
For girls of nine—O think what they have done,   180
And then run mad indeed, stark mad; for all
Thy bygone fooleries were but spices of it.
That thou betrayedst Polixenes, 'twas nothing;
That did but show thee of a fool, inconstant,
And damnable ingrateful. Nor was't much   185

170 *Enter Paulina*] ROWE 1709; *not in* F

the undeniable fact that Shakespeare's
sense can often be improved is surely not
a serious argument for editors to im-
prove it.

167 **commended** committed
169 **Through my rust** Again, the source
of much editorial fussing. F's spelling is
'through', but the word could be either
mono- or disyllabic, and was often
spelled 'thorough'. The editor of F2
treated it as a monosyllable and, as in l.
166 above, regularized the metre by
adding a word, reading 'Through my
dark rust'. The emendation was adopted
by Rowe, Capell and Rann, but rejected
by Malone and later editors, who instead regularized the line by printing
'thorough'. Once again, however, there
is nothing unmetrical about the line: a
single accented syllable is substituted for
the initial iamb; compare 'Good my

lord, give me thy favour still' (*Tempest*
4.1.204), and a multitude of other
examples. Moreover, in speaking, the
initial foot is heard as an iamb because
of the feminine ending of l. 168.
171 **lace** laces (of her bodice)
174 **What ... boiling?** F2, followed by
numerous editors well into the 19th
century, once again undertakes to regularize the metre by adding *burning?*
177 **most worst** The superlative is doubled
for emphasis; Abbott (11) quotes Jonson
on the practice, 'a certain kind of English Atticism, imitating the manner of
the *most ancientest and finest Grecians*'.
179 **green** immature
    idle silly, groundless (*OED* 2b, c)
182 **spices** slight tastes, samples (*OED*,
spice, 5b, c)
184 **of** for
185 **damnable** damnably (Abbott 1)

Thou wouldst have poisoned good Camillo's honour
To have him kill a king—poor trespasses,
More monstrous standing by, whereof I reckon
The casting forth to crows thy baby daughter
To be or none, or little, though a devil   190
Would have shed water out of fire ere done't.
Nor is't directly laid to thee, the death
Of the young prince, whose honourable thoughts—
Thoughts high for one so tender—cleft the heart
That could conceive a gross and foolish sire   195
Blemished his gracious dam. This is not, no,
Laid to thy answer; but the last—O lords,
When I have said, cry woe!—the Queen, the Queen,
The sweet'st, dear'st creature's dead, and vengeance for't
Not dropped down yet.

LORD   The higher powers forbid!   200

PAULINA
I say she's dead—I'll swear't. If word nor oath
Prevail not, go and see; if you can bring
Tincture or lustre in her lip, her eye,
Heat outwardly or breath within, I'll serve you
As I would do the gods. But O thou tyrant,   205
Do not repent these things, for they are heavier
Than all thy woes can stir; therefore betake thee
To nothing but despair. A thousand knees,
Ten thousand years together, naked, fasting,
Upon a barren mountain, and still winter   210
In storm perpetual could not move the gods
To look that way thou wert.

LEONTES   Go on, go on.

187 **To . . . king** As Malone pointed out,
no one has charged the King with this
except himself, in a speech delivered
while Paulina is off-stage.
188 **More . . . by** compared with the more
monstrous ones you have also committed
190 **or . . . or** either . . . or
191 **shed . . . fire** shed tears while burning
in hell-fire
done he had done
195 **conceive** understand that
196 **dam** Normally used of animals (as *sire*,
in the sense of a parent, also was);

when the word denoted a human
mother, it was usually contemptuous, as
in 2.3.92–5, 'This brat is none of mine,
| . . . Hence with it, and together with
the dam | Commit them to the fire'.
Paulina's sarcasm is the language of
Leontes.
197 **Laid . . . answer** a charge for you to
answer
198 **said** spoken
203 **Tincture** colour
207 **woes . . . stir** sorrows can move
210 **still** always

Thou canst not speak too much; I have deserved
All tongues to talk their bitt'rest.

LORD   Say no more;
Howe'er the business goes, you have made fault   215
I'th' boldness of your speech.

PAULINA   I am sorry for't;
All faults I make, when I shall come to know them,
I do repent. Alas, I have showed too much
The rashness of a woman—he is touched
To th' noble heart. What's gone and what's past help   220
Should be past grief. Do not receive affliction
At my petition; I beseech you, rather
Let me be punished, that have minded you
Of what you should forget. Now, good my liege,
Sir, royal sir, forgive a foolish woman.   225
The love I bore your Queen—lo, fool again!
I'll speak of her no more, nor of your children;
I'll not remember you of my own lord,
Who is lost too. Take your patience to you,
And I'll say nothing.

LEONTES   Thou didst speak but well   230
When most the truth, which I receive much better
Than to be pitied of thee. Prithee bring me
To the dead bodies of my Queen and son.
One grave shall be for both. Upon them shall
The causes of their death appear, unto   235
Our shame perpetual. Once a day I'll visit
The chapel where they lie, and tears shed there
Shall be my recreation. So long as nature
Will bear up with this exercise, so long
I daily vow to use it. Come, and lead me   240
To these sorrows.   *Exeunt*

---

214 **All ... bitt'rest** For the use of the noun with an infinitive as object, see Abbott 354.
220–1 **What's ... grief** Proverbial wisdom: Dent G453.
221–2 **Do ... petition** do not suffer as a result of my entreaty
223 **minded** reminded
228 **remember** remind
229 **Take ... you** make patience your own

230–1 **Thou ... truth** you spoke only well when you spoke most truthfully
238 **recreation** pastime, including its literal sense of 'restoration'
238–9 **nature ... with** my body can endure
239 **exercise** 'habitual occupation' (*OED* 2); also 'the practice and performance of rites and ceremonies' (*OED* 4)

3.3   *Enter Antigonus carrying the baby, and a Mariner*

ANTIGONUS

Thou art perfect, then, our ship hath touched upon

The deserts of Bohemia?

MARINER   Ay, my lord, and fear

We have landed in ill time—the skies look grimly

And threaten present blusters. In my conscience,

The heavens with that we have in hand are angry,   5

And frown upon's.

ANTIGONUS

Their sacred wills be done. Go, get aboard;

Look to thy barque; I'll not be long before

I call upon thee.

MARINER   Make your best haste, and go not

Too far i'th' land; 'tis like to be loud weather.   10

Besides, this place is famous for the creatures

Of prey that keep upon't.

ANTIGONUS   Go thou away,

I'll follow instantly.

MARINER   I am glad at heart

To be so rid o'th' business.   *Exit*

ANTIGONUS   Come, poor babe.

I have heard, but not believed, the spirits o'th' dead   15

May walk again. If such thing be, thy mother

3.3.0.1 *Enter . . . Mariner*] ROWE 1709;   *Enter Antigonus, a Marriner, Babe, Sheepe|-heard, and Clowne.* F

3.3.1 **perfect** certain

1–2 **our . . . Bohemia** For a discussion of this famous crux, see the Introduction, pp. 37–9.

4 **present** imminent
   In my conscience Both 'to my mind' and 'to my moral sense'.

10 **loud** noisy. There is no evidence that the word was used to mean windy, rough (Pafford) or stormy (Schanzer).

12 **keep** live

15–6 **I . . . again** Roman Catholic thinking admitted the existence of ghosts, but Protestantism was sceptical and in the official view, ghosts were delusions produced by the devil. To the drama of the period, however, they were indispensable, and Antigonus keeps all the options open. Like Horatio in the first scene of *Hamlet*, he is initially sceptical, but is

persuaded by 'the sensible and true avouch | Of mine own eyes' (1.1.55–6). This convinces Antigonus that the vision was an apparition, not a dream, and he takes it as conclusive evidence both of Hermione's death and, more surprisingly, of her guilt. At this point in the play, Hermione has certainly been represented as definitively dead; but apparitions of living people were not unknown. Walton's *Life of Donne* recounts how in Paris in 1612 the poet was visited by the spirit of his wife, who was alive in London at the time. David Novarr (*The Making of Walton's Lives* (Ithaca, 1958), p. 111) discusses the story, which he considers apocryphal because Walton got it at second hand; but the issue is not whether it actually happened to Donne, but that Walton

Appeared to me last night, for ne'er was dream
So like a waking. To me comes a creature,
Sometimes her head on one side, some another;
I never saw a vessel of like sorrow   20
So filled, and so becoming. In pure white robes,
Like very sanctity, she did approach
My cabin where I lay, thrice bowed before me,
And, gasping to begin some speech, her eyes
Became two spouts; the fury spent, anon   25
Did this break from her: 'Good Antigonus,
Since fate, against thy better disposition,
Hath made thy person for the thrower-out
Of my poor babe, according to thine oath,
Places remote enough are in Bohemia;   30
There weep, and leave it crying; and for the babe
Is counted lost for ever, Perdita
I prithee call't. For this ungentle business
Put on thee by my lord, thou ne'er shalt see
Thy wife Paulina more.' And so with shrieks   35
She melted into air. Affrighted much,
I did in time collect myself, and thought
This was so, and no slumber. Dreams are toys;
Yet for this once, yea superstitiously,
I will be squared by this. I do believe   40
Hermione hath suffered death, and that
Apollo would, this being indeed the issue
Of King Polixenes, it should here be laid,
Either for life or death, upon the earth
Of its right father. Blossom, speed thee well;   45
     He lays down the baby and a scroll

45.1 *He lays . . . scroll*] ROWE 1709 (*subs.*);   *not in* F

believed it and seventeenth-century
readers would not have found it incredible.

20–1 **vessel . . . filled** The metaphor of the
body as a vessel derives from biblical
usage (*OED* 3a–c). For the image, compare *Julius Caesar* 5.5.13–14, of Brutus:
'Now is that noble vessel full of grief, |
That it runs over even at his eyes.'
21 **becoming** beautifully appropriate
22 **very sanctity** true sanctity, sanctity itself

31 **for** because
32 **counted** reckoned, considered (*OED*,
count, 3)
   Perdita The name means 'lost'.
33 **ungentle** ignoble
38 **toys** trifles
39 **superstitiously**   idolatrously,   i.e.
against the truth of Protestant doctrine.
Compare 5.3.43.
40 **squared** guided, directed (*OED*, square,
v. II.4). Compare 5.1.52.
42 **issue** offspring

There lie, and there thy character; there these,
  He lays down a bundle
Which may, if fortune please, both breed thee, pretty,
And still rest thine. ⌈*Thunder*⌉ The storm begins—poor
  wretch,
That for thy mother's fault art thus exposed
To loss, and what may follow! Weep I cannot,   50
But my heart bleeds, and most accurst am I
To be by oath enjoined to this. Farewell;
The day frowns more and more—thou'rt like to have
A lullaby too rough. I never saw
The heavens so dim by day.
  ⌈*Storm, with a sound of dogs barking and hunting
  horns*⌉
                                A savage clamour!   55
Well may I get aboard!—This is the chase;
I am gone for ever!   *Exit pursued by a bear*
  Enter an Old Shepherd

46.1 *He lays . . . bundle*] JOHNSON; *not in* F   48 *Thunder*] BEVINGTON; *not in* F   55 *Storm
. . . horns*] This edition; *Noise without of Hunters and Dogs* STAUNTON; *not in* F   57.1 *Enter
. . . Shepherd*] ROWE; *Enter a shepherd* F2; *not in* F1

46 **character** written account. The word
literally means 'writing', and the
modern sense, 'personality' or 'inner nature', does not become primary until the
late 17th century.
47 **breed thee** pay for your upbringing
48 **still rest thine** i.e. there will be something left over
50 **loss** both ruin and estrangement (*OED*
I, 2c; compare 2.3.191)
  Weep I cannot As Hermione's appari-
tion had instructed him to do, l. 31.
56 **chase** Johnson explained, 'the animal
pursued'. All editors concur except
Schanzer, who objects that if the hunters are so close that they can be heard
off-stage, they would arrive on-stage in
time to prevent Antigonus from being
eaten. The logic is more rational than
dramatic, but the reading produced
thereby is not unattractive: the 'savage
clamour' (l. 55) then becomes the noise
of the bear, and 'This is the chase' is
explained as 'this is the hunt (and I am
the hunted animal)'.
57.1 **Exit . . . bear** This notorious stage
direction introduces the most famous of

a number of stage bears in the period.
There is a similar incident in the revised
Mucedorus, performed in 1610; in Jonson's masque *Oberon*, performed on New
Year's Day 1611, Oberon's chariot is
drawn by two polar bears; and Jonson's
Masque of Augurs, in 1622, included
John Urson and his troupe of dancing
bears. Like the seacoast of Bohemia, the
stage direction has been a touchstone for
the ambiguities of feeling aroused by the
play, though in this case the ambival-
ences are entirely modern: the bear was
not felt to be a problem until this century. Men in bear suits are, on our stage
at least, inescapably comic, and critics
who wish to keep the moment safe from
comedy have argued that the bear must
therefore have been a real one. Quiller-
Couch, in the Cambridge New Shakespeare, even located a hire service for
the bear, suggesting that the King's Men
had obtained a tame animal from the
nearby Bear-Pit in Southwark. Pafford,
though with some caution, concurs in
these arguments. But Nevill Coghill is
surely correct to insist that no bear has

OLD SHEPHERD I would there were no age between ten and
three-and-twenty, or that youth would sleep out the
rest; for there is nothing in the between but getting   60
wenches with child, wronging the ancientry, stealing,
fighting—hark you now! Would any but these boiled-
brains of nineteen and two-and-twenty hunt this
weather? They have scared away two of my best sheep,
which I fear the wolf will sooner find than the master;   65
if anywhere I have them, 'tis by the seaside, browsing
of ivy. Good luck, an't be thy will, what have we here?
Mercy on's, a bairn! A very pretty bairn—a boy, or a
child, I wonder? A pretty one, a very pretty one—sure
some scape; though I am not bookish, yet I can read   70
waiting-gentlewoman in the scape. This has been some
stair-work, some trunk-work, some behind-door work;

ever been tame enough to be a reliable
performer (*Sh. Survey* 11 (1958), 34–5),
and Schanzer observes that there is a
good deal of evidence of actors in bear-
skins on the Elizabethan stage, but none
that a real bear was ever used. As for the
question of inappropriate comedy, it is
not, of course, clear that Jacobean audiences inevitably found bear suits funny;
but neither is it clear that the moment
was not intended to be comic—Antigonus' death is being clowned up only
thirty lines later, and for Shakespeare's
audience the comedy could certainly
have started with the bear's entrance. In
a treatment of the question that opens it
up to a wider context, Louise G. Clubb
points out that in continental pastoral
drama bears are always both comic and
tragic, and in fact constitute a topos
marking the mixed genre of tragicomedy
('The Tragicomic Bear', *Comparative Literature Studies*, 9 (1972), 17–30). See
the Introduction, pp. 37 ff.

59–60 **the rest** what is 'in the between' (l.
60)
61 **ancientry** old people
62–3 **boiled-brains** The epithet is Shakespeare's coinage, and judging from analogous usage, the sense is probably
'muddle-heads', not hotheads, as it is
generally glossed; compare 'thy brains,
| Now useless, boiled within thy skull'
(*Tempest* 5.1.59–60), and 'Lovers and
madmen have such seething brains'

(*Dream* 5.1.4).
66–7 **by . . . ivy** Echoing *Pandosto*, 'browsing on the sea-ivy, whereon they greatly
do feed' (Appendix B, p. 249). Shakespeare is botanically more correct than
Greene, since there is no plant called
sea-ivy, though Pafford observes that
even ground ivy 'would probably not be
common on the shore'. Wild sheep,
however, will graze on seaweed, and
this may be the plant intended.
68 **bairn** child, a dialect word
69 **child** In dialect, a female child; *OED*
B.I. 1b cites only this passage before the
18th century, but Pafford adds an
example from Greene's *James IV* (pub.
1598), 'Hob your son, and Sib your nut-
brown child', where Sib is a daughter
(ed. N. Sanders, 1970, 5.4.103).
70 **scape** (the result of some) sexual trans-
gression (*OED* 2)
71–2 **some . . . behind-door work** i.e. a
clandestine affair, in which the couple
made love on the stairs, in a trunk,
behind doors. For work as sexual intercourse, compare the exchange between
Sly and Sinklo in the Induction to Mar-
ston's *The Malcontent* (ed. M. L. Wine,
Lincoln, Neb., 1964) 23–31:
SLY Oh, cousin, come, you shall sit between my legs here.
SINKLO No, indeed, cousin: the audience
will then take me for a viol-de-gamba,
and think that you play upon me.
SLY Nay, rather that I work upon you,
coz.

they were warmer that got this than the poor thing is
here. I'll take it up for pity; yet I'll tarry till my son
come; he hallooed but even now. Whoa-ho-hoa!   75
          Enter Clown
CLOWN Hilloa, loa!
OLD SHEPHERD What, art so near? If thou'lt see a thing to
    talk on when thou art dead and rotten, come hither.
    What ail'st thou, man?
CLOWN I have seen two such sights, by sea and by land!   80
    But I am not to say it is a sea, for it is now the sky;
    betwixt the firmament and it you cannot thrust a
    bodkin's point.
OLD SHEPHERD Why, boy, how is it?
CLOWN I would you did but see how it chafes, how it   85
    rages, how it takes up the shore; but that's not to the
    point. O, the most piteous cry of the poor souls!
    Sometimes to see 'em, and not to see 'em; now the ship
    boring the moon with her mainmast, and anon swal-
    lowed with yeast and froth, as you'd thrust a cork into   90
    a hogshead. And then for the land-service, to see how
    the bear tore out his shoulder-bone, how he cried to me
    for help and said his name was Antigonus, a noble-
    man! But to make an end of the ship, to see how the
    sea flapdragoned it; but first, how the poor souls   95
    roared, and the sea mocked them; and how the poor
    gentleman roared, and the bear mocked him; both
    roaring louder than the sea or weather.
OLD SHEPHERD Name of mercy, when was this, boy?
CLOWN Now, now; I have not winked since I saw these   100
    sights; the men are not yet cold under water, nor the
    bear half dined on the gentleman—he's at it now.
OLD SHEPHERD Would I had been by to have helped the old
    man.

73 **got** begot
75 **hallooed** called out
86 **takes up** The relevant senses are 'con-
    tends with', 'swallows up', 'rebukes'.
90 **yeast** foam. Compare 'yeasty waves',
    Macbeth 4.1.69.
91 **hogshead** huge cask of liquid
    land-service military service on land;
    the footsoldier Antigonus, as opposed to
    the sailors just described

95 **flapdragoned** swallowed. Flapdragon is
    a Christmas game 'in which they catch
    raisins out of burning brandy and, extin-
    guishing them by closing the mouth, eat
    them' (Johnson); it is also, by exten-
    sion, the raisin.
97 **gentleman . . . him** i.e. a bear-baiting
    in reverse, with the bear doing the bait-
    ing
100 **winked** closed my eyes, blinked

CLOWN I would you had been by the ship side to have   105
helped her; there your charity would have lacked
footing.

OLD SHEPHERD Heavy matters, heavy matters! But look
thee here, boy. Now bless thyself; thou metst with
things dying, I with things newborn. Here's a sight for   110
thee; look thee, a bearing-cloth for a squire's child;
look thee here, take up, take up, boy, open't.
⌜ *The Clown picks up the bundle* ⌉
So, let's see—it was told me I should be rich by the
fairies. This is some changeling; open't—what's within,
boy?   115
⌜ *The Clown unwraps the bundle* ⌉

CLOWN You're a made old man! If the sins of your youth
are forgiven you, you're well to live. Gold, all gold!

OLD SHEPHERD This is fairy gold, boy, and 'twill prove so.
Up with't, keep it close; home, home the next way. We
are lucky, boy, and to be so still requires nothing but   120
secrecy. Let my sheep go; come, good boy, the next
way home.

CLOWN Go you the next way with your findings, I'll go see
if the bear be gone from the gentleman, and how much
he hath eaten. They are never curst but when they are   125
hungry. If there be any of him left, I'll bury it.

OLD SHEPHERD That's a good deed. If thou mayst discern

112.1 *The . . . bundle*] This edition; *not in* F   115.1 *The . . . bundle*] BEVINGTON; *not in* F
116 made] THEOBALD; mad F

105–7 **would . . . footing** and would
  therefore have been all the more charitable, quibbling on the *foundation* of
  charities
109 **bless thyself** An exclamation of surprise (*OED* 10), like 'God bless us!'
111 **bearing-cloth** baptismal gown
114 **changeling** Fairies were said to take
  beautiful human children and leave ugly
  ones of their own in exchange; the
  noun was used to refer to both the child
  left and, as here, the child taken. See
  Dream 2.1.23.
116 **You're . . . man** i.e. your fortune is
  assured. Theobald's emendation of F's
  mad has been universally accepted. The
  shepherd in *Pandosto* declares himself

'made for ever' (Appendix B, p. 250).
116 **sins . . . youth** Echoing Job 20: 11,
  in the Bishops' Bible 'His bones are full
  of the sins of his youth'.
117 **well to live** well to do (Abbott 356)
119 **close** secret. Staunton observed that
  'to divulge the possession of fairies' gifts
  was supposed to entail misfortune', and
  cited Jonson, 'A prince's secrets are like
  fairy favours | Wholesome if kept, but
  poison if discovered'. I have been unable
  to locate the quotation.
  next nearest
120 **still** always
125 **curst** savage, vicious (*OED*, cursed,
  4b)

by that which is left of him what he is, fetch me to th'
sight of him.

CLOWN Marry, will I; and you shall help to put him i'th'   130
ground.

OLD SHEPHERD 'Tis a lucky day, boy, and we'll do good
deeds on't.   *Exeunt*

4.1   *Enter Time, the Chorus*
TIME
I that please some, try all; both joy and terror
Of good and bad, that makes and unfolds error,
Now take upon me, in the name of Time,
To use my wings. Impute it not a crime
To me or my swift passage that I slide   5
O'er sixteen years, and leave the growth untried
Of that wide gap, since it is in my power
To o'erthrow law, and in one self-born hour
To plant and o'erwhelm custom. Let me pass
The same I am ere ancient'st order was,   10
Or what is now received. I witness to
The times that brought them in; so shall I do
To th' freshest things now reigning, and make stale

---

128 **what he is** both 'who he is' and 'what
his rank is'
130 **Marry** certainly (originally an oath
sworn 'by the Virgin Mary')
4.1.0.1 **Time, the Chorus** The subtitle of
Pandosto reads 'The Triumph of Time.
Wherein is discovered by a pleasant history that although by the means of sinister fortune truth may be concealed, yet
by time, in spite of fortune, it is most
manifestly revealed'; the motto on the
title-page is '*Temporis filia veritas*', Truth
is the daughter of Time.
1 **try** test. 'Time tries all things' was
proverbial (Dent T336).
2 **makes . . . unfolds** For 'make' and
'unfold'; see Abbott 247, and note on
2.3.53.
3 **in the name** under the name: though
he carries his emblematic hourglass
(l. 16), Time also announces his identity. As with Rumour 'painted full of
tongues' in *2 Henry IV* (Induction 0.1–
2), the iconography, however traditional (and in modern accounts

self-explanatory), requires a verbal explanation to identify the figure for the
Renaissance audience.
4 **wings** Cesare Ripa makes Time winged
on the authority of Virgil, '*volat Tempus
irreparabile*' (Time flies inexorably), *Ico-
nologia* (Padua, 1611), p. 511; the Virgilian phrase is *fugit irreparabile Tempus*
(*Georgics* 3.284, and compare *Aeneid*
10.467).
6 **growth untried** developments unexam-
ined or not experienced. The *growth*
of the *gap* troubled 18th-century editors,
and Johnson observed that 'Our author
attends more to his ideas than to his
words.'
8 **self-born hour** hour to which I myself
gave birth. Capell ingeniously suggested
that the 'law' thus overthrown is the
dramatic rule of the unity of time (cited
in the *Variorum*).
10 **The same . . . was** who am the same
as I was at the beginning of time, before
the establishment of laws and customs
11 **received** accepted

The glistering of this present, as my tale
Now seems to it. Your patience this allowing,   15
I turn my glass, and give my scene such growing
As you had slept between; Leontes leaving,
Th'effects of his fond jealousies so grieving
That he shuts up himself. Imagine me,
Gentle spectators, that I now may be   20
In fair Bohemia; and remember well
I mentioned a son o'th' King's, which Florizel
I now name to you, and with speed so pace
To speak of Perdita, now grown in grace
Equal with wond'ring. What of her ensues   25
I list not prophesy, but let Time's news
Be known when 'tis brought forth. A shepherd's
      daughter,
And what to her adheres, which follows after,
Is th'argument of Time. Of this allow,
If ever you have spent time worse ere now;   30
If never, yet that Time himself doth say
He wishes earnestly you never may.   *Exit*

15 **seems to** seems stale in comparison with

16 **I ... glass** The time occupied by the play is thus half over, and that half has lasted an hour. If this is to be taken literally, it implies that the text must have been cut for performance by at least a third. The claim that theatrical performances lasted only two hours is all but universal in the period.

17 **As** as if

17–18 **Leontes ... grieving** (my scene now) leaves Leontes, the effects of whose foolish jealousies so grieve him

19 **Imagine me** F2, followed by many editors including Pafford, Schanzer and Bevington, removes the period after *himself* and ends the sentence here, so that it says 'Imagine me leaving Leontes'. But F's punctuation, which makes 'my scene' is unexceptionable, especially in a speech that is otherwise so contorted and elliptical.

22 **I mentioned** See 1.2.161 ff.; Time presents himself as narrating the play.
   Florizel The name, and the dramatic

situation, appear to come from the popular Spanish romance *Amadis de Grecia* (first published 1535), a continuation of the Amadis of Gaul story, in which Don Florisel is a prince disguised as a shepherd wooing a shepherdess who is in reality a princess.

23 **pace** proceed

25 **with wond'ring** to the growing wonder it inspires

26 **list not** do not intend to (Abbott 349)

27, 28 **daughter ... after** Often a rhyme, and possibly so here, though whether with a pronounced or unpronounced f is uncertain: *dafter* was a dialect spelling of daughter in the period, and after was not uncommonly pronounced 'arter'; see *Shrew* 1.1.237–8, *Lear* 1.4.297–301. *OED* notes that the words also rhyme in *Pilgrim's Progress*. Cercignani (p. 342) considers the case inconclusive.

28 **to her adheres** relates to or concerns her, a usage otherwise unrecorded

29 **argument** theme, subject (*OED* 6)

31 **yet that** yet allow that

4.2   *Enter Polixenes and Camillo*

POLIXENES I pray thee, good Camillo, be no more importunate. 'Tis a sickness denying thee anything, a death
to grant this.

CAMILLO It is fifteen years since I saw my country;
though I have for the most part been aired abroad, I   5
desire to lay my bones there. Besides, the penitent King,
my master, hath sent for me, to whose feeling sorrows
I might be some allay, or I o'erween to think so, which
is another spur to my departure.

POLIXENES As thou lov'st me, Camillo, wipe not out the   10
rest of thy services by leaving me now. The need I have
of thee thine own goodness hath made. Better not to
have had thee than thus to want thee; thou, having
made me businesses which none without thee can
sufficiently manage, must either stay to execute them   15
thyself or take away with thee the very services thou
hast done; which if I have not enough considered—as
too much I cannot—to be more thankful to thee shall
be my study, and my profit therein the heaping friendships. Of that fatal country Sicilia prithee speak no   20
more, whose very naming punishes me with the remembrance of that penitent, as thou call'st him, and
reconciled King my brother, whose loss of his most
precious Queen and children are even now to be afresh
lamented. Say to me, when saw'st thou the Prince   25
Florizel my son? Kings are no less unhappy, their issue
not being gracious, than they are in losing them when
they have approved their virtues.

4.2.4 **fifteen** In 4.1, Time gives the figure
as sixteen, as does Leontes at 5.3.31 and
Camillo at 5.3.50. The number was occasionally emended in the 18th and
19th centuries, but most modern editors
have left it unchanged, presumably regarding the slip, if it is one, as Shakespeare's. It may, however, be a scribal
or compositorial misreading of the
Roman numeral xvi for xv.
5 **been ... abroad** breathed foreign air
7 **feeling** deeply felt
8 **be ... allay** provide some means of
abatement
o'erween presume

13 **want** be without
14 **made me businesses** initiated projects
for me
17 **considered** rewarded
19–20 **heaping friendships** increase of
either your friendly services, or the
friendship between us
24 **are** For 'is'; see Abbott 412 (confusion
of proximity).
26–8 **Kings ... virtues** 'It is as hard for
kings to bear the disobedience and ill
conduct of their children as to lose them
when convinced of their virtues' (Kermode).

CAMILLO Sir, it is three days since I saw the prince. What
  his happier affairs may be are to me unknown, but I   30
  have missingly noted he is of late much retired from
  court, and is less frequent to his princely exercises than
  formerly he hath appeared.

POLIXENES I have considered so much, Camillo, and with
  some care, so far that I have eyes under my service   35
  which look upon his removedness; from whom I have
  this intelligence, that he is seldom from the house of a
  most homely shepherd—a man, they say, that from
  very nothing, and beyond the imagination of his neighbours, is grown into an unspeakable estate.   40

CAMILLO I have heard, sir, of such a man, who hath a
  daughter of most rare note. The report of her is extended
  more than can be thought to begin from such a cottage.

POLIXENES That's likewise part of my intelligence—but, I
  fear, the angle that plucks our son thither. Thou shalt   45
  accompany us to the place, where we will, not appearing what we are, have some question with the shepherd, from whose simplicity I think it not uneasy to get
  the cause of my son's resort thither. Prithee be my
  present partner in this business, and lay aside the   50
  thoughts of Sicilia.

CAMILLO I willingly obey your command.

POLIXENES My best Camillo! We must disguise ourselves.

                                            Exeunt

4.2.53.1 *Exeunt*] ROWE 1709; *Exit* F

30 **are** For 'is', as at line 24.
31 **missingly** i.e. missing him, 'with a
   sense of loss' (*OED*). The word is not
   recorded elsewhere.
32 **frequent to** frequently at
   exercises activities
35-6 **eyes . . . removedness** spies in my
   service who are watching him during
   his absences
37 **intelligence** information

37 **from** away from
38 **homely** simple
39 **very** absolutely
40 **is . . . estate** has come into an incredible fortune
42 **note** distinction (*OED sb.*² IV.19)
45 **angle** fish hook
47 **question** 'the action of questioning, in-
   terrogating, or examining a person . . .;
   hence talk, discourse' (*OED* 2)

4.3   *Enter Autolycus singing*

AUTOLYCUS

> When daffodils begin to peer,
>> With hey, the doxy over the dale,
> Why then comes in the sweet o'the year,
>> For the red blood reigns in the winter's pale.
>
> The white sheet bleaching on the hedge,   5
>> With hey, the sweet birds O how they sing!
> Doth set my pugging tooth on edge,
>> For a quart of ale is a dish for a king.
>
> The lark that tirra lirra chants,
>> With hey, with hey, the thrush and the jay,   10
> Are summer songs for me and my aunts
>> While we lie tumbling in the hay.

I have served Prince Florizel, and in my time wore
three-pile, but now I am out of service.

>> But shall I go mourn for that, my dear?   15
>> The pale moon shines by night,
>> And when I wander here and there,
>> I then do most go right.

4.3.10 With hey, with hey] F2 (with heigh, with heigh); With heigh F1

4.3.0.1 **Autolycus** Literally, 'the wolf himself', in Greek myth the maternal grandfather of Odysseus, and a famous thief and liar. See the Introduction, pp. 50 ff.

1 **peer** 'show itself, come in sight, appear' (*OED* v.² 3). Compare 'Flora | Peering in April's front', 4.4.2–3.

2 **doxy** In canting language, a beggar's mistress, or a beggar-maid, hence a prostitute, or more generally any available woman. Compare Dekker and Middleton's *The Roaring Girl* (ed. P. Mulholland, Manchester, 1987):
OMNES Doxy, Moll, what's that?
MOLL His wench. (5.1.147–8)

4 **pale** (*a*) pallor (*b*) enclave

7 **set . . . edge** To set on edge (or 'set an edge', F's reading) is literally to whet a knife; tooth = taste; hence 'whet my appetite for theft' of the valuable linens drying in the sun. 'To set one's teeth on edge' was proverbial, Dent T431.

7 **pugging** The word must mean thieving, but is otherwise unrecorded. In *The Roaring Girl*, 'puggard' appears in a list of cant words for thieves: 'lifters, nips, foists, puggards, curbers' (5.1.301). To pug is to pull or tug, but it is not clear that this is the same word.

8 **quart of ale** to be bought with the money realized by selling the sheets
dish . . . king Proverbial: Dent D363.1.

9 **tirra lirra** 'a representation of the note of the skylark' (*OED*)

10 **With hey, with hey** F2's doubling of the Folio's 'with heigh' to rectify the metre has been accepted by most editors, but it is more likely, as Dyce suggested, that the name of another bird has been dropped.

11 **aunts** wenches, mistresses (*OED*, aunt, 3). Compare 'doxy', line 2.

14 **three-pile** the thickest and most expensive velvet

18 **I . . . right** I do what is best for me

> If tinkers may have leave to live
>   And bear the sow-skin budget,   20
> Then my account I well may give,
>   And in the stocks avouch it.

My traffic is sheets—when the kite builds, look to lesser
linen. My father named me Autolycus, who, being as I
am littered under Mercury, was likewise a snapper-up   25
of unconsidered trifles. With die and drab I purchased
this caparison, and my revenue is the silly cheat.
Gallows and knock are too powerful on the highway;
beating and hanging are terrors to me. For the life to
come, I sleep out the thought of it. A prize, a prize!   30

Enter Clown

CLOWN Let me see, every 'leven wether tods, every tod
yields pound and odd shilling; fifteen hundred shorn,
what comes the wool to?

AUTOLYCUS (*aside*) If the springe hold, the cock's mine.

CLOWN I cannot do't without counters. Let me see, what   35
am I to buy for our sheep-shearing feast? (*He takes out*

36–7 *He . . . paper*] This edition; *not in* F

19 **tinkers** tinsmiths, who wander the
country but are not arrested for vagabondage

20 **bear . . . budget** carry their pigskin
toolbags; budget = pouch or bag—presumably Autolycus also carries one to
impersonate a tinker (see line 22) and to
hold what he steals

22 **in the stocks** where vagabonds were
put for punishment
avouch it i.e. swear I am a tinker, not
a vagabond, and thus entitled to be freed

23–4 **My . . . linen** 'Just as the kite steals
small pieces of linen to build its nest, my
business is the theft of sheets'

25 **littered . . . Mercury** Both fathered by
Mercury, as the mythical Autolycus was
(see the Introduction, p. 50), and born
when Mercury was in the ascendant.

26–7 **With . . . caparison** through dicing
and whoring I came to these rags. Caparison = originally the covering, often
decorative and ceremonial, for a horse,
and by extension, fancy clothing for
men and women (*OED* 1, 2).

27 **my . . . cheat** my source of income is
simple trickery (or cheating simple folk);
silly = simple, innocent, helpless, ignorant

28 **knock** i.e. the beating he may receive
from his intended victim

29–30 **For . . . it** as for the future (or the
afterlife), I don't worry about it. Com-
pare *Macbeth*: 'If th'assassination |
Could trammel up the consequence . . .
| We'd jump the life to come' (1.7.2–7).

31 **every . . . tods** every eleven sheep produce a tod (12.7 kilos, or 28 lb.) of wool

31–2 **every . . . shilling** i.e. wool sells for
21s. (£1.05) per tod; Pafford, citing J. E.
T. Rogers's *History of Agriculture* (Oxford, 1887), v. 408, notes that between
1572 and 1601 the price of wool at
Eton rose from 20s. 9d. to 25s. 6d. per
tod. For comparison, a penny was a
day's wage for an unskilled labourer.

34 **springe** trap
cock the woodcock, proverbially a
stupid bird (Tilley S788). Compare *Hamlet* 1.3.115, 'springes to catch wood-
cocks'.

35 **counters** pieces 'of metal, ivory,
or other material, formerly used in performing arithmetical operations' (*OED*,
counter, *sb.*[3])

36 **sheep-shearing feast** Sheep-shearing
was done any time between mid-May

a paper) Three pound of sugar, five pound of currants,
rice—what will this sister of mine do with rice? But my
father hath made her mistress of the feast, and she lays
it on. She hath made me four-and-twenty nosegays for   40
the shearers, three-man song men all, and very good
ones, but they are most of them means and basses—but
one puritan amongst them, and he sings psalms to
hornpipes. I must have saffron to colour the warden
pies; mace; dates, none, that's out of my note; nut-   45
megs, seven; a race or two of ginger, but that I may
beg; four pound of prunes, and as many raisins o'th'
sun.

AUTOLYCUS (*grovelling on the ground*) O, that ever I was
born!   50

CLOWN I'th' name of me!

AUTOLYCUS O, help me, help me! Pluck but off these rags,
and then death, death!

CLOWN Alack, poor soul, thou hast need of more rags to
lay on thee, rather than have these off.   55

AUTOLYCUS O sir, the loathsomeness of them offend me
more than the stripes I have received, which are mighty
ones and millions.

---

49 *grovelling . . . ground*] ROWE 1709; *not in* F

and the end of July, and was the occasion for a general celebration. Perdita's
flowers of midsummer (4.4.106–7) suggest a date in late July.

39–40 **lays it on** does it lavishly
41 **three-man song men** singers of part
   songs for three male voices, counter-
   tenor (or alto), tenor, and bass. The
   term 'three-man song' signified at various periods a round or madrigal, a har-
   monized song for three voices, and a
   piece with improvised parts in the alto
   and bass while the tenor carried the
   tune. For a discussion of the various
   changes in usage from the mid 16th
   century to the early 17th, see John Ste-
   vens, *Music and Poetry in the Early Tudor
   Court* (1961), pp. 286–7.
42–4 **means . . . hornpipes** Means are
   boy altos or adult counter-tenors, voices
   in the range between tenor and treble.
   The missing tenor part here is taken by

the psalm-singing puritan: in har-
monized Tudor psalmody, it was typically the tenor who carried the tune.
The puritan sings psalms *even* to hornpipes—i.e. he is not averse to music, but
no music is secular for him.

44 **warden** a variety of baking pears
45 **mace** the spice, the outer coating of
   nutmeg, not the herb
   out . . . note not on my list
46 **race** root
47–8 **raisins o'th' sun** sun-dried raisins
49–50 **that . . . born** Proverbial: Dent
   B140.1.
51 **I' . . . me** An otherwise unrecorded
   oath, and certainly one that would not
   have offended against the Act of Abuses
   (1606) forbidding profanity on the
   stage; compare 'for the life of me', and
   'Before me, she's a good wench' (*Twelfth
   Night* 2.3.172).
56 **offend** For 'offends' (Abbott 412, Confusion of proximity), as at 4.2.24 and 30.

CLOWN Alas, poor man, a million of beating may come to
a great matter.   60

AUTOLYCUS I am robbed, sir, and beaten, my money and
apparel ta'en from me, and these detestable things put
upon me.

CLOWN What, by a horseman or a footman?

AUTOLYCUS A footman, sweet sir, a footman.   65

CLOWN Indeed, he should be a footman, by the garments
he has left with thee—if this be a horseman's coat, it
hath seen very hot service. Lend me thy hand, I'll help
thee. Come, lend me thy hand.

He helps Autolycus up

AUTOLYCUS O good sir, tenderly, O!   70

CLOWN Alas, poor soul!

AUTOLYCUS O good sir, softly, good sir! I fear, sir, my
shoulder-blade is out.

CLOWN How now? Canst stand?

AUTOLYCUS Softly, dear sir; (*he picks the Clown's pocket*)   75
good sir, softly. You ha' done me a charitable office.

CLOWN Dost lack any money? I have a little money for
thee.

AUTOLYCUS No, good sweet sir; no, I beseech you, sir; I
have a kinsman not past three-quarters of a mile hence   80
unto whom I was going. I shall there have money, or
anything I want. Offer me no money, I pray you; that
kills my heart.

CLOWN What manner of fellow was he that robbed you?

AUTOLYCUS A fellow, sir, that I have known to go about   85
with troll-my-dames—I knew him once a servant of the
prince. I cannot tell, good sir, for which of his virtues it
was, but he was certainly whipped out of the court.

CLOWN His vices, you would say—there's no virtue
whipped out of the court; they cherish it to make it stay   90
there, and yet it will no more but abide.

69.1 *He helps . . . up*] ROWE 1709; *not in* F   75 *he picks . . . pocket*] CAPELL; *not in* F

64 **horseman . . . footman** highwayman
. . . footpad. The footpad would have the
poorer garments.
86 **troll-my-dames** or troll-madam, a
game played by women, in which a ball
was rolled either into holes or through

hoops on a board; hence sporting
women, whores
91 **will . . . abide** Usually explained as
'will do no more than pause', 'will only
stay briefly', but *abide* in this sense was
obsolete by the middle of the 16th cen-

AUTOLYCUS Vices I would say, sir. I know this man well.
He hath been since an ape-bearer; then a process-server,
a bailiff; then he compassed a motion of the Prodigal
Son, and married a tinker's wife within a mile where   95
my land and living lies; and having flown over many
knavish professions, he settled only in rogue. Some call
him Autolycus.

CLOWN Out upon him! Prig, for my life, prig! He haunts
wakes, fairs and bear-baitings.   100

AUTOLYCUS Very true, sir; he, sir, he; that's the rogue
that put me into this apparel.

CLOWN Not a more cowardly rogue in all Bohemia—if you
had but looked big and spit at him, he'd have run.

AUTOLYCUS I must confess to you, sir, I am no fighter. I   105
am false of heart that way, and that he knew, I warrant
him.

CLOWN How do you now?

AUTOLYCUS Sweet sir, much better than I was. I can stand
and walk. I will even take my leave of you and pace   110
softly towards my kinsman's.

CLOWN Shall I bring thee on the way?

AUTOLYCUS No, good-faced sir; no, sweet sir.

CLOWN Then fare thee well. I must go buy spices for our
sheep-shearing.   *Exit*   115

AUTOLYCUS Prosper you, sweet sir. Your purse is not hot
enough to purchase your spice. I'll be with you at your
sheep-shearing too—if I make not this cheat bring out
another, and the shearers prove sheep, let me be
unrolled and my name put in the book of virtue!   120

---

tury. Staunton's suggestion, 'will barely,
or only with difficulty, remain' seems
preferable.

93 **ape-bearer** keeper of a performing ape
process-server sheriff's officer who
serves summonses; synonymous with
'bailiff' immediately following

94 **compassed a motion** either acquired
or went about with a puppet-show

94–5 **Prodigal Son** The parable is in Luke
15: 11–32.

96 **living** estate (extending the sense of
land as productive property)

97 **in** upon that of

99 **prig** Here, thief, but the word was also

an opprobrious term for a tinker (*OED
sb.*[3] 1, 2), and is relevant to Autolycus'
determination to impersonate one if he
is apprehended (lines 19–22).

100 **wakes** both vigils for the dead and
country festivals

105–6 **I . . . heart** I have no courage

110–11 **pace softly** walk slowly

112 **bring** accompany

116–17 **not . . . spice** Spice is hot, whereas
empty purses were said to be cold; compare *1 Henry IV*, 'Hot livers, and cold
purses' (2.5.326), and *Timon* 3.4.17.

118 **cheat . . . out** swindle produce

120 **unrolled** removed from the roll of
thieves

(*Sings*)   Jog on, jog on the footpath way,
                      And merrily hent the stile-a;
                      A merry heart goes áll the day,
                      Your sad tires in a mile-a.   *Exit*

4.4   *Enter Florizel and Perdita*

FLORIZEL

These your unusual weeds to each part of you
Does give a life; no shepherdess, but Flora
Peering in April's front. This your sheep-shearing
Is as a meeting of the petty gods,
And you the queen on't.

PERDITA   Sir, my gracious lord,   5
To chide at your extremes it not becomes me—
O pardon that I name them! Your high self,
The gracious mark o'th' land, you have obscured
With a swain's wearing, and me, poor lowly maid,
Most goddess-like pranked up. But that our feasts   10
In every mess have folly, and the feeders
Digest it with a custom, I should blush

4.4.0.1 *Enter . . . Perdita*] ROWE 1709; *Enter Florizell, Perdita, Shepherd, Clowne, Polixenes,*
Camillo, Mopsa, Dorcas, Seruants, Autolicus. F   12 *Digest it*] F2 (disgest it); *Digest* F1

121 **Jog on** A tune with this title in John
    Playford's *Dancing Master* (1651) fits
    these words. The same tune, with varia-
    tions by Richard Farnaby, appears in the
    Fitzwilliam Virginal Book (1609–19)
    under the title 'Hanskin' (no. 197). (See
    Appendix C.)
122 **hent** grasp (to jump over)
123 **A . . . day** 'A merry heart lives long'
    was proverbial: Dent H320a.
4.4.0.1 The scene begins indoors (see lines
    183–4 and 337), but by the time the
    Clown and Shepherd enter at 678.1 it
    seems to be outside—see especially lines
    817–19.
  1 **weeds** garments; 'unusual' because
    she is garlanded with flowers
  2 **Does** Abbott 412 (Confusion of
    proximity); no emendation was con-
    sidered necessary until Theobald's time.
    Flora the nymph Chloris, transformed
    into the goddess of flowers by the love of
    Zephyrus, the west wind (see Ovid, *Fasti*
    5.195 ff.)
  3 **Peering . . . front** appearing as April
    begins (for 'peering' compare 4.3.1)

  4 **petty** lesser
  5 **on't** of it
  6 **extremes** exaggerations (*OED*, extreme,
    C. 5)
  8 **mark o'th' land** object of the whole
    country's attention; mark = 'the object
    desired or striven for' (*OED* 8)
  9 **swain** rustic, shepherd
 10 **pranked up** decked out (*OED*, prank, *v.*
    4); it is Florizel, therefore, who has
    dressed her as Flora (see above, line 2)
    But that were it not for the fact that
 11 **In . . . folly** Either 'foolish antics ac-
    company every dish' or 'every group of
    diners includes some who behave fool-
    ishly'. Most editors cite 1.2.224 in sup-
    port of the latter paraphrase, with 'mess'
    meaning a 'Company of persons [usually
    four] eating together' (*OED* II.4), though
    Schanzer, following Schmidt and Paf-
    ford, argues from 'the sequence of the
    metaphors' for the former, with 'mess'
    meaning a serving of food (*OED* I.1).
    'Digest it' (line 12), however, will sup-
    port either interpretation.
 12 **Digest . . . custom** swallow (i.e. ac-

To see you so attired, swoon, I think,
To show myself a glass.

FLORIZEL   I bless the time
When my good falcon made her flight across   15
Thy father's ground.

PERDITA   Now Jove afford you cause!
To me the difference forges dread—your greatness
Hath not been used to fear. Even now I tremble
To think your father by some accident
Should pass this way, as you did. O, the fates!   20
How would he look to see his work, so noble,
Vilely bound up? What would he say? Or how
Should I in these my borrowed flaunts behold
The sternness of his presence?

FLORIZEL   Apprehend
Nothing but jollity. The gods themselves,   25
Humbling their deities to love, have taken
The shapes of beasts upon them. Jupiter
Became a bull and bellowed; the green Neptune
A ram and bleated; and the fire-robed god,
Golden Apollo, a poor humble swain,   30
As I seem now. Their transformations
Were never for a piece of beauty rarer,
Nor in a way so chaste, since my desires

---

13 swoon] HANMER (*conj.* Theobald); sworne F

cept) it as customary (or from habit) at
such feasts. Dover Wilson and Quiller-
Couch observed that there are no parallels recorded to 'with a custom';
Shakespeare's usual expression is 'of
custom'. They proposed emending 'a
custom' to 'accustom', an obsolete word
for custom or habit; this reading is
adopted by Schanzer (though not by
Dover Wilson and Quiller-Couch themselves). But there are no parallels for
'with accustom' either: the usage in all
the *OED* citations is 'by accustom'.

13–14 **swoon . . . glass** Either 'swoon to
see myself in a glass' or 'swoon to recog-
nize in you a mirror of myself'. Theobald's emendation for F's 'sworne' has
been generally accepted, with the notable exceptions of Sisson (*New Readings*,
i. 199–200) and Bevington, who para-

phrase 'intended, I think, to show me
myself as in a mirror'.

17 **difference** i.e. in social class

21–2 **work . . . up** For the bookbinding
metaphor, compare *Romeo* 3.2.83–4,
'Was ever book containing such vile
matter | So fairly bound?'

23 **flaunts** finery (*OED* 2)

24 Compare *Pandosto*, Appendix B, pp.
260–1.

27–8 **Jupiter . . . bull** when he wooed Eu-
ropa; see Ovid, *Metamorphoses*, 2.847 ff.

28–9 **Neptune . . . ram** wooing Theo-
phane, the daughter of Bisaltis; *Metamorphoses*, 6.117

30 **Apollo . . . swain** Apollo tended the
flocks of Admetus; see Euripides' *Alcestis*.

32 **piece** masterpiece

33 **in a way** Both 'in a fashion' and 'on an
enterprise'.

33–5 **my . . . faith** Prospero twice

Run not before mine honour, nor my lusts
Burn hotter than my faith.

PERDITA   O, but sir,   35
Your resolution cannot hold when 'tis
Opposed, as it must be, by th' power of the King.
One of these two must be necessities,
Which then will speak, that you must change this
    purpose,
Or I my life.

FLORIZEL   Thou dear'st Perdita,   40
With these forced thoughts I prithee darken not
The mirth o'th' feast—or I'll be thine, my fair,
Or not my father's. For I cannot be
Mine own nor anything to any if
I be not thine. To this I am most constant,   45
Though destiny say no. Be merry, gentle;
Strangle such thoughts as these with anything
That you behold the while. Your guests are coming.
Lift up your countenance as it were the day
Of celebration of that nuptial which   50
We two have sworn shall come.

PERDITA   O Lady Fortune,
Stand you auspicious!

    Enter the Old Shepherd, Clown, Mopsa, Dorcas,
    Servants, ⌈*shepherds and shepherdesses*⌉*; Polixenes*
    and Camillo in disguise

FLORIZEL   See, your guests approach.

---

52 *Enter . . . disguise*] ROWE 1709 *(subs.) (after l.* 54); *Enter All* F2; *not in* F1

demands similar assurances from Ferdinand, *Tempest* 4.1.25–9 and 55–6.

35 **faith** fidelity to my promise (to marry
Perdita)

38 **One . . . two** each of these

39–40 **you . . . life** The syntax clearly in-
volves a zeugma ('you change your purpose or I change my life'), but the
overwhelming consensus of editors, with
Furness almost the sole exception, is
that Perdita is anticipating a death sentence—'her words, so emphatic and absolute at the end of her speech, can
surely refer to death alone' (Dover Wilson). The only evidence for this, how-

ever, is proleptic, Polixenes' threats at
lines 419–23, and there is no reason to
override Perdita's syntax in this way:
Polixenes' behaviour surely comes as a
surprise.

41 **forced** strained, unnatural (*OED* 3, 3c)

42–3 **or . . . Or** either . . . or

46 **gentle** Compare Antony to Cleopatra,
'Gentle, hear me', *Antony* 4.16.49.

47 **Strangle** stifle, check (*OED* 3, 3b). Com-
pare 'fear | That makes thee strangle
thy propriety', *Twelfth Night* 5.1.144–5.

49 **as** as if

52.1 **Mopsa, Dorcas** Mopsa is the shepherd's wife in *Pandosto*; the name had
earlier appeared in Sidney's *Arcadia*.

Address yourself to entertain them sprightly,
And let's be red with mirth.

OLD SHEPHERD

  Fie, daughter, when my old wife lived, upon 55
This day she was both pantler, butler, cook;
Both dame and servant; welcomed all, served all;
Would sing her song and dance her turn; now here
At upper end o'th' table, now i'th' middle;
On his shoulder, and his; her face o'fire 60
With labour, and the thing she took to quench it
She would to each one sip. You are retired,
As if you were a feasted one and not
The hostess of the meeting. Pray you bid
These unknown friends to's welcome, for it is 65
A way to make us better friends, more known.
Come, quench your blushes and present yourself
That which you are, mistress o'th' feast. Come on,
And bid us welcome to your sheep-shearing,
As your good flock shall prosper.

PERDITA (*to Polixenes*)   Sir, welcome. 70
It is my father's will I should take on me
The hostess-ship o'th' day. (*To Camillo*) You're
    welcome, sir.
Give me those flowers there, Dorcas. Reverend sirs,
For you there's rosemary and rue; these keep
Seeming and savour all the winter long. 75

61 it‸] FI; ~; F4

Dorcas, otherwise Tabitha, is the woman of Joppa 'full of good works' whom St Peter restores to life in Acts, 9: 36–41, and hence a prototype of Hermione.

53 **Address** prepare (*OED* 3)
54 **red** flushed (as the sign of excitement and a healthy complexion)
56 **pantler, butler** servants in charge of the pantry and cellar, hence of bread and liquor, respectively
57 **dame** mistress of the house
60 **On . . . his** at one man's shoulder (serving him), and then at another's
61 **With . . . it** Many 18th- and 19th-century editors, following F4, insert a strong mark of punctuation after 'it', so

that the wife becomes flushed from both labour and drink. Recent editors have preferred F's pointing, with the notable exception of Schanzer, who compares Cleopatra's fans, which 'did seem | To glow the delicate cheeks which they did cool, | And what they undid did' (*Antony* 2.2.210–12).
62 **She . . . sip** more likely 'she would drink to each in turn' than 'she would give one sip to each of the guests'
  retired withdrawn
65 **unknown . . . to's** For the construction, see Abbott 419a (transposition of adjectival phrases).
75 **Seeming and savour** appearance and scent

Grace and remembrance be to you both,
And welcome to our shearing.

POLIXENES   Shepherdess—
A fair one are you—well you fit our ages
With flowers of winter.

PERDITA   Sir, the year growing ancient,
Not yet on summer's death nor on the birth   80
Of trembling winter, the fairest flowers o'th' season
Are our carnations and streaked gillyvors,
Which some call nature's bastards; of that kind
Our rustic garden's barren, and I care not
To get slips of them.

POLIXENES   Wherefore, gentle maiden,   85
Do you neglect them?

PERDITA   For I have heard it said
There is an art which in their piedness shares
With great creating nature.

POLIXENES   Say there be,

76 **Grace and remembrance** Common-place significations of rue (the word means sorrow or repentance, hence implying the access of grace) and rosemary respectively: compare *Hamlet* 4.5.175–81: 'There's rosemary, that's for remembrance. . . . There's rue for you. . . . We may call it herb-grace'. Both have obvious relevance to Leontes. See the summary of popular flower symbolism in 'A Nosegay Always Sweet', published first in Clement Robinson's *Handful of Pleasant Delights* (1584), which observes that 'Rosemary is for remembrance between us day and night'.

79 **the . . . ancient** when autumn comes

82 **carnations . . . gillyvors** (= gilly-flowers, pinks) both cultivated forms of dianthus; the streaked gillyflower is described by Bacon as a natural hybrid: 'Take gillyflower seed of one kind of gillyflower . . . and sow it, and there will come up gillyflowers, some of one colour, and some of another . . . as purple, carnation of several stripes' (cited by Pafford, p. 170). The gillyflower or gillyvor was originally the term for clove, and thence was applied to any clove-scented plant; 'in dialects in which the word is still current, it is commonly applied either to the wallflower . . . or to

the white stock' (*OED*, gillyflower, 2). To Grigson, it is synonymous with stock (*The Englishman's Flora* (1955), p. 63).

83 **bastards** The term was used for both hybrids and counterfeits (*OED*, bastard, 2, 4).

87–103 The controversy between the claims of art and nature was a Renaissance topos. Analogues to Perdita's argument can be found in Montaigne, e.g. 'in [wild fruits] are the . . . natural properties most lively and vigorous, which in these we have bastardized, applying them to the pleasure of our corrupted taste' ('Of the Cannibals', *Essays*, trans. John Florio (1632), p. 102), and analogues to Polixenes' in Puttenham, e.g. 'art is an aid and coadjutor to nature, or peradventure a mean to supply her wants . . ., an alterer of them, and in some sort a surmounter of her skill, so as by means of it her own effects shall appear more beautiful or strange and miraculous' (*The Art of English Poesy*, ed. Willcock and Walker (1936), pp. 303 ff.); see Kermode's introduction to the Arden *Tempest* (London, 1954), pp. xxxv–xxxvi. For a discussion of the characteristically inconclusive debate, see the Introduction, p. 46.

87 **piedness** parti-colour

Yet nature is made better by no mean
But nature makes that mean; so over that art   90
Which you say adds to nature, is an art
That nature makes. You see, sweet maid, we marry
A gentler scion to the wildest stock,
And make conceive a bark of baser kind
By bud of nobler race. This is an art   95
Which does mend nature—change it rather—but
The art itself is nature.

PERDITA   So it is.

POLIXENES

Then make your garden rich in gillyvors,
And do not call them bastards.

PERDITA   I'll not put
The dibble in earth to set one slip of them;   100
No more than, were I painted, I would wish
This youth should say 'twere well, and only therefore
Desire to breed by me. Here's flowers for you,
Hot lavender, mints, savoury, marjoram,
The marigold that goes to bed wi'th' sun,   105
And with him rises weeping—these are flowers

98 your] F2; you F1

89 **mean** means
93 **gentler** more cultivated, with social overtones (compare 'nobler race', line 95)
100 **dibble** the gardener's tool for making
   holes to plant cuttings
101 **were I painted** if I were wearing
   make-up (and were thus, like the gilly-
   flowers, made attractive by art); but the
   art of painting is not 'nature'
104–27 Perdita's list of flowers descends
   from a long tradition of flower catalogues. Both Theocritus (Idyll 11.45,
   56–7) and Virgil (Eclogue 2.45–50)
   offer the beloved gifts of flowers; Bion's
   Lament for Adonis (75–6) decks the subject's bier with them, and Moschus' *Lament for Bion* (5–7) calls on the rose,
   hyacinth, and other flowers to mourn
   for him—compare Florizel's assumption
   in line 129 that Perdita is thinking of
   him as a corpse. The numerous Renaissance examples include Marot's elegy on
   the death of Louise of Savoy (225–40),
   Castiglione's *Alcon* (142–50), Spenser's
   April ecologue of the *Shepheardes Calen-*

der (60–3, 136–44) and *Lay of Clorinda*
(70–2). Notable later examples in-
fluenced by Shakespeare include Jonson's extraordinarily elaborated list in
Pan's Anniversary (21–40), and Milton's
in *Lycidas* (142–51). See the Introduction, pp. 43–5.

104 **Hot lavender** Plants, like people, had
   temperatures (or temperaments) determined by the proportion of humours
   they contained (see *OED*, temperature,
   4). According to Dodoens's *Herbal*
   (1578), p. 265, lavender is 'hot and dry
   in the second degree'.
105–6 **marigold . . . weeping** Nine-
   teenth-century editors debated whether
   the reference was not in fact to the
   sunflower, but Pafford quotes T. Hill's
   Profitable Art of Gardening (1597), pp.
   93–4, on the marigold or *calendula offici-
   nalis*: 'after the rising of the sun unto
   noon, this flower openeth larger and
   larger, but after the noon time unto the
   setting of the sun, the flower closeth and
   shutteth more and more so that after the

Of middle summer, and I think they are given
To men of middle age. You're very welcome.

CAMILLO
I should leave grazing were I of your flock,
And only live by gazing.

PERDITA   Out, alas!   110
You'd be so lean that blasts of January
Would blow you through and through. (*To Florizel*)
      Now, my fair'st friend,
I would I had some flowers o'th' spring, that might
Become your time of day; (*to the Shepherdesses*) and
      yours, and yours,
That wear upon your virgin branches yet   115
Your maidenheads growing—O Proserpina,
For the flowers now that frighted thou letst fall
From Dis's wagon! Daffodils,
That come before the swallow dares, and take
The winds of March with beauty; violets dim,   120
But sweeter than the lids of Juno's eyes

setting of the sun, the flower is then
wholly shut up together'. It 'rises weeping' presumably because it is wet with
morning dew.

108 **To . . . age** Perdita rectifies the impli-
cation of the 'flowers of winter' that
Polixenes and Camillo are elderly (see
lines 78–9).

110 **Out** A mild exclamation of reproach.

116–18 **Proserpina . . . wagon** The story
of the abduction of Proserpina by Dis, or
Pluto, is in Ovid, *Metamorphoses*, 5.391
ff. In Golding's translation (lines 491 ff.),
      While in this garden Proserpine was
      taking her pastime,
      In gathering either violets blue, or lilies
      white as lime . . .
      Dis spied her, loved her, caught her
      up . . .
      And as she from the upper part her
      garment would have rent,
      By chance she let her lap slip down, and
      out the flowers went.
For a discussion of the significance of the
Proserpina story to the play, see the
Introduction, pp. 44–6.

118–20 **Daffodils . . . March** According to
Gerard, 'They flower for the most part in
the spring, that is, from the beginning

of February unto the end of April'
(*Herbal . . . amended by Thomas Johnson*,
1597, i. 17). Attempts to regularize the
metre of l. 118 began with Hanmer
(1744) and Capell (1765), who read
'early daffodils'; Coleridge, who argued
that 'an epithet is wanted here, not
merely or chiefly for the metre, but for
the balance, for the aesthetic logic', suggested 'golden daffodils' (adopted by
Hudson, 1880); Keightley (1864)
printed 'yellow daffodils'. By 1931, and
the publication of Quiller-Couch and
Dover Wilson's New Shakespeare, the
line was being allowed to pass without
comment. (See Abbott 509, lines with
four accents.)

119 **take** affect, enchant. Compare *Tempest*
5.1.316–7, 'the story of your life, which
must | Take the ear strangely'; *Hamlet*
1.1.144, 'No fairy takes, nor witch hath
power to charm'.

120 **dim** Variously explained as modest,
homely, unassuming (in comparison
with daffodils); less persuasively, as
half-hidden (because they droop), or—
least persuasively—as the white variety
of violet praised by Bacon in *Of Gardens*.

121–2 **sweeter . . . breath** Schanzer explains, 'sweeter to *behold* than the lids of

Or Cytherea's breath; pale primroses,
That die unmarried ere they can behold
Bright Phoebus in his strength—a malady
Most incident to maids; bold oxlips and   125
The crown imperial; lilies of all kinds,
The flower-de-luce being one—O, these I lack
To make you garlands of, and my sweet friend,

Juno's eyes, sweeter to *smell* than the breath of Venus'. There has been much inconclusive comment on the selection of eyelids for special praise, but it is clear that these constituted a significant point of feminine beauty in the period. Malone compared Spenser: 'Upon her eyelids many graces sat, | Under the shadow of her even brows' (*Faerie Queene* 2.3.25), and the association of Juno with beautiful eyelids contributes to the praise of Thaisa and Marina in *Pericles*: 'her eyes as jewel-like, | And cased as richly, in pace another Juno' (Scene 21, 99–100 [i.e. 5.1.110–11]).

122 **Cytherea** Venus, from her birthplace out of sea-foam near the island of Cythera
pale primroses *Primula vulgaris*, not the lurid border flowers of modern gardens, but the fifth and seventh of Gerard's types of cowslips, 'the common whitish yellow field primrose', and 'a primrose with greenish flowers somewhat welted about the edges' (*Herbal*, 1597, ii. 118).

123–5 **That . . . maids** Primroses 'die unmarried ere they can behold | Bright Phoebus in his strength' because they are the earliest flowers of spring and have stopped blooming before the warm weather comes; the 'malady most incident to maids' is the green sickness, chlorosis, an anaemic condition affecting pubescent girls; the connection between the two is explained in Herrick's 'How Primroses Came Green':

Virgins, time past, known were these,
Troubled with green sicknesses,
Turned to flowers; still the hue,
Sickly girls, they bear of you.

Compare also Milton's 'rathe [early] primrose that forsaken dies' (*Lycidas*, l. 142), probably echoing Shakespeare—in the version preserved in the Trinity MS, the primrose dies 'unwedded'.

124 **Phoebus** Apollo as the sun god

125 **incident to** 'liable or apt to befall' (*OED* 1)
bold oxlips *Primula veris* x *vulgaris*: like the primrose, the oxlip in Gerard is a variety of cowslip, 'and differeth not from [field cowslips] save that the flowers are not so thick thrust together, and they are fairer, and not so many in number, and do not smell so pleasant as the other'. Steevens explained that the oxlip is 'bold' because it 'has not a weak flexible stalk like the cowslip, but erects itself boldly in the face of the sun' (cited in the *Variorum*)—the audacity is reflected in the gender implications of the names. In Grigson, the oxlip is 'the coarse hybrid between primrose and cowslip, which lacks the charm of either parent' (*The Englishman's Flora*, p. 267). Gerard adds a possibly relevant note: 'of [oxlips] we have one lately come into our gardens, whose flowers are curled and wrinkled after a most strange manner, which our women have named Jackanapes on horseback' (*Herbal*, 1597, ii. 118; the epithet was also used by 'the vulgar sort of women' for the marigold, ii. 112).

126 **crown imperial** *Fritillaria imperialis*: 'the flowers grow at the top of the stalk, encompassing it round in form of an imperial crown, . . . hanging their heads downward as it were bells; in colour it is yellowish . . . This plant . . . hath been brought from Constantinople amongst other bulbous roots, and made denizens in our London gardens.' They are, Gerard adds, 'greatly esteemed for the beautifying . . . of the bosoms of the beautiful' (*Herbal*, 1597, i. 28).

127 **flower-de-luce** or fleur-de-lis, the heraldic lily borne on the arms of France, but botanically the iris (*Herbal*, 1597, i. 10), and distinguished from the lily in, e.g., Jonson: 'Bring rich carnations, flower-de-luces, lilies' (*Pan's Anniversary*, 1620, l. 29), and Spenser: 'The lily, lady of the flowering field | The

To strew him o'er and o'er.

FLORIZEL　　　　　　　　　　　What, like a corpse?

PERDITA

No, like a bank for love to lie and play on,　　　　　130
Not like a corpse; or if, not to be buried,
But quick, and in mine arms. Come, take your
　　　flowers;
Methinks I play as I have seen them do
In Whitsun pastorals—sure this robe of mine
Does change my disposition.

FLORIZEL　　　　　　　　　　　What you do　　　　135
Still betters what is done. When you speak, sweet,
I'd have you do it ever; when you sing,
I'd have you buy and sell so, so give alms,
Pray so, and for the ord'ring your affairs,
To sing them too. When you do dance, I wish you　　140
A wave o'th' sea, that you might ever do
Nothing but that; move still, still so,
And own no other function. Each your doing,
So singular in each particular,
Crowns what you are doing in the present deeds,　　145
That all your acts are queens.

129, 131 corpse] F (coarse)

flower-de-luce, her lovely paramour' (*Faerie Queene* 2.6.16). To class it as a lily, therefore, is not botany but heraldry, and royal heraldry at that.

131-2 **not . . . quick** taking 'corpse' to mean 'the living body of a person' (*OED* 1)

132 **quick** alive

134 **Whitsun pastorals** Pentecost, or Whitsuntide, the seventh Sunday after Easter, was celebrated with plays and morris dances; compare Julia, dressed as a boy, in *Two Gentlemen* 4.4.155 ff.:

　　at Pentecost,
When all our pageants of delight were
　　played,
Our youth got me to play the woman's
　　part . . .

'Pastoral' specifically denoted a play depicting the life of shepherds, or the country life generally; but it was extended to cover almost any kind of recreative entertainment—Milton refers

to the Song of Solomon as 'a divine pastoral drama' (cited under *OED* 3).

135-6 **What . . . done** (*a*) 'each of your actions is better than the one before'; (*b*) 'whatever you do is done better than whatever anyone else does'; (*c*) 'the fact that it is you who perform an action makes it better—i.e. you bring something special to every action'

136 **Still** always

142 **Nothing . . . so** For the metrics, see Abbott 509: 'Lines with four accents are found where a number of short clauses . . . are connected together in one line, and must be pronounced slowly.'

still, still Connoting, as part of the wave image, both perpetual movement and stillness.

143-5 **Each . . . deeds** 'Your way of doing everything (so peculiarly your own in every particular) crowns what you are at present doing' (Furness); crowns = perfects, completes worthily (*OED*, crown, *v.*[1] 9).

PERDITA   O Doricles,
  Your praises are too large. But that your youth
  And the true blood which peeps fairly through't
  Do plainly give you out an unstained shepherd,
  With wisdom I might fear, my Doricles,   150
  You wooed me the false way.
FLORIZEL   I think you have
  As little skill to fear as I have purpose
  To put you to't. But come, our dance, I pray.
  Your hand, my Perdita—so turtles pair,
  That never mean to part.
PERDITA   I'll swear for 'em.   155
      ⌈ *Florizel and Perdita dance* ⌉
POLIXENES (*to Camillo*)
  This is the prettiest low-born lass that ever
  Ran on the greensward. Nothing she does or seems
  But smacks of something greater than herself,
  Too noble for this place.
CAMILLO   He tells her something
  That makes her blood look on't—good sooth, she is   160
  The queen of curds and cream.
CLOWN Come on, strike up!
DORCAS Mopsa must be your mistress; marry, garlic to
  mend her kissing with!

---

157 greensward] F (greene-sord)   160 on't] F; out THEOBALD

146 **Doricles** Florizel's name in disguise;
  Doric, from Doris, in Greece, was used to
  mean rustic, as the Doric order was the
  simplest of the Greek architectural orders.
147 **But that** if it were not for the fact that
148 **true blood** Both 'virtuous passion'
  and 'noble lineage'.
152 **skill** 'cause, reason, or ground'
  (*OED* 3)
154 **turtles** turtle-doves, said to be
  monogamous, and hence 'a type of con-
  jugal affection and constancy' (*OED* 1).
  'As true as a turtle to her mate' was
  proverbial, Dent T624. Compare
  5.3.132.
155 **I'll . . . 'em** I'll be sworn they do
160 **blood . . . on't** blush. Theobald's
  emendation 'look out' has been widely
  accepted, but both the apostrophe and
  the usage argue against it.

161 **queen . . . cream** The New Shakespeare editors quote Douce to the effect
  that the queen in western May games
  was called a 'white-pot queen'; 'white-
  pot in old cookery was a kind of custard,
  made in a crust or dish with cream,
  eggs, pulse of apples, sugar, spices, and
  sippets of white or manchet [fine wheat]
  bread' (*Illustrations of Shakespeare*, 1807,
  ii. 457). (See also the Stephen Batman
  citation in the *OED* under white-pot.)
162–7 Prose in F, but Pope, who assumed
  that whatever could be treated as verse
  should be, rearranged the passage accordingly, and has been widely followed,
  even, in this century, by the New
  Shakespeare editors and Bevington.
  Mopsa, Dorcas and the Clown do not
  speak verse elsewhere.
163 **marry** a mild exclamation, originally
  an oath sworn by the Virgin Mary

MOPSA Now, in good time!   165
CLOWN Not a word, a word; we stand upon our manners.
   Come, strike up!
      Music. Here a dance of Shepherds and Shepherdesses
POLIXENES
   Pray, good shepherd, what fair swain is this
   Which dances with your daughter?
OLD SHEPHERD
   They call him Doricles, and boasts himself   170
   To have a worthy feeding; but I have it
   Upon his own report, and I believe it—
   He looks like sooth. He says he loves my daughter;
   I think so too; for never gazed the moon
   Upon the water as he'll stand and read,   175
   As 'twere, my daughter's eyes; and to be plain,
   I think there is not half a kiss to choose
   Who loves another best.
POLIXENES   She dances featly.
OLD SHEPHERD
   So she does anything, though I report it
   That should be silent. If young Doricles   180
   Do light upon her, she shall bring him that
   Which he not dreams of.
      Enter Servant
SERVANT O master, if you did but hear the pedlar at the
   door you would never dance again after a tabor and
   pipe; no, the bagpipe could not move you. He sings   185

167.1 *Music*] MALONE; *not in* F

163–4 **garlic . . . with** give her garlic to
   sweeten her kisses

165 **in good time** An expression of indignation; compare Iago on Cassio: 'He
   in good time must his lieutenant be',
   Othello 1.1.31.
166 **stand upon** are particular about
   (Onions)
170 **boasts** 'Where there can be no doubt
   what is the nominative, it is sometimes
   omitted' (Abbott 399).
171 **have . . . feeding** own rich grazing
   land
173 **like sooth** truthful

175 **as** i.e. as steadfastly as
178 **another** the other (Abbott 88)
   featly elegantly
179–80 **though . . . silent** Proverbial: Dent
   S114.
184 **after** to
184–5 **tabor and pipe** A tabor is a drum
   that hangs at one's side, and the pipe is
   the tabor-pipe, designed to be played
   with one hand. The combination was
   associated with rustic dances. See *Tempest* 3.2.126.1; the Oxford edition includes an illustration of Will Kemp
   performing on the instruments.

several tunes faster than you'll tell money; he utters
them as he had eaten ballads, and all men's ears grew
to his tunes.

CLOWN He could never come better; he shall come in. I
love a ballad but even too well, if it be doleful matter   190
merrily set down, or a very pleasant thing indeed, and
sung lamentably.

SERVANT He hath songs for man or woman of all sizes—
no milliner can so fit his customers with gloves. He has
the prettiest love songs for maids, so without bawdry,   195
which is strange, with such delicate burdens of dildos
and fadings, 'jump her and thump her'; and where
some stretch-mouthed rascal would, as it were, mean

186 **tell** count
187 **as** as if
    ballads Broadside ballads (so called be-
    cause they were printed on one side of a
    large sheet of paper), on romantic
    themes, current events or prodigious
    happenings (see, e.g., lines 260, 273
    ff.), and set to popular tunes, were a
    staple of itinerant pedlars, both to per-
    form and sell.
187-8 **all . . . tunes** 'grew to' = were irre-
    sistibly attracted to; but also alluding to
    the story of Midas, who grew asses' ears
    as a punishment for preferring the sensual
    music of Pan to the rational music of
    Apollo (Ovid, *Metamorphoses*, 11.146 ff.)
190-2 **doleful . . . lamentably** Recalling
    the 'very tragical mirth' of *Pyramus and
    Thisbe*, *Dream* 5.1.57, but with a generic
    relevance as well to the play as a
    whole—in Sidney's words, to 'mongrel
    tragicomedy', 'mingling kings and
    clowns' (*Defense of Poesie*, in *Miscella-
    neous Prose*, ed. K. Duncan-Jones and
    Jan van Dorsten (Oxford, 1973),
    p. 114). See the Introduction, pp. 3–6.
194 **milliner** haberdasher; originally a
    vendor of fancy apparel of the sort
    manufactured at Milan (*OED* 2a)
196 **burdens** refrains
196-7 **dildos, fadings** Both terms are
    found in the refrains of 17th-century
    ballads the verses of which are not, for
    the most part, obscene (see Chappell,
    Popular Music of the Olden Time (1859),
    i. 234). In context, both are nonsense
    words, e.g.,

      With a hie, dildo, dill,
      Hie do, dil dur lie.

But obscene ballads are much less likely
to survive in printed sources, and 'dildo'
as a term for an artificial penis was
certainly in common usage by Shakespeare's time: Nashe's *Choice of Valen-
tines* (1593) uses the word twice (not
recorded in the *OED*), and Jonson has
'Madame, with a dildo, writ o' the
walls', *Alchemist* 5.5.42. In any case,
merely to take the word out of its context, as the Servant does, was thereby to
render it obscene. The fading, or fad-
ding, was the name of an Irish dance,
and 'With a fading' was the refrain of a
popular song said by the *OED* to be 'of
an indecent character' (fading *sb.*[1]), but
(as is usually the case when this claim is
made) no song is cited, and the songs
with this refrain in Chappell and in the
Pepys Ballads are not obscene. Frankie
Rubinstein's otherwise compendious
and ingenious *Dictionary of Shakespeare's
Sexual Puns* (1984) is eloquent on dildos,
burdens, even pins, but has no entry
whatever for fadings. Partridge suggests
that the word means having an orgasm
(compare 'dying'); he provides no
examples of its use in this sense, but the
context of the passage alone seems sufficient evidence of an indecent connota-
tion, even if only the one implied by the
juxtaposition of an otherwise innocent
word with 'dildo'—this, indeed, may be
the point of the joke. It is worth remarking, finally, that the association of bal-
ladry with bawdry was always present,
whatever the nominal subject matter.
198 **stretch-mouthed** bigmouth

mischief, and break a foul gap into the matter, he makes
the maid to answer, 'Whoop, do me no harm, good   200
man'—puts him off, slights him with 'Whoop, do me no
harm, good man'.

POLIXENES This is a brave fellow.

CLOWN Believe me, thou talkest of an admirable conceited
fellow. Has he any unbraided wares?   205

SERVANT He hath ribbons of all the colours i'th' rainbow;
points, more than all the lawyers in Bohemia can
learnedly handle, though they come to him by th'
gross; inkles, caddises, cambrics, lawns—why, he sings
'em over as they were gods or goddesses. You would   210
think a smock were a she-angel, he so chants to the
sleeve-hand and the work about the square on't.

CLOWN Prithee bring him in, and let him approach singing.

PERDITA Forewarn him that he use no scurrilous words
in's tunes.   *Exit Servant*   215

CLOWN You have of these pedlars that have more in them
than you'd think, sister.

PERDITA Ay, good brother, or go about to think.

215 *Exit Servant*] CAPELL; *not in* F

199 **break . . . matter** interpolate something indecent into the song. The ballad
is a dialogue between a man and
woman, with the man's incipient rib-
aldry repeatedly cut short by the
woman's reply. 'Gap' has been found
problematic, and in the 19th century
was often emended to 'jape', which is
not a possible form of 'gap' and is not
used by Shakespeare elsewhere.

200–1 **Whoop . . . man** A tune with this
title appears in William Corkine's *Ayres,
to sing and play to the lute and basse viol*
(1610), sig. IIb. Chappell (i. 208) cites a
version of the song in John Fry's *Pieces
of Ancient Poetry* (1814), adding that 'it
would not be desirable for republica-
tion'. The citation, however, is a red
herring; Fry's ballad is mildly bawdy,
but it is only sung to the tune of 'Whoop
do me no harm'; its subject is the Overbury scandal, and it therefore postdates
the play.

203 **brave** fine

204 **admirable conceited** marvellously
witty

205 **unbraided wares** Braided wares are

'goods that have changed colour, tarn-
ished, faded'; *OED*, braided cites Mars-
ton's *Scourge of Villainy* 1.3.185, 'To
yeeld his braided ware a quicker sale'.
Unbraided wares are therefore those that
are fresh, not shopworn.

206 **all . . . rainbow** Proverbial: Dent
C519.

207 **points** laces, with a pun on legal arguments

208–9 **by . . . gross** A gross is twelve
dozen; hence, in huge quantities.

209 **inkles** coarse linen tape
caddises caddis (= coarse cloth) ribbons, worsted tape used as garters; see
1 Henry IV 2.5.69–70 (2.4.69 in traditional numbering)
cambrics, lawns both kinds of fine
linen

210 **as** as if

212 **sleeve-hand** cuff
square the yoke of the dress (the piece
covering the bosom: *OED* 10a), here
embroidered

216 **You . . . that** some of these pedlars

218 **go about** would care

*Enter Autolycus wearing a false beard, carrying his
pack, singing*

AUTOLYCUS

Lawn as white as driven snow,
Cypress black as e'er was crow,   220
Gloves as sweet as damask roses,
Masks for faces and for noses,
Bugle-bracelet, necklace-amber,
Perfume for a lady's chamber,
Golden coifs and stomachers   225
For my lads to give their dears,
Pins and poking-sticks of steel;
What maids lack from head to heel—
Come buy of me, come, come buy, come buy;
Buy, lads, or else your lasses cry; come buy.   230

CLOWN If I were not in love with Mopsa, thou shouldst
take no money of me; but being enthralled as I am, it
will also be the bondage of certain ribbons and gloves.

MOPSA I was promised them against the feast, but they
come not too late now.   235

DORCAS He hath promised you more than that, or there
be liars.

MOPSA He hath paid you all he promised you; maybe he

218.1–2 *wearing . . . pack,*] OXFORD (*subs.*)   228 heel—] F (~:); ~ ‸ SCHANZER

219–30 The pedlar's pack song was a
popular topos; compare, e.g., Dow-
land's *Fine knacks for ladies*. A setting for
the song by John Wilson appears in
Cheerful Ayres or Ballads (1660); see
Appendix C.
219 **Lawn** fine linen
   white . . . snow Proverbial: Dent
   S591.
220 **Cypress** crape, fine gauze
   black . . . crow Proverbial: Dent
   C844.
221 **Gloves . . . roses** Gloves were commonly perfumed; 'sweet as a rose' was
   proverbial (Dent R178).
222 **for noses** as protection from the sun
223 **Bugle-bracelet** bracelets of glass
   beads
225 **coifs** close-fitting caps 'covering the
   top, back and sides of the head' (*OED*)
   stomachers ornamental coverings for
   the stomach and chest

227 **poking-sticks** rods used to iron
   starched ruffs
228 **What . . . heel** F ends the line with a
   colon, which most editors replace with
   a period or an exclamation point. But
   a colon is not the end of a sentence.
   Schanzer observes that the stop is intru-
   sive, and omits it entirely. The passage
   thus revised undeniably makes better
   sense, though possibly only to modern
   sensibilities. The musical setting, however, which, if not original, is at least
   very nearly contemporary, is emphatic
   about the pause after 'heel'. The dash of
   the present edition is intended to
   preserve both the pause and the ambiguous syntax.
   from . . . heel Proverbial: Dent T436.
232–3 **it . . . gloves** i.e. ribbons and gloves
   will have to be tied up into a parcel
234 **against** in time for

has paid you more, which will shame you to give him
again. 240
CLOWN Is there no manners left among maids? Will they
wear their plackets where they should bear their faces?
Is there not milking-time, when you are going to bed,
or kiln-hole to whistle of these secrets, but you must be
tittle-tattling before all our guests? 'Tis well they are 245
whisp'ring. Clammer your tongues, and not a word
more.
MOPSA I have done. Come, you promised me a tawdry-
lace and a pair of sweet gloves.
CLOWN Have I not told thee how I was cozened by the 250
way and lost all my money?
AUTOLYCUS And indeed, sir, there are cozeners abroad;
therefore it behoves men to be wary.
CLOWN Fear not thou, man; thou shalt lose nothing here.
AUTOLYCUS I hope so, sir, for I have about me many 255
parcels of charge.
CLOWN What hast here? Ballads?
MOPSA Pray now, buy some. I love a ballad in print, a-
life, for then we are sure they are true.

239 **paid you more** i.e. got you pregnant
241–2 **Will . . . faces?** A placket is both a
petticoat and the slit (or pocket) in a
petticoat, hence the vagina—compare
LLL, where Cupid is 'prince of plackets,
king of codpieces', 3.1.179; the line
means 'will they reveal what they
should keep hidden?' (see below, lines
605–7).
244 **kiln-hole** opening in an oven, conceived as an appropriate place for gossip; F's spelling, 'kill-hole', records the
17th-century pronunciation of kiln, still
standard in the US.
 whistle whisper (*OED* 10). The word
is not elsewhere used by Shakespeare in
this sense, but is common in the period
and needs no emendation. The *OED*
cites Sir John Hayward, 1599: 'Some of
the secrete counsailers . . . of the King,
whistled him in the eare, that his going
to Westminster was neither seemly nor
safe.'
246 **Clammer** or 'clamour', silence. The
OED cites John Taylor the Water Poet,
'Clamour the promulgation of your tongues' (clamour *v.*² 2). Warburton ex-

plained, 'The phrase is taken from ring-
ing. When bells are at the height, in
order to cease them, the repetition of the
strokes becomes much quicker than before; this is called *clamouring* them.'
Malone cited Johnson with a different
explanation: 'to *clam* a bell is to cover
the clapper with felt, which drowns the
blow and hinders the sound' (both cited
in the *Variorum*). Hanmer's emendation
to 'charm', once widely accepted, has
now been generally abandoned.
248–9 **tawdry-lace** for 'St Audrey's lace',
a silk neckerchief of the sort sold at St
Audrey's Fair held annually at Ely on 17
October, the saint's day. St Audrey (or
Etheldreda) was the founder of Ely
Cathedral; tawdry-lace commemorated
the manner of her death, of a tumour in
the neck, regarded as a punishment for
the elaborate necklaces she had worn in
her youth.
249 **sweet** perfumed
256 **parcels of charge** valuable goods
258–9 **a-life** 'a kind of oath, "on my life" '
(Abbott 24)

AUTOLYCUS Here's one to a very doleful tune, how a   260
usurer's wife was brought to bed of twenty money-bags
at a burden, and how she longed to eat adders' heads
and toads carbonadoed.

MOPSA Is it true, think you?

AUTOLYCUS Very true, and but a month old.   265

DORCAS Bless me from marrying a usurer!

AUTOLYCUS Here's the midwife's name to't, one Mistress
Taleporter, and five or six honest wives that were
present. Why should I carry lies abroad?

MOPSA Pray you now, buy it.   270

CLOWN Come on, lay it by, and let's first see more ballads.
We'll buy the other things anon.

AUTOLYCUS Here's another ballad, of a fish that appeared
upon the coast on Wednesday the fourscore of April
forty thousand fathom above water, and sung this   275
ballad against the hard hearts of maids. It was thought
she was a woman and was turned into a cold fish for
she would not exchange flesh with one that loved her.
The ballad is very pitiful, and as true.

DORCAS Is it true too, think you?   280

AUTOLYCUS Five justices' hands at it, and witnesses more
than my pack will hold.

CLOWN Lay it by too. Another.

AUTOLYCUS This is a merry ballad, but a very pretty one.

MOPSA Let's have some merry ones.   285

AUTOLYCUS Why, this is a passing merry one, and goes to
the tune of 'Two maids wooing a man'. There's scarce
a maid westward but she sings it—'tis in request, I can
tell you.

MOPSA We can both sing it. If thou'lt bear a part, thou   290
shalt hear; 'tis in three parts.

267 Mistress] F (Mist.)

262 **at a burden** in one birth
263 **carbonadoed** scored with a knife and
grilled
266 **Bless me** i.e. God keep me
268 **Taleporter** The name means tale-
bearer, gossip.
271 **lay it by** put it aside
274 **fourscore** eightieth
275 **fathom** A variable measure, originally
the length of the outstretched arms, in

Shakespeare's time usually reckoned at
six feet (nearly 2 metres). The fish's
position is thus about 45 miles (or 73
km.) above sea level.
281 **witnesses** testimonials (*OED*, witness, 2)
286 **passing** surpassingly, extremely
287 **tune . . . man** If this is a real tune,
neither it nor any other reference to it
has survived.
290 **bear** carry, sing

DORCAS We had the tune on't a month ago.
AUTOLYCUS I can bear my part; you must know 'tis my
occupation. Have at it with you.

Song

AUTOLYCUS
    Get you hence, for I must go   295
    Where it fits you not to know.
DORCAS
    Whither?
MOPSA   O whither?
DORCAS   Whither?
MOPSA
    It becomes thy oath full well
    Thou to me thy secrets tell.
DORCAS
    Me too; let me go thither.   300
MOPSA
    Or thou goest to th' grange or mill—
DORCAS
    If to either, thou dost ill—
AUTOLYCUS
    Neither.
DORCAS   What, neither?
AUTOLYCUS   Neither.
DORCAS
    Thou hast sworn my love to be.
MOPSA
    Thou hast sworn it more to me;   305
    Then whither goest? Say whither?

294.1 *Song*] F4; Song | Aut. F1 (*as speech headings to the first two lines of the song*)

292 **on't** of it
294 **Have . . . you** 'Let's have a go at it'
295–306 Not only the tune but the subject appears to be 'Two maids wooing a man' (see l. 287)—as Autolycus' line may imply: see *Macbeth* 1.3.86, 'To th' self-same tune and words'. Music for this song, and two early versions of the lyrics, one including additional verses, survive in manuscript sources; see Appendix C. Shakespeare may be using a popular song, as he does in *Othello* for Desdemona's 'Willow Song', and the Clown's promise that 'we'll have this song out anon by ourselves' does imply that there is more of it. But as Pafford points out, stage songs were often expanded in broadsheets, and if the song is original, the extra verses need not be.
296 **it . . . to** you need not
301 **Or . . . or** either . . . or

CLOWN We'll have this song out anon by ourselves; my
father and the gentleman are in sad talk, and we'll not
trouble them. Come, bring away thy pack after me;
wenches, I'll buy for you both. Pedlar, let's have the   310
first choice—follow me, girls.

Exit with Dorcas and Mopsa

AUTOLYCUS And you shall pay well for 'em.

Song

  Will you buy any tape, or lace for your cape,
    My dainty duck, my dear-a?
  Any silk, any thread, any toys for your head   315
    Of the new'st and fin'st, fin'st wear-a?
  Come to the pedlar, money's a meddler
    That doth utter all men's ware-a.   *Exit*

Enter Servant

SERVANT Master, there is three carters, three shepherds,
three neatherds, three swineherds that have made   320
themselves all men of hair. They call themselves saltiers, and they have a dance which the wenches say is
a gallimaufry of gambols, because they are not in't; but
they themselves are o'th' mind, if it be not too rough for
some that know little but bowling, it will please plenti-   325
fully.

OLD SHEPHERD Away! We'll none on't; here has been too
much homely foolery already. I know, sir, we weary
you.

POLIXENES You weary those that refresh us. Pray, let's see   330
these four threes of herdsmen.

---

308 gentleman] F (Gent.)   312.1 *Exit ... Mopsa*] ROWE 1709; *not in* F   318.1 *Enter
Servant*] ROWE 1709; *not in* F

307 **out** in full
308 **sad** serious
314 **duck** pet, darling
315 **toys** trifles, ornaments; but 'to have
toys in one's head' was a proverbial
warning against indulging idle fancies
(Dent T456.1)
317–18 **money's ... ware-a** 'money is
involved in everything, putting all men's
wares up for sale'; utter = 'to put
(goods, wares, etc.) forth or upon the
market' (*OED* I.1)

320 **neatherds** cowherds
320–1 **made ... hair** dressed themselves
in animal skins
321–2 **saltiers** leapers—presumably the
servant's error for 'satyrs' (see their
dance at 337.2)
323 **gallimaufry** hash, hodge-podge, ridiculous medley
325 **bowling** a gentle sport (as opposed to
satyric leaping)
328 **homely** rustic

SERVANT One three of them, by their own report, sir, hath
    danced before the King, and not the worst of the three
    but jumps twelve foot and a half by th' square.
OLD SHEPHERD Leave your prating; since these good men   335
    are pleased, let them come in—but quickly now.
SERVANT Why, they stay at door, sir.
       ⌈*He admits the dancers.*⌉
       Here a dance of twelve satyrs
POLIXENES (*to the Old Shepherd*)
    O, father, you'll know more of that hereafter.
    (*To Camillo*) Is it not too far gone? 'Tis time to part
        them.
    He's simple and tells much. (*To Florizel*) How now,
        fair shepherd,   340
    Your heart is full of something that does take
    Your mind from feasting. Sooth, when I was young,
    And handed love, as you do, I was wont
    To load my she with knacks. I would have ransacked
    The pedlar's silken treasury, and have poured it   345
    To her acceptance—you have let him go,
    And nothing marted with him. If your lass
    Interpretation should abuse and call this
    Your lack of love or bounty, you were straited
    For a reply, at least if you make a care   350
    Of happy holding her.

---

334 square] F (squire)   337.1 *He . . . dancers*] This edition; *He lets the herdsmen in* WILSON;
not in F

333 **danced . . . King** It seems likely
that this is a reference to the court performance of Ben Jonson and Inigo
Jones's *Oberon* on 1 January 1611,
which includes a dance of satyrs (see A.
H. Thorndike, 'Influence of the Court-
Masques on the Drama, 1608–14',
PMLA 15 (1900), 114–20). Since the
professional roles in the masque were
probably taken by the King's Men, the
argument is plausible, and has been
widely, though not universally, accepted. See the Introduction, pp. 79–80.
334 **by th' square** precisely. A square is a
carpenter's measure.
337 **at door** The article is often omitted
after prepositions in adverbial phrases;
see Abbott 90 and 143.

337.2 The music for the satyrs' dance in
    Oberon, by Robert Johnson, survives,
    and since Johnson wrote music for the
    King's Men (including the songs in *The
    Tempest*), the same music may have
    been used. See Appendix C.
340 **He's simple . . .** Referring to the old
    shepherd, whom Polixenes has been
    questioning about Florizel and Perdita.
343 **handed** handled, dealt with
344 **knacks** knicknacks, trifles
347 **nothing marted** made no bargain
348 **Interpretation . . . abuse** should
    misinterpret
349 **were straited** would be strapped,
    hard put
350–1 **make . . . her** care about keeping
    her happy

FLORIZEL   Old sir, I know
She prizes not such trifles as these are.
The gifts she looks from me are packed and locked
Up in my heart, which I have given already,
But not delivered. (*To Perdita*) O, hear me breathe my
          life   355
Before this ancient sir, who, it should seem,
Hath sometime loved: I take thy hand, this hand,
As soft as dove's down and as white as it,
Or Ethiopian's tooth, or the fanned snow that's bolted
By th' northern blasts twice o'er—
POLIXENES   What follows this?   360
(*To Camillo*) How prettily th'young swain seems to
          wash
The hand was fair before! (*To Florizel*) I have put you
          out;
But to your protestation—let me hear
What you profess.
FLORIZEL   Do, and be witness to't.
POLIXENES
And this my neighbour too?
FLORIZEL   And he, and more   365
Than he, and men—the earth, the heavens, and all—
That were I crowned the most imperial monarch,
Thereof most worthy, were I the fairest youth
That ever made eye swerve, had force and knowledge
More than was ever man's, I would not prize them   370
Without her love, for her employ them all,
Commend them, and condemn them to her service
Or to their own perdition.

356 who] F2; whom F1

353 **looks** looks for
356 **who** Almost all editors since F2
     (though not Schanzer) have thus
     emended F's *whom*, and in this case I am
     not about to defend it. But if it is an
     error, it is a remarkably characteristic
     one, and Schanzer's note, 'Shakespeare
     frequently uses *whom* where we should
     use "who" ', is, if unenlightening, cer-
     tainly correct. There are a number of
     places where the usage seems defen-
     sible; see the note on 3.2.32 (a passage

emended by Schanzer), and 420 below,
and 5.3.150.
358 **As . . . it** Both proverbial compli-
     ments: Dent D576.1, D573.2.
359 **fanned . . . bolted** winnowed . . . sifted.
     Compare *Dream* 3.2.142–3, 'high Taurus'
     snow, | Fanned with the eastern wind'.
362 **was** that was (Abbott 244)
372–3 **Commend . . . perdition** Either
     'commend them to her service' or 'con-
     demn them to destruction'. For the
     construction, compare 3.2.162–3.

POLIXENES   Fairly offered.

CAMILLO

This shows a sound affection.

OLD SHEPHERD   But my daughter,

Say you the like to him?

PERDITA   I cannot speak   375

So well, nothing so well; no, nor mean better.

By th' pattern of mine own thoughts I cut out

The purity of his.

OLD SHEPHERD   Take hands, a bargain;

And friends unknown, you shall bear witness to't—

I give my daughter to him, and will make   380

Her portion equal his.

FLORIZEL   O, that must be

I'th' virtue of your daughter. One being dead,

I shall have more than you can dream of yet;

Enough then for your wonder. But come on,

Contract us fore these witnesses.

OLD SHEPHERD   Come, your hand,   385

And daughter, yours.

POLIXENES   Soft, swain, awhile, beseech you.

Have you a father?

FLORIZEL

I have, but what of him?

POLIXENES

Knows he of this?

FLORIZEL

He neither does nor shall.   390

POLIXENES

Methinks a father

Is at the nuptial of his son a guest

That best becomes the table. Pray you once more,

378 **Take . . . bargain** 'Clap hands and a
bargain' was proverbial (Dent H109.1).
Compare 1.2.103.

383–4 **more . . . wonder** more than you
can dream of now, and enough to
amaze you then

385 **Contract . . . witnesses** Either a
promise to marry or a declaration of
marriage in the presence of witnesses
constituted a legally binding contract.
The first was a betrothal, and could be

abrogated under certain conditions, but
the second was a valid marriage subject
to the matrimonial law. Since the proceeding is interrupted, it is not clear
which sort of contract Florizel is about to
propose. Leontes describes Florizel as
both 'troth-plight' to Perdita and as his
son-in-law in 5.3.149–51; but at
5.1.204 Florizel denies that they are
married.

Is not your father grown incapable
Of reasonable affairs? Is he not stupid   395
With age and alt'ring rheums? Can he speak, hear?
Know man from man? Dispute his own estate?
Lies he not bedrid, and again does nothing
But what he did being childish?
FLORIZEL   No, good sir,
He has his health, and ampler strength indeed   400
Than most have of his age.
POLIXENES   By my white beard,
You offer him, if this be so, a wrong
Something unfilial. Reason my son
Should choose himself a wife, but as good reason
The father, all whose joy is nothing else   405
But fair posterity, should hold some counsel
In such a business.
FLORIZEL   I yield all this,
But for some other reasons, my grave sir,
Which 'tis not fit you know, I not acquaint
My father of this business.
POLIXENES   Let him know't.   410
FLORIZEL
He shall not.
POLIXENES   Prithee, let him.
FLORIZEL   No, he must not.
OLD SHEPHERD
Let him, my son; he shall not need to grieve
At knowing of thy choice.
FLORIZEL   Come, come, he must not.
Mark our contract.
POLIXENES (*removing his disguise*) Mark your divorce,
    young sir,
Whom son I dare not call—thou art too base   415

414 *removing . . . disguise*] ROWE 1709 (*subs.*); not in F

396 **alt'ring rheums** diseases that change
    his nature. Rheums are fluid secretions,
    and by extension the diseases that pro-
    duce these, such as colds and catarrh.
397 **Dispute . . . estate** discuss his own
    affairs. Compare *Romeo* 3.3.63, 'Let me
    dispute with thee of thy estate.'

403 **Something** somewhat
    Reason it is reasonable that. Compare
    K. John 5.2.130, 'He is prepared, and
    reason too he should.'
409 **I . . . acquaint** Abbott 305 ('Do'
    omitted before 'Not')

189

To be acknowledged, thou a sceptre's heir,
That thus affects a sheep-hook! Thou, old traitor,
I am sorry that by hanging thee I can
But shorten thy life one week. And thou fresh piece
Of excellent witchcraft, whom of force must know   420
The royal fool thou cop'st with—

OLD SHEPHERD   O, my heart!

POLIXENES

I'll have thy beauty scratched with briars and made
More homely than thy state. (*To Florizel*) For thee,
    fond boy,
If I may ever know thou dost but sigh
That thou no more shalt see this knack—as never   425
I mean thou shalt—we'll bar thee from succession,
Not hold thee of our blood, no, not our kin,
Far'r than Deucalion off. Mark thou my words;
Follow us to the court. (*To the Old Shepherd*) Thou,
    churl, for this time,
Though full of our displeasure, yet we free thee   430
From the dead blow of it. (*To Perdita*) And you,
    enchantment,
Worthy enough a herdsman—yea, him too

---

416 acknowledged] F2 (acknowledg'd); acknowledge FI   425 shalt see] ROWE 1709;
shalt neuer see F

417 **affects** desires; for the form, see Abbott 340
419 **piece** prototype, masterpiece
420 **witchcraft** For the charge of witchcraft as an explanation for socially disadvantageous affections, compare Brabanzio's tirade against Othello, 1.2.64 ff. See the Introduction, p. 60.
    whom See 3.2.32, 4.4.356, 5.3.150.
    of force perforce, necessarily
421 **cop'st** hast to do (*OED*, cope, v.² II.5)
423 **state** estate, position
    For as for
    fond foolish
425 **knack** The word combines the senses of trifle, toy (*OED* 3), choice dish, delicacy (3b), clever trick (1), originally with overtones of deceitfulness, which are relevant here.
428 **Far'r . . . off** Further off than Deucalion is in the past. Deucalion, the son of Prometheus, was the classical equivalent of Noah, who survived the universal

deluge and repeopled the earth. Polixenes' rejection of his son takes the world back as far as genealogy can go, to the flood. F's 'Farre', first modernized to 'far'r' by Whalley, is a comparative (OE 'ferror'); see Abbott 478.

429 **churl** peasant, possibly though not necessarily as a term of contempt; see *OED* 4, 5. The word originally meant simply 'man', and then an ordinary man as opposed to a nobleman or gentleman. By the 16th century it signified both a rustic and a boor or villain.
429–31 **for . . . it** See lines 448 ff. below.
431 **dead** mortal
432–4 **him . . . thee** 'indeed, you're worthy of Florizel—whose conduct has made him, save for the fact of his being my son, unworthy of you' (Kermode); 'our honour' is not necessarily a royal plural, since the honour involved—noble blood, position—is shared by Florizel

That makes himself, but for our honour therein,
Unworthy thee—if ever henceforth thou
These rural latches to his entrance open,   435
Or hoop his body more with thy embraces,
I will devise a death as cruel for thee
As thou art tender to't.   *Exit*
PERDITA   Even here undone!
I was not much afeared, for once or twice
I was about to speak and tell him plainly   440
The selfsame sun that shines upon his court
Hides not his visage from our cottage, but
Looks on alike. (*To Florizel*) Will't please you, sir, be
    gone?
I told you what would come of this. Beseech you,
Of your own state take care. This dream of mine   445
Being now awake, I'll queen it no inch farther,
But milk my ewes and weep.
CAMILLO   Why, how now, father!
Speak ere thou diest.
OLD SHEPHERD   I cannot speak nor think,
Nor dare to know that which I know. (*To Florizel*) O sir,
You have undone a man of fourscore-three   450
That thought to fill his grave in quiet, yea
To die upon the bed my father died,
To lie close by his honest bones; but now
Some hangman must put on my shroud and lay me
Where no priest shovels in dust. (*To Perdita*) O cursèd
    wretch,   455

436 hoop] POPE; hope F

438 **tender** 'acutely sensitive to pain' (*OED* IV.10c)
441–3 **sun . . . alike** Proverbial wisdom: Dent S985.
442 **his** its
445 **state** Both 'condition' and 'position'.
446 **queen it** behave like a queen. Quiller-Couch and Dover Wilson suggest that at this point she ('no doubt') removes her floral garland.
448 **ere . . . diest** But see 429–31: have both the shepherd and Camillo failed to take in the withdrawal of the death sentence? Or does 'for this time' (429)

merely imply a brief reprieve? Or, as with Hermione's death, does the play's argument change according to the dictates of dramatic effectiveness?
449 **Nor . . . I know** Compare 1.2.372.
452 **died** For the omission of the preposition, see Abbott 394.
454–5 **lay . . . dust** i.e. he would be buried as a common criminal, without a Christian service. In fact, as the *Variorum* observes, though in the first liturgy of Edward VI, 1549, the priest was instructed to cast earth upon the body, this was amended in 1552, after which

That knew'st this was the prince and wouldst
    adventure
To mingle faith with him! Undone, undone!
If I might die within this hour, I have lived
To die when I desire.   *Exit*

FLORIZEL (*to Perdita*)   Why look you so upon me?
  I am but sorry, not afeared; delayed,   460
But nothing altered. What I was, I am;
More straining on for plucking back, not following
My leash unwillingly.

CAMILLO   Gracious my lord,
  You know your father's temper. At this time
He will allow no speech—which I do guess   465
You do not purpose to him—and as hardly
Will he endure your sight as yet, I fear.
Then till the fury of his highness settle,
Come not before him.

FLORIZEL   I not purpose it.
  I think Camillo?

CAMILLO (*removing his disguise*) Even he, my lord.   470

PERDITA
  How often have I told you 'twould be thus?
How often said my dignity would last
But till 'twere known?

FLORIZEL   It cannot fail but by
  The violation of my faith, and then
Let nature crush the sides o'th' earth together,   475

464 your] F2; my F1   470 *removing . . . disguise*] This edition; *not in* F

the Prayer Book ordered merely that
'the earth should be cast upon the body
by some standing by'.

456 **adventure** dare
462 **plucking** dragging, pulling 'with a
forcible effort' (*OED*, pluck, 2). The
image is of a dog on a leash.
462–3 **not . . . unwillingly** i.e. not following it at all, not allowing himself to be
dragged away
468 **his highness** Both Polixenes' title and
his grandeur; compare 524.
470 **I . . . Camillo?** Florizel first recognizes
Camillo, who at this point would logically remove his disguise.

472 **dignity** high rank (*OED* 2)
475–6 **Let . . . within** According to Stoic
and Neoplatonic traditions, everything
living derives from the *logos spermatikos*,
'germinating reason', or in Latin *rationes
seminales*, defined by Marcus Aurelius as
'certain germs of future existences, en-
dowed with productive capacities of realization, change, and phenomenal
succession'. Augustine in *De Trinitate*
explains that 'some hidden seeds of all
things that are born corporeally and
visibly are concealed in the corporeal
elements of this world . . . For the creator of these invisible seeds is the creator
of all things himself; since whatever

And mar the seeds within. Lift up thy looks.
From my succession wipe me, father; I
Am heir to my affection.
CAMILLO   Be advised.
FLORIZEL
I am, and by my fancy. If my reason
Will thereto be obedient, I have reason.   480
If not, my senses, better pleased with madness,
Do bid it welcome.
CAMILLO   This is desperate, sir.
FLORIZEL
So call it, but it does fulfil my vow;
I needs must think it honesty. Camillo,
Not for Bohemia nor the pomp that may   485
Be thereat gleaned, for all the sun sees or
The close earth wombs or the profound seas hides
In unknown fathoms will I break my oath
To this my fair beloved. Therefore I pray you,
As you have ever been my father's honoured friend,   490
When he shall miss me—as in faith I mean not

comes forth to our sight by being born, receives the first beginnings of its course from hidden seeds' (see the discussion by Walter Clyde Curry, *Shakespeare's Philosophical Patterns*, 2nd edn. (Baton Rouge, 1959), pp. 30 ff.). These are Shakespeare's seeds, or (in *Macbeth* and *Lear*) 'germens'. Hence Florizel is proposing not only the destruction of the world, but of all potential life as well. Compare Banquo to the witches, 'If you can look into the seeds of time | And say which grain will grow and which will not' (*Macbeth* 1.3.56–7), and later Macbeth urging them to answer 'though the treasure | Of nature's germens tumble all together | Even till destruction sicken' (4.1.74–6); and Lear's invocation of universal chaos, 'Crack nature's moulds, all germens spill at once' (*Lear* 3.2.8).

478 **affection** passionate love
479 **fancy** By Shakespeare's time, the term combined the senses of imagination and love; it was originally the same word as fantasy, the power to create and apprehend images, as opposed to the verbal

power of reason (see *OED* 4, 8b)—love was assumed to be a function of vision; hence 'Who ever loved that loved not at first sight?' (Marlowe, *Hero and Leander*, i. 176, quoted in *As You Like it*, 3.5.83). In making reason subservient to fancy, Florizel is inverting the ethical hierarchy of the faculties.

487 **wombs** 'Any noun or adjective could be converted into a verb by the Elizabethan authors, generally in an active signification' (Abbott 290).

  hides Abbott 333 (Third person plural in -s)

490 **As . . . friend** Editors from the Second Folio on have from time to time been distressed by the alexandrine. F2, followed by Rowe and a number of 18th-century editions, omits 'honoured'; Dyce, followed most notably in this century by Schanzer, printed 'As you've e'er been'. Schanzer claims that the line is 'metrically quite un-Shakespearian', but this is an overstatement. Abbott observes that 'a proper Alexandrine with six accents . . . is seldom found in Shakespeare', but then proceeds to cite a healthy number of instances (see 495 ff.).

To see him any more—cast your good counsels
Upon his passion. Let myself and fortune
Tug for the time to come. This you may know
And so deliver: I am put to sea   495
With her who here I cannot hold on shore,
And most opportune to our need, I have
A vessel rides fast by, but not prepared
For this design. What course I mean to hold
Shall nothing benefit your knowledge, nor   500
Concern me the reporting.
CAMILLO   O my lord,
I would your spirit were easier for advice,
Or stronger for your need.
FLORIZEL   Hark, Perdita—
      (*To Camillo*) I'll hear you by and by.
        ⌈*He draws Perdita aside*⌉
CAMILLO   He's irremovable,
Resolved for flight. Now were I happy if   505
His going I could frame to serve my turn,
Save him from danger, do him love and honour,
Purchase the sight again of dear Sicilia
And that unhappy King, my master, whom
I so much thirst to see.
FLORIZEL   Now, good Camillo,   510
I am so fraught with curious business that
I leave out ceremony.
CAMILLO   Sir, I think
You have heard of my poor services i'th' love
That I have borne your father?
FLORIZEL   Very nobly
Have you deserved. It is my father's music   515
To speak your deeds, not little of his care

497 our] THEOBALD; her F   504 *He . . . aside*] CAPELL (*subs.*); *not in* F

494 **Tug** contend
495 **deliver** report
496 **who** Emended by F2 and many sub-
    sequent editors to 'whom'; but see Ab-
    bott 274.
497 **opportune** accented on the second
    syllable
500–1 **Shall . . . reporting** you need not

know, nor need I tell
502 **easier for** more at ease with
504 **irremovable** immovable
508 **Purchase** procure (*OED* 3)
511 **curious** Both 'anxious' and 'complex'
    (*OED* 1b, 10b).
512 **I . . . ceremony** I omit the courtesy
    due you

To have them recompensed as thought on.

CAMILLO   Well, my lord,

If you may please to think I love the King,
And through him what's nearest to him, which is
Your gracious self, embrace but my direction,   520
If your more ponderous and settled project
May suffer alteration. On mine honour,
I'll point you where you shall have such receiving
As shall become your highness, where you may
Enjoy your mistress, from the whom I see   525
There's no disjunction to be made but by—
As heavens forfend!—your ruin; marry her,
And, with my best endeavours in your absence,
Your discontenting father strive to qualify,
And bring him up to liking.

FLORIZEL   How, Camillo,   530

May this, almost a miracle, be done?—
That I may call thee something more than man,
And after that, trust to thee.

CAMILLO   Have you thought on

A place whereto you'll go?

FLORIZEL   Not any yet;

But as th'unthought-on accident is guilty   535
To what we wildly do, so we profess
Ourselves to be the slaves of chance, and flies
Of every wind that blows.

CAMILLO   Then list to me—

This follows, if you will not change your purpose,

517 **as . . . on** Either 'as soon as they are thought of', or 'as greatly as they are esteemed'.

521 **more ponderous** very serious

523 **receiving** a reception

524 **your highness** Compare l. 468 above.

529 **discontenting** discontented

    strive to qualify Rowe assumed that the striving was to be done by Camillo, and emended the phrase to read 'I'll strive to qualify'; the emendation is not strictly necessary, since the syntax could be 'I'll point you . . . and . . . strive'. Most 18th-century editors followed suit until Malone in 1790, who argued that the syntax is rather 'Marry her | And . . . strive'—it is Florizel who is to

do the striving. Pafford argues for Rowe's reading, Schanzer for Malone's. Since Camillo's projected abilities in the matter are called miraculous and more than human (lines 531–2), it looks as if Florizel, at least, understands Camillo to be offering to deal with Polixenes himself. Qualify = 'moderate or mitigate, . . . render less violent, severe or unpleasant' (*OED* 8).

535–6 **th'unthought . . . do** the unexpected mischance (of our discovery by Polixenes) is responsible for our rash actions. For 'guilty to' see Abbott 188.

537–9 **flies . . . blows** moths in the wind. compare Leontes' 'I am a feather for each wind that blows', 2.3.153.

But undergo this flight: make for Sicilia,   540
And there present yourself and your fair princess,
For so I see she must be, fore Leontes;
She shall be habited as it becomes
The partner of your bed. Methinks I see
Leontes opening his free arms and weeping   545
His welcomes forth; asks thee there, 'Son,
    forgiveness'—
As 'twere i'th' father's person; kisses the hands
Of your fresh princess; o'er and o'er divides him
'Twixt his unkindness and his kindness—th'one
He chides to hell, and bids the other grow   550
Faster than thought or time.
FLORIZEL   Worthy Camillo,
What colour for my visitation shall I
Hold up before him?
CAMILLO   Sent by the King your father
To greet him and to give him comforts. Sir,
The manner of your bearing towards him, with   555
What you, as from your father, shall deliver,
Things known betwixt us three, I'll write you down,
The which shall point you forth at every sitting

---

546 there ... forgiveness'—] F1 (there Sonne forgiuenesse,); the Sonne forgiuenesse F3; there 'Son, forgiveness!' ALEXANDER

545 **free** Relevant senses are noble, generous, magnanimous (*OED* 4).
546 **asks ... forgiveness** F3's emendation, 'asks thee, the son, forgiveness' was universally accepted until Peter Alexander devised a punctuation of the Folio line that made sense of it, whereby Camillo imagines Leontes speaking directly to Florizel and apologizing as if to his own son. If this is correct, it is both an oblique allusion to the death of Mamillius and an acknowledgment of how deeply 'twinned' the two childhood friends continue to be. Among recent editors, Alexander has been followed most notably by Pafford and Bevington. There is in fact no reason not to retain F's reading; once again, the claim that F3 provides a more felicitous line is no argument for emendation.
548 **fresh** blooming and young; also

newly-created (*OED* 2, 9b)
548–9 **divides ... kindness** talks alternately of his (former) inhumanity and his (present) tender feelings. *Kindness* implies something stronger than the modern term: family feeling in the largest sense, a natural affection deriving from a sense of shared humanity—the concept Hamlet invokes by calling Claudius 'less than kind' (1.2.65). Compare 'kindness, nobler ever than revenge', *As You Like It* 4.3.129.
551 **Faster** Both 'more quickly' and 'stronger'.
    Faster . . . thought 'As swift as thought' was proverbial (Dent T240).
552 **colour** plausible reason, pretext (*OED* 12)
556 **as** as if
558 **point ... forth** direct you
    sitting meeting (compare 'session')

What you must say, that he shall not perceive
But that you have your father's bosom there,   560
And speak his very heart.

FLORIZEL   I am bound to you—
There is some sap in this.

CAMILLO   A course more promising
Than a wild dedication of yourselves
To unpathed waters, undreamed shores, most certain
To miseries enough—no hope to help you,   565
But as you shake off one to take another;
Nothing so certain as your anchors, who
Do their best office if they can but stay you
Where you'll be loath to be. Besides, you know
Prosperity's the very bond of love,   570
Whose fresh complexion and whose heart together
Affliction alters.

PERDITA   One of these is true;
I think affliction may subdue the cheek,
But not take in the mind.

CAMILLO   Yea? Say you so?
There shall not at your father's house these seven years   575
Be born another such.

FLORIZEL   My good Camillo,
She's as forward of her breeding as
She is i'th' rear our birth.

CAMILLO   I cannot say 'tis pity
She lacks instructions, for she seems a mistress
To most that teach.

PERDITA   Your pardon, sir; for this   580

---

559 **that** so that
560 **bosom** 'the breast considered as the seat of thoughts and feelings'; 'the repository of secret thoughts and counsels' (*OED* 6, 6a)
562 **sap** life
568–9 **stay . . . be** i.e. although they save your ship from being wrecked, they also keep you where you do not wish to be
570–2 **Prosperity . . . alters** Proverbial wisdom: 'prosperity gets friends, but adversity tries them' (Dent P611; compare T301).

574 **take in** capture
575 **these seven years** Proverbial for a very long time; see Dent Y25.
577 **She's** Pope characteristically regularized the metre by emending to 'she is', a reading adopted by the majority of editors (though, recently, not by Oxford or Bevington). The hypermetric line following, however, has gone unnoticed.
577–8 **as . . . birth** as far ahead of her upbringing as she is beneath me in birth
579 **instructions** education

I'll blush you thanks.
FLORIZEL   My prettiest Perdita!
But O, the thorns we stand upon! Camillo—
Preserver of my father, now of me,
The medicine of our house—how shall we do?
We are not furnished like Bohemia's son,   585
Nor shall appear in Sicilia.
CAMILLO   My lord,
Fear none of this. I think you know my fortunes
Do all lie there; it shall be so my care
To have you royally appointed, as if
The scene you play were mine. For instance, sir,   590
That you may know you shall not want, one word—
                                        They talk aside

      Enter Autolycus
AUTOLYCUS Ha, ha, what a fool honesty is! And trust, his
sworn brother, a very simple gentleman. I have sold all
my trumpery; not a counterfeit stone, not a ribbon,
glass, pomander, brooch, table-book, ballad, knife, tape,   595
glove, shoe-tie, bracelet, horn-ring, to keep my pack
from fasting. They throng who should buy first, as if my
trinkets had been hallowed and brought a benediction
to the buyer; by which means I saw whose purse was
best in picture, and what I saw to my good use I   600
remembered. My clown, who wants but something to
be a reasonable man, grew so in love with the wenches'
song that he would not stir his pettitoes till he had both

591.1 *They . . . aside*] ROWE; *not in* F

582 **thorns . . . upon** Proverbial (Dent
T239); compare Sonnet 99, ll. 8–9:
'The roses fearfully on thorns did stand,
| One blushing shame, another white
despair'.
584 **medicine** Probably the doctor (*OED*
*sb.*²) rather than his potion, as in *Macbeth* 5.2.27 and *All's Well* 2.1.71.
585 **furnished** outfitted
Bohemia's the King of Bohemia's
586 **appear** appear as such
589 **royally appointed** equipped like a
prince—in fact, Florizel arrives in Sicily
'out of circumstance', and with a retinue 'but few, and those but mean'
(5.1.92–3)

592–614 The speech is based on passages
from Greene's *Third Part of Cony-catching*; see the Introduction, pp. 51–2.
592 **what . . . is** 'Honesty is a fool' was
proverbial (Dent H539.1).
595 **pomander** a ball of spices and perfume carried or worn round the neck or
at the waist to ward off disease
table-book notebook
597 **fasting** being empty
600 **best in picture** The phrase is elsewhere unparalleled; presumably 'best
looking', with a pun on 'best for picking'.
601 **wants but something** lacks only one
thing
603 **pettitoes** toes (normally of a pig)

tune and words, which so drew the rest of the herd to
me that all their other senses stuck in ears—you might   605
have pinched a placket, it was senseless; 'twas nothing
to geld a codpiece of a purse; I would have filed keys off
that hung in chains. No hearing, no feeling, but my
sir's song, and admiring the nothing of it. So that in this
time of lethargy I picked and cut most of their festival   610
purses; and had not the old man come in with a
hubbub against his daughter and the King's son and
scared my choughs from the chaff, I had not left a purse
alive in the whole army.

    Camillo, Florizel and Perdita come forward

CAMILLO

Nay, but my letters, by this means being there   615
So soon as you arrive, shall clear that doubt.

FLORIZEL

And those that you'll procure from King Leontes?—

CAMILLO

Shall satisfy your father.

PERDITA   Happy be you!

All that you speak shows fair.

CAMILLO (*seeing Autolycus*)   Who have we here?

We'll make an instrument of this, omit   620
Nothing may give us aid.

AUTOLYCUS (*aside*)

If they have overheard me now—why, hanging.

CAMILLO How now, good fellow, why shak'st thou so?
Fear not, man, here's no harm intended to thee.

AUTOLYCUS I am a poor fellow, sir.   625

CAMILLO Why, be so still; here's nobody will steal that
from thee. Yet for the outside of thy poverty we must

---

607 filed] F2 (fil'd); fill'd F1   614.1 *Camillo . . . forward*] THEOBALD; *not in* F   619 *seeing
Autolycus*] THEOBALD; *not in* F

---

605 **stuck in ears** stopped with hearing
606–7 **pinched . . . purse** placket = both
    pocket and vagina, purse = both wallet
    and scrotum. See above, lines 241–2.
607–8 **keys . . . hung** More sexual in-
    nuendo: key = penis, what fits the key-
    hole.
608–9 **my sir's** the clown's

609 **nothing** With a pun on 'noting', sing-
    ing.
610 **festival** i.e. full
613 **choughs** Used for both crows and
    jackdaws, birds easily attracted and
    caught.
627 **outside . . . poverty** your poor cloth-
    ing

make an exchange; therefore discase thee instantly—
thou must think there's a necessity in't—and change
garments with this gentleman. Though the pennyworth   630
on his side be the worst, yet hold thee, there's some
boot.

    He gives Autolycus money

AUTOLYCUS I am a poor fellow, sir. (*Aside*) I know ye well
enough.

CAMILLO Nay, prithee dispatch—the gentleman is half   635
flayed already.

AUTOLYCUS Are you in earnest, sir? (*Aside*) I smell the
trick on't.

FLORIZEL Dispatch, I prithee.

AUTOLYCUS Indeed, I have had earnest, but I cannot with   640
conscience take it.

CAMILLO Unbuckle, unbuckle.

    Florizel and Autolycus exchange garments

(*To Perdita*) Fortunate mistress—let my prophecy
Come home to ye!—you must retire yourself
Into some covert; take your sweetheart's hat   645
And pluck it o'er your brows, muffle your face,
Dismantle you, and, as you can, disliken
The truth of your own seeming, that you may—
For I do fear eyes over—to shipboard
Get undescried.

PERDITA   I see the play so lies   650
That I must bear a part.

CAMILLO   No remedy.

632.1 *He gives . . . money*] DYCE (*subs.*); *not in* F   636 flayed] F (fled)   642 *Florizel . . . garments*] CAPELL; *not in* F

628 **discase** undress. Compare *Tempest* 5.1.85. The word in this sense is apparently unique to Shakespeare, but Greene has Dorastus 'uncasing himself as secretly as might be' (Appendix B, p. 262).

630–1 **the . . . worst** he gets the worst of the bargain

631–2 **some boot** something extra; boot = 'that which is . . . given in addition to make up a deficiency in value' (*OED* 2)

633–4 **I . . . enough** 'I know thee well enough' was the proverbial recognition of villains (Dent K171.1).

636 **flayed** skinned, i.e. undressed

638 **on't** of it (Abbott 181)

640 **earnest** 'a sum of money . . . for the purpose of securing a bargain' (*OED*), the 'boot' of line 632

643–4 **let . . . ye** let my prediction (that you will be fortunate) prove true

645 **covert** hiding place

647–8 **Dismantle . . . seeming** change your clothes and make yourself as unlike your true appearance as you can

649 **eyes over** overseeing eyes, i.e. spies. Compare 4.2.35–6, and *LLL* 4.3.77, 'wretched fools' secrets heedfully o'er-eye'.

Have you done there?

FLORIZEL   Should I now meet my father
He would not call me son.

CAMILLO   Nay, you shall have no hat.

He gives the hat to Perdita

Come, lady, come. Farewell, my friend.

AUTOLYCUS Adieu, sir.   655

FLORIZEL

O Perdita, what have we twain forgot?—
Pray you, a word.

He draws her aside

CAMILLO

What I do next shall be to tell the King
Of this escape and whither they are bound;
Wherein my hope is I shall so prevail   660
To force him after, in whose company
I shall re-view Sicilia, for whose sight
I have a woman's longing.

FLORIZEL   Fortune speed us!
Thus we set on, Camillo, to th' seaside.

CAMILLO

The swifter speed the better.   665

Exeunt Florizel, Perdita and Camillo

AUTOLYCUS I understand the business, I hear it. To have
an open ear, a quick eye and a nimble hand is necessary
for a cutpurse; a good nose is requisite also, to smell
out work for th'other senses. I see this is the time that
the unjust man doth thrive. What an exchange had   670
this been, without boot! What a boot is here, with this
exchange! Sure the gods do this year connive at us, and

653.1 *He . . . Perdita*] CAPELL (subs.); *not in* F   657.1 *He . . . aside*] CAPELL; *not in* F
665.1 *Exeunt . . . Camillo*] CAPELL; *Exit* F

656 **what . . . forgot?** Steevens cited two
    parallels from *Merry Wives*, Dr Caius'
    'Od's me, *qu'ai-j'oublié?*' (1.4.58–9),
    and Mistress Quickly's 'Out upon't,
    what have I forgot?' (1.4.159–60), ob-
    serving that 'This is one of our author's
    dramatic expedients to introduce a con-
    versation apart, account for a sudden
    exit, etc.'
663 **I . . . longing** Women's longing was

proverbially overwhelming (Dent 421.1).
670 **unjust . . . thrive** The sentiment,
    though not the language, is biblical;
    compare Job 21: 7 (in the Bishops'
    Bible, 'Wherefore do the wicked live,
    and wax old, and grow in wealth?');
    also Psalms 73: 3 and Jeremiah 12: 1.
671 **boot** See above, line 632.
672 **connive** wink, look indulgently (*OED*
    1, 2)

we may do anything extempore. The prince himself is
about a piece of iniquity, stealing away from his father
with his clog at his heels. If I thought it were a piece of   675
honesty to acquaint the King withal, I would not do't.
I hold it the more knavery to conceal it; and therein am
I constant to my profession.

> *Enter Clown and Old Shepherd carrying a bundle and*
> *a box*

Aside, aside—here is more matter for a hot brain. Every
lane's end, every shop, church, session, hanging, yields   680
a careful man work.

CLOWN See, see, what a man you are now! There is no
    other way but to tell the King she's a changeling, and
    none of your flesh and blood.

OLD SHEPHERD Nay, but hear me—   685

CLOWN Nay, but hear me!

OLD SHEPHERD Go to, then.

CLOWN She being none of your flesh and blood, your flesh
    and blood has not offended the King, and so your flesh
    and blood is not to be punished by him. Show those   690
    things you found about her, those secret things, all but
    what she has with her. This being done, let the law go
    whistle, I warrant you.

OLD SHEPHERD I will tell the King all, every word, yea, and
    his son's pranks too—who, I may say, is no honest   695
    man, neither to his father nor to me, to go about to
    make me the King's brother-in-law.

CLOWN Indeed, brother-in-law was the farthest off you
    could have been to him; and then your blood had been
    the dearer by I know how much an ounce.   700

AUTOLYCUS (*aside*) Very wisely, puppies!

---

673 **extempore** without forethought—and
    by implication, without consequences
674 **about** engaged in
675 **clog** encumbrance, i.e. Perdita; 'to
    have a clog at one's heels' was prover-
    bial (Dent C426.1)
    If i.e. even if
680 **session** court session
683 **changeling** fairy child. See 3.3.114.
687 **Go to** go on
691–2 **but . . . her** Presumably Her-

mione's jewel, by which Perdita is later
identified (5.2.33), and which she is
wearing for the feast.
692–3 **go whistle** Proverbial for wasted
    effort (Dent W313).
700 **dearer . . . ounce** i.e. no dearer
    whatever. Hanmer, followed by many
    editors, emends to 'I know not how
    much', but this is removing the point of
    the joke.

OLD SHEPHERD Well, let us to the King. There is that in this
  fardel will make him scratch his beard.

AUTOLYCUS (*aside*) I know not what impediment this complaint may be to the flight of my master.   705

CLOWN Pray heartily he be at palace.

AUTOLYCUS (*aside*) Though I am not naturally honest, I am
  so sometimes by chance. Let me pocket up my pedlar's
  excrement.

  He takes off his false beard

  —How now, rustics, whither are you bound?   710

OLD SHEPHERD To th' palace, an it like your worship.

AUTOLYCUS Your affairs there, what, with whom, the
  condition of that fardel, the place of your dwelling, your
  names, your ages, of what having, breeding, and anything that is fitting to be known, discover!   715

CLOWN We are but plain fellows, sir.

AUTOLYCUS A lie; you are rough and hairy. Let me have
  no lying; it becomes none but tradesmen, and they
  often give us soldiers the lie, but we pay them for it with
  stamped coin, not stabbing steel, therefore they do not   720
  give us the lie.

CLOWN Your worship had like to have given us one, if you
  had not taken yourself with the manner.

709.1 *He takes . . . beard*] STEEVENS (*subs.*); *not in* F

703 **fardel** bundle
705 **my master** Autolycus thinks of himself as being in Florizel's service again—
  as, by the end of Act 4, he apparently is
  (see 4.3.13, 4.4.827).
706 **at palace** 'The is . . . omitted after
  prepositions in adverbial phrases' (Abbott 90); F prints an apostrophe before
  'palace'.
709 **excrement** beard; 'an outgrowth,
  said esp. of hair, nails, feathers'
  (*OED v.*²). Compare 'it will please
  his grace . . . to . . . dally with my
  excrement, with my mustachio', LLL
  5.1.96–9.
713 **condition . . . fardel** nature of that
  parcel
714 **having** wealth
715 **discover** reveal
717 **rough and hairy** Playing on the older
  sense of plain, 'smooth, . . . free from
  roughness' (*OED* 2).

718–20 **they . . . steel** they often cheat us
  soldiers, but we pay them for it with
  good money rather than with our
  swords. 'To give the lie', i.e. to accuse of
  lying, was grounds for a challenge to a
  duel.
720–1 **therefore . . . lie** i.e. they do not
  give it to us because we *pay* for it
722–3 **given . . . manner** accused us of
  lying if you had not caught yourself in
  time: 'With the manner' = in the act
  (from *mainour*, hand-work), legal termi-
  nology: 'the old law phrase, *to be taken
  as a thief with the mainour*, signifies to be
  taken in the very act' (Rushton, cited in
  the *Variorum*). Compare Costard discovered *in flagrante* with Jaquenetta,
  'The manner of it is, I was taken with
  the manner', LLL 1.1.199–200. The expression became proverbial: Dent
  M633.

OLD SHEPHERD Are you a courtier, an't like you, sir?

AUTOLYCUS Whether it like me or no, I am a courtier. Seest   725
thou not the air of the court in these enfoldings? Hath
not my gait in it the measure of the court? Receives not
thy nose court odour from me? Reflect I not on thy
baseness court-contempt? Think'st thou for that I insinuate to toze from thee thy business, I am therefore   730
no courtier? I am courtier cap-à-pie, and one that will
either push on or pluck back thy business there;
whereupon I command thee to open thy affair.

OLD SHEPHERD My business, sir, is to the King.

AUTOLYCUS What advocate hast thou to him?   735

OLD SHEPHERD I know not, an't like you.

CLOWN Advocate's the court word for a pheasant—say
you have none.

OLD SHEPHERD None, sir, I have no pheasant, cock nor hen.

AUTOLYCUS

How blessed are we that are not simple men!   740
Yet nature might have made me as these are,
Therefore I will not disdain.

CLOWN This cannot be but a great courtier.

OLD SHEPHERD His garments are rich, but he wears them
not handsomely.   745

CLOWN He seems to be the more noble in being fantastical.
A great man, I'll warrant—I know by the picking on's
teeth.

729–30 insinuate to toze] CAPELL; ~, at toaze F1; ~, or toaze F2

724 **an't like you** if you please

726 **enfoldings** garments

727 **measure** dignified step; measure = 'a
grave or stately dance' (*OED* 20)

729–30 **for ... toze** because I subtly
undertake to elicit. For *toze*, i.e. tease
out, see *OED* 1c. The Folio's 'insinuate
at' would require the substantive 'toz-
ing'; Capell's emendation 'to' is preferable to F2's 'or', adopted by most
editors.

731 **cap-à-pie** from head to foot; F's *pe*
suggests the pronunciation. 'To be
armed *cap à pie*' was proverbial (Dent
T436.1); compare *Hamlet* 1.2.200.

733 **open ... affair** explain your business

737 **pheasant** i.e. assuming that the shepherd would be expected to bring a gift of

game from the country. Sir Simonds
d'Ewes explains the connection between
advocates and poultry, describing 'bas-
ket justices', who 'for half a dozen of
chickens would dispense with a whole
dozen of penal statutes' (*Journals of Parliament*, cited in the *Variorum*). Compare
Jaques' 'justice, | In fair round belly
with good capon lined', *As You Like It*
2.7.153–4.

744 **garments are rich** They are, of
course, the garments of Florizel, but disguised as a shepherd.

746 **fantastical** eccentric in attire (see
OED, fantastic, 4)

747–8 **the ... teeth** his picking his teeth:
a fashionable affectation—the toothpick
was often worn in the hat

AUTOLYCUS The fardel there, what's i'th' fardel? Wherefore that box? 750

OLD SHEPHERD Sir, there lies such secrets in this fardel and box which none must know but the King, and which he shall know within this hour if I may come to th' speech of him.

AUTOLYCUS Age, thou hast lost thy labour. 755

OLD SHEPHERD Why, sir?

AUTOLYCUS The King is not at the palace; he is gone aboard a new ship, to purge melancholy and air himself; for if thou beest capable of things serious, thou must know the King is full of grief. 760

OLD SHEPHERD So 'tis said, sir—about his son, that should have married a shepherd's daughter.

AUTOLYCUS If that shepherd be not in handfast, let him fly; the curses he shall have, the tortures he shall feel, will break the back of man, the heart of monster. 765

CLOWN Think you so, sir?

AUTOLYCUS Not he alone shall suffer what wit can make heavy and vengeance bitter, but those that are germane to him, though removed fifty times, shall all come under the hangman—which, though it be great pity, yet it is 770 necessary. An old sheep-whistling rogue, a ram-tender, to offer to have his daughter come into grace! Some say he shall be stoned, but that death is too soft for him, say I. Draw our throne into a sheepcote! All deaths are too few, the sharpest too easy. 775

CLOWN Has the old man e'er a son, sir, do you hear, an't like you, sir?

AUTOLYCUS He has a son, who shall be flayed alive, then 'nointed over with honey, set on the head of a wasps'

749–50 **fardel, box** The fardel is the bundle of the infant Perdita's clothing; the box contains the gold left with her and her 'character' (3.3.46).

751 **there lies** Abbott 335 (quasi-singular verbs preceding plural subjects)

755 **Age** old man. Presumably an instance of Autolycus's fantastical usage, for which *OED* cites no parallels.
lost . . . labour Proverbial (Tilley L9).

757–60 Compare *Pandosto*, Appendix B, p. 264.

763 **in handfast** Loosely speaking, under arrest (*OED* 1b); the word seems to be related to the technical legal term *mainprize*, 'the action of procuring the release of a prisoner by becoming surety for his appearance' (*OED* 2), hence not free to depart.

767 **wit** invention, ingenuity

768 **heavy** painful
germane related

772 **offer** presume, propose

778–86 **flayed. . . death** The principal analogues cited for the punishment are

nest, then stand till he be three-quarters and a dram   780
dead, then recovered again with aqua vitae or some
other hot infusion, then, raw as he is, and in the hottest
day prognostication proclaims, shall he be set against a
brick wall, the sun looking with a southward eye upon
him, where he is to behold him with flies blown to   785
death. But what talk we of these traitorly rascals, whose
miseries are to be smiled at, their offences being so
capital? Tell me—for you seem to be honest, plain
men—what you have to the King. Being something
gently considered, I'll bring you where he is aboard,   790
tender your persons to his presence, whisper him in
your behalfs; and if it be in man besides the King to
effect your suits, here is man shall do it.

CLOWN He seems to be of great authority. Close with him,
give him gold; and though authority be a stubborn   795
bear, yet he is oft led by the nose with gold. Show the
inside of your purse to the outside of his hand, and no
more ado. Remember 'stoned' and 'flayed alive'.

OLD SHEPHERD An't please you, sir, to undertake the
business for us, here is that gold I have. I'll make it as   800
much more, and leave this young man in pawn till I
bring it you.

AUTOLYCUS After I have done what I promised?

Boccaccio, *Decameron* 2.9, a source for
Cymbeline, where Ambrogivolo, the Iachimo figure, is sentenced to a similar
death, and various atrocities committed
by the Spanish on American natives (see
J. D. Rogers, 'Voyages and Exploration',
in *Shakespeare's England*, i. 185).
Pafford, citing J. C. Maxwell, adds an
episode from William of Malmesbury's
Historiae Novellae; by Shakespeare's time
the torture had clearly become a topos
for the barbarity of foreigners.

780 **a dram** a little more (literally, one-
sixteenth of an ounce or 1.8 g.)
781 **aqua vitae** The term applied to any
distilled liquor, in the period primarily
brandy and whisky (usquebaugh).
782 **hot** pungent, acrid (*OED* 5)
783 **prognostication proclaims** forecast
in the almanac

785 **he** either the sun, or the Clown's father
   with . . . blown fly-blown, i.e. stung
   and swollen
786 **what** why
788 **capital** Both 'notable', and 'punish-
   able by death'.
789 **have to** have to do with
789–90 **Being . . . considered** 'for a bribe
   (consideration) suitable to a gentleman'.
   Pafford, followed by Bevington, proposes
   an unlikely alternative, 'being a gentleman of some influence'; but the Shepherd duly offers Autolycus the bribe at
   lines 799–800.
791 **tender . . . presence** present you to
   him
794 **Close . . . him** accept his offer
795–6 **though . . . nose** 'to lead (most
   commonly asses, but sometimes bears)
   by the nose' was proverbial (Dent N233)

OLD SHEPHERD Ay, sir.

AUTOLYCUS Well, give me the moiety. (*To the Clown*) Are   805
you a party in this business?

CLOWN In some sort, sir; but though my case be a pitiful
one, I hope I shall not be flayed out of it.

AUTOLYCUS O, that's the case of the shepherd's son—hang
him, he'll be made an example.   810

CLOWN Comfort, good comfort! (*Aside to the Shepherd*) We
must to the King and show our strange sights. He must
know 'tis none of your daughter nor my sister; we are
gone else.—Sir, I will give you as much as this old man
does when the business is performed, and remain, as he   815
says, your pawn till it be brought you.

AUTOLYCUS I will trust you. Walk before toward the seaside; go on the right hand—I will but look upon the
hedge, and follow you.

CLOWN We are blessed in this man, as I may say, even   820
blessed.

OLD SHEPHERD Let's before, as he bids us. He was provided
to do us good.   *Exeunt Shepherd and Clown*

AUTOLYCUS If I had a mind to be honest, I see Fortune
would not suffer me—she drops booties in my mouth. I   825
am courted now with a double occasion, gold, and a
means to do the prince my master good—which who
knows how that may turn back to my advancement? I
will bring these two moles, these blind ones, aboard
him. If he think it fit to shore them again, and that the   830
complaint they have to the King concerns him nothing,
let him call me rogue for being so far officious; for I am
proof against that title and what shame else belongs
to't. To him will I present them; there may be matter
in it.   *Exit*   835

823 *Exeunt . . . Clown*] ROWE 1709; *Exeunt* F2; *not in* F1   835 *Exit*] ROWE 1709; *Exeunt.* F

805 **the moiety** Lit. half; the first instal-
ment, as promised in ll. 800–1.
807 **case** Both 'situation' and 'skin'.
814 **gone** lost
818–20 **look . . . hedge** i.e. to urinate (as
a way of providing an exit for the clowns
without him)
825 **booties** the plural of booty

826 **with . . . occasion** by a doubly good
fortune
828 **turn back** redound
829 **moles . . . ones** The blindness of
moles was proverbial: Dent M1034.
830 **shore them** put them ashore
833 **proof . . . title** i.e. I am used to being
called a rogue

5.1   *Enter Leontes, Cleomenes, Dion, Paulina, Servants*

CLEOMENES

Sir, you have done enough, and have performed
A saint-like sorrow. No fault could you make
Which you have not redeemed; indeed, paid down
More penitence than done trespass. At the last,
Do as the heavens have done, forget your evil;   5
With them forgive yourself.

LEONTES   Whilst I remember
Her and her virtues, I cannot forget
My blemishes in them, and so still think of
The wrong I did myself, which was so much
That heirless it hath made my kingdom, and   10
Destroyed the sweet'st companion that e'er man
Bred his hopes out of. True?

PAULINA   Too true, my lord.
If one by one you wedded all the world,
Or from the all that are took something good
To make a perfect woman, she you killed   15
Would be unparalleled.

LEONTES   I think so. Killed?
She I killed? I did so, but thou strik'st me

5.1.0.1 *Enter . . . Servants*] ROWE 1709; F *adds* 'Florizel, Perdita.'   12 of. True? |
PAULINA Too] F (of, true. | PAULINA Too); of. | PAULINA True, too THEOBALD

5.1.3 **paid down** fully paid (compare the
    modern 'paid up')
  5 **Do . . . evil** As the repentant are
    assured by the Book of Common Prayer,
    Visitation of the Sick: 'merciful God,
    which . . . dost so put away the sins of
    those which truly repent, that thou re-
    memberest them no more' (cited by
    Noble, *Shakespeare's Biblical Knowledge*,
    p. 248).
  8 **in them** as regards them (Abbott 162).
    Compare 'Our fears in Banquo | Stick
    deep', *Macbeth* 3.1.50–1.
14–15 **from . . . woman** Compare Ferdi-
    nand on Miranda: 'O you, | So perfect
    and so peerless, are created | Of every
    creature's best' (*Tempest* 3.1.46–8), and
    Orlando's poem to Rosalind, *As You Like
    It* 3.2.139 ff. Johnson, glossing the *Tem-
    pest* passage, cited 'the picture of Venus
    by Apelles', which synthesized the most
    perfect features of the most beautiful

women he could find. Bacon alludes to
the story in *Of Beauty*, where it serves as
a pejorative example of artistic trifling:
'There is no excellent beauty that hath
not some strangeness in the proportion.
A man cannot tell whether Apelles or
Albert Dürer were the more trifler,
whereof the one [i.e. Dürer] would make
a personage by geometrical proportions,
the other, by taking the best parts out of
divers faces, to make one excellent' (*Essays* XLIII). In all the ancient sources,
the story is about Zeuxis, not Apelles,
and the painting is of Helen. Cicero
recounts it in *De Inventione* 2.1; Pafford
cites a version from Pliny. To transfer
the image from Helen to Venus as the
prototype of female beauty was also
necessarily to change the artist: it was
Apelles whose most famous painting
was of Aphrodite.

Sorely to say I did. It is as bitter
Upon thy tongue as in my thought. Now, good now,
Say so but seldom.

CLEOMENES   Not at all, good lady.   20
You might have spoken a thousand things that would
Have done the time more benefit, and graced
Your kindness better.

PAULINA   You are one of those
Would have him wed again.

DION   If you would not so,
You pity not the state, nor the remembrance   25
Of his most sovereign name, consider little
What dangers by his highness' fail of issue
May drop upon his kingdom and devour
Incertain lookers-on. What were more holy
Than to rejoice the former Queen is well?   30
What holier than, for royalty's repair,
For present comfort and for future good,
To bless the bed of majesty again
With a sweet fellow to't?

PAULINA   There is none worthy,
Respecting her that's gone. Besides, the gods   35
Will have fulfilled their secret purposes;
For has not the divine Apollo said,
Is't not the tenor of his oracle,
That King Leontes shall not have an heir
Till his lost child be found? Which that it shall   40
Is all as monstrous to our human reason
As my Antigonus to break his grave
And come again to me, who, on my life,
Did perish with the infant. 'Tis your counsel
My lord should to the heavens be contrary,   45

---

19 **good now** 'interjectional expression denoting entreaty, expostulation'
(Onions). Compare *Antony* 1.3.78–9,
'Good now, play one scene | Of excellent
dissembling'.

26 **consider little** you little consider

27 **fail** This is the noun in Shakespeare's
time. See 2.3.169.

28–9 **devour . . . lookers-on** destroy the
spectators, unsure of what to do (in the

absence of a secure succession)

30 **well** Either in heaven, or simply 'well
out of it'; compare *Antony*, 2.5.31–2,
'we use | To say the dead are well'.
Tilley and Dent record as proverbial 'He
is well since he is in heaven' (H347).

35 **Respecting** compared with

36 **Will . . . purposes** will have their secret purposes fulfilled

45 **contrary** Commonly (as here), though

Oppose against their wills. (*To Leontes*) Care not for
    issue;
The crown will find an heir. Great Alexander
Left his to th' worthiest; so his successor
Was like to be the best.
LEONTES   Good Paulina,
Who hast the memory of Hermione,   50
I know, in honour, O that ever I
Had squared me to thy counsel! Then, even now,
I might have looked upon my Queen's full eyes,
Have taken treasure from her lips—
PAULINA   And left them
More rich for what they yielded.
LEONTES   Thou speak'st truth.   55
No more such wives, therefore no wife. One worse,
And better used, would make her sainted spirit
Again possess her corpse, and on this stage,
Where we offenders now appear, soul-vexed,
And begin, 'Why to me?'
PAULINA   Had she such power,   60

not invariably, accented on the second
syllable.

47–8 **Alexander . . . worthiest** The story
is not in Plutarch; Pafford cites a version
of it from John Brende's translation of
Quintus Curtius, *The Historie . . . contein-
ing the Actes of . . . Alexander* (1602):
when Alexander was dying, 'they demanded whom he would leave his king-
dome? He said: to the worthiest' (fol.
300ᵛ).

52 **squared me to** been guided by (compare 3.3.40)

56–60 **One . . . me** The syntax is, 'One
worse would make her spirit again possess her corpse, and, soul-vexed, [do so]
on this [very] stage where we appear,
and begin . . .'. The passage is undeniably awkward; the syntax, however,
is no more strained than that of much
else in the play, and its grammar, in
fact, is unexceptionable. The speech has
been much debated and emended,
though it was not found problematic
before Theobald, who considered the
difficulty to be grammatical, and printed
'stage, | (Where we offend her now)
appear . . .'; this was adopted by War-

burton, Johnson, and numerous others
until late in the 19th century. Hanmer
dealt with the crux by simply expanding
the parenthesis, '(Where we offenders
now appear soul-vex'd)'; despite (or
perhaps because of) its simplicity, this
was not subsequently found persuasive.
Other emendations include Rann's
'(Were we offenders now)', adopted by
Pafford; Dover Wilson and Quiller-
Couch's 'Where we offenders move'
(following Moorman), adopted by
Schanzer; and the original Cambridge's
'Where we're offenders now, appear' followed by Bevington. Wells and Taylor's
old-spelling Shakespeare prints '(Where
we offendors morne) appeare', explaining that ' "Morne" (i.e. "mourne")
could be misread "nowe".' No doubt it
could, but the emendation is clearly ar-
bitrary, and the argument from hypothetical handwriting will support any
number of alternative possibilities, including all those here cited. The problem
is not grammatical, it is why Leontes
should refer to himself, his court, and
especially Paulina, as 'offenders'. If the
Folio reading is correct, this may be a
simple acknowledgement that, in con-

She had just cause.

LEONTES   She had, and would incense me
To murder her I married.

PAULINA   I should so.
Were I the ghost that walked, I'd bid you mark
Her eye, and tell me for what dull part in't
You chose her; then I'd shriek, that even your ears   65
Should rift to hear me, and the words that followed
Should be, 'Remember mine.'

LEONTES   Stars, stars,
And all eyes else dead coals—fear thou no wife;
I'll have no wife, Paulina.

PAULINA   Will you swear
Never to marry but by my free leave?   70

LEONTES
Never, Paulina, so be blessed my spirit.

PAULINA
Then good my lords, bear witness to his oath.

CLEOMENES
You tempt him over-much.

PAULINA   Unless another
As like Hermione as is her picture
Affront his eye.

CLEOMENES   Good madam—

PAULINA   I have done.   75

61 just cause] F3; just such cause F1   75 Good . . . done] CAPELL; Good Madame, I haue
done. | *Paul.* F

trast with the saintliness of Hermione's
spirit, we are all sinners. Alternatively, it
may imply that we offend her memory
by merely discussing the question of
remarriage. Or it may express Leontes'
conviction that our continued life constitutes a continuing affront to her
offended spirit. The argument against
the Folio reading, that Hermione's spirit
would not take offence since the idea of
remarriage is being rejected, and that
Paulina is in any case not at fault, is
scarcely relevant: this is a play in which
reproach is so generalized that every
major character is at some point declared criminally guilty of something;
and the attempt to make 'we offenders
now' mean 'we who would be offenders

if we agreed to a remarriage' surely
assumes a kind of psychological neatness to both the play and its syntax that
is quite alien to it throughout. There is,
in short, no reason to emend.

60 **Why to me?** Why have you done this to
me? Compare the opening of Jonson's *Exe-
cration Upon Vulcan*, 'And why to me this'.

61 **just cause** F's 'just such cause' has
been, since F3, and with the notable
exception of Theobald, considered a
printer's error, adopted from the 'such'
in the previous line.

66 **rift** gape open
67 **mine** my eyes
73 **tempt** try
75 **Affront** confront. Compare *Hamlet*

Yet if my lord will marry—if you will, sir,
No remedy but you will—give me the office
To choose you a queen. She shall not be so young
As was your former, but she shall be such
As, walked your first queen's ghost, it should take joy   80
To see her in your arms.

LEONTES   My true Paulina,
We shall not marry till thou bidd'st us.

PAULINA   That
Shall be when your first queen's again in breath;
Never till then.

　　　Enter a Servant

SERVANT
One that gives out himself Prince Florizel,   85
Son of Polixenes, with his princess—she
The fairest I have yet beheld—desires access
To your high presence.

LEONTES   What with him? He comes not
Like to his father's greatness. His approach,
So out of circumstance, and sudden, tells us   90
'Tis not a visitation framed, but forced
By need and accident. What train?

SERVANT   But few,
And those but mean.

LEONTES   His princess, say you, with him?

3.1.32–3, 'That he ... may here | Af-
front Ophelia'.

75 **Good . . . done** F gives the whole to
Cleomenes; the decision to split the passage between him and Paulina was
Capell's; it has been followed by most
editors, and seems to me to make the
best sense dramatically. But Knight registered a strong and reasonable dissent:
'The vehemence of Paulina overbears
the interruption of Cleomenes, and he
says, "I have done." The modern editors
give "I have done" to Paulina; when
she is evidently going on, perfectly re-
gardless of any opposition.' Forster objected that ' "Yet" [line 76] introduces a
concession on her part, which properly
follows the "I have done" ' (both cited in
the *Variorum*), but as Wells and Taylor
observe, 'Paulina's concession from a

position of strength is no less effective,
and is consistent with the comedy in her
presentation.' Theatrically, either reading makes good sense.

84.1 **Servant** Theobald, followed by many
editors, changed 'Servant' to 'Gentleman', to take account of the familiarity
of his tone and of the subsequent allusion to his verses on Hermione (ll. 100–
1), but the change is unnecessary: the
King's servants are gentlemen.
85 **gives out** announces
88 **What** what company
90 **out of circumstance** unceremonious.
Circumstance = 'the "ado" made about
anything; formality, ceremony' (*OED*
II. 7).
91 **framed** planned
92 **train** retinue

SERVANT

Ay, the most peerless piece of earth, I think,
That e'er the sun shone bright on.

PAULINA   O Hermione,   95
As every present time doth boast itself
Above a better gone, so must thy grave
Give way to what's seen now. *(To the Servant)* Sir,
    you yourself
Have said, and writ so—but your writing now
Is colder than that theme—she had not been,   100
Nor was not to be equalled; thus your verse
Flowed with her beauty once. 'Tis shrewdly ebbed
To say you have seen a better.

SERVANT   Pardon, madam.
The one I have almost forgot—your pardon;
The other, when she has obtained your eye,   105
Will have your tongue too. This is a creature,
Would she begin a sect, might quench the zeal
Of all professors else, make proselytes
Of who she but bid follow.

PAULINA   How—not women!

SERVANT

Women will love her that she is a woman   110
More worth than any man; men, that she is
The rarest of all women.

LEONTES   Go, Cleomenes;
Yourself, assisted with your honoured friends,

---

94 **piece** masterpiece. Compare *Tempest*
1.2.56, 'Thy mother was a piece of
virtue'. Dent records both 'a peerless
piece' and 'a piece of earth' as proverbial
(P289.1, P290.1).

97 **thy grave** i.e. you in your grave—the
container for the thing contained

100 **that theme** the subject of your verse
(who is dead)

100–1 **she . . . equalled** All editors since
Hanmer, with the exception of Schanzer
and the Oxford editors, treat this as a
quotation from the gentleman-servant's
poem. Schanzer, however, observes that
the tenses are wrong: 'what the Gentleman must have written is "she has not
been, nor is not to be, equalled" ', and

Paulina's version of the line is therefore
not verbatim but indirect discourse.

102 **shrewdly** Relevant senses range from
opprobrium to praise: maliciously (*OED*
1), severely (2, 3), seriously (5), astute-
ly, sagaciously (7).

108 **professors else** members of other
sects; professor = 'a professed member
of a religious order' (*OED*).

109 **who** For 'whom': Abbott 274.
women! Most editors retain F's question mark, but the punctuation is ambiguous, the question mark often
standing for an exclamation point, and
Paulina's banter is surely exclamatory,
not interrogative.

Bring them to our embracement.

Exit Cleomenes with others

Still, 'tis strange
He thus should steal upon us.

PAULINA   Had our prince,   115
Jewel of children, seen this hour, he had paired
Well with this lord. There was not full a month
Between their births.

LEONTES   Prithee no more, cease; thou know'st
He dies to me again when talked of. Sure
When I shall see this gentleman, thy speeches   120
Will bring me to consider that which may
Unfurnish me of reason. They are come.

Enter Florizel, Perdita, Cleomenes and others

Your mother was most true to wedlock, prince,
For she did print your royal father off,
Conceiving you. Were I but twenty-one,   125
Your father's image is so hit in you,
His very air, that I should call you brother,
As I did him, and speak of something wildly
By us performed before. Most dearly welcome,
And your fair princess—goddess! O! Alas,   130
I lost a couple that 'twixt heaven and earth
Might thus have stood, begetting wonder, as
You, gracious couple, do; and then I lost—
All mine own folly—the society,
Amity too, of your brave father, whom,   135
Though bearing misery, I desire my life
Once more to look on him.

FLORIZEL   By his command
Have I here touched Sicilia, and from him
Give you all greetings that a king, at friend,
Can send his brother; and but infirmity,   140
Which waits upon worn times, hath something seized

114 *Exit . . . others*] JOHNSON (*subs.*);   *Exit* F (*after* 'us', *l.* 115)

126 **hit** perfectly achieved
135–7 **whom . . . him** 'I desire to go on
living, though I endure misery, in order
to look on him once more.' The concluding 'him' is redundant; for the construction, see Abbott 248 and 249 (Relative

with supplementary pronoun).
139 **at friend** in the way of friendship
(Abbott 143)
140 **but** were it not that
141 **waits . . . times** accompanies old age
141–2 **something . . . ability** partly re-

His wished ability, he had himself
The lands and waters 'twixt your throne and his
Measured to look upon you, whom he loves—
He bade me say so—more than all the sceptres   145
And those that bear them living.
LEONTES   O my brother,
Good gentleman, the wrongs I have done thee stir
Afresh within me, and these thy offices,
So rarely kind, are as interpreters
Of my behindhand slackness. Welcome hither,   150
As is the spring to th'earth. And hath he too
Exposed this paragon to th' fearful usage—
At least ungentle—of the dreadful Neptune,
To greet a man not worth her pains, much less
Th'adventure of her person?
FLORIZEL   Good my lord,   155
She came from Libya.
LEONTES   Where the warlike Smalus,
That noble, honoured lord, is feared and loved?
FLORIZEL
Most royal sir, from thence; from him whose
      daughter
His tears proclaimed his, parting with her; thence,
A prosperous south wind friendly, we have crossed   160
To execute the charge my father gave me
For visiting your highness. My best train
I have from your Sicilian shores dismissed,
Who for Bohemia bend to signify
Not only my success in Libya, sir,   165

---

158 Most . . . daughter] HANMER; *two lines in* F, . . . Sir, | From   159 his, parting]
HANMER; his parting F

moved the ability he wishes he had (to
visit you)

144 **Measured** travelled
148 **offices** kindnesses (*OED* 1)
149 **rarely** exceptionally
149-50 **are . . . slackness** reveal to me
      how remiss I have been (in attentions
      towards Polixenes)
150-1 **Welcome . . . earth** A variation on
      the proverbial 'welcome as flowers in
      May' (Dent F390).

155 **adventure** hazard
156 **Smalus** No source has been found for
      Smalus, but Pafford notes that in the life
      of Dion, Plutarch refers to a voyage from
      Libya to a Sicilian town governed by a
      Carthaginian named Synalus, and sug-
      gests a compositor's misreading of *yn* for
      m. This, of course, would put the war-
      like Smalus in Sicily, not Libya, but
      Pafford is suggesting only that the
      name, like a number of others in the
      play, comes from Plutarch.

But my arrival, and my wife's, in safety
Here where we are.
LEONTES   The blessèd gods
Purge all infection from our air whilst you
Do climate here! You have a holy father,
A graceful gentleman, against whose person,   170
So sacred as it is, I have done sin,
For which the heavens, taking angry note,
Have left me issueless; and your father's blessed,
As he from heaven merits it, with you,
Worthy his goodness. What might I have been,   175
Might I a son and daughter now have looked on,
Such goodly things as you!
      Enter a Lord
LORD   Most noble sir,
That which I shall report will bear no credit,
Were not the proof so nigh. Please you, great sir,
Bohemia greets you from himself by me,   180
Desires you to attach his son, who has,
His dignity and duty both cast off,
Fled from his father, from his hopes, and with
A shepherd's daughter.
LEONTES   Where's Bohemia? Speak.
LORD
Here in your city; I now came from him.   185
I speak amazedly, and it becomes
My marvel and my message. To your court
Whiles he was hast'ning, in the chase, it seems,
Of this fair couple, meets he on the way
The father of this seeming lady and   190
Her brother, having both their country quitted
With this young prince.
FLORIZEL   Camillo has betrayed me,
Whose honour and whose honesty till now
Endured all weathers.
LORD   Lay't so to his charge;

169 **climate** 'sojourn in a particular re-
    gion' (*OED*, citing only this passage).
    Compare 'wombs', 4.4.487, and see
    Abbott 290.
170 **graceful** full of divine grace (*OED* 1),

virtuous (2)
176 **son and daughter** See ll. 207–8.
181 **attach** arrest
186–7 **becomes . . . marvel** befits my
    amazement

He's with the King your father.

LEONTES   Who? Camillo?   195

LORD

Camillo, sir; I spake with him, who now
Has these poor men in question. Never saw I
Wretches so quake—they kneel, they kiss the earth,
Forswear themselves as often as they speak;
Bohemia stops his ears, and threatens them   200
With divers deaths in death.

PERDITA   O my poor father!
The heaven sets spies upon us, will not have
Our contract celebrated.

LEONTES   You are married?

FLORIZEL

We are not, sir, nor are we like to be.
The stars, I see, will kiss the valleys first;   205
The odds for high and low's alike.

LEONTES   My lord,
Is this the daughter of a king?

FLORIZEL   She is,
When once she is my wife.

LEONTES

That 'once' I see by your good father's speed
Will come on very slowly. I am sorry,   210
Most sorry you have broken from his liking,
Where you were tied in duty, and as sorry

197 **Has . . . question** is questioning these
    poor men
203 **You . . . married?** See 4.4.385.
206 **The . . . alike** A baffling piece of wis-
    dom, much debated. Douce observed
    that loaded dice were called 'high and
    low', and Dover Wilson and Quiller-
    Couch cite *Merry Wives* 1.3.81, 'high
    and low beguiles the rich and poor'. The
    parallel is persuasive, though only Ker-
    mode among recent editors has found it
    conclusive evidence that the reference is
    to dice—I tend to agree, but even so, the
    meaning of Florizel's line is not thereby
    rendered self-evident. The sense is ob-
    viously that we are bound to lose, with
    'the odds' presumably what they would
    be if we were playing against an oppon-
    ent who used loaded dice. Dover Wilson
    and Quiller-Couch gloss the line 'For-

tune is a cheater who beguiles princes
and shepherds alike with his false dice',
but this requires 'high and low' to be
simultaneously dice and social ine-
quities, which strikes me as unlikely—
the *Merry Wives* passage includes both
'high and low' and 'rich and poor', and
is clearly not redundant. Without the
dice, plausible interpretations include
'fortune is the same for the noble and
the humble (therefore my princely birth
is no advantage to me)', and 'the chan-
ces of high and low (being united in
marriage) are as good as those that the
stars will kiss the valleys'.
207–8 **daughter . . . wife** 'Daughter' and
'son' could be used for 'daughter-in-law'
and 'son-in-law' (hence the irony of
l. 176).

Your choice is not so rich in worth as beauty
That you might well enjoy her.
FLORIZEL   Dear, look up.
Though fortune, visible an enemy,   215
Should chase us with my father, power no jot
Hath she to change our loves. Beseech you, sir,
Remember since you owed no more to Time
Than I do now. With thought of such affections
Step forth mine advocate—at your request   220
My father will grant precious things as trifles.
LEONTES
Would he do so, I'd beg your precious mistress,
Which he counts but a trifle.
PAULINA   Sir, my liege,
Your eye hath too much youth in't. Not a month
Fore your queen died, she was more worth such gazes   225
Than what you look on now.
LEONTES   I thought of her
Even in these looks I made. But your petition
Is yet unanswered. I will to your father.
Your honour not o'erthrown by your desires,
I am friend to them and you; upon which errand   230
I now go toward him, therefore follow me,
And mark what way I make. Come, good my lord.
                                                    Exeunt

5.2   *Enter Autolycus and a Gentleman*

AUTOLYCUS Beseech you, sir, were you present at this
     relation?
FIRST GENTLEMAN I was by at the opening of the fardel,
     heard the old shepherd deliver the manner how he

---

213 **worth** rank
214 **look up** Proverbial for 'keep your
     spirits up' (Dent L431.1).
215–16 **visible . . . Should** should become
     a visible enemy, and
216 **jot** smallest bit. From *iota*, the smallest
     letter in the Greek alphabet.
218–19 **since . . . now** when you were no
     older than I am now
222–7 This is the only remnant of Pan-
     dosto's incenstuous passion for Fawnia;

see Appendix B, pp. 267–8.
229 **Your . . . desires** Either 'provided
     your love has not been dishonourable
     (i.e. unchaste)', recalling Prospero's
     warnings to Ferdinand against pre-mari-
     tal sex, or simply 'provided your wishes
     are not incompatible with your rank'.
232 **what . . . make** how far I succeed
5.2.2 relation narration
     4 **deliver** recount

found it; whereupon, after a little amazedness, we were   5
all commanded out of the chamber. Only this, methought I heard the shepherd say he found the child.

AUTOLYCUS I would most gladly know the issue of it.

FIRST GENTLEMAN I make a broken delivery of the business; but the changes I perceived in the King and   10
Camillo were very notes of admiration. They seemed
almost with staring on one another to tear the cases of
their eyes. There was speech in their dumbness, language in their very gesture; they looked as they had
heard of a world ransomed, or one destroyed. A notable   15
passion of wonder appeared in them, but the wisest
beholder that knew no more but seeing could not say if
th'importance were joy or sorrow—but in the extremity
of the one it must needs be.

Enter another Gentleman

Here comes a gentleman that haply knows more. The   20
news, Ruggiero?

SECOND GENTLEMAN Nothing but bonfires. The oracle is
fulfilled, the King's daughter is found; such a deal of
wonder is broken out within this hour that ballad-
makers cannot be able to express it.   25

Enter another Gentleman

Here comes the Lady Paulina's steward; he can deliver
you more. How goes it now, sir? This news, which is
called true, is so like an old tale that the verity of it is
in strong suspicion. Has the King found his heir?

THIRD GENTLEMAN Most true, if ever truth were pregnant   30
by circumstance. That which you hear you'll swear you
see, there is such unity in the proofs. The mantle of

5.2.20 haply] F (happily)

8 **issue** outcome

9 **broken delivery** disjointed report

11 **notes of admiration** indications
of wonder; specifically, exclamation
points: note = 'a sign or character
(other than a letter) used in writing or
printing' (*OED* 10). Compare Jonson in
The English Grammar, 'If a Sentence be
with an *Interrogation*, we use this note
(?) . . . . If it be pronounced with an
Admiration, then thus (!)' (*Ben Jonson*,

ed. Herford and Simpson, viii. 552–3).

12–13 **cases . . . eyes** their eyelids

17 **no . . . seeing** no more than he could
see

18 **importance** implications

18–19 **in . . . one** the most extreme degree
of either one

30–1 **pregnant by circumstance** made
clear by detailed evidence; pregnant =
'of an argument, proof, evidence, reason, etc.: . . . clear, obvious' (*OED*)

Queen Hermione's; her jewel about the neck of it; the
letters of Antigonus found with it, which they know to
be his character; the majesty of the creature in resem-   35
blance of the mother; the affection of nobleness which
nature shows above her breeding; and many other
evidences proclaim her with all certainty to be the
King's daughter. Did you see the meeting of the two
Kings?   40

SECOND GENTLEMAN No.

THIRD GENTLEMAN Then have you lost a sight which was
to be seen, cannot be spoken of. There might you have
beheld one joy crown another so and in such manner
that it seemed sorrow wept to take leave of them, for   45
their joy waded in tears. There was casting up of eyes,
holding up of hands, with countenance of such distraction that they were to be known by garment, not by
favour. Our King, being ready to leap out of himself for
joy of his found daughter, as if that joy were now   50
become a loss cries, 'O, thy mother, thy mother!'; then
asks Bohemia forgiveness, then embraces his son-in-
law; then again worries he his daughter with clipping
her. Now he thanks the old shepherd, which stands by
like a weather-beaten conduit of many kings' reigns. I   55
never heard of such another encounter, which lames
report to follow it, and undoes description to do it.

SECOND GENTLEMAN What, pray you, became of Antigonus, that carried hence the child?

THIRD GENTLEMAN Like an old tale still, which will have   60
matter to rehearse though credit be asleep and not an
ear open—he was torn to pieces with a bear. This
avouches the shepherd's son, who has not only his

---

35 **character** handwriting. For the letters,
see 3.3.46.
36 **affection of** disposition toward (*OED* 5)
47 **countenance** Either 'demeanour', or
perhaps simply 'faces', an implied plural: 'The plural and possessive cases of
nouns in which the singular ends in s,
se, ss, ce, and ge, are frequently written,
and still more frequently pronounced,
without the additional syllable' (Abbott
471).
49 **favour** features

49–50 **leap . . . joy** Varying the proverbial
'leap out of his skin for joy' (Dent S507).
53 **clipping** embracing
54 **which** For 'who', Abbott 265.
55 **conduit** fountain or water-spout. Compare *Romeo* 3.5.129, 'How now, a conduit, girl? What, still in tears?'
57 **undoes . . . it** unfits the power of description to describe it
61 **credit** belief
62 **with** by (Abbott 193)

innocence, which seems much, to justify him, but a
handkerchief and rings of his that Paulina knows.   65
FIRST GENTLEMAN What became of his barque and his
  followers?
THIRD GENTLEMAN Wrecked the same instant of their
  master's death, and in the view of the shepherd; so that
  all the instruments which aided to expose the child were   70
  even then lost when it was found. But O, the noble
  combat that 'twixt joy and sorrow was fought in
  Paulina! She had one eye declined for the loss of her
  husband, another elevated that the oracle was fulfilled.
  She lifted the princess from the earth, and so locks her   75
  in embracing as if she would pin her to her heart, that
  she might no more be in danger of losing.
FIRST GENTLEMAN The dignity of this act was worth the
  audience of kings and princes, for by such was it acted.
THIRD GENTLEMAN One of the prettiest touches of all, and   80
  that which angled for mine eyes—caught the water,
  though not the fish—was when at the relation of the
  Queen's death, with the manner how she came to't
  bravely confessed and lamented by the King, how
  attentiveness wounded his daughter; till from one sign   85
  of dolour to another she did, with an 'Alas!', I would
  fain say bleed tears; for I am sure my heart wept blood.
  Who was most marble there changed colour. Some
  swooned, all sorrowed; if all the world could have
  seen't, the woe had been universal.   90
FIRST GENTLEMAN Are they returned to the court?
THIRD GENTLEMAN No. The princess hearing of her
  mother's statue, which is in the keeping of Paulina—a
  piece many years in doing and now newly performed by
  that rare Italian master Giulio Romano, who, had he   95

---

64 **innocence** 'freedom from cunning or
    artifice; guilelessness, simplicity'
    (*OED* 3)
73–4 **one ... elevated** Compare Claudius
    'With one auspicious and one dropping
    eye', *Hamlet* 1.2.11. 'To cry with one
    eye and laugh with the other' was
    proverbial (Dent E248).
77 **losing** being lost. Compare 'Women are
    angels, wooing' (for 'being wooed'),
    Troilus 1.2.282. See Abbott 372: 'It

would sometimes appear that Shakespeare fancied that *-ing* was equivalent
to *-en*, the old affix of the Passive
Participle.'
94 **performed** completed
95 **Giulio Romano** (1499–1546), one of
    the most famous Italian artists of the
    16th century, pupil and heir of Raphael,
    and the only contemporary artist men-
    tioned by Shakespeare. Both the ana-
    chronism and the fact that Giulio was

himself eternity and could put breath into his work,
would beguile nature of her custom, so perfectly he is
her ape. He so near to Hermione hath done Hermione
that they say one would speak to her and stand in hope
of answer. Thither with all greediness of affection are   100
they gone, and there they intend to sup.

SECOND GENTLEMAN I thought she had some great matter
there in hand, for she hath privately twice or thrice a
day ever since the death of Hermione visited that
removed house. Shall we thither, and with our com-   105
pany piece the rejoicing?

FIRST GENTLEMAN Who would be thence that has the
benefit of access? Every wink of an eye, some new grace
will be born—our absence makes us unthrifty to our
knowledge. Let's along.   *Exeunt Gentlemen*   110

AUTOLYCUS Now had I not the dash of my former life in
me, would preferment drop on my head. I brought the
old man and his son aboard the prince, told him I heard
them talk of a fardel and I know not what; but he at

---

110 *Exeunt Gentlemen*] ROWE; *Exit.* F

---

notable as a painter and architect but
not as a sculptor have prompted endless
commentary, and continue to do so.
However, Elze in 1874 was only the first
of a number of scholars to cite Giulio's
epitaph, quoted in Vasari, beginning
'*Videbat Jupiter corpora sculpta pictaque* |
Spirare aedes mortalium aequarier coelo |
Julii virtute Romani': 'Jupiter saw
sculpted and painted bodies breathe and
the houses of mortals made equal to
those in heaven through the skill of
Giulio Romano.' Giulio was, then,
known in the 16th century as a sculptor. This would seem to provide all the
explanation necessary for why Shakespeare should have credited him with
the ability to create living statues, if not
for why there are no extant records of
his sculptures. For a summary of the
debate, and an authoritative discussion
of the topos from Ovid's Pygmalion story
on, see Leonard Barkan, 'Living Sculptures: Ovid, Michelangelo and *The
Winter's Tale*', *ELH* 48 (1981), 639–67.
As for the anachronism, the question of
why Giulio is invoked rather than Zeuxis

can hardly be a real one in a play in
which the Delphic oracle shares the
stage with the kingdom of Bohemia. For
a discussion of the choice of Giulio as the
artist, and of the relation of Paulina's
supposed statue to the Jacobean passion
for collecting, and for collecting Italian
art in particular, see the Introduction,
pp. 53–62. Ross Duffin points out that
there is at least a musical overtone in
the account of the statue in 5.2.93–5, 'a
piece . . . now newly performed by . . .
Giulio Romano', and observes that the
famous singer and composer Giulio Cac-
cini (*c.*1545–1618) was also known
as Giulio Romano. See 'An Encore for
Shakespeare's Rare Italian Master', *The
Elizabethan Review* (Spring, 1994), pp.
21–5.

97–8 **is her ape** imitates nature
100 **greediness of affection** eager love
106 **piece** piece out, add to
109 **unthrifty to** wasting the chance to
    add to
111 **dash** taint

that time overfond of the shepherd's daughter—so he   115
then took her to be—who began to be much seasick,
and himself little better, extremity of weather continuing, this mystery remained undiscovered. But 'tis all
one to me, for had I been the finder-out of this secret, it
would not have relished among my other discredits.   120

Enter Old Shepherd and Clown

Here come those I have done good to against my will,
and already appearing in the blossoms of their fortune.

OLD SHEPHERD Come, boy, I am past more children, but
thy sons and daughters will be all gentlemen born.

CLOWN You are well met, sir. You denied to fight with me   125
this other day because I was no gentleman born. See
you these clothes? Say you see them not, and think me
still no gentleman born—you were best say these robes
are not gentlemen born. Give me the lie, do, and try
whether I am not now a gentleman born.   130

AUTOLYCUS I know you are now, sir, a gentleman born.

CLOWN Ay, and have been so any time these four hours.

OLD SHEPHERD And so have I, boy.

CLOWN So you have; but I was a gentleman born before
my father, for the King's son took me by the hand and   135
called me brother, and then the two Kings called my
father brother, and then the prince my brother and the
princess my sister called my father father, and so we
wept; and there was the first gentlemanlike tears that
ever we shed.   140

OLD SHEPHERD We may live, son, to shed many more.

CLOWN Ay, or else 'twere hard luck, being in so preposterous estate as we are.

AUTOLYCUS I humbly beseech you, sir, to pardon me all
the faults I have committed to your worship, and to give   145
me your good report to the prince my master.

120 **relished** tasted right
124 **gentlemen born** Not according to Elizabethan usage. Douce cited *The Booke of
Honour and Armes*, 1590: 'In saying a
gentleman borne, we meane he must be
descended from three degrees of gentry,
both on the mother's and father's side'

(quoted in the *Variorum*). 'It takes three
generations to make a gentleman' was
proverbial (Dent G58.1).
129 **Give me the lie** accuse me of lying
(and thereby agree to fight me)
142–3 **preposterous** For 'prosperous'.

OLD SHEPHERD Prithee, son, do; for we must be gentle
now we are gentlemen.

CLOWN Thou wilt amend thy life?

AUTOLYCUS Ay, an it like your good worship.   150

CLOWN Give me thy hand. I will swear to the prince thou
art as honest a true fellow as any is in Bohemia.

OLD SHEPHERD You may say it, but not swear it.

CLOWN Not swear it now I am a gentleman? Let boors
and franklins say it, I'll swear it.   155

OLD SHEPHERD How if it be false, son?

CLOWN If it be ne'er so false, a true gentleman may swear
it in the behalf of his friend. And I'll swear to the prince
thou art a tall fellow of thy hands, and that thou wilt
not be drunk—but I know thou art no tall fellow of thy   160
hands, and that thou wilt be drunk—but I'll swear it,
and I would thou wouldst be a tall fellow of thy hands.

AUTOLYCUS I will prove so, sir, to my power.

CLOWN Ay, by any means prove a tall fellow. If I do not
wonder how thou dar'st venture to be drunk, not being   165
a tall fellow, trust me not. Hark, the Kings and the
princes, our kindred, are going to see the Queen's
picture. Come, follow us; we'll be thy good masters.

Exeunt

5.3   *Enter Leontes, Polixenes, Florizel, Perdita, Camillo,*
Paulina, Lords, etc.

LEONTES

O grave and good Paulina, the great comfort
That I have had of thee!

PAULINA   What, sovereign sir,

5.3.0.1–2 *Enter . . . etc.*] ROWE; F *adds after 'Paulina': Hermione (like a Statue:)*

150 **an it like** if it please
154 **Not . . . gentleman** Swearing, like
duelling, was a prerogative of
gentlemen, as Cloten, in characteristically boorish fashion, insists:
'When a gentleman is disposed to swear
it is not for any standers-by to curtail his
oaths' (*Cymbeline* 2.1.10–11).
154–5 **boors and franklins** peasants and
yeomen
159 **tall . . . hands** brave man. Compare
'manhandle', which originally meant

'handle in an appropriately manly
fashion'. Furness cites Cotgrave's *Dictionary* (1611), '*Homme à la main*, A
man of execution or valour; a man of
his hands'. Tilley and Dent record the
expression as proverbial (M163).
163 **to** to the extent of
166 **trust me not** or 'never trust me',
proverbial assurances (Dent T558.1)
168 **picture** The term could be used of a
statue or effigy; see *OED* 1d.

I did not well, I meant well; all my services
You have paid home. But that you have vouchsafed,
With your crowned brother and these your contracted   5
Heirs of your kingdoms, my poor house to visit,
It is a surplus of your grace which never
My life may last to answer.
LEONTES   O Paulina,
We honour you with trouble; but we came
To see the statue of our Queen. Your gallery   10
Have we passed through, not without much content
In many singularities, but we saw not
That which my daughter came to look upon,
The statue of her mother.
PAULINA   As she lived peerless,
So her dead likeness I do well believe   15
Excels whatever yet you looked upon,
Or hand of man hath done; therefore I keep it
Lonely, apart. But here it is—prepare
To see the life as lively mocked as ever
Still sleep mocked death.
            Paulina draws a curtain, and reveals Hermione
            standing like a statue
                              Behold, and say 'tis well.   20
I like your silence; it the more shows off
Your wonder. But yet speak—first you, my liege.
Comes it not something near?
LEONTES   Her natural posture.
Chide me, dear stone, that I may say indeed
Thou art Hermione—or rather, thou art she   25
In thy not chiding; for she was as tender
As infancy and grace. But yet, Paulina,
Hermione was not so much wrinkled, nothing

18 Lonely] HANMER; Louely F   20 *Paulina . . . statue*] ROWE; *not in* F

5.3.4 **paid home** fully repaid. 'To pay
home' was proverbial (Dent H 535.1).
9 **We . . . trouble** what you call an honour is a trouble to you. Compare 'The
love that follows us sometime is our
trouble', *Macbeth* 1.6.11.
12 **singularities** rarities
15 **dead** The word also meant perfect,
exact (*OED* 31); compare the modern

'dead ringer'.
18 **Lonely** separate (*OED* 2). Hanmer's
emendation of F's 'louely' has been
generally accepted.
19 **lively mocked** accurately counterfeited
(*OED*, mock, 4)
20 **sleep . . . death** 'Sleep is the image of
death' was proverbial (Dent S527).

225

So agèd as this seems.
POLIXENES   O, not by much.
PAULINA

So much the more our carver's excellence,   30
Which lets go by some sixteen years, and makes her
As she lived now.
LEONTES   As now she might have done,
So much to my good comfort as it is
Now piercing to my soul. O, thus she stood,
Even with such life of majesty—warm life   35
As now it coldly stands—when first I wooed her.
I am ashamed. Does not the stone rebuke me
For being more stone than it? O royal piece!
There's magic in thy majesty, which has
My evils conjured to remembrance, and   40
From thy admiring daughter took the spirits,
Standing like stone with thee.
PERDITA   And give me leave,
And do not say 'tis superstition, that
I kneel and then implore her blessing. Lady,
Dear Queen, that ended when I but began,   45
Give me that hand of yours to kiss.
PAULINA   O, patience—
The statue is but newly fixed; the colour's
Not dry.
CAMILLO

My lord, your sorrow was too sore laid on,
Which sixteen winters cannot blow away,   50
So many summers dry. Scarce any joy
Did ever so long live; no sorrow
But killed itself much sooner.

32 **As** as if
38 **more . . . it** Compare the proverbial
'heart of stone', Dent H310.1, 311.
piece masterpiece
41–2 **admiring . . . thee** The ability of
wonder to turn one to stone was proverbial, Dent S893.1. Compare Jonson,
Poetaster, To the Reader, 68: 'then turn
stone with wonder!' See the Introduction, pp. 61–2.
43 **superstition** The act of kneeling to the
statue would constitute idol worship,

with Roman Catholic overtones; compare Antigonus' determination 'superstitiously' to believe he has seen the ghost
of Hermione, 3.3.39.
47 **fixed** set, completed; or perhaps 'the
paint has only just been applied', an
earlier usage than those recorded in
OED, fix, 4b, 5. Elizabethan and Jacobean effigies (like ancient Greek statues)
were invariably painted to look lifelike.
51 **dry** cannot dry up

POLIXENES   Dear my brother,
 Let him that was the cause of this have power
 To take off so much grief from you as he   55
 Will piece up in himself.
PAULINA   Indeed, my lord,
 If I had thought the sight of my poor image
 Would thus have wrought you—for the stone is
      mine—
 I'd not have showed it.
      She moves to draw the curtain
LEONTES   Do not draw the curtain.
PAULINA
 No longer shall you gaze on't, lest your fancy   60
 May think anon it moves.
LEONTES   Let be, let be.
 Would I were dead, but that methinks already—
 What was he that did make it?—See, my lord,
 Would you not deem it breathed, and that those veins
 Did verily bear blood?
POLIXENES   Masterly done!   65
 The very life seems warm upon her lip.
LEONTES
 The fixure of her eye has motion in't,
 As we are mocked with art.
PAULINA   I'll draw the curtain.
 My lord's almost so far transported that
 He'll think anon it lives.
LEONTES   O sweet Paulina,   70
 Make me to think so twenty years together!
 No settled senses of the world can match
 The pleasure of that madness. Let't alone.
PAULINA
 I am sorry, sir, I have thus far stirred you, but
 I could afflict you farther.

---

59 *She . . . curtain*] COLLIER (*subs.*); *not in* F

54 **him** i.e. myself
56 **piece . . . himself** add to his own
58 **wrought** affected (compare modern 'overwrought')
62 **Would . . . already** Staunton effectively ended a century of debate with the

explanation 'May I die if I do not think it moves *already*' (cited in the *Variorum*).
67 **fixure** fixity
68 **As** thus (Abbott 110)
72 **settled . . . world** calm mind in the world

LEONTES   Do, Paulina,   75
For this affliction has a taste as sweet
As any cordial comfort. Still methinks
There is an air comes from her. What fine chisel
Could ever yet cut breath? Let no man mock me,
For I will kiss her.
PAULINA   Good my lord, forbear.   80
The ruddiness upon her lip is wet;
You'll mar it if you kiss it, stain your own
With oily painting. Shall I draw the curtain?
LEONTES
No, not these twenty years.
PERDITA   So long could I
Stand by, a looker-on.
PAULINA   Either forbear,   85
Quit presently the chapel, or resolve you
For more amazement. If you can behold it,
I'll make the statue move indeed, descend
And take you by the hand—but then you'll think,
Which I protest against, I am assisted   90
By wicked powers.
LEONTES   What you can make her do
I am content to look on, what to speak
I am content to hear; for 'tis as easy
To make her speak as move.
PAULINA   It is required
You do awake your faith. Then all stand still—   95
Or those that think it is unlawful business
I am about, let them depart.
LEONTES   Proceed.
No foot shall stir.
PAULINA   Music; awake her—strike!
        Music

96 Or] HANMER; On: F   98.1 *Music*] ROWE; *not in* F

77 **cordial** restorative (literally 'reviving
   the heart')
86 **presently** immediately
   chapel Not simply a removed room, but
   specifically a place of worship, not
   necessarily Christian (see *OED* 6).
90–1 **I . . . powers** See lines 110–11.

96 **Or those** Hanmer's emendation of F's
   'On: those' has been generally accepted.
   unlawful business See lines 110–11.
98.1 **Music** Cerimon similarly invokes
   music for the resuscitation of Thaisa
   (*Pericles*, Scene 12.86 ff. [3.2.86 ff.]),
   and in the quarto text, the Doctor

(*To Hermione*) 'Tis time; descend; be stone no more;
    approach;
Strike all that look upon with marvel—come,   100
I'll fill your grave up. Stir—nay, come away,
Bequeath to Death your numbness, for from him
Dear life redeems you. (*To Leontes*) You perceive she stirs.
    Hermione descends
Start not; her actions shall be holy as
You hear my spell is lawful. Do not shun her   105
Until you see her die again, for then
You kill her double. Nay, present your hand.
When she was young you wooed her; now in age
Is she become the suitor?
LEONTES   O, she's warm!
If this be magic, let it be an art   110
Lawful as eating.
POLIXENES   She embraces him.
CAMILLO
She hangs about his neck—
If she pertain to life, let her speak too!
POLIXENES
Ay, and make it manifest where she has lived,
Or how stol'n from the dead.
PAULINA   That she is living,   115
Were it but told you, should be hooted at
Like an old tale; but it appears she lives,
Though yet she speak not. Mark a little while.
(*To Perdita*) Please you to interpose, fair madam; kneel
And pray your mother's blessing. (*To Hermione*) Turn,   120
    good lady;

103.1 *Hermione descends*] ROWE (*subs.*); *not in* F

awakes Lear with music (Scene 21.23).

101 **I'll ... up** i.e. you will no longer be
   dead
102 **him** death
106 **then** i.e. if you do
110–11 **magic ... Lawful** Though the
   practice of magic was illegal, prosecutions diminished significantly after about
   1585, and very few cases are recorded
   in the early 17th century. Martin In-

gram concludes that 'in late Elizabethan
and early Stuart times witchcraft and
magical practices were not of major
concern either to the ecclesiastical
authorities or to the majority of the
people' (*Church Courts, Sex and Marriage
in England*, 1570–1640 (Cambridge,
1987), p. 97). See the Introduction,
p. 61.
113 **pertain** belong, with a legal overtone,
   'be entitled' (*OED* 1, 2)

Our Perdita is found.

HERMIONE   You gods look down,
And from your sacred vials pour your graces
Upon my daughter's head! Tell me, mine own,
Where hast thou been preserved, where lived, how
    found
Thy father's court? For thou shalt hear that I,   125
Knowing by Paulina that the oracle
Gave hope thou wast in being, have preserved
Myself to see the issue.

PAULINA   There's time enough for that,
Lest they desire upon this push to trouble
Your joys with like relation. Go together,   130
You precious winners all; your exultation
Partake to everyone. I, an old turtle,
Will wing me to some withered bough, and there
My mate, that's never to be found again,
Lament till I am lost.

LEONTES   O peace, Paulina.   135
Thou shouldst a husband take by my consent,
As I by thine a wife. This is a match,
And made between's by vows. Thou hast found
    mine—
But how is to be questioned, for I saw her,
As I thought, dead, and have in vain said many   140
A prayer upon her grave. I'll not seek far—
For him, I partly know his mind—to find thee
An honourable husband. Come, Camillo,

---

122 vials] F (viols)

121-2 **You . . . graces** Compare Gonzalo's
    invocation of grace upon Ferdinand and
    Miranda, 'Look down, you gods, | And
    on this couple drop a blessèd crown',
    Tempest 5.1.204–5.
126 **Knowing . . . oracle** Hermione was
    in fact present at the reading of the
    oracle, 3.2.130–5.
127 **in being** alive
129–30 **Lest . . . relation** Generally ex-
    plained, 'lest at this critical moment the
    observers should wish to interrupt your
    joy by telling their stories too' (for 'push'

see *OED sb.*[1] 6). But Bevington offers an
    attractive alternative, modernizing F's
    'least' not to 'lest', but to 'least': 'the
    last thing they desire at this dramatic
    moment is to interrupt your joys with a
    narrative of that sort'.
132 **Partake to** share with, communicate
    to (*OED* 2)
    turtle turtle dove, emblematic of con-
    stancy; compare 4.4.154.
135 **lost** dead
142 **For** as for

And take her by the hand, whose worth and honesty
Is richly noted, and here justified   145
By us, a pair of kings. Let's from this place.
(*To Hermione*) What! Look upon my brother. Both
    your pardons
That e'er I put between your holy looks
My ill suspicion. This your son-in-law,
And son unto the King, whom heavens directing,   150
Is troth-plight to your daughter. Good Paulina,
Lead us from hence, where we may leisurely
Each one demand and answer to his part
Performed in this wide gap of time since first
We were dissevered. Hastily lead away.   *Exeunt*   155

144–6 **whose ... kings** Dover Wilson and Quiller-Couch, following Mason and followed by Schanzer, argue that this praise refers to Camillo, not to Paulina. This is grammatically conceivable, but far-fetched; the immediate antecedent, 'her', makes perfectly good sense both logically and dramatically.

145 **noted** well known
    justified confirmed

149 **This** Many editors insert an apostrophe to indicate the omission of 'is', but

the syntax as it stands is unexceptionable: 'This your son-in-law . . . is troth-plight to your daughter.'

150 **whom ... directing** with the heavens guiding him. Editors who add the apostrophe to 'This' in the preceding line thereby produce another ungrammatical *whom* for *who*; see 3.2.32, 4.4.356 and 420.

151 **troth-plight** betrothed; see 1.2.275 and 4.4.385. 'Son-in-law' in line 149 is proleptic.

SIMON FORMAN'S ACCOUNT OF *THE WINTER'S TALE*

FROM Simon Forman's *Booke of Plaies and Notes thereof per formans for Common Pollicie*, Bodleian Ashmole MS 208, fols. 201ᵛ–202ʳ. Reprinted in Chambers, *William Shakespeare*, ii. 340–1; the present text has been modernized.

In *The Winter's Tale* at the Globe 1611 the 15 of May Wednesday, observe there how Leontes the King of Sicilia was overcome with jealousy of his wife with the King of Bohemia, his friend that came to see him, and how he contrived his death and would have had his cupbearer to have poisoned, who gave the King of Bohemia warning thereof and fled with him to Bohemia.

Remember also how he sent to the oracle of Apollo, and the answer of Apollo, that she was guiltless and that the King was jealous, etc., and how except the child was found again that was lost the King should die without issue, for the child was carried into Bohemia and there laid in a forest and brought up by a shepherd. And the King of Bohemia his son married that wench, and how they fled into Sicilia to Leontes, and the shepherd having showed the letter of the nobleman by whom Leontes sent a was [away?] that child, and the jewels found about her, she was known to be Leontes' daughter, and was then sixteen years old.

Remember also the rogue that came in all tattered like colt-pixie,[1] and how he feigned him sick and to have been robbed of all that he had, and how he cozened the poor man of all his money, and after came to the sheep-shear with a pedlar's pack and there cozened them again of all their money, and how he changed apparel with the King of Bohemia his son, and then how he turned courtier, etc. Beware of trusting feigned beggars or fawning fellows.

---

[1] A mischievous sprite or hobgoblin, especially in the shape of a ragged colt luring men to follow it and then disappearing (*OED*).

ROBERT GREENE'S *PANDOSTO*

GREENE'S novel was first published in 1588, and had gone through five editions by the time *The Winter's Tale* was written. These exhibit only minor differences, one of which, however, is significant: in the first three editions, the words of the oracle read as they do in Shakespeare, that 'the King shall live without an heir'; in the fourth edition, 1607, however, the oracle says 'the King shall die without an heir'. It is clear, therefore, that Shakespeare was working from an earlier edition.

This text, prepared by Stanley Wells, is a modernization of the 1588 edition. The only surviving copy of the book, in the British Library, is imperfect, lacking all of sheet B; the text has therefore been augmented where necessary by reference to the Folger Shakespeare Library's copy of the second edition, 1592. Introductory matter has been omitted. Passages from the novel that have close parallels in the play are footnoted.

Pandosto. The Triumph of Time

THE HISTORY OF DORASTUS AND FAWNIA

Among all the passions wherewith human minds are perplexed, there is none that so galleth with restless despite as that infectious sore of jealousy, for all other griefs are either to be appeased with sensible persuasions, to be cured with wholesome counsel, to be relieved in want, or by tract of time to be worn out, jealousy only excepted, which is so sauced with suspicious doubts and pinching mistrust that whoso seeks by friendly counsel to raze out this hellish passion, it forthwith suspecteth that he giveth this advice to cover his own guiltiness. Yea, whoso is pained with this restless torment doubteth all, distrusteth himself, is always frozen with fear and fired with suspicion, having that wherein consisteth all his joy to be the breeder of his misery. Yea, it is such a heavy enemy to that holy estate of matrimony, sowing between the married couple such deadly seeds of secret hatred as, love being once razed out by spiteful distrust, there oft ensueth bloody revenge, as this ensuing history manifestly proveth, wherein Pandosto, furiously incensed by causeless jealousy, procured the death of his most loving and loyal wife, and his own endless sorrow and misery.

In the country of Bohemia there reigned a king called Pandosto, whose fortunate success in wars against his foes, and bountiful courtesy towards his friends in peace, made him to be greatly feared and loved of all men. This Pandosto had to wife a lady called Bellaria, by birth royal, learned by education, fair by nature, by virtues famous, so that it was hard to judge whether her beauty, fortune, or virtue won the greatest commendations. These two, linked together in perfect love, led their lives with such fortunate content that their subjects greatly rejoiced to see their quiet disposition. They had not been married long but Fortune, willing to increase their happiness, lent them a son so adorned with the gifts of nature as the perfection of the child greatly augmented the love of the parents and the joy of their commons,[1] in so much that the Bohemians, to show their inward joys by outward actions, made bonfires and triumphs throughout all the kingdom, appointing jousts and tourneys for the honour of their young prince; whither resorted not only his nobles, but also divers kings and princes which were his neighbours, willing to show their friendship they owed to Pandosto, and to win fame and glory by their prowess and valour.

Pandosto, whose mind was fraught with princely liberality, entertained the kings, princes, and noblemen with such submiss courtesy and magnifical bounty that they all saw how willing he was to gratify their good wills, making a general feast for his subjects, which continued by the space of twenty days; all which time the jousts and tourneys were kept, to the great content both of the lords and ladies there present.

This solemn triumph being once ended, the assembly taking their leave of Pandosto and Bellaria, the young son, who was called Garinter,[2] was nursed up in the house to the great joy and content of the parents. Fortune, envious of such happy success, willing to show some sign of her inconstancy, turned her wheel and darkened their bright sun of prosperity with the misty clouds of mishap and misery. For it so happened that Egistus, King of Sicilia, who in his youth had been brought up with Pandosto, desirous to show that neither tract of time nor distance of place could diminish their former friendship,[3] provided a navy of ships and sailed into Bohemia to visit his old friend and companion who, hearing of his arrival, went himself in person, and his wife Bellaria, accompanied with a great train of lords and ladies, to meet Egistus, and, espying him, alighted from his horse, embraced him very lovingly, protesting that nothing in the world could have happened more acceptable to him than his coming, wishing his wife to welcome his old friend and acquaintance, who, to show how she liked him whom her husband loved, entertained him with such familiar courtesy as Egistus perceived himself to be very well welcome.[4]

[1] 1.1.31–41
[2] The name (like that of Shakespeare's Florizel) is from *Amadis de Grecia.*
[3] 1.1.21 ff.
[4] 3.2.61–9

After they had thus saluted and embraced each other, they mounted again on horseback and rode toward the city, devising and recounting how, being children, they had passed their youth in friendly pastimes; where, by the means of the citizens, Egistus was received with triumphs and shows in such sort that he marvelled how on so small a warning they could make such preparation. Passing the streets thus with such rare sights, they rode on to the palace, where Pandosto entertained Egistus and his Sicilians with such banqueting and sumptuous cheer, so royally, as they all had cause to commend his princely liberality; yea, the very basest slave that was known to come from Sicilia was used with such courtesy that Egistus might easily perceive how both he and his were honoured for his friend's sake.

Bellaria, who in her time was the flower of courtesy, willing to show how unfeignedly she loved her husband by his friend's entertainment, used him likewise so familiarly that her countenance bewrayed how her mind was affected towards him, oftentimes coming herself into his bedchamber to see that nothing should be amiss to mislike him.

This honest familiarity increased daily more and more betwixt them, for Bellaria noting in Egistus a princely and bountiful mind adorned with sundry and excellent qualities, and Egistus finding in her a virtuous and courteous disposition, there grew such a secret uniting of their affections that the one could not well be without the company of the other, in so much that, when Pandosto was busied with such urgent affairs that he could not be present with his friend Egistus, Bellaria would walk with him into the garden,[1] where they two in private and pleasant devices would pass away the time to both their contents. This custom still continuing betwixt them, a certain melancholy passion entering the mind of Pandosto drave him into sundry and doubtful thoughts. First, he called to mind the beauty of his wife Bellaria, the comeliness and bravery of his friend Egistus, thinking that love was above all laws, and therefore to be stayed with no law; that it was hard to put fire and flax together without burning; that their open pleasures might breed his secret displeasures. He considered with himself that Egistus was a man, and must needs love; that his wife was a woman and therefore subject unto love; and that where fancy forced, friendship was of no force.

These and suchlike doubtful thoughts a long time smothering in his stomach began at last to kindle in his mind a secret mistrust which, increased by suspicion, grew at last to a flaming jealousy that so tormented him as he could take no rest. He then began to measure all their actions, and to misconstrue of their too private familiarity, judging that it was not for honest affection but for disordinate fancy, so that he

[1] 1.2.176

began to watch them more narrowly to see if he could get any true or certain proof to confirm his doubtful suspicion.

While thus he noted their looks and gestures, and suspected their thoughts and meanings, they two silly souls (who doubted nothing of this his treacherous intent) frequented daily each other's company, which drave him into such a frantic passion that he began to bear a secret hate to Egistus and a louring countenance to Bellaria, who, marvelling at such unaccustomed frowns,[1] began to cast beyond the moon, and to enter into a thousand sundry thoughts which way she should offend her husband. But finding in herself a clear conscience, ceased to muse until such time as she might find fit opportunity to demand the cause of his dumps.

In the mean time Pandosto's mind was so far charged with jealousy that he did no longer doubt, but was assured (as he thought) that his friend Egistus had entered a wrong point in his tables,[2] and so had played him false play. Whereupon—desirous to revenge so great an injury—he thought best to dissemble the grudge with a fair and friendly countenance, and so, under the shape of a friend, to show him the trick of a foe. Devising with himself a long time how he might best put away Egistus without suspicion of treacherous murder, he concluded at last to poison him;[3] which opinion pleasing his humour, he became resolute in his determination, and, the better to bring the matter to pass, he called unto him his cupbearer,[4] with whom in secret he broke the matter, promising to him for the performance thereof to give him a thousand crowns of yearly revenues.

His cupbearer—either being of a good conscience, or willing for fashion's sake to deny such a bloody request—began with great reasons to persuade Pandosto from his determinate mischief, showing him what an offence murder was to the gods, how such unnatural actions did more displease the heavens than men, and that causeless cruelty did seldom or never escape without revenge. He laid before his face that Egistus was his friend, a king, and one that was come into his kingdom to confirm a league of perpetual amity betwixt them; that he had and did show him a most friendly countenance; how Egistus was not only honoured of his own people by obedience, but also loved of the Bohemians for his courtesy; and that if now he should without any just or manifest cause poison him, it would not only be a great dishonour to his majesty, and a means to sow perpetual enmity between the Sicilians

---

[1] 1.2.148, 364–5

[2] The metaphor is from backgammon: the tables are the two halves of the board, and the points are the divisions on it. To 'enter' a wrong point is to cheat by moving one's man into a space it is not entitled to by the throw of the dice.

[3] 1.2.313 ff.

[4] 1.2.341

and the Bohemians, but also his own subjects would repine at such treacherous cruelty.

These and suchlike persuasions of Franion—for so was his cupbearer called—could no whit prevail to dissuade him from his devilish enterprise, but—remaining resolute in his determination, his fury so fired with rage as it could not be appeased with reason—he began with bitter taunts to take up his man, and to lay before him two baits: preferment, and death; saying that if he would poison Egistus, he should advance him to high dignities; if he refused to do it of an obstinate mind, no torture should be too great to requite his disobedience.

Franion, seeing that to persuade Pandosto any more was but to strive against the stream, consented as soon as opportunity would give him leave to dispatch Egistus, wherewith Pandosto remained somewhat satisfied, hoping that now he should be fully revenged of such mistrusted injuries; intending also as soon as Egistus was dead to give his wife a sop of the same sauce, and so be rid of those which were the cause of his restless sorrow.

While thus he lived in this hope, Franion, being secret in his chamber, began to meditate with himself in these terms:

'Ah Franion, treason is loved of many, but the traitor hated of all. Unjust offences may for a time escape without danger, but never without revenge; thou art servant to a king, and must obey at command; yet, Franion, against law and conscience it is not good to resist a tyrant with arms, nor to please an unjust king with obedience. What shalt thou do? Folly refuseth gold, and frenzy preferment; wisdom seeketh after dignity, and counsel looketh for gain. Egistus is a stranger to thee, and Pandosto thy sovereign: thou hast little cause to respect the one, and oughtest to have great care to obey the other. Think this, Franion: that a pound of gold is worth a ton of lead, great gifts are little gods, and preferment to a mean man is a whetstone to courage. There is nothing sweeter than promotion, nor lighter than report. Care not then though most count thee a traitor, so all call thee rich. Dignity, Franion, advanceth thy posterity, and evil report can hurt but thyself. Know this: where eagles build, falcons may prey; where lions haunt, foxes may steal. Kings are known to command, servants are blameless to consent. Fear not thou then to lift at Egistus. Pandosto shall bear the burden. Yea, but Franion, conscience is a worm that ever biteth, but never ceaseth. That which is rubbed with the stone galactites[1] will never be hot. Flesh dipped in the sea Aegeum will never be sweet. The herb tragion,[2] being once bit with

---

[1] 'a precious stone of a white colour' (*OED*). No authority for its anti-caloric properties has been found.

[2] any of a variety of bitter herbs

an aspis,[1] never groweth, and conscience once stained with innocent blood is always tied to a guilty remorse. Prefer thy content before riches, and a clear mind before dignity. So, being poor, thou shalt have rich peace, or else rich, thou shalt enjoy disquiet.'

Franion having muttered out these or suchlike words—seeing either he must die with a clear mind or live with a spotted conscience—he was so cumbered with divers cogitations that he could take no rest until at last he determined to break the matter to Egistus; but fearing that the King should either suspect or hear of such matters, he concealed the device till opportunity would permit him to reveal it. Lingering thus in doubtful fear, in an evening he went to Egistus' lodging, and—desirous to break with him of certain affairs that touched the King—after all were commanded out of the chamber, Franion made manifest the whole conspiracy which Pandosto had devised against him, desiring Egistus not to account him a traitor for betraying his master's counsel, but to think that he did it for conscience, hoping that, although his master—inflamed with rage, or incensed by some sinister reports or slanderous speeches— had imagined such causeless mischief, yet, when time should pacify his anger and try those talebearers but flattering parasites, then he would count him as a faithful servant, that with such care had kept his master's credit.

Egistus had not fully heard Franion tell forth his tale but a quaking fear possessed all his limbs, thinking that there was some treason wrought, and that Franion did but shadow his craft with these false colours. Wherefore he began to wax in choler, and said that he doubted not Pandosto, sith he was his friend, and there had never as yet been any breach of amity. He had not sought to invade his lands, to conspire with his enemies, to dissuade his subjects from their allegiance, but in word and thought he rested his at all times. He knew not therefore any cause that should move Pandosto to seek his death, but suspected it to be a compacted knavery of the Bohemians to bring the King and him at odds.

Franion staying him in the midst of his talk told him that to dally with princes was with the swans to sing against[2] their death, and that if the Bohemians had intended any such secret mischief, it might have been better brought to pass than by revealing the conspiracy; therefore his majesty did ill to misconstrue of his good meaning; sith his intent was to hinder treason, not to become a traitor; and—to confirm his premises—if it please his majesty to flee into Sicilia for the safeguard of his life, he would go with him; and if then he found not such a practice to be pretended, let his imagined treachery be repaid with most monstrous torments.

[1] asp   [2] at the moment of

Egistus, hearing the solemn protestation of Franion, began to consider that in love and kingdoms neither faith nor law is to be respected; doubting that Pandosto thought by his death to destroy his men, and with speedy war to invade Sicilia. These and such doubts thoroughly weighed, he gave great thanks to Franion, promising if he might with life return to Syracuse, that he would create him a duke in Sicilia, craving his counsel how he might escape out of the country. Franion, who (having some small skill in navigation) was well acquainted with the ports and havens, and knew every danger in the sea, joining in counsel with the master of Egistus' navy, rigged all their ships, and setting them afloat let them lie at anchor, to be in the more readiness when time and wind should serve.[1]

Fortune, although blind, yet by chance favouring this just cause, sent them within six days a good gale of wind, which Franion seeing fit for their purpose, to put Pandosto out of suspicion, the night before they should sail he went to him and promised that the next day he would put the device in practice, for he had got such a forcible poison as the very smell thereof should procure sudden death. Pandosto was joyful to hear this good news, and thought every hour a day till he might be glutted with bloody revenge; but his suit had but ill success, for Egistus—fearing that delay might breed danger, and willing that the grass should not be cut from under his feet—taking bag and baggage, with the help of Franion, conveyed himself and his men out of a postern gate[2] of the city, so secretly and speedily that without any suspicion they got to the seashore, where, with many a bitter curse taking their leave of Bohemia, they went aboard, weighing their anchors, and hoisting sail, they passed as fast as wind and sea would permit towards Sicilia, Egistus being a joyful man that he had safely passed such treacherous perils.

But as they were quietly floating on the sea, so Pandosto and his citizens were in an uproar, for—seeing that the Sicilians without taking their leave were fled away by night—the Bohemians feared some treason, and the King thought that without question his suspicion was true,[3] seeing his cupbearer had betrayed the sum of his secret pretence. Whereupon he began to imagine that Franion and his wife Bellaria had conspired with Egistus, and that the fervent affection she bare him was the only means of his secret departure, in so much that, incensed with rage, he commanded that his wife should be carried to strait prison until they heard further of his pleasure. The guard, unwilling to lay their hands on such a virtuous princess and yet fearing the King's fury, went very sorrowfully to fulfil their charge.

Coming to the Queen's lodging, they found her playing with her young son Garinter, unto whom with tears doing the message, Bella-

[1] I.2.444–6   [2] I.2.459   [3] 2.1.36 ff.

ria—astonished at such a hard censure, and finding her clear conscience a sure advocate to plead in her case—went to the prison most willingly, where with sighs and tears she passed away the time till she might come to her trial.[1]

But Pandosto (whose reason was suppressed with rage, and whose unbridled folly was incensed with fury), seeing Franion had betrayed his secrets, and that Egistus might well be railed on, but not revenged; determined to wreak all his wrath on poor Bellaria.[2] He therefore caused a general proclamation to be made through all his realm that the Queen and Egistus had by the help of Franion not only committed most incestuous adultery, but also had conspired the King's death. Whereupon the traitor Franion was fled away with Egistus, and Bellaria was most justly imprisoned.[3]

This proclamation being once blazed through the country, although the virtuous disposition of the Queen did half discredit the contents, yet the sudden and speedy passage of Egistus, and the secret departure of Franion, induced them, the circumstances thoroughly considered, to think that both the proclamation was true, and the King greatly injured. Yet they pitied her case, as sorrowful that so good a lady should be crossed with such adverse fortune. But the King, whose restless rage would admit no pity, thought that, although he might sufficiently requite his wife's falsehood with the bitter plague of pinching penury, yet his mind should never be glutted with revenge till he might have fit time and opportunity to repay the treachery of Egistus with a fatal injury.

But a curst cow hath oft-times short horns, and a willing mind but a weak arm; for Pandosto—although he felt that revenge was a spur to war, and that envy always proffereth steel—yet he saw that Egistus was not only of great puissance and prowess to withstand him but had also many kings of his alliance to aid him,[4] if need should serve, for he was married to the Emperor's daughter of Russia.[5] These and suchlike considerations something daunted Pandosto his courage, so that he was content rather to put up a manifest injury with peace than hunt after revenge with dishonour and loss; determining, since Egistus had escaped scot free, that Bellaria should pay for all at an unreasonable price.

Remaining thus resolute in this determination, Bellaria—continuing still in prison, and hearing the contents of the proclamation, knowing that her mind was never touched with such affection, nor that Egistus had ever offered her such discourtesy—would gladly have come to her answer, that both she might have known her unjust accusers, and cleared herself of that guiltless crime. But Pandosto was so inflamed with

---

[1] 2.1.1 ff.   [2] 2.3.3–9   [3] 3.2.12–20   [4] 2.3.20–1   [5] 3.2.117

rage and infected with jealousy as he would not vouchsafe to hear her nor admit any just excuse, so that she was fain to make a virtue of her need, and with patience to bear these heavy injuries.

As thus she lay crossed with calamities—a great cause to increase her grief—she found herself quick with child; which as soon as she felt stir in her body, she burst forth into bitter tears, exclaiming against fortune in these terms:

'Alas Bellaria, how unfortunate art thou because fortunate! Better hadst thou been born a beggar than a prince. So shouldst thou have bridled Fortune with want where now she sporteth herself with thy plenty. Ah, happy life, where poor thoughts and mean desires live in secure content, not fearing Fortune because too low for Fortune! Thou seest now, Bellaria, that care is a companion to honour, not to poverty; that high cedars are frushed[1] with tempests when low shrubs are not touched with the wind. Precious diamonds are cut with the file when despised pebbles lie safe in the sand. Delphos is sought to by princes, not beggars, and Fortune's altars smoke with kings' presents, not with poor men's gifts. Happy are such, Bellaria, that curse Fortune for contempt, not fear, and may wish they were, not sorrow they have been. Thou art a princess, Bellaria, and yet a prisoner, born to the one by descent, assigned to the other by despite, accused without cause, and therefore oughtest to die without care; for patience is a shield against Fortune, and a guiltless mind yieldeth not to sorrow. Ah, but infamy galleth unto death, and liveth after death. Report is plumed with Time's feathers, and envy oftentimes soundeth Fame's trumpets. Thy suspected adultery shall fly in the air, and thy known virtues shall lie hid in the earth. One mole staineth a whole face, and what is once spotted with infamy can hardly be worn out with time. Die then, Bellaria, Bellaria, die; for if the gods should say thou art guiltless, yet envy would hear the gods but never believe the gods. Ah, hapless wretch, cease these tears! Desperate thoughts are fit for them that fear shame, not for such as hope for credit. Pandosto hath darkened thy fame, but shall never discredit thy virtues. Suspicion may enter a false action, but proof shall never put in his plea. Care not then for envy, sith report hath a blister on her tongue; and let sorrow bite them which offend, not touch thee that are faultless. But alas, poor soul, how canst thou but sorrow? Thou art with child, and by him that instead of kind pity pincheth thee in cold prison.'

And with that such gasping sighs so stopped her breath that she could not utter any more words but—wringing her hands, and gushing forth streams of tears—she passed away the time with bitter complaints.

The jailer, pitying these her heavy passions, thinking that if the King knew she were with child he would somewhat appease his fury and

---

[1] bruised

release her from prison,[1] went in all haste and certified Pandosto what the effect of Bellaria's complaint was; who no sooner heard the jailer say she was with child but, as one possessed with a frenzy, he rose up in a rage, swearing that she and the bastard brat she was withal should die, if the gods themselves said no, thinking assuredly by computation of time that Egistus, and not he, was father to the child. This suspicious thought galled afresh this half-healed sore, in so much as he could take no rest until he might mitigate his choler with a just revenge, which happened presently after. For Bellaria was brought to bed of a fair and beautiful daughter, which no sooner Pandosto heard but he determined that both Bellaria and the young infant should be burnt with fire.[2]

His nobles, hearing of the King's cruel sentence, sought by persuasions to divert him from this bloody determination, laying before his face the innocency of the child and the virtuous disposition of his wife, how she had continually loved and honoured him so tenderly that without due proof he could not nor ought not to appeach her of that crime.[3] And if she had faulted, yet it were more honourable to pardon with mercy than to punish with extremity, and more kingly to be commended of pity than accused of rigour. And as for the child, if he should punish it for the mother's offence, it were to strive against nature and justice; and that unnatural actions do more offend the gods than men; how causeless cruelty nor innocent blood never scapes without revenge.

These and suchlike reasons could not appease his rage, but he rested resolute in this, that, Bellaria being an adultress, the child was a bastard, and he would not suffer that such an infamous brat should call him father. Yet at last, seeing his noblemen were importunate upon him, he was content to spare the child's life, and yet to put it to a worser death. For he found out this device, that seeing, as he thought, it came by Fortune, so he would commit it to the charge of Fortune; and therefore he caused a little cock-boat to be provided, wherein he meant to put the babe, and then send it to the mercy of the seas and the destinies.[4] From this his peers in no wise could persuade him, but that he sent presently two of his guard to fetch the child; who being come to the prison, and with weeping tears recounting their master's message, Bellaria no sooner heard the rigorous resolution of her merciless husband but she fell down in a sound, so that all thought she had been dead, yet at last being come to herself, she cried and screeched out in this wise:

'Alas, sweet infortunate babe, scarce born before envied by Fortune: would the day of thy birth had been the term of thy life, then shouldst thou have made an end to care, and prevented thy father's rigour. Thy faults cannot yet deserve such hateful revenge, thy days are too short for so sharp a doom, but thy untimely death must pay thy mother's

---

[1] 2.2.30 ff.   [2] 2.3.94–5   [3] 2.1.126 ff.   [4] 2.3.173–82

debts, and her guiltless crime must be thy ghastly curse. And shalt thou, sweet babe, be committed to Fortune when thou art already spited by Fortune? Shall the seas be thy harbour, and the hard boat thy cradle? Shall thy tender mouth instead of sweet kisses be nipped with bitter storms? Shalt thou have the whistling winds for thy lullaby, and the salt sea foam instead of sweet milk? Alas, what destinies would assign such hard hap? What father would be so cruel? Or what gods will not revenge such rigour? Let me kiss thy lips, sweet infant, and wet thy tender cheeks with my tears, and put this chain about thy little neck, that, if Fortune save thee, it may help to succour thee. Thus, since thou must go to surge in the gastful[1] seas, with a sorrowful kiss I bid thee farewell, and I pray the gods thou mayst fare well.'

Such and so great was her grief that—her vital spirits being suppressed with sorrow—she fell again down in a trance, having her senses so sotted with care that, after she was revived, yet she lost her memory, and lay for a great time without moving as one in a trance. The guard left her in this perplexity and carried the child to the King who, quite devoid of pity, commanded that without delay it should be put in the boat, having neither sail nor other to guide it, and so to be carried into the midst of the sea, and there left to the wind and wave as the destinies please to appoint. The very shipmen, seeing the sweet countenance of the young babe, began to accuse the King of rigour, and to pity the child's hard fortune, but fear constrained them to that which their nature did abhor, so that they placed it in one of the ends of the boat, and with a few green boughs made a homely cabin to shroud it as they could from wind and weather. Having thus trimmed the boat they tied it to a ship, and so haled it into the main sea and then cut in sunder the cord, which they had no sooner done but there arose a mighty tempest which tossed the little boat so vehemently in the waves that the shipmen thought it could not continue long without sinking, yea the storm grew so great that with much labour and peril they got to the shore. But leaving the child to her fortunes, again to Pandosto who, not yet glutted with sufficient revenge, devised which way he should best increase his wife's calamities.

But first, assembling his nobles and counsellors, he called her for the more reproach into open court, where it was objected against her that she had committed adultery with Egistus, and conspired with Franion to poison Pandosto, her husband, but, their pretence being partly spied, she counselled them to fly away by night for their better safety. Bellaria, who, standing like a prisoner at the bar, feeling in herself a clear conscience to withstand her false accusers, seeing that no less than death could pacify her husband's wrath, waxed bold and desired that she

---

[1] dreadful

might have law and justice, for mercy she neither craved nor hoped for, and that those perjured wretches which had falsely accused her to the King might be brought before her face, to give in evidence. But Pandosto, whose rage and jealousy was such as no reason nor equity could appease, told her that, for her accusers, they were of such credit as their words were sufficient witness, and that the sudden and secret flight of Egistus and Franion confirmed that which they had confessed; and as for her, it was her part to deny such a monstrous crime, and to be impudent in forswearing the fact, since she had passed all shame in committing the fault; [1] but her stale countenance should stand for no coin, for as the bastard which she bare was served, so she should with some cruel death be requited.

Bellaria, no whit dismayed with this rough reply, told her husband Pandosto that he spake upon choler and not conscience; for her virtuous life had been ever such as no spot of suspicion could ever stain. And if she had borne a friendly countenance to Egistus, it was in respect he was his friend, and not for any lusting affection. Therefore if she were condemned without any further proof, it was rigour and not law. [2]

The noblemen which sat in judgement said that Bellaria spake reason, and entreated the King that the accusers might be openly examined and sworn, and if then the evidence were such as the jury might find her guilty—for seeing she was a prince, she ought to be tried by her peers—then let her have such punishment as the extremity of the law will assign to such malefactors. The King presently made answer that in this case he might and would dispense with the law, and that, the jury being once panelled, they should take his word for sufficient evidence, otherwise he would make the proudest of them repent it.

The noblemen, seeing the King in choler, were all whist; but Bellaria, whose life then hung in the balance, fearing more perpetual infamy than momentary death, told the King, if his fury might stand for a law, that it were vain to have the jury yield their verdict, and therefore she fell down upon her knees and desired the King that for the love he bare to his young son Garinter, whom she brought into the world, that he would grant her a request, which was this: that it would please his majesty to send six of his noblemen whom he best trusted to the isle of Delphos, there to enquire of the oracle of Apollo whether she had committed adultery with Egistus, or conspired to poison him with Franion; [3] and if the god Apollo, who by his divine essence knew all secrets, gave answer that she was guilty, she were content to suffer any torment, were it never so terrible. The request was so reasonable that Pandosto could not for shame deny it, unless he would be counted of all his subjects more wilful than wise. He therefore agreed that with as

---

[1] 3.2.53–6   [2] 3.2.107–12   [3] 2.1.183

much speed as might be there should be certain ambassadors dispatched to the isle of Delphos; and in the mean season he commanded that his wife should be kept in close prison.

Bellaria, having obtained this grant, was now more careful for her little babe that floated on the seas than sorrowful for her own mishap. For of that she doubted, of herself she was assured, knowing if Apollo should give oracle according to the thoughts of the heart, yet the sentence should go on her side, such was the clearness of her mind in this case. But Pandosto, whose suspicious head still remained in one song, chose out six of his nobility, whom he knew were scarce indifferent men in the Queen's behalf, and, providing all things fit for their journey, sent them to Delphos. They, willing to fulfil the King's command, and desirous to see the situation and custom of the island, dispatched their affairs with as much speed as might be, and embarked themselves to this voyage, which, the wind and weather serving fit for their purpose, was soon ended. For within three weeks they arrived at Delphos,[1] where they were no sooner set on land but with great devotion they went to the temple of Apollo, and there offering sacrifice to the god and gifts to the priest, as the custom was, they humbly craved an answer of their demand. They had not long kneeled at the altar but Apollo with a loud voice said, 'Bohemians, what you find behind the altar, take, and depart.' They forthwith obeying the oracle found a scroll of parchment wherein was written these words in letters of gold:

The Oracle.
Suspicion is no proof; jealousy is an unequal judge; Bellaria is chaste; Egistus blameless; Franion a true subject; Pandosto treacherous; his babe an innocent; and the King shall live without an heir if that which is lost be not found.[2]

As soon as they had taken out this scroll, the priest of the god commanded them that they should not presume to read it before they came in the presence of Pandosto, unless they would incur the displeasure of Apollo. The Bohemian lords carefully obeying his command, taking their leave of the priest, with great reverence departed out of the temple and went to their ships, and as soon as wind would permit them, sailed toward Bohemia, whither in short time they safely arrived and, with great triumph issuing out of their ships, went to the King's palace, whom they found in his chamber accompanied with other noblemen.

Pandosto no sooner saw them but with a merry countenance he welcomed them home, asking what news. They told his majesty that they had received an answer of the god written in a scroll, but with this charge: that they should not read the contents before they came in the

---

[1] 2.3.196–8   [2] 3.2.130–4

presence of the King, and with that they delivered him the parchment. But his noblemen entreated him that sith therein was contained either the safety of his wife's life and honesty, or her death and perpetual infamy, that he would have his nobles and commons assembled in the judgement hall, where the Queen brought in as prisoner should hear the contents. If she were found guilty by the oracle of the god, then all should have cause to think his rigour proceeded of due desert. If her grace were found faultless, then she should be cleared before all, sith she had been accused openly.[1]

This pleased the King so that he appointed the day and assembled all his lords and commons, and caused the Queen to be brought in before the judgement seat, commanding that the indictment should be read wherein she was accused of adultery with Egistus and of conspiracy with Franion. Bellaria, hearing the contents, was no whit astonished, but made this cheerful answer:

'If the divine powers be privy to human actions—as no doubt they are—I hope my patience shall make Fortune blush, and my unspotted life shall stain spiteful discredit. For although lying report hath sought to appeach mine honour, and suspicion hath intended to soil my credit with infamy, yet where virtue keepeth the fort, report and suspicion may assail but never sack. How I have led my life before Egistus' coming, I appeal, Pandosto, to the gods and to thy conscience. What hath passed betwixt him and me the gods only know, and I hope will presently reveal. That I loved Egistus I cannot deny; that I honoured him I shame not to confess; to the one I was forced by his virtues, to the other for his dignities. But as touching lascivious lust, I say Egistus is honest, and hope myself to be found without spot. For Franion, I can neither accuse him nor excuse him, for I was not privy to his departure, and that this is true which I have here rehearsed, I refer myself to the divine oracle.'[2]

Bellaria had no sooner said but the King commanded that one of his dukes should read the contents of the scroll, which after the commons had heard, they gave a great shout, rejoicing and clapping their hands that the Queen was clear of that false accusation. But the King, whose conscience was a witness against him of his witless fury and false suspected jealousy, was so ashamed of his rash folly that he entreated his nobles to persuade Bellaria to forgive and forget these injuries, promising not only to show himself a loyal and loving husband but also to reconcile himself to Egistus and Franion, revealing then before them all the cause of their secret flight, and how treacherously he thought to have practised his death, if the good mind of his cupbearer had not prevented his purpose.[3] As thus he was relating the whole matter, there was word brought him that his young son Garinter was suddenly dead,

[1] 3.2.4–7   [2] 3.2.27–33, 60–4, 72–5, 113   [3] 3.2.151–68

which news so soon as Bellaria heard, surcharged before with extreme joy, and now suppressed with heavy sorrow, her vital spirits were so stopped that she fell down presently dead, and could be never revived.[1] This sudden sight so appalled the King's senses that he sank from his seat in a sound so as he was fain to be carried by his nobles to his palace, where he lay by the space of three days without speech. His commons were as men in despair, so diversely distressed. There was nothing but mourning and lamentation to be heard throughout all Bohemia—their young prince dead, their virtuous queen bereaved of her life, and their King and sovereign in great hazard. This tragical discourse of Fortune so daunted them as they went like shadows, not men. Yet somewhat to comfort their heavy hearts, they heard that Pandosto was come to himself and had recovered his speech, who as in a fury brayed out these bitter speeches:

'O miserable Pandosto, what surer witness than conscience? What thoughts more sour than suspicion? What plague more bad than jealousy? Unnatural actions offend the gods more than men, and causeless cruelty never scapes without revenge. I have committed such a bloody fact as repent I may, but recall I cannot. Ah jealousy, a hell to the mind and a horror to the conscience, suppressing reason, and inciting rage: a worse passion than frenzy, a greater plague than madness. Are the gods just? Then let them revenge such brutish cruelty. My innocent babe I have drowned in the seas; my loving wife I have slain with slanderous suspicion; my trusty friend I have sought to betray, and yet the gods are slack to plague such offences. Ah, unjust Apollo, Pandosto is the man that hath committed the fault, why should Garinter, silly[2] child, abide the pain? Well, sith the gods mean to prolong my days to increase my dolour, I will offer my guilty blood a sacrifice to those sackless[3] souls whose lives are lost by my rigorous folly.'

And with that he reached at a rapier to have murdered himself, but his peers (being present) stayed him from such a bloody act, persuading him to think that the commonwealth consisted on his safety, and that those sheep could not but perish that wanted a shepherd; wishing that if he would not live for himself, yet he should have care of his subjects, and to put such fancies out of his mind, sith in sores past help, salves do not heal but hurt, and in things past cure, care is a corrosive. With these and suchlike persuasions the King was overcome and began somewhat to quiet his mind, so that as soon as he could go abroad he caused his wife to be embalmed and wrapped in lead with her young son Garinter, erecting a rich and famous sepulchre wherein he entombed them both, making such solemn obsequies at her funeral as all Bohemia might

---

[1] 3.2.141–6   [2] guiltless   [3] innocent

perceive he did greatly repent him of his forepast folly, causing this epitaph to be engraven on her tomb in letters of gold:

[*The Epitaph.*]

Here lies entombed Bellaria fair,
   Falsely accused to be unchaste;
Cleared by Apollo's sacred doom,
   Yet slain by jealousy at last.

Whate'er thou be that passest by,
Curse him that caused this queen to die.

This epitaph being engraven, Pandosto would once a day repair to the tomb and there with watery plaints bewail his misfortune, coveting no other companion but sorrow, nor no other harmony but repentance.[1] But leaving him to his dolorous passions, at last let us come to show the tragical discourse of the young infant.

Who, being tossed with wind and wave, floated two whole days without succour, ready at every puff to be drowned in the sea, till at last the tempest ceased and the little boat was driven with the tide into the coast of Sicilia, where sticking upon the sands, it rested. Fortune, minding to be wanton, willing to show that as she hath wrinkles on her brows, so she hath dimples in her checks, thought after so many sour looks to lend a feigned smile, and after a puffing storm to bring a pretty calm; she began thus to dally.

It fortuned a poor mercenary shepherd that dwelled in Sicilia, who got his living by other men's flocks, missed one of his sheep, and, thinking it had strayed into the covert that was hard by, sought very diligently to find that which he could not see, fearing either that the wolves or eagles had undone him (for he was so poor as a sheep was half his substance), wandered down toward the sea cliffs to see if perchance the sheep was browsing on the sea-ivy,[2] whereon they greatly do feed; but not finding her there, as he was ready to return to his flock he heard a child cry; but knowing there was no house near, he thought he had mistaken the sound and that it was the bleating of his sheep. Wherefore, looking more narrowly, as he cast his eye to the sea he spied a little boat from whence, as he attentively listened, he might hear the cry to come.

Standing a good while in amaze, at last he went to the shore and, wading to the boat, as he looked in he saw the little babe lying all alone, ready to die for hunger and cold, wrapped in a mantle of scarlet, richly embroidered with gold,[3] and having a chain about the neck. The shepherd (who before had never seen so fair a babe nor so rich jewels) thought assuredly that it was some little god, and began with great devotion to knock on his breast. The babe, who writhed with the head to seek for the pap, began again to cry afresh, whereby the poor man knew that it was a child which by some sinister means was driven thither by distress of weather, marvelling how such a silly infant, which by the mantle and the chain could not be but born of noble parentage,[1] should be so hardly crossed with deadly mishap. The poor shepherd, perplexed thus with divers thoughts, took pity of the child and determined with himself to carry it to the King, that there it might be brought up according to the worthiness of birth, for his ability could not afford to foster it, though his good mind was willing to further it.

Taking therefore the child in his arms, as he folded the mantle together the better to defend it from cold there fell down at his foot a very fair and rich purse, wherein he found a great sum of gold; which sight so revived the shepherd's spirits as he was greatly ravished with joy and daunted with fear: joyful to see such a sum in his power, and fearful, if it should be known, that it might breed his further danger. Necessity wished him at the least to retain the gold, though he would not keep the child; the simplicity of his conscience feared him from such a deceitful bribery. Thus was the poor man perplexed with a doubtful dilemma, until at last the covetousness of the coin overcame him—for what will not the greedy desire of gold cause a man to do? So that he was resolved in himself to foster the child, and with the sum to relieve his want.

Resting thus resolute in this point, he left seeking of his sheep and as covertly and secretly as he could went by a by-way to his house, lest any of his neighbours should perceive his carriage. As soon as he was got home, entering in at the door, the child began to cry, which his wife hearing, and seeing her husband with a young babe in his arms, began to be somewhat jealous, yet marvelling that her husband should be so wanton abroad sith he was so quiet at home. But as women are naturally given to believe the worst, so his wife, thinking it was some bastard, began to crow against her goodman, and taking up a cudgel (for the most master went breechless) sware solemnly that she would make clubs trumps if he brought any bastard brat within her doors. The goodman, seeing his wife in her majesty with her mace in her hand, thought it was time to bow for fear of blows, and desired her to be quiet, for there was none such matter; but if she could hold her peace, they were made for ever.[2] And with that he told her the whole matter: how he had found the child in a little boat, without any succour, wrapped in that costly mantle, and having that rich chain about the neck. But at last, when he showed her the purse full of gold, she began to simper something sweetly and, taking her husband about the neck, kissed him after her homely fashion, saying that she hoped God had seen their

---

[1] 3.3.111   [2] 3.3.116

want, and now meant to relieve their poverty, and, seeing they could get no children, had sent them this little babe to be their heir.

'Take heed in any case,' quoth the shepherd, 'that you be secret,[1] and blab it not out when you meet with your gossips; for if you do, we are like not only to lose the gold and jewels, but our other goods and lives.'

'Tush,' quoth his wife, 'profit is a good hatch[2] before the door. Fear not, I have other things to talk of than of this. But, I pray you, let us lay up the money surely, and the jewels, lest by any mishap it be spied.'

After that they had set all things in order, the shepherd went to his sheep with a merry note, and the good wife learned to sing lullaby at home with her young babe, wrapping it in a homely blanket instead of a rich mantle, nourishing it so cleanly and carefully as it began to be a jolly girl, insomuch that they began both of them to be very fond of it, seeing, as it waxed in age, so it increased in beauty. The shepherd every night at his coming home would sing and dance it on his knee, and prattle, that in a short time it began to speak and call him 'Dad,' and her 'Mam'.

At last when it grew to ripe years, that it was about seven years old, the shepherd left keeping of other men's sheep and, with the money he found in the purse, he bought him the lease of a pretty farm and got a small flock of sheep which, when Fawnia—for so they named the child—came to the age of ten years, he set her to keep, and she with such diligence performed her charge as the sheep prospered marvellously under her hand. Fawnia thought Porrus had been her father and Mopsa her mother (for so was the shepherd and his wife called) and honoured and obeyed them with such reverence that all the neighbours praised the dutiful obedience of the child. Porrus grew in short time to be a man of some wealth and credit;[3] for Fortune so favoured him in having no charge but Fawnia that he began to purchase land, intending after his death to give it to his daughter, so that divers rich farmers' sons came as wooers to his house; for Fawnia was something cleanly attired, being of such singular beauty and excellent wit that whoso saw her would have thought she had been some heavenly nymph, and not a mortal creature. Insomuch that, when she came to the age of sixteen years, she so increased with exquisite perfection both of body and mind as her natural disposition did bewray that she was born of some high parentage; but the people, thinking she was daughter to the shepherd Porrus, rested only amazed at her beauty and wit. Yea, she won such favour and commendations in every man's eye as her beauty was not only praised in the country but also spoken of in the court.[4] Yet such was her submiss

[1] 3.3.120–21
[2] wicket, gate. To have a hatch before the door = to keep silent.
[3] 4.2.38–40
[4] 4.2.41–2

modesty that, although her praise daily increased, her mind was no whit puffed up with pride, but humbled herself as became a country maid and the daughter of a poor shepherd. Every day she went forth with her sheep to the field, keeping them with such care and diligence as all men thought she was very painful, defending her face from the heat of the sun with no other veil but with a garland made of boughs and flowers, which attire became her so gallantly as she seemed to be the goddess Flora herself[1] for beauty.

Fortune, who all this while had showed a friendly face, began now to turn her back and to show a louring countenance, intending as she had given Fawnia a slender check, so she would give her a harder mate; to bring which to pass, she laid her train on this wise.

Egistus had but one only son called Dorastus, about the age of twenty years, a prince so decked and adorned with the gifts of nature, so fraught with beauty and virtuous qualities as not only his father joyed to have so good a son, and all his commons rejoiced that God had lent them such a noble prince to succeed in the kingdom.[2] Egistus, placing all his joy in the perfection of his son, seeing that he was now marriageable, sent ambassadors to the King of Denmark to entreat a marriage between him and his daughter, who, willingly consenting, made answer that the next spring, if it please Egistus with his son to come into Denmark, he doubted not but they should agree upon reasonable conditions. Egistus, resting satisfied with this friendly answer, thought convenient in the meantime to break with his son. Finding therefore on a day fit opportunity, he spake to him in these fatherly terms:

'Dorastus, thy youth warneth me to prevent the worst, and mine age to provide the best. Opportunities neglected are signs of folly; actions measured by time are seldom bitten with repentance. Thou art young, and I old. Age hath taught me that which thy youth cannot yet conceive. I therefore will counsel thee as a father, hoping thou wilt obey as a child. Thou seest my white hairs are blossoms for the grave, and thy fresh colour fruit for time and fortune, so that it behoveth me to think how to die, and for thee to care how to live. My crown I must leave by death, and thou enjoy my kingdom by succession, wherein I hope thy virtue and prowess shall be such as, though my subjects want my person, yet they shall see in thee my perfection. That nothing either may fail to satisfy thy mind or increase thy dignities; the only care I have is to see thee well married before I die, and thou become old.'

Dorastus (who from his infancy delighted rather to die with Mars in the field than to dally with Venus in the chamber), fearing to displease his father, and yet not willing to be wed, made him this reverent answer:

[1] 4.4.1–3   [2] 1.1.32–41

'Sir, there is no greater bond than duty, nor no straiter law than nature. Disobedience in youth is often galled with despite in age. The command of the father ought to be a constraint to the child. So parents' wills are laws, so they pass not all laws. May it please your grace therefore to appoint whom I shall love, rather than by denial I should be appeached of disobedience I rest content to love, though it be the only thing I hate.'

Egistus, hearing his son to fly far from the mark, began to be somewhat choleric, and therefore made him this hasty answer:

'What, Dorastus, canst thou not love? Cometh this cynical passion of prone desires, or peevish forwardness? What, dost thou think thyself too good for all, or none good enough for thee? I tell thee, Dorastus, there is nothing sweeter than youth, nor swifter decreasing while it is increasing. Time passed with folly may be repented but not recalled. If thou marry in age, thy wife's fresh colours will breed in thee dead thoughts and suspicion, and thy white hairs her loathsomeness and sorrow. For Venus' affections are not fed with kingdoms or treasures, but with youthful conceits and sweet amours. Vulcan was allotted to shake the tree, but Mars allowed to reap the fruit. Yield, Dorastus, to thy father's persuasions, which may prevent thy perils. I have chosen thee a wife fair by nature, royal by birth, by virtues famous, learned by education, and rich by possessions, so that it is hard to judge whether her bounty or fortune, her beauty or virtue, be of greater force. I mean, Dorastus, Euphania, daughter and heir to the King of Denmark.'

Egistus pausing here a while, looking when his son should make him answer, and seeing that he stood still as one in a trance, he shook him up thus sharply:

'Well, Dorastus, take heed; the tree alpya[1] wasteth not with fire, but withereth with the dew. That which love nourisheth not perisheth with hate. If thou like Euphania, thou breedest my content, and in loving her thou shalt have my love; otherwise . . .'—and with that he flung from his son in a rage, leaving him a sorrowful man in that he had by denial displeased his father, and half angry with himself that he could not yield to that passion whereto both reason and his father persuaded him.

But see how Fortune is plumed with Time's feathers, and how she can minister strange causes to breed strange effects. It happened not long after this that there was a meeting of all the farmers' daughters in Sicilia, whither Fawnia was also bidden as the mistress of the feast,[2] who, having attired herself in her best garments, went among the rest of her companions to the merry meeting, there spending the day in such homely pastimes as shepherds use.

---

[1] untraced; not recorded in the *OED*   [2] 4.4.68

As the evening grew on and their sports ceased, each taking their leave at other, Fawnia, desiring one of her companions to bear her company, went home by the flock to see if they were well folded; and as they returned it fortuned that Dorastus (who all that day had been hawking,[1] and killed store of game) encountered by the way these two maids, and casting his eye suddenly on Fawnia he was half afraid, fearing that with Acteon he had seen Diana; for he thought such exquisite perfection could not be found in any mortal creature.

As thus he stood in amaze, one of his pages told him that the maid with the garland on her head was Fawnia, the fair shepherd, whose beauty was so much talked of in the court. Dorastus, desirous to see if nature had adorned her mind with any inward qualities as she had decked her body with outward shape, began to question with her whose daughter she was, of what age, and how she had been trained up; who answered him with such modest reverence and sharpness of wit that Dorastus thought her outward beauty was but a counterfeit to darken her inward qualities, wondering how so courtly behaviour could be found in so simple a cottage, and cursing Fortune that had shadowed wit and beauty with such hard fortune.

As thus he held her a long while with chat, Beauty, seeing him at discovert,[2] thought not to lose the vantage, but struck him so deeply with an envenomed shaft as he wholly lost his liberty and became a slave to love, which before contemned love; glad now to gaze on a poor shepherd, who before refused the offer of a rich princess; for the perfection of Fawnia had so fixed his fancy as he felt his mind greatly changed, and his affections altered, cursing love that had wrought such a change, and blaming the baseness of his mind that would make such a choice. But thinking these were but passionate toys that might be thrust out at pleasure, to avoid the siren that enchanted him he put spurs to his horse and bade this fair shepherd farewell.

Fawnia, who all this while had marked the princely gesture of Dorastus, seeing his face so well featured and each limb so perfectly framed, began greatly to praise his perfection, commending him so long till she found herself faulty, and perceived that if she waded but a little further she might slip over her shoes. She therefore, seeking to quench that fire which never was put out, went home and, feigning herself not well at ease, got her to bed where, casting a thousand thoughts in her head, she could take no rest; for if she waked, she began to call to mind his beauty, and thinking to beguile such thoughts with sleep, she then dreamed of his perfection. Pestered thus with these unacquainted passions, she passed the night as she could in short slumbers.

[1] 4.4.14–16 [2] off his guard

Dorastus, who all this while rode with a flea in his ear,[1] could not by any means forget the sweet favour of Fawnia, but rested so bewitched with her wit and beauty as he could take no rest. He felt fancy to give the assault, and his wounded mind ready to yield as vanquished. Yet he began with divers considerations to suppress this frantic affection, calling to mind that Fawnia was a shepherd, one not worthy to be looked at of a prince, much less to be loved of such a potentate; thinking what a discredit it were to himself, and what a grief it would be to his father; blaming Fortune and accusing his own folly that should be so fond as but once to cast a glance at such a country slut.

As thus he was raging against himself, Love (fearing if she dallied long to lose her champion) stepped more nigh and gave him such a fresh wound as it pierced him at the heart, that he was fain to yield maugre his face,[2] and to forsake the company and get him to his chamber, where being solemnly set, he burst into these passionate terms:

'Ah, Dorastus, art thou alone? No, not alone, while thou art tired with these unacquainted passions. Yield to fancy thou canst not, by thy father's counsel, but in a frenzy thou art by just destinies. Thy father were content if thou couldst love, and thou therefore discontent, because thou dost love. O, divine love—feared of men because honoured of the gods; not to be suppressed by wisdom, because not to be comprehended by reason; without law, and therefore above all law!

'How now, Dorastus, why dost thou blaze that with praises which thou hast cause to blaspheme with curses? Yet why should they curse love that are in love? Blush, Dorastus, at thy fortune, thy choice, thy love; thy thoughts cannot be uttered without shame, nor thy affections without discredit. Ah, Fawnia, sweet Fawnia, thy beauty, Fawnia!

'Shamest not thou, Dorastus, to name one unfit for thy birth, thy dignities, thy kingdoms? Die, Dorastus, Dorastus, die! Better hadst thou perish with high desires than live in base thoughts. Yea, but beauty must be obeyed, because it is beauty; yet framed of the gods to feed the eye, not to fetter the heart. Ah, but he that striveth against love shooteth with them of Scyrum against the wind,[3] and with the cockatrice[4] pecketh against the steel. I will therefore obey, because I must obey. Fawnia, yea Fawnia, shall be my fortune, in spite of Fortune. The gods above disdain not to love women beneath. Phoebus liked Sibylla, Jupiter Io, and why not I then Fawnia?—one something inferior to these in

---

[1] Proverbial: anything disquieting or agitating.

[2] despite his determination

[3] i.e. ineffectively. Scyros is the Aegean island where Achilles hid to avoid military service, but the allusion is untraced.

[4] basilisk. Its ineffective assault on steel is also mentioned in Lyly's *Campaspe* (*Works*, ed. Bond, ii. 342).

birth, but far superior to them in beauty; born to be a shepherd but worthy to be a goddess.

'Ah, Dorastus, wilt thou so forget thyself as to suffer affection to suppress wisdom, and love to violate thine honour? How sour will thy choice be to thy father, sorrowful to thy subjects, to thy friends a grief, most gladsome to thy foes? Subdue then thy affections, and cease to love her whom thou couldst not love unless blinded with too much love.

'Tush, I talk to the wind, and in seeking to prevent the causes I further the effects. I will yet praise Fawnia, honour—yea, and love—Fawnia, and at this day follow content, not counsel. Do, Dorastus, thou canst but repent.'

And with that his page came into the chamber, whereupon he ceased from his complaints, hoping that time would wear out that which Fortune had wrought.

As thus he was pained, so poor Fawnia was diversely perplexed; for the next morning, getting up very early, she went to her sheep, thinking with hard labours to pass away her new-conceived amours, beginning very busily to drive them to the field, and then to shift the folds. At last, wearied with toil, she sat her down, where, poor soul, she was more tried with fond affections; for love began to assault her insomuch that, as she sat upon the side of a hill, she began to accuse her own folly in these terms:

'Infortunate Fawnia, and therefore infortunate because Fawnia, thy shepherd's hook showeth thy poor state, thy proud desires an aspiring mind. The one declareth thy want, the other thy pride. No bastard[1] hawk must soar so high as the hobby, no fowl gaze against the sun but the eagle. Actions wrought against nature reap despite, and thoughts above Fortune, disdain.

'Fawnia, thou art a shepherd, daughter to poor Porrus. If thou rest content with this, thou art like to stand; if thou climb, thou art sure to fall. The herb aneta,[2] growing higher than six inches, becometh a weed. Nilus flowing more than twelve cubits procureth a dearth. Daring affections that pass measure are cut short by time or Fortune. Suppress then, Fawnia, those thoughts which thou mayst shame to express. But ah, Fawnia, love is a lord who will command by power and constrain by force.

'Dorastus, ah Dorastus is the man I love, the worse is thy hap, and the less cause hast thou to hope. Will eagles catch at flies, will cedars stoop to brambles, or mighty princes look at such homely trulls? No, no, think this: Dorastus' disdain is greater than thy desire. He is a prince respecting his honour, thou a beggar's brat forgetting thy calling. Cease then not only to say, but to think to love Dorastus, and dissemble thy

---

[1] inferior, low-born   [2] or anet, dill

love, Fawnia; for better it were to die with grief than to live with shame. Yet in despite of love I will sigh to see if I can sigh out love.'

Fawnia, somewhat appeasing her griefs with these pithy persuasions, began after her wonted manner to walk about her sheep and to keep them from straying into the corn, suppressing her affection with the due consideration of her base estate, and with the impossibilities of her love, thinking it were frenzy, not fancy, to covet that which the very destinies did deny her to obtain.

But Dorastus was more impatient in his passions; for love so fiercely assailed him that neither company nor music could mitigate his martyrdom, but did rather far the more increase his malady. Shame would not let him crave counsel in this case, nor fear of his father's displeasure reveal it to any secret friend, but he was fain to make a secretary of himself, and to participate his thoughts with his own troubled mind. Lingering thus awhile in doubtful suspense, at last, stealing secretly from the court without either men or page, he went to see if he could espy Fawnia walking abroad in the field. But, as one having a great deal more skill to retrieve the partridge with his spaniels than to hunt after such a strange prey, he sought, but was little the better; which cross luck drove him into a great choler, that he began both to accuse love and Fortune. But as he was ready to retire he saw Fawnia sitting all alone under the side of a hill, making a garland of such homely flowers as the fields did afford. This sight so revived his spirits that he drew nigh, with more judgement to take a view of her singular perfection, which he found to be such as in that country attire she stained all the courtly dames of Sicilia.

While thus he stood gazing with piercing looks on her surpassing beauty, Fawnia cast her eye aside and spied Dorastus, which sudden sight made the poor girl to blush, and to dye her crystal cheeks with a vermilion red which gave her such a grace as she seemed far more beautiful. And with that she rose up, saluting the prince with such modest courtesies as he wondered how a country maid could afford such courtly behaviour. Dorastus, repaying her courtesy with a smiling countenance, began to parley with her on this manner:

'Fair maid,' quoth he, 'either your want is great, or a shepherd's life very sweet, that your delight is in such country labours. I cannot conceive what pleasure you should take, unless you mean to imitate the nymphs, being yourself so like a nymph. To put me out of this doubt, show me what is to be commended in a shepherd's life, and what pleasures you have to countervail these drudging labours.'

Fawnia with blushing face made him this ready answer:

'Sir, what richer state than content, or what sweeter life than quiet? We shepherds are not born to honour, nor beholden unto beauty—the less care we have to fear fame or fortune. We count our attire brave enough if warm enough, and our food dainty, if to suffice nature. Our greatest enemy is the wolf, our only care in safe keeping our flock. Instead of courtly ditties, we spend the days with country songs. Our amorous conceits are homely thoughts, delighting as much to talk of Pan and his country pranks as ladies to tell of Venus and her wanton toys. Our toil is in shifting the folds and looking to the lambs, easy labours; oft singing and telling tales, homely pleasures; our greatest wealth not to covet, our honour not to climb, our quiet not to care. Envy looketh not so low as shepherds; shepherds gaze not so high as ambition. We are rich in that we are poor with content, and proud only in this: that we have no cause to be proud.'

This witty answer of Fawnia so inflamed Dorastus' fancy as he commended himself for making so good a choice, thinking, if her birth were answerable to her wit and beauty, that she were a fit mate for the most famous prince in the world. He therefore began to sift her more narrowly on this manner:

'Fawnia, I see thou art content with country labours, because thou knowest not courtly pleasures. I commend thy wit and pity thy want; but wilt thou leave thy father's cottage, and serve a courtly mistress?'

'Sir,' quoth she, 'beggars ought not to strive against fortune, nor to gaze after honour, lest either their fall be greater or they become blind. I am born to toil for the court, not in the court, my nature unfit for their nurture; better live then in mean degree than in high disdain.'

'Well said, Fawnia,' quoth Dorastus, 'I guess at thy thoughts; thou art in love with some country shepherd.'

'No sir,' quoth she, 'shepherds cannot love that are so simple, and maids may not love that are so young.'

'Nay, therefore,' quoth Dorastus, 'maids must love because they are young; for Cupid is a child, and Venus, though old, is painted with fresh colours.'

'I grant,' quoth she, 'age may be painted with new shadows, and youth may have imperfect affections; but what art concealeth in one, ignorance revealeth in the other.'

Dorastus, seeing Fawnia held him so hard, thought it was vain so long to beat about the bush. Therefore he thought to have given her a fresh charge, but he was so prevented by certain of his men who, missing their master, came posting to seek him, seeing that he was gone forth all alone; yet before they drew so nigh that they might hear their talk, he used these speeches:

'Why, Fawnia, perhaps I love thee, and then thou must needs yield; for thou knowest I can command and constrain.'

'Truth, sir,' quoth she, 'but not to love; for constrained love is force, not love. And know this, sir, mine honesty is such as I had rather die than be a concubine even to a king, and my birth is so base as I am unfit to be a wife to a poor farmer.'

'Why then,' quoth he, 'thou canst not love Dorastus?'

'Yes,' said Fawnia, 'when Dorastus becomes a shepherd—' and with that the presence of his men broke off their parle, so that he went with them to the palace and left Fawnia sitting still on the hillside, who, seeing that the night drew on, shifted her folds and busied herself about other work to drive away such fond fancies as began to trouble her brain.

But all this could not prevail, for the beauty of Dorastus had made such a deep impression in her heart as it could not be worn out without cracking, so that she was forced to blame her own folly in this wise:

'Ah, Fawnia, why dost thou gaze against the sun, or catch at the wind? Stars are to be looked at with the eye, not reached at with the hand; thoughts are to be measured by fortunes, not by desires; falls come not by sitting low, but by climbing too high. What then, shall all fear to fall, because some hap to fall? No, luck cometh by lot, and fortune windeth those threads which the Destinies spin. Thou art favoured, Fawnia, of a prince, and yet thou art so fond to reject desired favours. Thou hast denial at thy tongue's end, and desire at thy heart's bottom—a woman's fault, to spurn at that with her foot which she greedily catcheth at with her hand. Thou lovest Dorastus, Fawnia, and yet seemst to lour. Take heed—if he retire, thou wilt repent; for unless he love, thou canst but die. Die then, Fawnia, for Dorastus doth but jest. The lion never preyeth on the mouse, nor falcons stoop not to dead stales.[1] Sit down then in sorrow, cease to love, and content thyself that Dorastus will vouchsafe to flatter Fawnia, though not to fancy Fawnia. Hey ho! Ah, fool, it were seemlier for thee to whistle as a shepherd than to sigh as a lover'; and with that she ceased from these perplexed passions, folding her sheep, and hying home to her poor cottage.

But such was the incessant sorrow of Dorastus to think on the wit and beauty of Fawnia, and to see how fond he was being a prince, and how froward she was being a beggar, that he began to lose his wonted appetite, to look pale and wan; instead of mirth, to feed on melancholy; for courtly dances to use cold dumps;[2] insomuch that not only his own men but his father and all the court began to marvel at his sudden change, thinking that some lingering sickness had brought him into this state. Wherefore he caused physicians to come; but Dorastus neither would let them minister nor so much as suffer them to see his urine, but remained still so oppressed with these passions as he feared in himself a farther inconvenience. His honour wished him to cease from such folly, but love forced him to follow fancy. Yea, and in despite of honour love

---

[1] decoys   [2] both plaintive music and low spirits

won the conquest, so that his hot desires caused him to find new devices; for he presently made himself a shepherd's coat, that he might go unknown and with the less suspicion to prattle with Fawnia, and conveyed it secretly into a thick grove hard joining to the palace, whither, finding fit time and opportunity, he went all alone and, putting off his princely apparel, got on those shepherd's robes and, taking a great hook in his hand, which he had also gotten, he went very anciently[1] to find out the mistress of his affections. But as he went by the way, seeing himself clad in such unseemly rags he began to smile at his own folly, and to reprove his fondness in these terms:

'Well said, Dorastus—thou keepest a right decorum, base desires and homely attires! Thy thoughts are fit for none but a shepherd, and thy apparel such as only become a shepherd. A strange change, from a prince to a peasant! What is it—thy wretched fortune or thy wilful folly? Is it thy cursed destinies or thy crooked desires that appointeth thee this penance? Ah, Dorastus, thou canst but love, and unless thou love, thou art like to perish for love. Yet, fond fool, choose flowers, not weeds; diamonds, not pebbles; ladies which may honour thee, not shepherds which may disgrace thee. Venus is painted in silks, not in rags; and Cupid treadeth on disdain when he reacheth at dignity. And yet, Dorastus, shame not at thy shepherd's weed. The heavenly gods have sometime earthly thoughts. Neptune became a ram, Jupiter a bull, Apollo a shepherd; they gods, and yet in love;[2] and thou a man, appointed to love.'

Devising thus with himself he drew nigh to the place where Fawnia was keeping her sheep, who, casting her eye aside and seeing such a mannerly shepherd perfectly limbed and coming with so good a pace, she began half to forget Dorastus and to favour this pretty shepherd, whom she thought she might both love and obtain. But as she was in these thoughts, she perceived then it was the young prince Dorastus; wherefore she rose up and reverently saluted him. Dorastus, taking her by the hand, repaid her courtesy with a sweet kiss and, praying her to sit down by him, he began thus to lay the battery:

'If thou marvel, Fawnia, at my strange attire, thou wouldst more muse at my unaccustomed thoughts. The one disgraceth but my outward shape; the other disturbeth my inward senses. I love Fawnia, and therefore what love liketh I cannot mislike. Fawnia, thou hast promised to love, and I hope thou wilt perform no less. I have fulfilled thy request, and now thou canst but grant my desire. Thou wert content to love Dorastus when he ceased to be a prince and granted to become a shepherd, and see, I have made the change, and therefore hope not to miss of my choice.'

---

[1] old-fashionedly   [2] 4.4.25–31

'Truth,' quoth Fawnia, 'but all that wear cowls are not monks; painted eagles are pictures, not eagles; Zeuxis' grapes were like grapes, yet shadows. Rich clothing make not princes, nor homely attire beggars. Shepherds are not called shepherds because they wear hooks and bags, but that they are born poor and live to keep sheep; so this attire hath not made Dorastus a shepherd, but to seem like a shepherd.'

'Well, Fawnia,' answered Dorastus, 'were I a shepherd, I could not but like thee, and being a prince, I am forced to love thee. Take heed, Fawnia: be not proud of beauty's painting; for it is a flower that fadeth in the blossom. Those which disdain in youth are despised in age. Beauty's shadows are tricked up with Time's colours which, being set to dry in the sun, are stained with the sun, scarce pleasing the sight ere they begin not to be worth the sight—not much unlike the herb ephemeron[1] which flourisheth in the morning and is withered before the sun setting. If my desire were against law, thou mightest justly deny me by reason; but I love thee, Fawnia, not to misuse thee as a concubine but to use thee as my wife. I can promise no more, and mean to perform no less.'

Fawnia, hearing this solemn protestation of Dorastus, could no longer withstand the assault but yielded up the fort in these friendly terms:

'Ah, Dorastus, I shame to express that thou forcest me with thy sugared speech to confess. My base birth causeth the one, and thy high dignities the other. Beggars' thoughts ought not to reach so far as kings, and yet my desires reach as high as princes; I dare not say, Dorastus, I love thee, because I am a shepherd; but the gods know I have honoured Dorastus (pardon if I say amiss), yea and loved Dorastus with such dutiful affection as Fawnia can perform or Dorastus desire. I yield, not overcome with prayers but with love, resting Dorastus' handmaid ready to obey his will, if no prejudice at all to his honour nor to my credit.'

Dorastus, hearing this friendly conclusion of Fawnia, embraced her in his arms, swearing that neither distance, time, nor adverse fortune should diminish his affections, but that, in despite of the destinies, he would remain loyal unto death. Having thus plight their troth each to other, seeing they could not have the full fruition of their love in Sicilia for that Egistus' consent would never be granted to so mean a match, Dorastus determined, as soon as time and opportunity would give them leave, to provide a great mass of money and many rich and costly jewels (for the easier carriage) and then to transport themselves and their treasure into Italy, where they should lead a contented life until such time as either he could be reconciled to his father or else by succession

[1] or ephemerum; the English name is said by Gerard to be 'quick-fading flower'; both he and the *OED* are vague about its botanical credentials. *Herbal* (1633), p. 492.

come to the kingdom. This device was greatly praised of Fawnia; for she feared, if the King his father should but hear of the contract, that his fury would be such as no less than death would stand for payment. She therefore told him that delay bred danger, that many mishaps did fall out between the cup and the lip, and that to avoid danger it were best with as much speed as might be to pass out of Sicilia, lest Fortune might prevent their pretence with some new despite. Dorastus, whom love pricked forward with desire, promised to dispatch his affairs with as great haste as either time or opportunity would give him leave; and so resting upon this point, after many embracings and sweet kisses they departed.

Dorastus, having taken his leave of his best beloved Fawnia, went to the grove where he had his rich apparel, and there uncasing himself as secretly as might be, hiding up his shepherd's attire till occasion should serve again to use it he went to the palace, showing by his merry countenance that either the state of his body was amended or the case of his mind greatly redressed. Fawnia, poor soul, was no less joyful that, being a shepherd, Fortune had favoured her so as to reward her with the love of a prince, hoping in time to be advanced from the daughter of a poor farmer to be the wife of a rich king, so that she thought every hour a year till by their departure they might prevent danger, not ceasing still to go every day to her sheep, not so much for the care of her flock as for the desire she had to see her love and lord Dorastus who oftentimes, when opportunity would serve, repaired thither to feed his fancy with the sweet content of Fawnia's presence; and although he never went to visit her but in his shepherd's rags, yet his oft repair made him not only suspected but known to divers of their neighbours who, for the good will they bare to old Porrus, told him secretly of the matter, wishing him to keep his daughter at home lest she went so oft to the field that she brought him home a young son; for they feared that, Fawnia being so beautiful, the young prince would allure her to folly. Porrus was stricken into a dump at these news, so that, thanking his neighbours for their good will, he hied him home to his wife, and, calling her aside, wringing his hands and shedding forth tears, he brake the matter to her in these terms:

'I am afraid, wife, that my daughter Fawnia hath made herself so fine that she will buy repentance too dear. I hear news which, if they be true, some will wish they had not proved true. It is told me by my neighbours that Dorastus, the King's son, begins to look at our daughter Fawnia, which if it be so, I will not give her a halfpenny for her honesty at the year's end. I tell thee, wife, nowadays beauty is a great stale[1] to trap young men, and fair words and sweet promises are two great enemies to a maiden's honesty, and, thou knowest, where poor men entreat and

---

[1] See above, p. 259, n. 1.

cannot obtain, there princes may command, and will obtain. Though kings' sons dance in nets,[1] they may not be seen; but poor men's faults are spied at a little hole. Well, it is a hard case where kings' lusts are laws, and that they should bind poor men to that which they themselves wilfully break.'

'Peace, husband,' quoth his wife, 'take heed what you say. Speak no more than you should, lest you hear what you would not. Great streams are to be stopped by sleight, not by force, and princes to be persuaded by submission, not by rigour. Do what you can, but no more than you may, lest in saving Fawnia's maidenhead you lose your own head. Take heed, I say, it is ill jesting with edged tools, and bad sporting with kings. The wolf had his skin pulled over his ears for but looking into the lion's den.'

'Tush, wife,' quoth he, 'thou speakest like a fool. If the King should know that Dorastus had begotten our daughter with child (as I fear it will fall out little better), the King's fury would be such as no doubt we should both lose our goods and lives. Necessity therefore hath no law, and I will prevent this mischief with a new device that is come in my head, which shall neither offend the King nor displease Dorastus. I mean to take the chain and the jewels that I found with Fawnia, and carry them to the King, letting him then to understand how she is none of my daughter, but that I found her beaten up with the water alone in a little boat wrapped in a rich mantle wherein was enclosed this treasure. By this means I hope the King will take Fawnia into his service; and we, whatsoever chanceth, shall be blameless.'

This device pleased the good wife very well, so that they determined as soon as they might know the King at leisure to make him privy to this case. In the meantime Dorastus was not slack in his affairs, but applied his matters with such diligence that he provided all things fit for their journey. Treasure and jewels he had gotten great store, thinking there was no better friend than money in a strange country. Rich attire he had provided for Fawnia, and (because he could not bring the matter to pass without the help and advice of someone) he made an old servant of his called Capnio, who had served him from his childhood, privy to his affairs who, seeing no persuasions could prevail to divert him from his settled determination, gave his consent, and dealt so secretly in the cause that within short space he had gotten a ship ready for their passage.

The mariners, seeing a fit gale of wind for their purpose, wished Capnio to make no delays lest, if they pretermitted[2] this good weather, they might stay long ere they had such a fair wind. Capnio, fearing that his negligence should hinder the journey, in the night time conveyed the trunks full of treasure into the ship, and by secret means let Fawnia

---

[1] i.e. with practically no disguise (*OED*, net, 2b)
[2] failed to take advantage of

understand that the next morning they meant to depart. She upon this news slept very little that night, but got up very early and went to her sheep, looking every minute when she should see Dorastus, who tarried not long, for fear delay might breed danger, but came as fast as he could gallop and without any great circumstance took Fawnia up behind him and rode to the haven where the ship lay, which was not three-quarters of a mile distant from that place. He no sooner came there but the mariners were ready with their cock-boat to set them aboard where, being couched together in a cabin, they passed away the time in recounting their old loves till their man Capnio should come.

Porrus, who had heard that this morning the King would go abroad to take the air, called in haste to his wife to bring him his holiday hose and his best jacket, that he might go like an honest substantial man to tell his tale. His wife, a good cleanly wench, brought him all things fit and sponged him up very handsomely, giving him the chains and jewels in a little box, which Porrus (for the more safety) put in his bosom. Having thus all his trinkets in a readiness, taking his staff in his hand he had his wife kiss him for good luck, and so he went towards the palace. But as he was going, Fortune, who meant to show him a little false play, prevented his purpose in this wise.

He met by chance in his way Capnio who—trudging as fast as he could with a little coffer under his arm to the ship, and spying Porrus (whom he knew to be Fawnia's father) going towards the palace—being a wily fellow began to doubt the worst, and therefore crossed him the way and asked him whither he was going so early this morning.[1]

Porrus (who knew by his face that he was one of the court), meaning simply told him that the King's son Dorastus dealt hardly with him; for he had but one daughter, who was a little beautiful, and that his neighbours told him the young prince had allured her to folly; he went therefore now to complain to the King how greatly he was abused.

Capnio (who straightway smelt the whole matter) began to soothe him in his talk, and said that Dorastus dealt not like a prince to spoil any poor man's daughter in that sort. He therefore would do the best for him he could, because he knew he was an honest man. 'But', quoth Capnio, 'you lose your labour in going to the palace, for the King means this day to take the air of the sea, and to go aboard of a ship that lies in the haven.[2] I am going before, you see, to provide all things in a readiness, and if you will follow my counsel, turn back with me to the haven, where I will set you in such a fit place as you may speak to the King at your pleasure.'[3]

Porrus, giving credit to Capnio's smooth tale, gave him a thousand thanks for his friendly advice, and went with him to the haven, making

---

[1] 4.4.710 ff.   [2] 4.4.757–8   [3] 4.4.790–3

all the way his complaints of Dorastus, yet concealing secretly the chain and the jewels. As soon as they were come to the seaside the mariners, seeing Capnio came aland with their cock-boat, who, still dissembling the matter, demanded of Porrus if he would go see the ship; who, unwilling and fearing the worst because he was not well acquainted with Capnio, made his excuse that he could not brook the sea, therefore would not trouble him.

Capnio, seeing that by fair means he could not get him aboard, commanded the mariners that by violence they should carry him into the ship, who like sturdy knaves hoisted the poor shepherd on their backs, and, bearing him to the boat, launched from the land.

Porrus, seeing himself so cunningly betrayed, durst not cry out (for he saw it would not prevail) but began to entreat Capnio and the mariners to be good to him and to pity his estate; he was but a poor man that lived by his labour. They, laughing to see the shepherd so afraid, made as much haste as they could, and set him aboard. Porrus was no sooner in the ship but he saw Dorastus walking with Fawnia; yet he scarce knew her; for she had attired herself in rich apparel which so increased her beauty that she resembled rather an angel than a mortal creature.[1]

Dorastus and Fawnia were half astonished to see the old shepherd, marvelling greatly what wind had brought him thither, till Capnio told them all the whole discourse; how Porrus was going to make his complaint to the King, if by policy he had not prevented him; and therefore now, sith he was aboard, for the avoiding of further danger it were best to carry him into Italy.

Dorastus praised greatly his man's device, and allowed of his counsel, but Fawnia (who still feared Porrus as her father) began to blush for shame that by her means he should either incur danger or displeasure.

The old shepherd, hearing this hard sentence—that he should on such a sudden be carried from his wife, his country and kinsfolk, into a foreign land amongst strangers—began with bitter tears to make his complaint, and on his knees to entreat Dorastus that, pardoning his unadvised folly, he would give him leave to go home; swearing that he would keep all things as secret as they could wish. But these protestations could not prevail, although Fawnia entreated Dorastus very earnestly, but the mariners hoisting their mainsails weighed anchors, and haled into the deep, where we leave them to the favour of the wind and seas, and return to Egistus, who, having appointed this day to hunt in one of his forests, called for his son Dorastus to go sport himself, because he saw that of late he began to lour. But his men made answer that he was gone abroad none knew whither, except he were gone to the grove to walk all alone, as his custom was to do every day.

[1] Compare 5.2.111 ff.

The King, willing to waken him out of his dumps, sent one of his men to go to seek him; but in vain, for at last he returned, but find him he could not, so that the King went himself to go see the sport, where passing away the day, returning at night from hunting he asked for his son, but he could not be heard of; which drave the King into a great choler. Whereupon most of his noblemen and other courtiers posted abroad to seek him; but they could not hear of him through all Sicilia, only they missed Capnio his man, which again made the King suspect that he was not gone far.

Two or three days being passed and no news heard of Dorastus, Egistus began to fear that he was devoured with some wild beasts, and upon that made out a great troop of men to go seek him; who coasted through all the country and searched in every dangerous and secret place until at last they met with a fisherman that was sitting in a little covert hard by the seaside mending his nets when Dorastus and Fawnia took shipping; who, being examined if he either knew or heard where the King's son was, without any secrecy at all revealed the whole matter: how he was sailed two days past, and had in his company his man Capnio, Porrus, and his fair daughter Fawnia.

This heavy news was presently carried to the King who, half dead for sorrow, commanded Porrus' wife to be sent for. She, being come to the palace, after due examination confessed that her neighbours had oft told her that the King's son was too familiar with Fawnia, her daughter, whereupon her husband, fearing the worst, about two days past, hearing the King should go an-hunting, rose early in the morning and went to make his complaint; but since she neither heard of him nor saw him. Egistus, perceiving the woman's unfeigned simplicity, let her depart without incurring further displeasure, concealing such secret grief for his son's reckless folly that he had so forgotten his honour and parentage by so base a choice to dishonour his father and discredit himself, that with very care and thought he fell into a quartan fever,[1] which was so unfit for his aged years and complexion that he became so weak as the physicians would grant him no life.

But his son Dorastus little regarded either father, country, or kingdom in respect of his lady Fawnia; for Fortune, smiling on this young novice, lent him so lucky a gale of wind for the space of a day and a night that the mariners lay and slept upon the hatches. But on the next morning, about the break of day, the air began to overcast, the winds to rise, the seas to swell; yea, presently there arose such a fearful tempest as the ship was in danger to be swallowed up with every sea, the mainmast with the violence of the wind was thrown overboard, the sails were torn,

[1] So called because it is 'characterised by the occurrence of a paroxysm every fourth (in modern reckoning, every third) day' (*OED*).

the tacklings went in sunder, the storm raging still so furiously that poor Fawnia was almost dead for fear, but that she was greatly comforted with the presence of Dorastus. The tempest continued three days, all which time the mariners every minute looked for death, and the air was so darkened with clouds that the master could not tell by his compass in what coast they were. But upon the fourth day, about ten of the clock, the wind began to cease, the sea to wax calm, and the sky to be clear, and the mariners descried the coast of Bohemia, shooting off their ordnance for joy that they had escaped such a fearful tempest.

Dorastus, hearing that they were arrived at some harbour, sweetly kissed Fawnia and bade her be of good cheer. When they told him that the port belonged unto the chief city of Bohemia, where Pandosto kept his court, Dorastus began to be sad, knowing that his father hated no man so much as Pandosto, and that the King himself had sought secretly to betray Egistus. This considered, he was half afraid to go on land, but that Capnio counselled him to change his name and his country until such time as they could get some other barque to transport them into Italy. Dorastus, liking this device, made his case privy to the mariners, rewarding them bountifully for their pains, and charging them to say that he was a gentleman of Trapalonia called Meleagrus. The shipmen, willing to show what friendship they could to Dorastus, promised to be as secret as they could or he might wish, and upon this they landed in a little village a mile distant from the city; where after they had rested a day, thinking to make provision for their marriage, the fame of Fawnia's beauty was spread throughout all the city so that it came to the ears of Pandosto[1] who, then being about the age of fifty, had notwithstanding young and fresh affections; so that he desired greatly to see Fawnia; and to bring this matter the better to pass, hearing they had but one man and how they rested at a very homely house, he caused them to be apprehended as spies and sent a dozen of his guard to take them, who being come to their lodging told them the King's message. Dorastus, no whit dismayed, accompanied with Fawnia and Capnio went to the court (for they left Porrus to keep the stuff), who being admitted to the King's presence, Dorastus and Fawnia with humble obeisance saluted his majesty.

Pandosto, amazed at the singular perfection of Fawnia, stood half astonished viewing her beauty, so that he had almost forgot himself what he had to do. At last with stern countenance he demanded their names, and of what country they were, and what caused them to land in Bohemia.

'Sir,' quoth Dorastus, 'know that my name Meleagrus is, a knight born and brought up in Trapalonia; and this gentlewoman who I mean

[1] 5.1.93–5

to take to my wife is an Italian born in Padua, from whence I have now brought her. The cause I have so small a train with me is for that, her friends unwilling to consent, I intended secretly to convey her into Trapalonia, whither as I was sailing by distress of weather I was driven into these coasts. Thus have you heard my name, my country, and the cause of my voyage.' Pandosto, starting from his seat as one in choler, made this rough reply:

'Meleagrus, I fear this smooth tale hath but small truth, and that thou coverest a foul skin with fair paintings. No doubt this lady by her grace and beauty is of her degree more meet for a mighty prince than for a simple knight, and thou, like a perjured traitor, hast bereft her of her parents, to their present grief and her ensuing sorrow. Till, therefore, I hear more of her parentage and of thy calling, I will stay you both here in Bohemia.'

Dorastus, in whom rested nothing but kingly valour, was not able to suffer the reproaches of Pandosto, but that he made him this answer:

'It is not meet for a king without due proof to appeach any man of ill behaviour, nor upon suspicion to infer belief. Strangers ought to be entertained with courtesy, not to be entreated with cruelty, lest, being forced by want to put up injuries, the gods revenge their cause with rigour.'

Pandosto, hearing Dorastus utter these words, commanded that he should straight be committed to prison until such time as they heard further of his pleasure; but as for Fawnia, he charged that she should be entertained in the court with such courtesy as belonged to a stranger and her calling. The rest of the shipmen he put into the dungeon.

Having thus hardly handled the supposed Trapalonians, Pandosto, contrary to his aged years, began to be somewhat tickled with the beauty of Fawnia,[1] insomuch that he could take no rest, but cast in his old head a thousand new devices. At last he fell into these thoughts:

'How art thou pestered, Pandosto, with fresh affections and unfit fancies, wishing to possess with an unwilling mind, and in a hot desire troubled with a cold disdain! Shall thy mind yield in age to that thou hast resisted in youth? Peace, Pandosto, blab not out that which thou mayst be ashamed to reveal to thyself. Ah, Fawnia is beautiful, and it is not for thine honour, fond fool, to name her that is thy captive and another man's concubine. Alas, I reach at that with my hand which my heart would fain refuse, playing like the bird ibis in Egypt, which hateth serpents yet feedeth on their eggs.

'Tush, hot desires turn oftentimes to cold disdain. Love is brittle where appetite, not reason, bears the sway. Kings' thoughts ought not to climb so high as the heavens, but to look no lower than honour. Better it is to

---

[1] Compare 5.1.222–7.

peck at the stars with the young eagles than to prey on dead carcases with the vultures. 'Tis more honourable for Pandosto to die by concealing love than to enjoy such unfit love. Doth Pandosto then love? Yea. Whom? A maid unknown, yea, and perhaps immodest, straggled out of her own country; beautiful, but not therefore chaste; comely in body, but perhaps crooked in mind. Cease then, Pandosto, to look at Fawnia, much less to love her. Be not overtaken with a woman's beauty, whose eyes are framed by art to enamour, whose heart is framed by nature to enchant, whose false tears know their true times, and whose sweet words pierce deeper than sharp swords.'

Here Pandosto ceased from his talk but not from his love; for although he sought by reason and wisdom to suppress this frantic affection, yet he could take no rest, the beauty of Fawnia had made such a deep impression in his heart. But on a day, walking abroad into a park which was hard adjoining to his house, he sent by one of his servants for Fawnia, unto whom he uttered these words:

'Fawnia, I commend thy beauty and wit, and now pity thy distress and want; but if thou wilt forsake Sir Meleagrus—whose poverty (though a knight) is not able to maintain an estate answerable to thy beauty—and yield thy consent to Pandosto, I will both increase thee with dignities and riches.'

'No sir,' answered Fawnia; 'Meleagrus is a knight that hath won me by love, and none but he shall wear me. His sinister mischance shall not diminish my affection, but rather increase my good will. Think not, though your grace hath imprisoned him without cause, that fear shall make me yield my consent. I had rather be Meleagrus' wife and a beggar than live in plenty and be Pandosto's concubine.'

Pandosto, hearing the assured answer of Fawnia, would notwithstanding prosecute his suit to the uttermost, seeking with fair words and great promises to scale the fort of her chastity, swearing that if she would grant to his desire, Meleagrus should not only be set at liberty but honoured in his court amongst his nobles. But these alluring baits could not entice her mind from the love of her new-betrothed mate, Meleagrus; which Pandosto seeing, he left her alone for that time to consider more of the demand. Fawnia, being alone by herself, began to enter into these solitary meditations:

'Ah, infortunate Fawnia, thou seest to desire above fortune is to strive against the gods and fortune. Who gazeth at the sun weakeneth his sight. They which stare at the sky fall oft into deep pits. Hadst thou rested content to have been a shepherd, thou needst not to have feared mischance. Better had it been for thee by sitting low to have had quiet than by climbing high to have fallen into misery. But alas, I fear not mine own danger but Dorastus' displeasure. Ah, sweet Dorastus, thou art a prince but now a prisoner, by too much love procuring thine own loss. Hadst thou not loved Fawnia, thou hadst been fortunate. Shall I then be false to him that hath forsaken kingdoms for my cause? No; would my death might deliver him, so mine honour might be preserved.'

With that, fetching a deep sigh, she ceased from her complaints and went again to the palace, enjoying a liberty without content, and proffered pleasure with small joy.

But poor Dorastus lay all this while in close prison, being pinched with a hard restraint and pained with the burden of cold and heavy irons, sorrowing sometimes that his fond affection had procured him this mishap, that, by the disobedience of his parents, he had wrought his own despite; another while cursing the gods and fortune that they should cross him with such sinister chance; uttering at last his passions in these words:

'Ah, unfortunate wretch, born to mishap, now thy folly hath his desert. Art thou not worthy for thy base mind to have bad fortune? Could the destinies favour thee which hast forgot thine honour and dignities? Will not the gods plague him with despite that paineth his father with disobedience? Oh gods, if any favour or justice be left, plague me but favour poor Fawnia, and shroud her from the tyrannies of wretched Pandosto; but let my death free her from mishap, and then welcome death.'

Dorastus, pained with these heavy passions, sorrowed and sighed, but in vain, for which he used the more patience. But again to Pandosto who, broiling at the heat of unlawful lust, could take no rest, but still felt his mind disquieted with his new love, so that his nobles and subjects marvelled greatly at this sudden alteration, not being able to conjecture the cause of this his continued care. Pandosto, thinking every hour a year till he had talked once again with Fawnia, sent for her secretly into his chamber, whither though Fawnia unwillingly coming, Pandosto entertained her very courteously, using these familiar speeches, which Fawnia answered as shortly in this wise:

Pandosto: Fawnia, are you become less wilful and more wise, to prefer the love of a king before the liking of a poor knight? I think ere this you think it is better to be favoured of a king than of a subject.

Fawnia: Pandosto, the body is subject to victories, but the mind not to be subdued by conquest. Honesty is to be preferred before honour, and a dram of faith weigheth down a ton of gold. I have promised Meleagrus to love, and will perform no less.

Pandosto: Fawnia, I know thou art not so unwise in thy choice as to refuse the offer of a king, nor so ingrateful as to despise a good turn. Thou art now in that place where I may command, and yet thou seest I entreat; my power is such as I may compel by force, and yet I sue by prayers. Yield, Fawnia, thy love to him which burneth in thy love,

Meleagrus shall be set free, thy countrymen discharged, and thou both loved and honoured.

Fawnia: I see, Pandosto, where lust ruleth it is a miserable thing to be a virgin. But know this, that I will always prefer fame before life, and rather choose death than dishonour.

Pandosto seeing that there was in Fawnia a determinate courage to love Meleagrus, and a resolution without fear to hate him, flung away from her in a rage swearing if in short time she would not be won with reason, he would forget all courtesy, and compel her to grant by rigour. But these threatening words no whit dismayed Fawnia, but that she still both despited and despised Pandosto. While thus these two lovers strove, the one to win love, the other to live in hate, Egistus heard certain news by merchants of Bohemia that his son Dorastus was imprisoned by Pandosto, which made him fear greatly that his son should be but hardly entreated. Yet, considering that Bellaria and he was cleared by the oracle of Apollo from that crime wherewith Pandosto had unjustly charged them, he thought best to send with all spend to Pandosto, that he should set free his son Dorastus, and put to death Fawnia and her father Porrus.

Finding this by the advice of counsel the speediest remedy to release his son, he caused presently two of his ships to be rigged and thoroughly furnished with provision of men and victuals, and sent divers of his nobles ambassadors into Bohemia, who, willing to obey their king and receive their young prince, made no delays, for fear of danger, but, with as much speed as might be, sailed towards Bohemia. The wind and seas favoured them greatly, which made them hope of some good hap; for within three days they were landed; which Pandosto no sooner heard of their arrival but he in person went to meet them,[1] entreating them with such sumptuous and familiar courtesy that they might well perceive how sorry he was for the former injuries he had offered to their king, and how willing, if it might be, to make amends.

As Pandosto made report to them how one Meleagrus, a knight of Trapalonia, was lately arrived with a lady called Fawnia in his land, coming very suspiciously, accompanied only with one servant and an old shepherd, the ambassadors perceived by the half what the whole tale meant, and began to conjecture that it was Dorastus, who, for fear to be known, had changed his name. But dissembling the matter, they shortly arrived at the court, where, after they had been very solemnly and sumptuously feasted, the noblemen of Sicilia being gathered together they made report of their embassage, where they certified Pandosto that Meleagrus was son and heir to the King Egistus, and that his name was Dorastus; how contrary to the King's mind he had privily conveyed

[1] 5.1.228–31

away that Fawnia, intending to marry her, being but daughter to that poor shepherd Porrus. Whereupon the King's request was that Capnio, Fawnia, and Porrus might be murdered and put to death, and that his son Dorastus might be sent him in safety.[1]

Pandosto having attentively and with great marvel heard their embassage, willing to reconcile himself to Egistus and to show him how greatly he esteemed his favour, although love and fancy forbade him to hurt Fawnia, yet in despite of love he determined to execute Egistus' will without mercy; and therefore he presently sent for Dorastus out of prison, who marvelling at this unlooked-for courtesy, found at his coming to the King's presence that which he least doubted of, his father's ambassadors; who no sooner saw him but with great reverence they honoured him; and Pandosto, embracing Dorastus, set him by him very lovingly in a chair of estate.

Dorastus, ashamed that his folly was betrayed, set a long time as one in a muse, till Pandosto told him the sum of his father's embassage, which he had no sooner heard but he was touched at the quick for the cruel sentence that was pronounced against Fawnia. But neither could his sorrow nor persuasions prevail; for Pandosto commanded that Fawnia, Porrus, and Capnio should be brought to his presence; who were no sooner come but Pandosto, having his former love turned to a disdainful hate, began to rage against Fawnia in these terms:

'Thou disdainful vassal, thou currish kite, assigned by the destinies to base fortune, and yet with an aspiring mind gazing after honour: how durst thou presume, being a beggar, to match with a prince—by thy alluring looks to enchant the son of a king to leave his own country to fulfil thy disordinate lusts? O despiteful mind! A proud heart in a beggar is not unlike to a great fire in a small cottage, which warmeth not the house, but burneth it. Assure thyself thou shalt die; and thou, old doting fool, whose folly hath been such as to suffer thy daughter to reach above thy fortune, look for no other meed but the like punishment.[2] But Capnio, thou which hast betrayed the King and hast consented to the unlawful lust of thy lord and master, I know not how justly I may plague thee. Death is too easy a punishment for thy falsehood, and to live, if not in extreme misery, were not to show thee equity. I therefore award that thou shall have thine eyes put out, and continually, while thou diest, grind in a mill like a brute beast.' The fear of death brought a sorrowful silence upon Fawnia and Capnio, but Porrus, seeing no hope of life, burst forth into these speeches:

'Pandosto, and ye noble ambassadors of Sicilia, seeing without cause I am condemned to die, I am yet glad I have opportunity to disburden my conscience before my death. I will tell you as much as I know, and

[1] 5.1.179 ff.   [2] Compare 4.4.417–38.

yet no more than is true. Whereas I am accused that I have been a supporter of Fawnia's pride, and she disdained as a vile beggar, so it is that I am neither father unto her nor she daughter unto me. For so it happened that I, being a poor shepherd in Sicilia, living by keeping other men's flocks, one of my sheep straying down to the seaside, as I went to seek her I saw a little boat driven upon the shore, wherein I found a babe of six days old wrapped in a mantle of scarlet, having about the neck this chain. I, pitying the child and desirous of the treasure, carried it home to my wife, who with great care nursed it up and set it to keep sheep. Here is the chain and the jewels, and this Fawnia is the child whom I found in the boat. What she is, or of what parentage, I know not, but this I am assured: that she is none of mine.'

Pandosto would scarce suffer him to tell out his tale but that he enquired the time of the year, the manner of the boat, and other circumstances; which when he found agreeing to his count, he suddenly leapt from his seat and kissed Fawnia, wetting her tender cheeks with his tears, and crying 'My daughter Fawnia, ah sweet Fawnia, I am thy father, Fawnia!' This sudden passion of the King drave them all into amaze, especially Fawnia and Dorastus.[1] But when the King had breathed himself awhile in this new joy, he rehearsed before the ambassadors the whole matter—how he had entreated his wife Bellaria for jealousy, and that this was the child whom he sent to float in the seas.

Fawnia was not more joyful that she had found such a father than Dorastus was glad he should get such a wife. The ambassadors rejoiced that their young prince had made such a choice, that those kingdoms which through enmity had long time been dissevered should now through perpetual amity be united and reconciled. The citizens and subjects of Bohemia, hearing that the King had found again his daughter which was supposed dead, joyful that there was an heir apparent to his kingdom, made bonfires and shows throughout the city. The courtiers and knights appointed jousts and tourneys to signify their willing minds in gratifying the King's hap.

Eighteen days being past in these princely sports, Pandosto, willing to recompense old Porrus, of a shepherd made him a knight. Which done, providing a sufficient navy to receive him and his retinue, accompanied with Dorastus, Fawnia, and the Sicilian ambassadors, he sailed towards Sicilia, where he was most princely entertained by Egistus who, hearing this comical event, rejoiced greatly at his son's good hap, and without delay, to the perpetual joy of the two young lovers, celebrated the marriage; which was no sooner ended but, Pandosto calling to mind how first he betrayed his friend Egistus, how his jealousy was the cause

[1] 5.2.49 ff.

of Bellaria's death, that, contrary to the law of nature, he had lusted after his own daughter, moved with these desperate thoughts he fell in a melancholy fit and—to close up the comedy with a tragical stratagem—he slew himself, whose death being many days bewailed of Fawnia, Dorastus, and his dear friend Egistus, Dorastus, taking his leave of his father, went with his wife and the dead corpse into Bohemia where, after they were sumptuously entombed, Dorastus ended his days in contented quiet.

THE MUSIC

The Winter's Tale calls for a good deal of music, all of it in Act 4, with the exception of the viol music to which Hermione is restored in 5.3. All that survives that can reasonably be thought to belong to the original production are three songs and a dance: 'Jog on, jog on the footpath way', 4.3.121–4; 'Lawn as white as driven snow', 4.4.219–30; the trio 'Get you hence, for I must go', 4.4.295–306, said to be 'to the tune of "Two maids wooing a man" '; and the music for the dance of satyrs at 4.4.337.2. Of these, 'Jog on' and 'Get you hence' are popular ballad tunes, certainly not composed for the play, though the words of the latter presumably originate with it, and a song with this text (and, in one manuscript, an additional stanza; see below) is preserved in a version which Ian Spink, in the standard edition of Robert Johnson's lute songs, believes is 'probably' by Johnson, who also composed music for *The Tempest*, presented in the same year as *The Winter's Tale*.[1] The setting of 'Lawn as white as driven snow' by John Wilson (1595–1674), Professor of Music at Oxford from 1656 to 1661 and successor to Henry Lawes as Gentleman of the Chapel Royal under Charles II, was first printed in 1659, but was presumably composed earlier. It is certainly conceivable, if unlikely, that he contributed a song setting to the King's Men at the age of sixteen;[2] and if he is the Jack Wilson cited in F's text of *Much Ado* as providing the music in 2.3 (see the stage direction at 2.3.35.2), presumably a boy singer, his setting of 'Lawn as white' may preserve a version of an original by Johnson.[3] Spink, however, assumes, reasonably, that the setting is later, composed for an early revival. It is, in any case, close enough to a contemporary setting to be worth including, given the meagreness of what survives. *The Satyrs' Masque* is part of the music provided by Robert Johnson for Ben Jonson and Inigo Jones's *Oberon*, performed before the King at Whitehall on New Year's

[1] Ian Spink, ed., Robert Johnson, *Ayres Songs and Dialogues*: The English Lute Songs, second series, 17 (1961), p. 74.

[2] Pafford, in the article on the songs cited below, confusingly claims he was born 'in 1585 or 1595', apparently conflating him with another John Wilson, born in 1585, who was a member of Shakespeare's company. The two are distinguished in T. W. Baldwin, *The Organisation and Personnel of the Shakespearean Company* (Princeton, 1927), pp. 420–1.

[3] Howell Chickering takes this view in a well-argued and cogent overview of the musical situation, for the most part about *The Tempest* but bearing as well on *The Winter's Tale;* see 'Hearing Ariel's Songs', *Journal of Medieval and Renaissance Studies*, 24 (1994), pp. 131–72.

Day 1611, to which there seems to be an allusion in 4.4.333. Since Johnson was employed by the King's Men at the time, there is a reasonable possibility that his satyrs' music of several months earlier would have been used again.

The words and music to 'Jog on' appear in a number of versions in the period, usually separately. The song is a catch, a round 'in which the words are so arranged as to produce ludicrous effects, one singer catching at the words of another' (*OED*). The transcription given here is from *Catch that Catch Can or The Musical Companion* (1667), a three-part version with additional stanzas, in which the piece is ascribed to John Hilton. Hilton (d. 1657) was a well known composer of madrigals, ayres, catches and rounds, active as early as 1601, when he contributed madrigals to *The Triumphs of Orianna*. As with all extant versions of the song, the words differ somewhat from those sung by Autolycus. The earliest surviving version of the tune is found in the *Fitzwilliam Virginal Book*, entitled *Hanskin*, as the basis for a set of variations by Richard Farnaby; the tune is elsewhere referred to as *Sir Francis Drake* and *Eighty-eight*, suggesting that it long predates both the play and John Hilton. 'Lawn as white as driven snow' appears in John Wilson's *Cheerfull Ayres or Ballads* (Oxford, 1660 [1659]), pp. 64–6. The modernized transcriptions of these two songs are by Michelle Dulak. The version of 'Get you hence' included here is that of Ian Spink in his edition of Johnson's *Ayres, Songs and Dialogues*, no. 23, pp. 62–3. *The Satyrs' Masque* is from Andrew Sabol's *Four Hundred Songs and Dances from the Stuart Masque* (Providence, RI, 1978), no. 107, pp. 209–10.[1]

I am indebted for musicological guidance to Professor Anthony Newcomb.

---

[1] A discussion of the music, including a list of later settings, is by J. H. P. Pafford, 'Music, and the Songs in *The Winter's Tale*', *ShQ* 10 (1959), 161–75. Practical realizations of all the music required by the play in performance, based where possible on the original sources, are included in Andrew Charlton, *Music in the Plays of Shakespeare: A Practicum* (New York, 1991).

1. 'Jog on'

See 4.3.121–4. From *Catch that Catch Can or The Musical Companion* (1667), 85. Transcription by Michelle Dulak.

a. 3. Voc.   Mr. John Hilton

2. 'Lawn as white as driven snow'
See 4.4.219–30. From John Wilson, *Cheerfull Ayres or Ballads* (Oxford, 1660 [1659]), pp. 64–6. Transcription by Michelle Dulak.

3. 'Get you hence'

See 4.4.295–306. From *Robert Johnson, Ayres Songs and Dialogues*, ed. Ian Spink (Stainer and Bell, 1961), pp. 62–3. © Stainer and Bell Ltd. Reprinted by permission. Sole American agent, Galaxy Music Corporation, New York. The version of the song in the New York Public Library Drexel MS Dx. 4041, [unnumbered] fols. 127–9, includes a second stanza, which does not entirely fit the music; see Spink, p. 174, and John P. Cutts, 'An Unpublished Contemporary Setting of a Shakespeare Song', *ShS* 9 (1956), 86–9. The words, without repeats, are included below.

It befits thy oath full well, _____ Thou to me thy

sec — rets tell: And me too, let me go thither. If thou — go'st to

6.b.4 – 9.b.3: originally a course higher in *Drex 1.*
12.b.3 originally a course lower in MS

© 1961 by Stainer & Bell Ltd.

grange, or _____ mill; If to _____ ei - ther, thou dost — ill.

Nei - ther, What nei - ther? _____ Nei - ther. Thou hast vow'd thy _____

love to _____ me; Thou hast sworn _____ my — love to _____

16.b.1: originally a course lower in MS
25.b.1-2: note values not halved here

Additional stanza

Never more for lasses' sake
Will I dance at fair or wake.
Ah me!
Oh, ah me!
Ah me!
Who shall then wear a raced[1] shoe?
Or what shall the bagpipe do?
Recant or else you slay me.
If thou leave our arbour[2] green,
Where shall Phill or Friz[3] be seen?
Sleeping.
What, sleeping?
Sleeping.
No, I'll warrant thee; sitting sadly,
Or idly walking madly,
In some dark corner weeping.

[1] fancy (*OED*, race, *v.*³, 1b)
[2] Pafford's emendation for the manuscript's 'andorne'
[3] The manuscript reads 'fill or frize', presumably women's names. Fill = Phillida or Phyllis; Friz appears as a country woman's name in *The Two Noble Kinsmen* 3.5.25.

4. The Satyrs' Masque

See 4.4.337.2. From *Four Hundred Songs and Dances from the Stuart Masque*, ed. Andrew Sabol (Providence, 1978), no. 107, pp. 209–10. Reprinted by permission of Andrew Sabol and the University Press of New England.

INDEX

THIS is a selective guide to points in the Introduction and Commentary of more than routine note. Asterisks identify words which supplement the *Oxford English Dictionary*.

Index

Index

neat, 1.2.122
neatherds, 4.4.320
Neptune, 4.4.28
next, 3.3.119
note, 1.2.2; 4.2.42
noted, 5.3.145
notes of admiration, 5.2.11
Nunn, Trevor, p. 76

occasion, 4.4.828
Odysseus, p. 50
Oedipus, p. 34
o'ercharged, 3.2.148
o'erdyed, 1.2.131
o'erween, 4.2.8
offices, 5.1.148
officious, 2.3.158
of force, 4.4.421
on (=resulting from), 2.2.22
on't, 2.2.30; 2.3.15; 3.1.14; 4.4.5,
 160, 292, 639
open, 4.4.735
opportune, 4.4.499
oracles, pp. 31–2, 67, 78, 79
Oresteia, p. 3
Othello, pp. 6, 17, 18–19, 22–3, 26,
 60
otium, p. 43
out (*adv.*), 4.4.301
out (=mistaken), 2.1.72
out (*expletive*), 4.4.110
outside, 4.4.628
overture, 2.1.172
Ovid, pp. 44, 50–1
owe, 3.2.37
oxlips, 4.4.125

pace, 4.1.23; 4.3.110
paddling, 1.2.114
Pafford, J. H. P., pp. 38, 80, 82
paid down, 5.1.3
paid home, 5.3.4
painted, 4.4.101
pale, 4.3.4
Palma Giovane, p. 55
Pandosto (Greene), pp. 7, 31–2, 37,
 38, 42, 45, 51, 58, 234–74
pantler, 4.4.56
parasite, 1.2.166
parcels, 4.4.256
Parliament, pp. 13–14, 27
partake to, 5.3.132
parties, 2.3.21

Partlet, 2.3.75
pash, 1.2.127
passing, 4.4.286
pastoral, pp. 5, 37–47, 50, 64
pastorals, 4.4.134
Pastor Fido (Guarini), pp. 37, 63
patience, 3.2.31
pattern (*v.*), 3.2.35
Paulina, pp. 53–62
pawn, 2.3.165
peer (*v.*), 4.3.1
peering, 4.4.3
Perdita, 3.3.32
perfect, 3.3.1
performed, 5.2.94
Pericles, pp. 2, 6, 11, 41, 61
personal, 1.1.25
pertain, 5.3.113
pettitoes, 4.4.604
petty, 4.4.4
pheasant, 4.4.739
Philammon, pp. 50–1
Phoebus, 4.4.124
picture, 4.4.601; 5.2.168
piece (*sb.*), 4.4.32; 4.4.420; 5.1.94;
 5.3.38
piece (*v.*), 5.2.106
piedness, 4.4.87
pin and web, 1.2.288
pinched, 2.1.51
pipe, 4.4.185
place, 2.1.83
places, 1.2.433
placket, 4.4.607
plackets, 4.4.242
Platter, Thomas, p. 4
plucking, 4.4.463
point forth, 4.4.560
points, 4.4.207
poking-sticks, 4.4.227
Polyphemus, p. 43
pomander, 4.4.596
ponderous, 4.4.523
Pope, Alexander, p. 2
post (=haste), 2.1.182
posterns, 1.2.433, 2.1.52
pranked up, 4.4.10
predominant, 1.2.200
pregnant, 5.2.30
preposterous, 5.2.142–3
presence, 4.4.793
present, 1.2.278; 2.3.183; 3.3.4
presently, 2.2.46; 5.3.86